STATE OF THE
WORLD
1993

STATE OF THE WORLD

1993

A Worldwatch Institute Report on Progress Toward a Sustainable Society

PROJECT DIRECTOR
Lester R. Brown

ASSOCIATE PROJECT DIRECTORS
Christopher Flavin
Sandra Postel

EDITOR
Linda Starke

CONTRIBUTING RESEARCHERS
Lester R. Brown
Alan Thein Durning
Christopher Flavin
Hilary F. French
Jodi Jacobson
Nicholas Lenssen
Marcia D. Lowe
Sandra Postel
Michael Renner
Peter Weber
John E. Young

W·W·NORTON & COMPANY
NEW YORK   LONDON

The text of this book is composed in Baskerville, with the display set in Caslon.
Composition and manufacturing by the Haddon Craftsmen, Inc.

First Edition

ISBN 0-393-03439-9 (cloth)
ISBN 0-393-30963-0 (paper)

W. W. Norton & Company, Inc., 500 Fifth Avenue, New York, N.Y. 10110
W. W. Norton & Company Ltd., 10 Coptic Street, London WC1A 1PU

1 2 3 4 5 6 7 8 9 0

 This book is printed on recycled paper

Acknowledgments

This is the tenth edition of *State of the World*. By all rights, we should reprint here the acknowledgments of the nine earlier editions, for truly we could not have produced the book you hold in your hands without the unwavering support during the last decade of hundreds of chapter reviewers, scores of people at the foundations that have provided funds for our research, a few dozen former staff members, and the 10 distinguished individuals who form the Worldwatch Board of Directors. To them all, we offer thanks for helping us make *State of the World* the most widely translated and read annual assessment in the world today.

This year, we are pleased to have received core funding support for the book from the Rockefeller Brothers Fund and the Winthrop Rockefeller Trust. Additional research support that contributed to various specific chapters was received from the Ford and the Curtis and Edith Munson foundations. The Institute also acknowledges with thanks general support for its work received from the Geraldine R. Dodge, George Gund, William and Flora Hewlett, W. Alton Jones, John D. and Catherine T. MacArthur, Andrew W. Mellon, Edward John Noble, Public Welfare, Surdna, Turner, and Frank Weeden foundations and the Pew Charitable Trusts. Roy Young again supported our work with a personal donation.

1992 was a time of change on many levels. The Earth Summit in Rio moved the international community closer to accord on some vital global environmental issues. The U.S. election moved environment to the center stage of national debate due to Vice President Gore's longstanding concern about this subject. And at the most local level, we moved offices: after 18 years of watching the world from the seventh floor, with satellite offices for the last few years on the sixth floor, we are now all happily ensconced on the eighth floor at 1776 Massachusetts Avenue. Moving only one floor away takes as much effort as moving across town, of course. For managing this disrupting event in the midst of the deadline for *State of the World*, we owe particular thanks to Worldwatch Vice President and Treasurer Blondeen Gravely. She was more than ably assisted by Barbara Fallin, our Assistant Treasurer. Reah Janise Kauffman, Corporate Secretary and Assistant to the President, coordinated the all-important task of getting the computer system up and running after the move.

In addition to moving, we are responding to the heaviest load of orders Worldwatch has ever experienced, in good part in reaction to the publication of the other annual report we have just launched, *Vital Signs*. Handling all these requests is the responsibility of Publications Sales Coordinator Gloria Grant, with the help of Joseph Gravely, Millicent Johnson, and Greg Lee. Our thanks go to this team and to Charline Burgess, our Receptionist, and James

Porter, our Library Assistant. *World Watch* magazine continues to generate enormous interest and orders for subscriptions, due to the hard work of Managing Editor James Gorman, assisted by Ed Ayres and Carla Atkinson. Ed also edits the Worldwatch Paper Series. The outreach team that so successfully lets the world know of all these publications—Carole Douglis, Steve Kaufman, and Denise Byers Thomma—deserves special thanks for coping with a growing load of work.

Helping authors with research for their chapters is a time-consuming and often demanding task. Therefore we acknowledge here with special thanks the efforts of Vikram Akula (for Chapters 5 and 7), Derek Denniston (Chapter 6), Vicki Elkin (Chapters 3 and 4), Heather Hanford (Chapters 2 and 3 and, as our librarian, for our research materials in general), Hal Kane (Chapter 1), Ann Misch (Chapter 8), and Megan Ryan (Chapters 9 and 10). The index has again this year been prepared by Julie Phillips. Additional research help is often provided by Magnar Norderhaug, who keeps us up to date on developments in Europe.

At W.W. Norton & Company, for 10 years we have relied heavily on the patience and understanding of Iva Ashner and Andrew Marasia for turning a manuscript around in record short order. A special thanks goes to independent editor Linda Starke, who for all 10 editions of *State of the World* has been responsible for shepherding chapters from early drafts through printed copy, and for dealing firmly but gracefully with authors who want to rewrite up to the last possible minute. The book's readability and consistency are in large part due to Linda—and we look forward to another decade of her careful eye and organized mind.

As always, we rely on numerous people outside the Institute to review chapters in draft, often assuming they will drop everything and give us their reaction in just a few days. For being willing to do so this year, we thank John Ambler, Saul Arlosoroff, Robert Buddemeier, Julian Burger, Tom Burke, Ross Capon, John Cavanagh, E. Walter Coward, Jr., Colin Crawford, Zvy Dubinsky, Don Dumond, Maureen Eldredge, John Elkington, Jodi Felberg, Gail Fondahl, Rodney Fujita, Ashok Gadgil, Robert Hitchcock, Robert Housman, Stewart Hudson, Barbara Johnston, Stephen Karekezi, H. Jeffrey Leonard, Owen Lynch, Ted Macdonald, Joel Makower, Ruth Meinzen-Dick, Deborah Moore, Harriet Parcells, Gunther Pauli, John Ryan, Shira Saperstein, Ken Scott, Jael Silliman, Bruce Smart, Marnie Stetson, Richard Tapper, Frederik van Bolhuis, Amy Vickers, Susan Wells, and Clive Wilkinson.

Finally, we would like to dedicate this tenth edition of *State of the World* to the memory of a former colleague: David Macgregor. During his two years at Worldwatch, David helped us launch this series, devised our first ever direct mail campaign, and edited Worldwatch Papers on photovoltaics, soil erosion, and population policies, among other topics. His wit, generosity of spirit, and good humor in times of stress will long be remembered. David died this June after a struggle with AIDS for nearly a decade, during which he never lost that wittiness and the will to remain strong for others. His loss is felt deeply by his friends and former colleagues.

Lester R. Brown, Christopher Flavin, and Sandra Postel

Contents

List of Tables and Figures

LIST OF TABLES

LIST OF FIGURES

Foreword

It doesn't seem possible that this is the tenth *State of the World* report! Maybe that's because we have had so much fun writing it each year and interacting with readers around the world.

Sometimes in life, new undertakings exceed expectations. Such is the case with *State of the World*. We hoped it would be widely translated, but we never imagined it would be published in 27 languages, with a first printing each year in English of 100,000 copies. And we could not have dreamed that it would spawn "Race to Save the Planet," a 10-part series on public television.

We started this series because we were concerned by the lack of information on global environmental conditions and trends. Environmental literacy, even among national political leaders, was at the time limited. Our concern was shared by the staff and directors of the Rockefeller Brothers Fund. Indeed, the idea for *State of the World* originated in a discussion with Larry Rockefeller, one of the directors. William Dietel, then president of the Fund, offered to help put together a package of funding that would make the report possible, and off we went.

Since that first report, we have watched many environmental issues emerge and evolve. As we worked on *State of the World 1984*, the first in the series, we debated whether we should include in the forestry chapter a reference to a new and disturbing survey: a team of German scientists reported that 8 percent of West Germany's forests were showing signs of damage. Although it was widely known that acid rain could render freshwater lakes lifeless, the team's view that it could also cause wholesale damage to forests was new. In this *State of the World*, we report the results of a new study, which finds that forests are suffering from sulfur deposition in every country in Europe and that the productivity of the continent's forests has been reduced by 16 percent.

When we were working on the first *State of the World*, stratospheric ozone depletion and the risks associated with the resulting increased ultraviolet radiation reaching the earth's surface were of little more than academic interest. In 1985, two British scientists reported finding an "ozone hole" over Antarctica. Since then, a steady stream of reports has chronicled the progressive depletion of the protective ozone layer.

In *State of the World 1984*, we reported that the earth was losing 11 million hectares of tropical forest per year. Now the annual figure is 17 million hectares. A decade ago, few people were deeply troubled about the destruction of tropical rain forests. Today, public concern about this loss and its potential consequences is worldwide.

Over the past decade, countless thousands of plant and animal species have disappeared. They are literally countless because we have never taken an inventory of the earth's biological resources. In last year's *State of the World*, we reported that three fourths of the 9,000 known bird species in the world are declining in numbers or are threatened with extinction.

In *State of the World 1989*, we noted that severe heat and drought in the summer of 1988 had pulled the U.S. grain harvest below domestic consumption levels for the first time in history. No one knows if this was a preview of global warming and far hotter summers to come. If it was, then the argument for replacing fossil fuels with solar-derived energy sources is even stronger than we had thought.

In the first report, we estimated that soil erosion was costing the world's farmers some 24 billion tons of topsoil in excess of new soil formation. Now we can assess the economic costs of this continuing heavy loss. In Chapter 1 of this edition, we report on a U.N. study indicating that land degradation in arid and semiarid regions costs some $42 billion a year in reduced crop and livestock productivity, an amount equal to the value of the U.S. grain harvest.

Contributing to many of these trends is the relentless growth in population. In 1984, when we published the first *State of the World*, some 80 million people were added to the world. The annual addition is projected to exceed 92 million in 1993.

Over the years we have chronicled some promising new trends as well. When we launched the series, the generation of electricity from wind turbines was minuscule and solar thermal power was limited to pilot projects. Today, California alone generates enough electricity from wind power and solar thermal plants to meet the needs of nearly 2 million of its residents.

Ten years ago, nuclear power was still seen by many as the logical replacement for fossil fuels. But the explosion at Chernobyl in 1986 sounded the death knell for the industry. In contrast to the late seventies and early eighties, when construction of 20–30 new plants began each year, new starts have dropped to scarcely one a year during the early nineties.

The world's policy response to these issues has also evolved during the last decade. In 1987, countries gathered in Montreal and agreed to sharply reduce production of the family of chemicals threatening the ozone layer, cutting it in half by 1998. The alarming reports of accelerated depletion of stratospheric ozone since then have quickened the phaseout. Between 1988, the peak year of production, and 1991, world production of chlorofluorocarbons fell by an astounding 46 percent.

Since 1984, many national governments have begun to take the threat of global warming seriously. Wishing to avoid the economic disruption associated with rising global temperatures, more than a dozen countries have now adopted goals to reduce carbon emissions over the next decade or so. Leading this group is Germany, which is committed to a 20-percent reduction by 2005.

With soil erosion, global losses continue to be heavy, but the United States has made impressive progress. The 1985 Conservation Reserve Program provided for the conversion of some 14 million hectares of highly erodible cropland to either grassland or woodland. The result was a reduction of U.S. soil losses by at least one third. In the second phase of the program, from 1990 to 1995, soil losses could be cut by another third. This adds up to a remarkable achievement, a substantial contribution to world food security.

Environmental initiatives notwithstanding, all the major trends of degradation that existed a decade ago have continued. The earth's forests continue to shrink, its deserts continue to expand, and a third of all cropland continues to erode excessively. The number of plant and animal species with which we share the planet is diminishing. The concentration of greenhouse gases in the atmosphere climbs higher each year. And almost every new assessment of the ozone layer's health indicates accelerating depletion.

One of these years we would like to write an upbeat *State of the World*, one reporting that some of the trends of global degradation have been reversed. Unfortunately, not enough people are working yet to reverse the trends of decline for us to write such a report. We are falling far short in our efforts. On the plus side, concern about the earth's future is continuing to rise throughout the world, giving us hope that the degradation will one day be reversed.

One of the manifestations of rising concern that we see directly is the growing interest in *State of the World*. As noted earlier, this edition of our annual report will be brought out by commercial publishers in some 27 languages, including all the major ones—Spanish, Portuguese, French, Italian, Chinese, Japanese, Arabic, Indonesian, German, Polish, and Russian—in addition to English. Now appearing in almost every language in which there is a publishing industry of any size, *State of the World* has acquired a semiofficial status, widely read and used throughout the world. Over the past decade thousands of environmental action groups have sprung up around the world, many of them local, single-issue groups. Eager to reverse a damaging local environmental trend, they need information to help guide their actions.

For them, having *State of the World* available in the local language is invaluable.

In some countries, such as Finland and Argentina, *State of the World* has become a best seller, though only in Finland has it occupied the top slot on the nonfiction best seller list. The first Polish edition sold out in a few weeks and thereafter was available only on the black market at three times the original price. And the first children's version of *State of the World*, adapted from the original, will soon appear in Japanese. There are even multiple editions in some languages: the Spanish edition is published in Barcelona, Mexico City, and Buenos Aires, while three separate English editions appear—for the United States and Canada, for India, and for the United Kingdom and other Commonwealth countries.

When we launched *State of the World* we hoped it would be used in colleges and universities, but we did not anticipate that by 1989 it would be used in more than a thousand courses in 584 U.S. colleges and universities. Leading the way were University of Michigan, Purdue University, and Pennsylvania State University with 13, 10, and 9 courses, respectively. Although this annual report was not designed as a textbook, its integrative, interdisciplinary approach is apparently highly valued by professors in many fields. Its use as a supplemental text to frame the specialized subject matter in individual courses makes it one of the most widely adopted textbooks in the United States.

Further underlining its usefulness was an international survey conducted by a group at Pennsylvania State University, which asked some 235 environmental leaders to select the most influential environmental books. *State of the World* ranked third on the all-time list of 500 books, behind *Sand County Almanac* by

Aldo Leopold and *Silent Spring* by Rachel Carson.

Over the years, more and more concerned individuals have voluntarily purchased large quantities for distribution to key decision makers. In the United States, Ted Turner led the way with the purchase of some 1,400 copies of *State of the World 1984*. These were given to the heads of the Fortune 500, members of the U.S. Congress, state governors, and others. Turner described *State of the World* as "the most important book he had read in years." In 1992 Turner upped his purchase for the Cable News Network to 700, giving a copy to each of the network's editors and senior reporters.

In Norway, business executive Raymond Rooth annually distributes 900 copies of the Norwegian edition to key individuals. Bjorn Stigson, a director of ABB Flakt, gives 500 copies to policymakers in Sweden. An Iranian physician, G. Baski, purchased 1,000 copies of the Persian edition for distribution to key people throughout his country, including leading government officials. And in Belgium, Ecover, a manufacturer of environmentally friendly cleaning products, distributes copies of the Dutch and French editions to members of the country's bilingual national parliament.

Beginning in 1991, the aid agencies of Norway, Sweden, and Denmark started distributing *State of the World* and other Worldwatch publications to key individuals and officials in some 24 developing countries where they operate. They reason that a modest investment in dissemination of environmental information in these countries can pay handsome dividends in policymaking.

During the last decade, there have been many exciting milestones along the way. One of the earliest came in 1989 when course adoptions in U.S. colleges and universities passed the 1,000 mark for the first time. A second came in 1990, when *State of the World* appeared in more languages than *Reader's Digest*.

The rising demand for *State of the World* and the associated Worldwatch Papers reflects a great hunger for environmental information. This led us in 1988 to start a third publication, the bimonthly magazine *World Watch*, as a way to maintain a continuous flow of fresh information to activists and policymakers throughout the world. For those interested in more in-depth treatment of specific issues, we added in 1991 the Environmental Alert series of books, a set of short, topical volumes on subjects such as the consumer society, water, energy, and population.

In 1992, we launched a new annual—*Vital Signs: The Trends That Are Shaping Our Future*. It aims to provide historical data on key trends, such as carbon emissions, the world fish catch, population growth, global military expenditures, production of chlorofluorocarbons, wind electric generation, and grain production. Designed as a handy reference for the growing number of people concerned about the future of the planet, this annual serves as a companion volume to *State of the World*.

One of the reasons *State of the World* is popular is its integrative, interdisciplinary character, which makes it ideal for policymakers who are concerned with all dimensions of issues. With a publishing schedule shorter than that of some monthly magazines, *State of the World* is also timely. In a volume published in English in early January and in several other languages in February, readers are astounded at references to events as recent as mid-November.

As noted earlier, one of these years we would like to write about the reversal of the many global environmental trends that are undermining our future, but that time does not appear to be imminent.

Time and leadership are among the scarcest of resources. On at least one front, we can take heart from the new leaders assuming office in Washington and from their commitment to environmental issues. Perhaps in a future *State of the World* we will be able to report that policy changes they have introduced helped set the world on the right track. Whether the world has time to make the needed changes remains to be seen.

Lester R. Brown
Christopher Flavin
Sandra Postel

Worldwatch Institute
1776 Massachusetts Ave., NW
Washington, DC 20036

December 1992

STATE OF THE
WORLD
1993

1

A New Era Unfolds

Lester R. Brown

In early 1992, the U.S. National Academy of Sciences and the Royal Society of London issued a report that began: "If current predictions of population growth prove accurate and patterns of human activity on the planet remain unchanged, science and technology may not be able to prevent either irreversible degradation of the environment or continued poverty for much of the world."[1]

It was a remarkable statement, an admission that science and technology can no longer ensure a better future unless population growth slows quickly and the economy is restructured. This abandonment of the technological optimism that has permeated so much of the twentieth century by two of the world's leading scientific bodies represents a major shift, but perhaps not a surprising one given the deteriorating state of the planet. That they chose to issue a joint statement, their first ever, reflects the deepening concern about the future among scientists.

This concern is not limited to the scientific community. People everywhere are worried about the planet's continuing deterioration. Attendance at the U.N. Conference on Environment and Development and the parallel nongovernmental events in June in Rio de Janeiro totalled 35,000 people, dwarfing the turnout at the predecessor meetings in Stockholm in 1972. Some 106 heads of state and government participated in the Earth Summit, the largest gathering of national political leaders in history. The 9,000 journalists in Rio for the meetings exceeded the number of total participants in Stockholm.[2]

Despite the intensifying global interest in the planet's future, the U.N. conference fell short of both hopes and expectations. Many of the difficulties centered on the U.S. insistence that goals and timetables for restricting carbon emissions be removed from the climate treaty, leaving it little more than a statement of good intentions. The convention designed to protect biological diversity had some flaws, but perhaps the most serious one was the missing U.S. signature.

The Earth Summit was not a total loss by any means. The climate treaty, which was signed by 154 participating countries, including the United States, recognizes that global warming is a serious issue. And it does provide for setting up an international system for governments to report each year on changes in carbon emissions. This information flow itself

Units of measure throughout this book are metric unless common usage dictates otherwise.

will focus attention on the threat of climate change.[3]

The Rio conference was a time for taking stock of environmental gains and losses. Individual countries presented national state-of-the-environment reports, typically emphasizing their achievements. The descriptions included countless examples of local gains in achieving cleaner air and water, greater recycling of materials, and reforestation.

These improvements notwithstanding, the broad indicators showed a continuing wholesale deterioration in the earth's physical condition. During the 20 years since Stockholm, farmers have lost nearly 500 billion tons of topsoil through erosion at a time when they were called on to feed 1.6 billion additional people. Atmospheric concentrations of carbon dioxide (CO_2), the principal greenhouse gas, climbed 9 percent. In Rio, the risks to life on earth posed by the loss of stratospheric ozone and the associated increase of ultraviolet radiation were on everyone's mind, a threat not even imagined in 1972.[4]

The environmental concerns that brought delegates to Rio exist in part because of an economic accounting system that misleads and a biological accounting system that is largely nonexistent. The internationally accepted system of national economic accounting used to calculate gross national product (GNP) rightly subtracts the depreciation of plant and equipment from the overall output of goods and services. But it takes no account of the depreciation of natural capital, such as the loss of topsoil from erosion, the destruction of forests by acid rain, or the depletion of the protective stratospheric ozone layer. As a result, the economic accounting system now used by governments greatly overstates progress. Failing to reflect reality, it generates environmentally destructive economic policies.

The biological accounting system is fragmentary at best. No one knows how many species of plants and animals are lost each year; indeed, lacking a global inventory of the earth's biological resources, no one even knows how many species there are. Visual evidence, occasional national surveys, and satellite data tell us that forests are disappearing in many countries. Similarly, incomplete data indicate that grasslands are deteriorating. Closely associated with the reduced grass and tree cover is the loss of topsoil. Despite the essential economic role of soil, no global data gathering system measures its gains or losses.

Nor does the biological accounting system warn when carrying capacity thresholds are crossed. We learn that cattle numbers are excessive only when the rangeland begins to deteriorate. We discover that demands on forests are excessive only when they begin to disappear. We find that we have been overfishing only when the catch drops precipitously. Lacking information on sustainable yields, governments have permitted demands on these natural systems to become excessive, leading to their gradual destruction.

The result of this flawed economic accounting system and largely nonexistent biological accounting system is widespread degradation and destruction of the economy's environmental support systems. Industrial firms are allowed to internalize profits while externalizing costs, passing on to society such expenses as those for health care associated with polluted air or those arising from global warming.

An expanding economy based on such an incomplete accounting system would be expected to slowly undermine itself, eventually collapsing as support systems are destroyed. And that is just what is happening. The environmentally destructive activities of recent decades are now showing up in reduced productivity of croplands, forests, grasslands, and fisheries; in the mounting cleanup costs of toxic waste sites; in rising health care costs for cancer, birth defects, allergies, emphysema, asthma, and other respiratory diseases; and in the spread of hunger.

Rapid population growth, environmental degradation, and deepening poverty are reinforcing each other in a downward spiral in many countries. In its *World Development Report 1992*, the World Bank reported that per capita GNP had fallen in 49 countries during the eighties. Almost all these nations, containing 846 million people, are low-income, largely agrarian economies experiencing rapid population growth and extensive degradation of their forests, grasslands, and croplands.[5]

As the Royal Society/National Academy statement implies, it may not be possible to reverse this fall in living standards of nearly one sixth of humanity if rapid population growth continues and existing patterns of economic activity are not changed. Just how difficult it will be is only now becoming clear. There is also a real risk that the demographic pressures and environmental deterioration that are replacing progress with decline will spread, enveloping even more of humanity during the nineties.

ENVIRONMENTAL DEGRADATION: THE ECONOMIC COSTS

Many people have long understood, at least intuitively, that continuing environmental degradation would eventually exact a heavy economic toll. Unfortunately, no global economic models incorporate the depletion and destruction of the earth's natural support systems.

Only now can we begin to piece together information from several recent independent studies to get a sense of the worldwide economic effects of environmental degradation. Among the most revealing of these are studies on the effects of air pollution and acid rain on forests in Europe, of land degradation on livestock and crop production in the world's dryland regions, of global warming on the U.S. economy, and of pollution on health in Russia.

Every country is practicing the environmental equivalent of deficit financing in one form or another.

These reports and other data show that the fivefold growth in the world economy since 1950 and the increase in population from 2.6 billion to 5.5 billion have begun to outstrip the carrying capacity of biological support systems and the ability of natural systems to absorb waste without being damaged. In country after country, demands for crops and for the products of grasslands, forests, and fisheries are exceeding the sustainable yield of these systems. Once this happens, the resource itself begins to shrink as natural capital is consumed. Overstocking grasslands, overcutting forests, overplowing, and overfishing are now commonplace. Every country is practicing the environmental equivalent of deficit financing in one form or another.[6]

Perhaps the most visible environmental deficit is deforestation, the result of tree cutting and forest clearing that exceeds natural regrowth and tree planting. Each year this imbalance now costs the world some 17 million hectares of tropical forests alone. Over a decade, the destruction of tropical forests clears an area the size of Malaysia, the Philippines, Ghana, the Congo, Ecuador, El Salvador, and Nicaragua. Once tropical forests are burned off or clear-cut, the land rapidly loses its fertility, since most of the nutrients in these ecosystems are stored in the vegetation. Although these soils can be farmed for 3–5 years before fertility drops and can be grazed for 5–10 years before becoming wasteland, they typically will not sustain productivity over the long term. Clearing tropical forests is, in effect, the conversion of a highly productive ecosystem into wasteland in exchange for a short-term economic gain.[7]

As timber resources are depleted in the Third World, transforming countries that traditionally exported forest products into importers, logging companies are turning to remote temperate-zone forests. Canada, for example, is now losing 200,000 hectares a year as cutting exceeds regeneration by a wide margin. Similarly, as Japanese and Korean logging firms move into Siberia, the forests there are also beginning to shrink.[8]

It is not only the axe and the chainsaw that threaten forests, but also emissions from power plant smokestacks and automobile exhaust pipes. In Europe, air pollution and acid rain are damaging and destroying the region's traditionally well managed forests. Scientists at the International Institute for Applied Systems Analysis (IIASA) in Austria have estimated the effect on forest productivity of sulfur dioxide emissions from fossil-fuel-burning power plants, factories, and automobiles. They concluded that 75 percent of Europe's forests are now experiencing damaging levels of sulfur deposition. Forests in every country on the continent are affected—from Norway and Portugal in the west to the European part of the former Soviet Union in the east.[9]

The IIASA study estimated that losses associated with the deterioration of Europe's forests total $30.4 billion each year, roughly equal to the annual output of the German steel industry. (See Table 1–1.) The researchers note that the loss of raw or unprocessed wood from a 16-percent reduction in the annual harvest is $6.3 billion. The loss in value added as it is converted to lumber or pulp comes to $7.2 billion. Other losses associated with dying forests, including the costs of increased flooding, soil losses, and the silting of rivers, reach $16.9 billion a year. With Europe's forest industries employing some 5 million people, the effects of diminished productivity on employment are obvious. An IIASA staffer notes, "What emerges is a startling picture of forests crippled by air pollutants at immense cost to European industry and society."[10]

If damage from nitrogen oxides had been included, the losses would be far greater. Even more alarming, the IIASA

Table 1–1. Annual Losses Due to Forest Damage in Europe from Sulfur Deposition[1]

Loss	Amount of Loss
	(billion dollars)
Losses of Unprocessed Wood	6.3
Losses from Value Added in Basic Processing of Wood (into lumber, paper pulp, and so on)	7.2
Other Costs (including damage from floods, losses of soil from erosion, silting of rivers, and so on)	16.9
Total	30.4

[1]Does not include damage from nitrogen oxides.
SOURCE: Constructed from data in "The Price of Pollution," *Options* (International Institute for Applied Systems Analysis), September 1990.

team estimates that adoption of the most effective pollution control technologies available would still leave nitrogen oxides deposition at half and sulfur deposition at one fourth the current levels, which would continue to threaten the long-term viability of Europe's forests.[11]

Land degradation is also taking a heavy economic toll, particularly in the drylands that account for 41 percent of the earth's land area. In the early stages the costs show up as lower land productivity. But if the process continues unarrested, it eventually creates wasteland, destroying the soil as well as the vegetation. Using data for 1990, a U.N. assessment of the earth's dryland regions estimated that the degradation of irrigated cropland, rainfed cropland, and rangeland now costs the world more than $42 billion a year in lost crop and livestock output, a sum that approximates the value of the U.S. grain harvest. (See Table 1–2.)[12]

In Africa, where land degradation is most visible, the annual loss of rangeland productivity is estimated at $7 billion, more than the GNP of Ethiopia and Uganda combined. And lost productivity on Africa's rainfed cropland, largely from soil erosion, totals $1.9 billion, roughly the same as Tanzania's GNP. In Asia, the losses are larger mainly because of the waterlogging and salting of irrigated land: for irrigated land, rainfed cropland, and rangeland, they total nearly $21 billion a year—by far the largest of any geographic region.[13]

These losses are from the degradation of drylands only. The deterioration in humid regions of the world, which includes the U.S. Corn Belt and most of Europe's rich agricultural regions, also takes a heavy toll, though no one has calculated it.

Excessive demand directly threatens the productivity of oceanic fisheries as well. The U.N. Food and Agriculture Organization (FAO), which monitors oceanic fisheries, indicates that 4 out of 17

Table 1–2. Annual Losses in Crop and Livestock Production from Land Degradation in Dryland Regions

Continent	Irrigated Land	Rainfed Cropland	Rangeland	Total[1]
	(billion dollars)			
Africa	0.5	1.9	7.0	9.3
Asia	8.0	4.6	8.3	20.9
Australia	0.1	0.5	2.5	3.1
Europe	0.5	0.4	0.6	1.5
North America	1.5	0.4	2.9	4.8
South America	0.3	0.2	2.1	2.7
Total[1]	10.8	8.2	23.2	42.3

[1]Columns may not add up to totals due to rounding.
SOURCE: H. Dregne et al., "A New Assessment of the World Status of Desertification," *Desertification Control Bulletin*, No. 20, 1991.

of the world's fishing zones are now overfished. It also reports that most traditional marine fish stocks have reached full exploitation. Atlantic stocks of the heavily fished bluefin tuna have been cut by a staggering 94 percent. It will take years for such species to recover, even if fishing were to stop altogether.[14]

Depletion of the cod and haddock fisheries off Nova Scotia has led to heavy layoffs in the fishing and fish processing industries.

Dwindling fish stocks are affecting many national economies. In Canada, for example—where the fishing industry traditionally landed roughly 1.5 million tons of fish a year, worth $3.1 billion—depletion of the cod and haddock fisheries off the coast of Nova Scotia has led to shrinking catches and heavy layoffs in the fishing and fish processing industries. In July 1992, in an unprecedented step, Canada banned all cod fishing off the coast of Newfoundland and Labrador for two years in a bid to save the fishery. To cushion the massive layoffs in the industry, the mainstay of Newfoundland's economy, Ottawa authorized a $400-million aid package for unemployment compensation and retraining.[15]

As overfishing of the North Atlantic by U.S., Canadian, and European fleets decimated stocks there during the seventies, the ships turned to the South Atlantic, particularly to the fisheries off the African coast. Unable to control fishing in the 200-mile Exclusive Economic Zones granted by the 1979 Law of the Sea Treaty, some African countries saw their fisheries decimated. Namibia, for instance, watched the catch in its zone fall from nearly 2 million tons in 1980 to less than 100,000 tons a decade later. After banning European ships from its

waters in 1990, stocks started to recover.[16]

Inland fisheries are also suffering from environmental mismanagement—water diversion, acidification, and pollution. The Aral Sea, located between Kazakstan and Uzbekistan, as recently as 1960 yielded 40 million kilograms of fish per year. Shrinking steadily over the last three decades as the river water feeding it was diverted for irrigation, the sea has become increasingly salty, eventually destroying the fish stock. Today it is effectively dead. A similar situation exists in Pakistan, where Deg Nullah, a small but once highly productive freshwater lake that yielded 400,000 kilograms of fish annually, is now barren—destroyed by pollution. Acidification is also taking a toll. Canada alone now counts 14,000 dead lakes.[17]

In the United States, pollution has severely affected the Chesapeake Bay, one of the world's richest estuaries. Its fabulously productive oyster beds, which yielded 8 million bushels per year a century ago, now produce scarcely a million bushels. Elsewhere, fish have survived, such as in the U.S. Great Lakes and New York's Hudson River, but many species are unsafe for human consumption because of pollution with PCBs and other toxic chemicals. Half the shellfish-growing areas off Nova Scotia in eastern Canada have been closed because of contamination.[18]

The rising atmospheric concentration of greenhouse gases is potentially the most economically disruptive and costly change that has been set in motion by our modern industrial society. William Cline, an economist with the Washington-based Institute for International Economics, has looked at the long-term economic effects of global warming. As part of this study he analyzed the effect of a doubling of greenhouse gases on the U.S. economy, which could come as early as 2025. He estimates that heat stress and drought would cost U.S. farmers $18 billion in output, that increased electricity for air conditioning would require an additional $11 billion, and that dealing with sea level rise would cost an estimated $7 billion per year. In total, Cline estimates the cost at nearly $60 billion, roughly 1 percent of the 1990 U.S. GNP. (See Table 1–3.)

Not all countries would be affected equally. Some island countries, such as the Republic of the Maldives in the Indian Ocean, would become uninhabit-

Table 1–3. Annual U.S. Economic Losses from Global Warming with Doubling of Greenhouse Gases

Source of Loss	Amount of Loss
	(billion dollars)
Agricultural Losses due to Heat Stress and Drought	18
Increased Electricity for Air Conditioning	11
Sea Level Rise	7
Curtailed Water Supply from Reduced Runoff	7
Increased Urban Air Pollution	4
Reduced Lumber Yield from Forests	3
Other (includes hurricane and forest fire damage, and increased mortality due to heat stress)	8
Total	58

SOURCE: William Cline, *Global Warming: The Economic Stakes* (Washington, D.C.: Institute for International Economics, 1992).

able. Low-lying deltas, such as in Egypt and Bangladesh, would be inundated, displacing millions of people. In the end, rising seas in a warming world would be not only economically costly, but politically disruptive as well.

Every society is paying a price for environmental pollution. Contamination of air, water, and soil by toxic chemicals and radioactivity, along with increased ultraviolet radiation, is damaging human health, running up health care costs. An assessment of urban air quality jointly undertaken by the World Health Organization and the United Nations Environment Programme reports that 625 million people are exposed to unhealthy levels of sulfur dioxide from fossil fuel burning. More than a billion people, a fifth of the planet's population, are exposed to potentially health-damaging levels of air pollutants of all kinds. One study for the United States estimates that air pollution may cost the nation as much as $40 billion annually in health care and lost productivity.[19]

In Bulgaria, research that was declassified following democratization showed that those living near heavy industrial complexes had asthma rates nine times higher than people living elsewhere. Skin diseases occurred seven times as often. Liver disease was four times as frequent, and nervous system diseases three times as high.[20]

New data from Russia, Europe's largest country, show all too well the devastating effect of pollution by chemical and organic toxins on human health. At an October 1992 news conference, Vladimir Pokrovsky, head of the Russian Academy of Medical Sciences, shocked the world with his frankness, "We have already doomed ourselves for the next 25 years." He added: "The new generation is entering adult life unhealthy. The Soviet economy was developed at the expense of the population's health." Data released by the Academy show 11 percent of Russian infants suffering from birth defects. With half the drinking water and a tenth of the food supply contaminated, 55 percent of school-age children suffer health problems. The Academy reported that the increase in illness and early death among those aged 25–40 was particularly distressing. The bottom line is that Russian life expectancy is now falling.[21]

Another source of higher future health care costs is stratospheric ozone depletion. Epidemiologists at the U.S. Environmental Protection Agency (EPA) estimate that the upward revision in early 1991 of the rate of ozone loss could mean an additional 200,000 skin cancer fatalities in the United States over the next five decades. Worldwide, this translates into millions of deaths. The number of people with cataracts would also increase dramatically in a world where people are exposed to greater doses of ultraviolet radiation than ever recorded. Other associated health care costs include a projected higher incidence of infectious diseases associated with the suppression of immune systems, the economic costs of which are difficult to even estimate.[22]

In addition to the environmental deficits the world is now experiencing, huge environmental cleanup bills are accumulating. For example, the estimated costs for cleaning up hazardous waste sites in the United States center on $750 billion, roughly three fourths the 1990 U.S. federal budget. And a national survey in Norway has discovered some 7,000 hazardous waste sites, the product of decades of irresponsible dumping. Cleanup is estimated to cost tiny Norway $3–6 billion.[23]

There is no reason to believe that these bills for the United States and Norway are very different from those of other industrial countries. In a world generating more than a million tons of hazardous waste a day, much of it care-lessly disposed of, the costs of cleanup are enormous. The alternative to cleaning up these sites is to ignore them and let toxic wastes eventually leak into underground aquifers. One way or another, society will pay—either in cleanup bills or in rising health care costs.[24]

In addition to toxic chemical wastes, damaging nuclear waste is also a threat to human health. National governments in countries with nuclear power plants have failed to design a system for safely disposing of their wastes. At present, radiated fuel at most plants is stored in pools of cooling water at the site itself. No one has yet put a price tag on safely disposing of nuclear waste and decommissioning the nuclear power plants that generate it. Coping with the health problems associated with nuclear waste is being left to future generations, a part of the nuclear legacy.

Several military powers face the related threat of radiation wastes generated at nuclear weapons manufacturing facilities, which are released into the surrounding areas. In the United States, the cleanup bill for all these sites, including some of the more publicized ones such as Rocky Flats in Colorado and the Savannah River site in South Carolina, is estimated at $200 billion. For the former Soviet Union, where the management of radioactive waste has been even more irresponsible, the costs are likely to be far greater. Again, the question is not whether society will pay the bill for nuclear wastes, but whether it will be in the form of cleanup or in rising health care costs in exposed communities.[25]

The environmental deficits and debts that the world has incurred in recent decades are enormous, often dwarfing the economic debts of nations. Perhaps more important is the often overlooked difference between economic deficits and environmental ones. Economic debts are something we owe each other. For every borrower there is a lender; resources simply change hands. But environmental debts, especially those that lead to irreversible damage or losses of natural capital, can often be repaid only in the deprivation and ill health of future generations.

GROWTH IN FOOD OUTPUT SLOWING

Of the major economic sectors, the one most vulnerable to environmental degradation is agriculture, simply because it is so directly dependent on natural systems and resources. Environmental degradation, along with emerging agronomic constraints, is slowing the growth in world food output.

The production of grain, which dominates human diets, expanded at 3 percent a year from 1950 until 1984, when per capita output peaked at 344 kilograms. From then until 1992, it grew less than 1 percent annually, scarcely half the rate of population. (See Table 1–4.) For soybeans, the world's leading protein crop, growth averaged 5 percent a year from 1950 to 1980. Over the next 12 years, it averaged 2 percent annually. Slower growth of grain and soybean production, both of which are used as feed, helps explain the slowdown in meat production growth from 3.4 percent a year between 1950 and 1986 to 2 percent annually during the following six years.

This slower growth has several causes, but two stand out. One is that the growth in the use of key inputs—cropland, irrigation water, and fertilizer—has slowed

Table 1–4. Growth in Production of Principal Foods and in Use of Agricultural Resources, 1950–92

Commodity/Resources	Rapid Growth Period		Slow Growth Period	
	Years	Annual Rate	Years	Annual Rate
		(percent)		(percent)
Principal Food Commodities				
Grain Production	1950–84	+ 2.9	1984–92	+ 0.7
Soybean Production	1950–80	+ 5.1	1980–92	+ 2.2
Meat Production	1950–86	+ 3.4	1986–92	+ 2.0
World Fish Catch	1950–88	+ 4.0	1988–92	− 0.8
Principal Agricultural Resources				
Grainland Area	1950–81	+ 0.7	1981–92	− 0.5
Irrigated Area	1950–78	+ 2.8	1978–92	+ 1.2
Fertilizer Use	1950–84	+ 6.7	1984–92	+ 0.7

SOURCES: Various annual publications of the U.N. Food and Agriculture Organization and unpublished annual printouts from the U.S. Department of Agriculture.

dramatically. And two, the many forms of environmental degradation—soil erosion, aquifer depletion, air pollution, ozone depletion, and hotter summers— are taking a toll on agricultural output.

Between 1950 and 1981 the grain harvested area expanded some 24 percent. In the next 11 years, it actually declined slightly. While new cropland is being added in some countries, it is being lost in others from land degradation or conversion to nonfarm uses. On balance, there is little prospect for markedly increasing the world cropland area during the nineties.[26]

As growth in the cropland area was coming to a halt, that in irrigated area was slowing dramatically. Between 1950 and 1978 irrigated area expanded by 2.8 percent a year, enlarging the area per person by nearly one third. Annual growth since 1978 of 1.2 percent, less than that of population, has shrunk irrigated area per person by 6 percent.[27]

The halt in cropland expansion and the slower growth of irrigation are combining with the falling yield response to additional fertilizer to slow the growth in the use of this other key input. During the sixties and seventies, using more fertilizer sharply boosted crop output, making the annual rise in fertilizer use one of the most predictable of world economic trends. Today, using more fertilizer in agriculturally advanced countries has little effect on crop yields. Worldwide, from 1950 to 1984 growth in fertilizer use averaged nearly 7 percent a year. From 1984 to 1992, it expanded less than 1 percent annually.[28]

U.S. fertilizer use during the early nineties, averaging 21 million tons per year, is slightly lower than the 22 million tons a year used in the early eighties. Similar trends are emerging in Western Europe and Japan. Agricultural reforms launched in the Soviet Union in 1988, which included a shift to the much higher world market price for fertilizer, sharply lowered use there. Between 1988 and 1991, fertilizer use fell 23 percent as Soviet farmers eliminated the excessive, often uneconomical, use of this input. World Bank efforts to eliminate fertilizer subsidies in other countries, such as Mexico and Indonesia, have also contributed to this trend.[29]

With the cropland area no longer expanding, all growth in output must now come from raising productivity on existing cropland. But the declining potential for profitably using more fertilizer calls into question farmers' ability to increase production enough to feed the billions of people to be added to world population in the decades ahead.

As noted earlier, the growth in oceanic food sources has also slowed dramatically. After expanding at nearly 4 percent a year from 1950 to 1988 and climbing from 22 million to 99 million tons, the catch has actually declined, dropping per capita fish availability an estimated 7 percent over the ensuing four years. If the oceans cannot sustain a catch of more than 100 million tons, as FAO marine biologists believe, then this per capita decline will continue as world population grows.[30]

The second cause of slower food production growth is environmental degradation, which is damaging agriculture more than ever before. Worldwide, farmers are losing an estimated 24 billion tons of topsoil from cropland each year. With one hectare-inch of topsoil weighing 400 tons, this annual loss can be visualized as one inch lost from 60 million hectares, an area equal to roughly half of China's cropland. A compilation of more than a dozen U.S. studies analyzing the effect of erosion on land productivity found that losing an inch of topsoil reduces corn and wheat yields an average of 6 percent.[31]

The World Bank, citing studies for Costa Rica, Malawi, Mali, and Mexico, concludes that annual losses of agricultural productivity from soil erosion equal 0.5–1.5 percent of those countries' gross domestic product. To some degree, the effect of soil losses can be offset by using more fertilizer, but this too has its limits. With the effect of fertility loss accumulating over time, it is not surprising that the growth in world food output is slowing.[32]

Air pollution, now almost as pervasive as soil erosion, is also lowering agricultural productivity. In some parts of the world, it takes an even greater crop toll than soil erosion does. In Sweden, where air pollution is moderate compared with some industrial countries, yields of the more sensitive food crops such as potatoes and oats are suffering. Air pollution reduced the output of all cereals by 350,000 tons per year, 6 percent of the annual harvest there. In heavily industrialized Czechoslovakia, with some of the world's worst air pollution, crop yields are also suffering. Czech scientists estimate an annual harvest loss of all crops as a result of air pollution at $192 million.[33]

For the United States, where some 70 monitoring stations indicate crop-damaging concentrations of ground-level ozone in every part of the country, the financial loss is far greater. A joint study by EPA and the U.S. Department of Agriculture indicates that crops are affected in varying degrees depending on their sensitivity to air pollutants. Overall, the study estimates that the annual crop harvest in the United States is down at least 5 percent because of air pollution and perhaps as much as 10 percent. Applying these proportions to the annual harvest, with a market value around $70 billion, yields a loss of $3.5–7 billion from air pollution. Worldwide, losses must be several times this amount.[34]

Although the effect of soil erosion and air pollution on harvests has long been known, that of exposure to increased ultraviolet radiation resulting from strato-

spheric ozone losses is only beginning to unfold. Two multiyear projects researching this effect, one by the Commonwealth Scientific and Industrial Research Organization in Australia and the other at the International Rice Research Institute in the Philippines, are still in the early stages. Preliminary results show that with both wheat and rice, the world's leading food staples, exposure to increased ultraviolet radiation impairs photosynthesis, which in turn stunts growth. The next stage of these projects will measure the effect of increased dosages of ultraviolet radiation on crop yields.[35]

Since there are only a few monitoring stations that measure ultraviolet radiation at ground level, scientists do not know exactly how much additional radiation is reaching the earth's surface during the most vulnerable plant growth phases. With losses of stratospheric ozone projected to continue for several decades, even if chlorofluorocarbon (CFC) production is halted soon, the potential effects on agriculture deserve far more monitoring and research.

With both wheat and rice, exposure to increased ultraviolet radiation stunts growth.

In addition to soil erosion, air pollution, and ozone depletion, other forms of environmental degradation—such as increased flooding due to deforestation, the depletion of aquifers, losses in genetic diversity of various crops, and the hotter summers that are in prospect—will hinder the world's ability to feed ever growing numbers.

The loss of momentum in food production growth, specifically the 6-percent decline in grain output per person between 1984 and 1992, is perhaps the most disturbing economic trend in the world today. The decline in low-income countries has been even more pronounced—and more worrying. In the short run, world food supplies can be redistributed by shipping food from surplus countries, such as the United States, to countries where hunger is growing. But the only lasting solution is accelerated agricultural development and slower population growth in these countries. Failure to slow world population growth during the eighties, the loss of economic momentum, and the cumulative effect of environmental degradation may ultimately be measured in hunger— and will be seen in the emaciated bodies of those trapped in the decline.[36]

THE END OF RAPID GNP GROWTH

As noted earlier, our existing economic accounting system makes it difficult to assess the effect on the economy of both environmental degradation and the inherent constraints imposed by the carrying capacity of natural systems. We know that they will constrain future expansion of food and other essential commodities, but we do not know how much. Until we have an accounting system that incorporates natural capital depreciation and losses, we cannot measure progress or decline accurately. For the time being, then, policymakers are forced to rely on GNP, which overstates progress.

More and more evidence indicates that the productivity of the earth's biological systems is emerging as a constraint on the growth of the economy and ultimately on that of population. This is most evident in the Third World, where the falling productivity of forests, grasslands, and, in some countries, croplands is reducing living standards.

In scores of developing countries, per capita grain production has been falling far longer than it has for the world as a whole. In Africa, the decline has been under way since 1970, dropping an average of roughly 1 percent a year. Such a decrease in a largely agrarian society is often followed by a decline in per capita GNP. Indeed, of the 49 countries where per capita GNP fell during the eighties, the great majority had experienced a drop in per capita grain production. Globally, if growth in grain output cannot be raised from the 1 percent annually of the last several years to something close to the 3 percent a year that was helping eradicate hunger from mid-century until 1984, slow agricultural growth will become a severe constraint on world economic growth.[37]

A major subsector within agriculture, the production of beef and mutton on grasslands, is also pushing against nature's boundaries. With only rare exceptions, the world's grasslands are now either fully used or overused; in many areas they cannot sustain even the present output. A study of rangeland productivity in Pakistan's semiarid regions reports that overgrazing has reduced productivity to 15–40 percent of its potential. It describes the livestock sector as "caught in a downward spiral of too many sick animals chasing too little feed." Oceanic fisheries, like grasslands, are also being pushed to their limits. Little future growth can be expected.[38]

Beef and mutton production can be expanded in the future, but only by feeding more grain. Similarly for seafood, future growth in marine protein supplies almost certainly will have to come from fish farming. Both putting more cattle and sheep in feedlots and expanding fish farming require more grain and soybean meal, which further intensifies the competition with humans for grain.

With forests, the demand for firewood

and lumber exceeds forest regeneration by a wide margin in China, the Indian subcontinent, and semiarid Africa—areas that contain nearly half of humanity. Many developing countries that once exported forest products, such as Nigeria, are now importers. Of the 33 remaining Third World exporters of forest products, only 10 are projected to still be in that position by the end of this decade. With productive forests shrinking, the prospect for rapid long-term expansion of this sector is not good.[39]

Slower growth in agriculture affects the entire economy since the farm sector accounts for anywhere from a high of 60 percent or more of some African economies to less than 3 percent of the U.S. economy. The modest U.S. number greatly understates agriculture's role since the food sector, principally the food processing and retail industries, depend on it. The farm/food sector, taken collectively, accounts for easily one tenth of U.S. economic output.[40]

Agriculture also supplies industrial raw materials. Farms and forests together supply cotton and wool for the textile industries, leather for the leather goods industries, lumber for construction, wood pulp for paper, and many other basic inputs. Indeed, with the important exceptions of minerals and petrochemical products, virtually all the raw materials used in industry are of biological origin, coming from the agricultural and forestry sectors. Slower growth in world farm output thus affects not only the food prospect, but the industrial growth prospect as well.

In addition to the constraints imposed by the maximum sustainable yield of forests, grasslands, and fisheries, the amount of fresh water produced by the hydrological cycle is impairing economic expansion in many countries. In more and more locations, the threefold growth in world water use since mid-century is pushing demand beyond the amount that the hydrological cycle can supply. Water scarcity and falling water tables are now commonplace in the former Soviet Asian republics, the Middle East, North China, parts of India, North Africa, parts of sub-Saharan Africa, and the southwestern United States. (See Chapter 2.)[41]

Many developing countries that once exported forest products, such as Nigeria, are now importers.

Pollution cleanup costs are siphoning public capital away from investment in education, health care, and other key needs. Societies everywhere are facing huge cleanup costs for toxic chemical waste sites and areas contaminated with nuclear radiation. In some countries the costs total in the billions of dollars; in larger industrial economies, such as the United States, they total in the hundreds of billions.[42]

The costs of environmentally induced illnesses, both those of health care and lost labor productivity, are everywhere on the rise. Because of the long delays between exposure to carcinogenic or other health-damaging pollutants and the manifestation of illness, the full effect is only beginning to be felt. Thus far, epidemiologists are picking up increases in respiratory illnesses (such as bronchitis, asthma, and emphysema), nervous system disorders, allergies, skin diseases, liver disease, cancers of every kind, and birth defects, among others. When the health care costs of environmentally induced illnesses already reported and those associated with the projected increased exposure to ultraviolet radiation are totalled, they will represent an enormous drain on the financial resources of societies everywhere.

These illnesses will also take a heavy toll on labor force productivity.[43]

Even a cursory glance at global economic growth by decade since mid-century shows the emergence of a disturbing trend for the world's poor. (See Table 1–5.) World economic growth exceeded that of population by more than 3 percent during the fifties and sixties, providing a substantial gain in living standards for much of humanity. During the seventies, this was roughly cut in half; it dropped further during the eighties. And the nineties are not off to a good start. As a result of the global recession, per capita income fell by over 2 percent from 1990 to 1992. Even with a strong rebound, it could be mid-decade before incomes regain their 1990 level, giving the world five years with no improvement in living standards.

The world has experienced three major global recessions since mid-century, periods in which average income per person dropped for the world. The first two, in 1974–76 and 1980–81, were the result of oil price shocks. The reces-

Table 1–5. World Economic Growth by Decade, 1950–92

Decade	Annual Growth of World Economy	Annual Growth Per Person
	(percent)	(percent)
1950–60	4.9	3.1
1960–70	5.2	3.2
1970–80	3.4	1.6
1980–90	2.9	1.1
1990–92	0.6	− 1.1

SOURCES: World Bank, Department of Socio-Economic Data, unpublished printout, February 1992; International Monetary Fund, *World Economic Outlook October 1992* (Washington, D.C.: 1992); world product in 1950 from Herbert R. Block, *The Planetary Product in 1980: A Creative Pause?* (Washington, D.C.: U.S. Department of State, 1981); population data from Population Reference Bureau, *World Population Data Sheets* (Washington, D.C.: various years).

sion of the early nineties appears to be largely tied to economic mismanagement in the United States, where a huge fiscal deficit is crippling the economy, in Japan, where the deflation of overvalued real estate prices is undermining confidence, and in Germany, where unification costs are higher than expected. At the same time, however, environmental degradation in its many forms and the constraints imposed by natural systems are slowing long-term economic expansion, making it easier for the economy to fall into a recession.[44]

The economic effect of environmental degradation is certain to grow as the costs accumulate and as the damage materializes from such big-ticket items as stratospheric ozone depletion and global warming. This will affect not only the expansion of food output, but also the ability of national economies to provide housing, health care, education, and other essential goods and services.

Now directly affecting national and global economic trends, environmental degradation can no longer be considered a peripheral issue. If destruction of the economy's support systems continues, growth in economic output could fall below that of population, pulling average incomes down for the entire world. The bottom line is that the world is entering a new era, one in which future economic progress depends on reversing environmental degradation. This in turn is contingent on new economic and population policies.

THE SHAPE OF A NEW WORLD

That the existing economic system is slowly beginning to self-destruct as it undermines its environmental support systems is evident. The challenge is to design and build an economic system that is environmentally sustainable. Can we envision what this would look like? Yes. And can we devise a strategy for getting from here to there in the time that is available? Again, the answer is yes.

The basic components of an effort to build an environmentally sustainable global economy are rather straightforward. They include reestablishing climate stability, protecting the stratospheric ozone layer, restoring the earth's tree cover, stabilizing soils, safeguarding the earth's remaining biological diversity, and restoring the traditional balance between births and deaths. Endowed with a certain permanence, this new society will be a far more appealing, satisfying one than the ephemeral, throwaway society we now live in. Space constraints preclude detailed information on the shape of a sustainable economy, but brief descriptions of what the energy sector would look like and how population growth can be stabilized give a partial glimpse of this future world.[45]

In this new world, energy would be used far more efficiently. (See Chapter 6.) Traditional incandescent light bulbs, for example, would be replaced by the latest compact fluorescents, which provide the same light but use only a quarter as much electricity. In sector after sector—transportation, manufacturing, housing, agriculture—energy would be used with an efficiency dwarfing that of today.[46]

Recognizing that fossil fuels are no longer environmentally feasible and that nuclear power is not economically or environmentally viable, the only option is solar energy. This energy source takes many forms: hydropower, wind power, solar thermal power plants, firewood, photovoltaic cells, agricultural wastes, rooftop solar water heaters, alcohol fuels from sugar cane, and many more. All are likely to play a role. Hydropower already

supplies one fifth of the world's electricity. The world's wind power potential may be far greater.[47]

The costs of photovoltaic cells are coming down fast, and these are likely to play an important role eventually. But for large-scale production during this decade, solar thermal power plants of the sort built in southern California will probably have the edge. The latest of these converts a phenomenal 22 percent of sunlight into electricity and produces it for 8¢ per kilowatt hour, well below the 12¢ for electricity from new nuclear plants in the state, but still above the 6¢ for that from coal-fired plants.[48]

As costs continue to drop, the resulting cheap solar electricity permits the production of hydrogen fuel from the simple electrolysis of water. Hydrogen provides a means of both storing solar energy and transporting it efficiently over long distances, either by pipeline or by tanker, much the same way that natural gas is transported.

Fortunately, all the world's major population concentrations are located near areas rich in sunlight. For the densely populated northeastern United States and industrial Midwest, it is the sun-drenched Southwest. Natural gas pipelines that already link Texas-Oklahoma gas fields to these regions might one day carry hydrogen fuel. For the European Community, the source will be southern Spain, which has a solar regime similar to southern California's, and the coast of North Africa. The electricity can be either fed directly into the European grid or converted into hydrogen for the natural gas pipeline network that already ties Europe together. For the Commonwealth of Independent States, the Asian republics are rich in sunlight. For India, the Thar Desert in the northwest could someday easily supply its energy needs.

China, and possibly Japan, can turn to central and northwest China, a largely desert region. For Japan, investing in solar-hydrogen facilities in central China could make this region a future source of hydrogen, much as the Middle East now supplies it with oil. In addition, it could help China shift away from its projected heavy use of coal, thus helping reduce the damaging air pollution and acid rain at home and in both Korea and Japan.

Natural gas can serve as a bridging fuel, linking the fossil fuel era with the solar age. Shifting from coal or oil to natural gas sharply reduces air pollution and carbon emissions per unit of energy produced. And the facilities and pipelines now used to store and transport natural gas can one day be used for hydrogen.

Only a reorientation of development strategies that concentrates resources on raising female literacy and improving the status of women can succeed.

Cheap solar electricity and the hydrogen produced with it provide the diversity of fuels needed to run a modern industrial economy. Transport vehicles can be powered either with electric motors or hydrogen engines, both of which are already in use on a small scale. Electricity can operate highly efficient electric arc steel furnaces, an advanced steel-making technology that thrives on steel scrap and now accounts for 38 percent of U.S. steel production. Both electricity and hydrogen can also be used to heat homes and satisfy other needs of a modern industrial society. The solar thermal technology is already economically competitive in some situations.[49]

The second major challenge in building a new world is to reestablish the balance between births and deaths that prevailed throughout most of our existence as a species. This complex undertaking involves raising public understanding of the social consequences of having large families, filling the family planning gap, giving equal opportunities to women, and creating the other social conditions that encourage the shift to small families. (See Chapter 4.)

Few national political leaders have a well-developed sense of the relationship between population size and the sustainable yield thresholds of basic life-support systems. National projections that include demographic, environmental, and economic trends and their interaction over time would help boost understanding of the population threat among both the public and the leaders they elect. Relating future population growth to the availability of cropland, fresh water, forest products, and grazing area along with the need for classrooms, health care, and jobs can serve as a guide to responsible policies.

At least one government, working with the World Conservation Union, has recently undertaken such an exercise. In a 1992 study, the government of Pakistan concluded that the country might be able to support an increase from 122 million at present to the 200 million projected by 2013, if resources are managed carefully, but that there is no possibility of sustaining the 400 million projected by 2040 if current growth trends continue. Their assessment of potential population support capacities by agro-ecological zones suggests that food shortages will come first in the more ecologically fragile low rainfall regions, and then spread, achieving massive dimensions and enveloping the entire country.[50]

One of the great tragedies of the last decade has been the withdrawal of all U.S. financial support for the U.N. Population Fund and the International Planned Parenthood Federation, the two principal agencies engaged in family planning internationally. This is one reason that up to 300 million of the world's women do not yet have access to family planning services. Demographic surveys indicate that one in four births in the Third World is unplanned and unwanted, which explains in part the millions of street children there. Simply eliminating unwanted births would cut world population growth by more than a third.[51]

As economic and social conditions improve and as women are given equal rights and choices, fertility levels decrease, moving societies toward population stability. Unfortunately, the improvements that normally drive the demographic transition are not occurring in large parts of the Third World. Only a reorientation of development strategies that concentrates resources on raising female literacy and improving the status of women can succeed. In summary, raising public understanding of the population threat, filling the gap in the availability of family planning services, and creating the social conditions conducive to lower fertility are keys to an environmentally sustainable future.

Glimpses of what our new world would look like can be seen here and there: Japan, for example, set the international standard for energy efficiency and, in the process, strengthened its competitive position in world markets. California, with its rapidly growing solar and wind industries, provides a window on future energy sources. Its solar thermal electric generating capacity of 350 megawatts and its wind generating capacity of 1,600 megawatts are enough to satisfy the residential needs of nearly 2 million people, easily enough for San Francisco, San Diego, and Sacramento combined.[52]

On population, Thailand stands out, having halved its population growth rate in less than 15 years. In the effort to stabilize soils, the United States is leading the way; its innovative Conservation Reserve Program adopted in 1985 reduced soil erosion by one third by 1990 and may cut it by another third by 1995. In the effort to reduce garbage, Germany is a model with its comprehensive program designed to force companies to assume responsibility for disposing of the packaging used with their products. With beverage containers, Denmark has gone even further—banning those that are not refillable.[53]

In the end, we need not merely a vision, but a shared vision, one that guides and unites us in our day-to-day decision making. Such a vision, a common blueprint, can infuse society with a sense of purpose as we try to build a new world, one much more attractive than today's. This sense of common purpose and excitement is essential if we are to create an environmentally sustainable economic system.

FACING UP TO CHANGE

We cannot claim that we have not been warned of the need for a fundamental redirection in development of the global economy. The deterioration in living conditions for much of humanity during the eighties and early nineties will continue if economies are not restructured. The fall in incomes in 49 countries between 1980 and 1990 was not an accident or a statistical quirk. It was too large, involving too many countries and too many people, and occurred over too long a time. The great majority of these countries are poor ones where livelihoods are directly dependent on the productivity of croplands, grasslands, and forests. It is in these largely agrarian economies that the link between deteriorating natural systems and living conditions is most direct, and the effects most visible.[54]

Even a casual survey of the planet's physical condition shows the costs of burning fossil fuels are rising on many fronts. At some point, the economic costs of deteriorating forests, dying lakes, damaged crops, respiratory illnesses, increasing temperatures, rising sea level, and other destructive effects of fossil fuel use become unacceptably high. Basic economics argues for a switch to solar energy. Rather than wondering if we can afford to respond to these threats, policymakers should consider the costs of not responding. If the eventual consequence of failing to respond is catastrophe, the answer is obvious.

We are facing great change. On that there is little doubt. If we try to build the new economic system slowly, time will run out and environmental deterioration will lead to economic decline. The question is whether we will initiate the changes in time and manage the process, or whether the forces of deterioration and decline will prevail, acquiring a momentum of their own.

Rather than wondering if we can afford to respond to these threats, policymakers should consider the costs of not responding.

It is not clear what the deterioration/decline scenario would look like since we have little experience in the modern era with which to judge it. Will our social institutions be overwhelmed by deterioration and decline? Would this scenario look like Lebanon over the past two decades? Mozambique, Peru, Somalia, or Sudan in recent years? Yugoslavia in 1992? Will it be a world where dying ecosystems and rising sea levels generate massive flows of environmental refugees, movements that generate social conflicts and overwhelm national borders? Precisely because this is an out-of-control scenario, it is difficult to visualize the form it will take.

Getting off the deterioration/decline path requires an enormous effort, one akin to mobilizing for war. Turning things around begins with us as individuals. We each can do many things. We can recycle, use energy and water more efficiently, and limit our families to two children. Although these individual actions are necessary, they are not sufficient. They will not bring about the basic structural changes in the economy needed to make it sustainable. For this, only citizen action to press governments to adopt policies that will transform the economy will suffice.

The overriding need is for a new view of the world, one that reflects environmental realities and that redefines security by recognizing that the overwhelming threat to our future is not military aggression but the environmental degradation of the planet. With this official recognition by national political leaders comes a need to push the United Nations to the fore, giving it a major role in maintaining stability and protecting national borders. Fortunately, a move to strengthen the U.N. peacekeeping capacity is already under way. (See Chapter 8.) Investing this responsibility in the UN would then permit the international community to concentrate on the steps needed to save the planet. Moving away from a world of nations in a state of permanent military preparedness, ready to wage war at a moment's notice, to one in which the United Nations assumes the responsibility for keeping the peace, much as its founders envisaged, would free up a vast array of resources for reversing the destruction of the earth. Each dollar invested in a strong U.N. peacekeeping force could easily reduce national military expenditures by $10.

The question is not only what do we need to do, but how can we do it quickly—before time runs out and the entire world is caught in the downward spiral that already has roughly one sixth of humanity in its grip. Among the principal policy instruments that can convert an economic system that is slowly self-destructing into one that is environmentally sustainable are regulations and tax policy. Until now, governments have relied heavily on regulation, but the record of the last two decades shows that this is not a winning strategy.

Regulations clearly do have some role to play. Environmentally damaging chemicals, such as CFCs, can be banned. Regulations are needed on the handling of toxic waste and radioactive materials—things too dangerous to leave to the marketplace. Energy efficiency standards for automobiles and household appliances cut carbon emissions, air pollution, and acid rain.

To transform the economy quickly, however, by far the most effective instrument is tax policy, specifically the partial replacement of income taxes with environmental taxes. An advantage of using tax policy is that it permits the market to work unimpeded, preserving its inherent efficiency. Today, governments tax income because it is an easy way to collect revenue, even though it serves no particular social purpose. Replacing a portion of income taxes with environmental taxes would help to transform the economy quickly. This shift would encourage work and savings and would discourage environmentally destructive activities. In short, it would foster productive activities and discourage destructive ones, guiding both corporate investments (see Chapter 10) and consumer expenditures.

Among the activities that would be taxed are the burning of fossil fuels, the production of hazardous chemical waste, the generation of nuclear waste, pesticide use, and the use of virgin raw materials. The adoption of a carbon tax, which would discourage the burning of fossil fuels, is now being actively considered in both the European Community and Japan. Even a modest carbon tax would quickly tip the scales away from investment in fossil fuel production and toward investment in energy efficiency and renewable energy sources. Within a year of adoption of an international carbon tax, literally scores of solar thermal plants could be under construction.[55]

The measure of individuals or nations is whether they respond to the great issues of their time. For our generation, the great issues are environment and poverty. We will be judged by whether we can reverse the environmental degradation of the planet and eradicate the dehumanizing poverty that is now engulfing more and more of the world's people.

We know what we have to do. And we know how to do it. If we fail to convert our self-destructing economy into one that is environmentally sustainable, future generations will be overwhelmed by environmental degradation and social disintegration. Simply stated, if our generation does not turn things around, our children may not have the option of doing so.

2

Facing Water Scarcity

Sandra Postel

"When the well's dry," American inventor and diplomat Benjamin Franklin once said, "we know the worth of water." Unfortunately, much of the world is now in danger of learning Franklin's lesson the hard way. For decades, water has been wasted, mismanaged, and overused—and the consequences are beginning to hit home.

Water scarcity typically conjures up visions of drought, the temporary dry spells that nature inflicts from time to time. But while droughts capture headlines and grab our attention, the far greater threat posed by our escalating water consumption goes largely unnoticed.

Signs of water stress abound. Water tables are falling, lakes are shrinking, and wetlands are disappearing. Engineers propose "solving" water problems by building ever more mammoth river diversion schemes, with exorbitant price tags and damaging environmental effects. Around Beijing, New Delhi, Phoenix, and other water-short cities, competition is brewing between city-dwellers and farmers who lay claim to the same limited supply. And people in the Mid-

dle East have heard more than one leader voice the possibility of going to war over scarce water.

In each major area of water use—agriculture, industry, and cities—demands have increased rapidly. (See Figure 2–1.) Global water use has more than tripled since 1950, and now stands at an estimated 4,340 cubic kilometers per year—eight times the annual flow of the Mississippi River. This total includes only what is removed from rivers, lakes, and groundwater, and amounts to 30 percent of the world's stable renewable supply. But we actually rely on a far larger share since water bodies dilute pollution, generate electricity, and support fisheries and wildlife. And because of improved living standards, world water demand has been growing faster than population: at 800 cubic meters a year, per capita use today is nearly 50 percent higher than it was in 1950, and in most of the world continues to climb.[1]

For decades, planners have met this rising demand by turning to ever more and larger "water development" projects, particularly dams and river diversions. Engineers have built more than 36,000 large dams around the world to control floods and to provide hydroelectric power, irrigation, industrial supplies, and drinking water to a growing

This chapter is adapted from *Last Oasis: Facing Water Scarcity* (New York: W.W. Norton & Co., 1992).

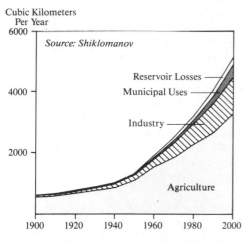

Cubic Kilometers
Per Year

Source: Shiklomanov

Reservoir Losses

Municipal Uses

Industry

Agriculture

**Figure 2-1. Estimated Annual World Water Use,
Total and by Sector, 1900–2000**

global population and economy. Rare is the river that now runs freely toward the sea, and many that still do are slated to come under control soon.[2]

But limits to this ever-expanding supply are swiftly coming to light. Engineers naturally first selected the easiest and least-costly sites for water development. Over time, water projects have become increasingly complex, expensive to build, and more damaging to the environment. Fewer dams and diversion projects are making it off the drawing boards, and most that do will deliver water at a far higher price than in the past.

Worldwide, the rate of dam construction during the last decade has averaged only half that during the preceding 25 years—170 annually, compared with some 360 a year from 1951 to 1977. In Australia, North America, and Western Europe, few affordable and acceptable sites remain for damming and diverting more river water. In many developing countries, too, large projects are coming under closer scrutiny because of their social and ecological costs. For instance, an independent review of India's huge Sardar Sarovar dam commissioned by

the World Bank concluded in mid-1992 that "it would be prudent if the necessary studies were done and the data made available for informed decision-making before further construction takes place. Implementation requires that the Bank take a step back."[3]

Meeting human needs while facing up to water's limits—economic, ecological, and political—entails developing a wholly new relationship to water. Historically, we have managed water with a frontier philosophy, manipulating natural systems to whatever degree engineering know-how would permit. Modern society has come to view water only as a resource that is there for the taking, rather than a life-support system that underpins the natural world we depend on. Instead of continuously reaching out for more, we must begin to look within—within our regions, our communities, our homes, and ourselves—for ways to meet our needs while respecting water's life-sustaining functions.

SIGNS OF UNSUSTAINABILITY

Although water is a renewable resource, it is also a finite one. The water cycle makes available only so much each year in a given location. That means supplies per person, a broad indicator of water security, drop as population grows. Thus per capita water supplies worldwide are a third lower now than in 1970 due to the 1.8 billion people added to the planet since then.[4]

One of the clearest signs of water scarcity is the increasing number of countries in which population has surpassed the level that can be sustained comfortably with the water available. As a rule of thumb, hydrologists designate water-stressed countries as those with annual supplies of 1,000–2,000 cubic meters per person. When the figure drops below 1,000 cubic meters (about 725 gallons per person a day), nations are considered water-scarce—that is, lack of water becomes a severe constraint on food production, economic development, and protection of natural systems.[5]

Today, 26 countries, collectively home to 232 million people, fall into the water-scarce category. (See Table 2–1.) As many of them have very high population growth rates, their water problems are deepening fast. Africa has the largest number of water-scarce countries, 11 in all, and, given current population projections, six others there will join the list by 2010. At that time, the total number of Africans living in water-scarce countries will climb to 400 million, some 37 percent of the continent's projected population.[6]

Nine out of the 14 countries in the Middle East already face water-short conditions, making this the most concentrated region of scarcity in the world. Populations in several of them are projected to double within 25 years; a rapid tightening of supplies is thus inevitable. With virtually all Middle East rivers being shared by several nations, tensions over water rights are a potent political force throughout the region, and could ignite during this decade.[7]

Although the population-water equation suggests where to expect trouble, numerous physical symptoms of water stress already exist—and not just in water-scarce countries, but in parts of water-wealthy ones as well. Among the most pervasive problems is that of declining water tables, which results when groundwater is used faster than nature replenishes it. If pumping is not brought into balance with recharge, eventually the underground supply becomes too expensive to keep tapping, too salty to use as it is pulled up from greater depths, or simply too depleted. Overuse

of groundwater is now ubiquitous in parts of China, India, Mexico, Thailand, the western United States, north Africa, and the Middle East.[8]

Some of the most troubling cases of unsustainable groundwater use involve "fossil" aquifers, underground reservoirs that hold water hundreds or thousands of years old and that receive little replenishment from rainfall today. Like oil reserves, these aquifers are essentially nonrenewable: pumping water from them depletes the supply in the same way that extractions from an oil well do. Farms and cities that depend on this water will eventually face the problem of what to do when the wells run dry.

The arid kingdom of Saudi Arabia now mines fossil groundwater to meet 75 percent of its water needs, and that dependence is growing as a result of government efforts to encourage large-scale wheat production in the desert. Though the kingdom imports barley and other food crops, it became self-sufficient in wheat in 1984, and has since joined the ranks of the world's top wheat exporters. In early 1992, King Fahd authorized payments totalling $2.1 billion for 1991's record 4-million-ton wheat crop, which was worth only one fourth as much at the world market price.[9]

Groundwater depletion in Saudi Arabia has been averaging about 5.2 billion cubic meters a year, and that rate is projected to increase by nearly half during the nineties. Assuming 80 percent of the reserve can be exploited, the supply would be exhausted in 52 years. At the faster extraction rates projected for 2000–10, it would dry up much sooner. And even before that happens, the groundwater will likely become too salty to use without expensive treatment. Thus, little of the Saudi's grain can be considered a reliable portion of the long-term food supply—either for Saudis or for those countries receiving its exports.[10]

Table 2–1. Water-Scarce Countries, 1992, With Projections for 2010[1]

Region/Country	Per Capita Renewable Water Supplies		Change
	1992	2010	
	(cubic meters per person)		(percent)
Africa			
Algeria	730	500	−32
Botswana	710	420	−41
Burundi	620	360	−42
Cape Verde	500	290	−42
Djibouti	750	430	−43
Egypt	30	20	−33
Kenya	560	330	−41
Libya	160	100	−38
Mauritania	190	110	−42
Rwanda	820	440	−46
Tunisia	450	330	−27
Middle East			
Bahrain	0	0	0
Israel	330	250	−24
Jordan	190	110	−42
Kuwait	0	0	0
Qatar	40	30	−25
Saudi Arabia	140	70	−50
Syria	550	300	−45
United Arab Emirates	120	60	−50
Yemen	240	130	−46
Other			
Barbados	170	170	0
Belgium	840	870	+ 4
Hungary	580	570	− 2
Malta	80	80	0
Netherlands	660	600	− 9
Singapore	210	190	−10
Additional Countries by 2010			
Malawi	1,030	600	−42
Sudan	1,130	710	−37
Morocco	1,150	830	−28
South Africa	1,200	760	−37
Oman	1,250	670	−46
Somalia	1,390	830	−40
Lebanon	1,410	980	−30
Niger	1,690	930	−45

[1]Countries with per capita renewable water supplies of less than 1,000 cubic meters per year. Does not include water flowing in from neighboring countries.

SOURCE: Worldwatch Institute, based on data from World Resources Institute, *World Resources 1992–93* (New York: Oxford University Press, 1992), and from Population Reference Bureau, *1992 World Population Data Sheet* (Washington, D.C.: 1992).

Other places dependent on fossil groundwater include the north African nation of Libya and the northwestern corner of Texas, where the amount of water in that state's portion of the Ogallala aquifer has already been diminished by a fourth. Unsustainable use of groundwater, however, is not limited to fossil aquifers; it occurs anywhere groundwater is pumped faster than nature recharges it. In Beijing, China, water tables have been dropping 1–2 meters a year, and a third of the wells have reportedly gone dry. Groundwater pumping in Mexico City exceeds recharge by 50–80 percent, which has led to falling groundwater levels, aquifer compaction, and land subsidence that has caused the famous Metropolitan Cathedral to slump.[11]

More water devoted to human needs means less for sustenance of ecosystems—and in many areas, nature is losing out fast.

As demands continue to rise and water supply projects get more difficult to build, water budgets are becoming badly imbalanced in many regions. From southern California to Israel, from northern China to parts of India, shortages are becoming chronic and rationing a way of life. In China, for instance, planners project that Beijing's total water demand in 2000 could outstrip available supplies by 70 percent. Israel's annual water use already exceeds its renewable supply by some 300 million cubic meters, or 15 percent. With the projected influx of up to 1 million Soviet Jews over the next decade, its yearly water deficit will worsen greatly.[12]

Shrinking groundwater reserves, falling water tables, and projected demands that far exceed available supplies are clear signals of water stress. But perhaps the most worrying sign of trouble comes from examining the health of aquatic environments. The damming, diverting, and polluting of watercourses with little regard for the environmental services they provide and the species they support has wreaked havoc on the world's wetlands, deltas, lakes, and riverine habitats.

A distressing conflict has emerged over two of water's roles: as a commodity serving the economic aims of greater agricultural productivity, industrial expansion, and urban growth, and as a key life-support for all species and natural communities. Mounting scarcity has thrown this friction into sharp relief. More water devoted to human needs means less for sustenance of ecosystems—and in many areas, nature is losing out fast.

The infamous shrinking Aral Sea in central Asia is but the most dramatic in a long list of natural areas destroyed, degraded, or at grave risk from human use and abuse of water. Among them are many unique wild places—including California's Mono Lake, south Florida's Everglades, Spain's Doñana wetlands, and Sudan's Sudd swamps—that are home to astounding numbers and varieties of bird and wildlife species.[13]

Botswana's Okavango Delta, for instance, Africa's largest oasis, is world-renowned for its zebras, antelope, elephants, Cape buffalo, and other diverse wildlife. During the dry season, animals migrate from the nearby Kalahari Desert and the wildlife population supported by the delta climbs some tenfold. The government of this southern African nation has proposed siphoning off some of the delta's water by diverting the Boro River to expand irrigation by 1 million hectares, provide drinking water to the northern city of Maun, and increase supplies to the Orapa diamond mine, all of which would shrink the wetland habitat.[14]

For the time being, the diversion project has been put on hold. When the government invited local people to voice their views on the plan in early 1991, they resoundingly opposed it. Among the most vocal were herders and fishers, whose livelihoods depend directly on the integrity of the delta. In mid-1992, after release of a report by the World Conservation Union showing less need for the water supply scheme than originally thought, the government cancelled the project. But with rich cattle barons and a lucrative diamond mine standing to benefit from more water, the Okavango oasis could again be threatened by water exploitation.[15]

Similar tales could be told in many areas of a tug-of-war between the water demands of conventional economic development and those of aquatic ecosystems. A more pervasive sign of the severely compromised health of the water environment is the number of aquatic species now in jeopardy. In North America, for example, the American Fisheries Society lists 364 species of fish as endangered, threatened, or of special concern—the vast majority of them at risk because of habitat destruction. An estimated one third of the continent's fish, two thirds of its crayfish, and nearly three fourths of its mussels are now "rare or imperiled." They often reach such status by way of incremental human actions that end up undermining their basic habitat requirements—be it the timing, quantity, or quality of water's flow.[16]

Of the many varieties of native fish species at risk in North America, perhaps the most notable for their cultural and recreational values are several species of salmon in the western United States. The winter run of chinook salmon in California's Sacramento River declined from 120,000 in the sixties to just 400 today, and the species was added to the federal endangered list in 1989. In 1991, just four adult Snake River sockeye salmon made it from the Pacific Ocean past eight federal dams in the Columbia River basin to their primordial spawning ground at Idaho's Redfish Lake. On the brink of extinction, the Snake River sockeye was listed as endangered in November 1991. And as of early July 1992, steps were being taken to move the Snake River chinook salmon from threatened to endangered status.[17]

Each wetland, lake, or aquatic species at risk presents a crucial test of whether a region's people and economy can adapt to the ecological needs of a healthy aquatic system. Only in rare instances are public values and future generations winning out over private rights to dam and divert natural watercourses. And a growing movement to protect property rights from government actions to safeguard the environment, especially in the United States, could tip this balance even further away from ecosystem protection. Unfortunately, protecting aquatic environments and their species is still often viewed as a luxury that can be traded off against pressing economic goals, rather than as essential to preserving the environmental foundation all else rests upon.

WATER-THRIFTY FOOD PRODUCTION

With agriculture claiming two thirds of all the water removed from rivers, lakes, streams, and aquifers, making irrigation more efficient is a top priority in moving toward more sustainable water use. The possible savings—ranging from 10 to 50 percent—constitute a large and mostly unexploited new source of supply. Reducing irrigation needs by a tenth, for instance, would free up enough water to roughly double domestic water use worldwide.[18]

A wide variety of measures exist to boost agriculture's water productivity. They include new and improved irrigation technologies, better management practices by farmers and water managers, and changes in the institutions that govern the distribution and use of irrigation water. Although some gains have been made in each area, there is a vast potential yet to tap.

Not surprisingly, some of the biggest technological successes in improving irrigation efficiency have occurred where water scarcity poses serious threats to farming. In northwest Texas, for instance, supplied by the dwindling Ogallala aquifer, many farmers have adapted old-fashioned furrow systems to a new surge technique that reduces percolation losses at the head of the field and distributes water more uniformly. This has reduced their water use by 15–50 percent while cutting their pumping costs. For those in the Texas Plains, where savings have averaged 25 percent, the initial investment of about $30 per hectare is typically recouped within the first year.[19]

Many irrigators in northwest Texas have moved from high-pressure sprinklers, which typically register efficiencies of 60–70 percent, to low-pressure ones that boost efficiency to around 80 percent. A relatively new sprinkler design, known as low-energy precision application (LEPA), offers even greater savings. LEPA sprinklers deliver water closer to the crops by means of drop tubes extending vertically from the sprinkler arm. When used with water-conserving land preparation methods, LEPA can achieve efficiencies as high as 95 percent. Adapting an existing sprinkler for LEPA costs Texas farmers $60–160 per hectare; the water, energy, and yield gains typically pay back the initial investment in two to four years.[20]

Added up, irrigation efficiency improvements have helped stem the Ogallala aquifer's depletion. Since it peaked in 1974, water use in the Texas High Plains has fallen by 43 percent. Two thirds of this is due to cutbacks in irrigated area, but one third is attributed to conservation. On average, farmers used 16 percent less water per irrigated hectare during 1979–89 than they did in 1964–74. The average annual rate of Ogallala depletion in the state has fallen from nearly 2 billion cubic meters during the late sixties to 241 million cubic meters in recent years.[21]

Israel has brought about what is widely perceived as an agricultural miracle over the last three decades. Although it remains to be seen whether its success in making the desert bloom will prove sustainable, Israel has developed technologies, methods, and scientific capabilities in irrigation that could prove invaluable to much of the world as the era of water constraints unfolds.

Among the most heralded of its accomplishments is the development of "drip irrigation." Under this method, water is delivered directly to crops' roots through a network of porous or perforated piping installed on or below the soil surface. This keeps evaporation and seepage losses extremely low. Because water is applied frequently at low doses, optimal moisture conditions are maintained for the crop, which boosts yields, and salt does not accumulate in the root zone. Modern Israeli farms often have highly automated drip systems, with computers and monitors sensing when and how much water to apply and determining the precise amount of nutrients to add. Israeli farmers now liken their irrigation practices to "feeding the plant with a teaspoon."[22]

Following its commercial development in Israel in the sixties, drip and other "microirrigation" techniques began to spread. Since the mid-seventies, their use has grown twenty-eightfold, with nearly 1.6 million hectares watered by drip and micro-sprinklers in 1991. (See Table 2–2.) Drip systems often achieve efficiencies in the range of 95 percent. Because it is relatively expensive, however, with the initial outlay typically running $1,500–3,000 per hectare, drip irrigation is mostly used on higher-valued fruit and vegetable crops. But more than 130,000 hectares of cotton, sugar, sweet corn, and other field

Table 2–2. Use of Microirrigation, Leading Countries and World, 1991[1]

Country	Area Under Microirrigation	Share of Total Irrigated Area Under Microirrigation[2]
	(hectares)	(percent)
United States	606,000	3.0
Spain	160,000	4.8
Australia	147,000	7.8
Israel[3]	104,302	48.7
South Africa	102,250	9.0
Egypt	68,450	2.6
Mexico	60,600	1.2
France	50,953	4.8
Thailand	41,150	1.0
Colombia	29,500	5.7
Cyprus	25,000	71.4
Portugal	23,565	3.7
Italy	21,700	0.7
Brazil	20,150	0.7
China	19,000	<0.1
India	17,000	<0.1
Jordan	12,000	21.1
Taiwan	10,005	2.4
Morocco	9,766	0.8
Chile	8,830	0.7
Other	39,397	—
World[4]	1,576,618	0.7

[1]Microirrigation includes primarily drip (surface and subsurface) methods and micro-sprinklers. [2]Irrigated areas are for 1989, the latest available. [3]Israel's drip and total irrigated area down 18 and 15 percent, respectively, from 1986, reflecting severe water allocation cutbacks due to drought. [4]13,820 hectares (11,200 of them in the Soviet Union) were reported in 1981 by countries that did not report at all in 1991; world total does not include this area.
SOURCE: Worldwatch Institute, based on Dale Bucks, Microirrigation Working Group, International Commission on Irrigation and Drainage, Beltsville, Md., private communication, June 22, 1992, and on irrigated area from U.N. Food and Agriculture Organization, *1990 Production Yearbook* (Rome: 1991), with adjustments from the U.S. Department of Agriculture for the United States and Taiwan.

crops are now watered by drip as well. Israel has around half its total irrigated land under drip, which has helped its farmers reduce their water use on each irrigated hectare by one third even while increasing crop yields.[23]

New technologies that build efficiency into their designs—like surge, LEPA, and drip irrigation—can help make crop production less demanding of the world's water supply. Equally important, however, is raising the efficiency of the extensive surface canal systems that dominate the world's irrigated lands. Much land slated for irrigation, and often counted as receiving it, gets insufficient water or none at all because irrigation works are poorly maintained and operated. University of Sussex researcher Robert Chambers estimates, for example, that at least a quarter of the area declared irrigated in India yields far below its potential because of "tail-end deprivation"—lack of water toward the back of a canal system. "Tail-enders" suffer reduced livelihoods as a result, since equitable and reliable irrigation is a key to raising incomes, generating employment, and, because it allows year-round crop production, promoting social stability.[24]

Much land slated for irrigation gets insufficient water or none at all because irrigation works are poorly maintained and operated.

Many problems with large canal systems arise because irrigation officials rarely have any incentive to improve the performance of projects they administer. Their operating budgets, for example, may come from a state or national treasury and bear no relation to how well the system functions. Irrigation fees collected from farmers may go back into a general treasury, rather than being used to operate and maintain the local system. And since farmers have little say in how their projects are managed and are not charged for water according to their use, they, too, have little incentive to use water wisely. In short, there is little accountability of those in control, and little control by those who are supposed to benefit.

The potential gains of correcting such deficiences are as large as the task is difficult. Chambers estimates, for instance, that management improvements in India could allow an additional 8 million hectares to receive irrigation water from existing canal projects. That would expand India's irrigated area by 19 percent, and perhaps double the yield from the newly irrigated land—without developing any new water sources.[25]

Especially in government-run projects, some form of "water users association" is necessary for farmers to have a say in management decisions. Such an organization also provides a mechanism for collecting fees to cover operation and maintenance costs and for involving farmers directly in maintenance activities. Many studies have shown that when farmers actively participate in projects and have some responsibility for their operation, canals and other infrastructure function better, a greater proportion of the project area gets irrigated, and crop yields rise.[26]

Besides efficiency improvements, another way to stretch freshwater supplies is to use treated municipal wastewater for irrigation. Farmers worldwide spend heavily on chemical fertilizers to give their crops the nitrogen, phosphorus, and potassium that domestic wastewater contains in large amounts. By using municipal water supplies twice—once for domestic use and again for irrigation—would-be pollutants become valuable fertilizers, rivers and lakes are protected from contamination, the irrigated land boosts crop production, and the reclaimed water becomes a reliable, local supply.

At least 500,000 hectares of cropland in some 15 countries are now being irrigated with municipal wastewater. Although this amounts to just two tenths of 1 percent of the world's irrigated area, in dry regions wastewater can supply an important share of agriculture's water.[27]

Israel has the most ambitious wastewater reuse effort in the world. Already, some 70 percent of the nation's sewage gets treated and reused to irrigate 19,-000 hectares of agricultural land. With no new sources of fresh water to tap, Israel plans to expand the use of reclaimed wastewater greatly by the end of the decade. Virtually all of it will go to agriculture, which is projected to be allocated 38 percent less fresh water in 2000 than it received in 1984. If the nation achieves its targets, reclaimed wastewater will meet more than 16 percent of Israel's total water needs by the end of the nineties.[28]

Unfortunately, the reuse practices of many developing countries are far from safe and sanitary. Most of the wastewater flowing from their urban centers gets no treatment, and in water-short areas it is often applied raw to edible crops. Raw sewage from Santiago, Chile, for instance, makes up almost the entire flow of the Rio Mapocho during the dry season. This water irrigates about 16,000 hectares of vegetable and salad crops headed for city markets, a practice linked to typhoid fever outbreaks in Santiago in the mid-eighties.[29]

By not making wastewater reuse a part of water planning and management, developing countries put their urban and rural populations at risk. As World Bank wastewater specialists Carl Bartone and Saul Arlosoroff note: "Examples abound of local farmers breaking into sewer interceptors both within and on the outskirts of urban areas to steal the effluents for watering their crops. These are often vegetable crops destined for local markets that will be consumed raw. In addition, . . . highly polluted rivers serve as major water sources for large-scale irrigation projects."[30]

When designed and operated properly, waste stabilization ponds that biologically treat wastewater offer a low-cost way to keep sewage out of rivers and streams, safeguard human health from disease-causing organisms, and produce a nutrient-rich source of irrigation water. Studies have shown them capable of treating wastewater up to the World Health Organization's standards for irrigation of crops not eaten raw. Care must always be taken to prevent heavy metals from getting into wastewater destined for irrigation. Cadmium, copper, nickel, zinc, and other heavy metals can accumulate in crops and soils, or percolate to groundwater and contaminate a drinking supply. A key to safe reuse is thus preventing untreated industrial effluent, which often contains heavy metals, from mixing with domestic wastewater.[31]

Finally, producing enough food for the world's expanding population while economizing on water will also require boosting yields on the 84 percent of the world's cropland watered only by rainfall. The drylands of Africa, western India, north-central China, and southwestern Latin America present formidable challenges to crop production. Altogether, arid and semiarid lands cover about a third of the earth's land surface and are home to some 600 million people, including many of the world's poorest farmers. For them, conservation and more efficient use of scarce water is quite literally a matter of life and death.[32]

Attention is turning now to the potential of smaller-scale projects—micro dams, shallow wells, low-cost pumps, moisture-conserving land techniques, and a wide variety of "rainwater harvesting" methods—to make food production more secure for dryland dwellers. Many of these efforts have proved more cost-effective and less disruptive to local communities than the massive schemes that dominated development efforts during the past few decades. And their smaller size and use of local resources tend to make them less damaging to the environment.

Rural families in the Burkina Faso province of Yatenga, for instance, have been helped by the construction of stone walls, known as bunds, along contour lines across their fields. The bunds cause rainwater to spread out and slowly infiltrate the soil rather than running off the field. When accompanied by deep planting holes that concentrate rainfall runoff around the crops, bunds can raise yields 30–60 percent even in the first year. Equally important, the treatments help prevent total crop failure in very dry years, greatly enhancing household food security. By the end of 1989, 8,000 hectares in more than 400 Yatenga villages were benefiting from these techniques.[33]

Pollution control laws have not only helped clean up rivers, lakes, and streams, they have promoted more efficient water use.

People in the Machakos district of southern Kenya have reaped similar benefits from terracing, another effective way to capture rainwater and raise productivity on sloping dry lands. Since the mid-eighties, they have built an average of 1,000 kilometers of terraces each year, and an estimated 70 percent of all cropland in the district is now terraced. As Will Critchley reports in *Looking After Our Land: Soil and Water Conservation in Dryland Africa*, the few studies that have examined production gains suggest in-creases in average corn yields of at least 50 percent.[34]

In much of sub-Saharan Africa, the use of simple, low-cost wells and pumps to tap shallow groundwater or local rivers and streams offers great potential to increase food production and cash income for farm families. In Nigeria, for instance, farmers had established more than 8,600 wells in three northern states by the late eighties, each capable of irrigating up to 2 hectares of land. In contrast to the large government schemes, which have averaged $30,000 per hectare of public money, these small-scale efforts have cost farmers $1,000–2,000 per hectare, including the pumps. Yields have increased 25–40 percent in the wet season, and farmers have added a dry-season crop, giving them more cash and security.[35]

INDUSTRIAL RECYCLING

Making the myriad products we use in everyday life—from clothes and computers to paper, plastics, and televisions—requires copious amounts of water. Producing 1 kilogram of paper can take as much as 700 kilograms of water. And making a ton of steel can take 280 tons of water.[36]

Collectively, industries account for nearly a quarter of the world's water use. In most industrial countries, they are the biggest user—frequently accounting for 50–80 percent of total demand, compared with 10–30 percent in much of the Third World. As developing countries industrialize, however, their water demands for thermoelectric power generation, manufacturing, mining, and materials processing are rising rapidly.[37]

In contrast to the water used in agriculture, only a small fraction of industrial water is actually consumed. Most of it is used for cooling, processing, and other activities that may heat or pollute water, but do not use it up. This allows a factory to recycle its supplies, thereby getting more output from each cubic meter delivered or allocated to it. U.S. steelmakers, for instance, have reduced their water intake to 14 tons per ton of steel, securing the remainder from recycling.[38]

So far, the main impetus for industrial water recycling has come from pollution control laws. Most of the world's wealthier countries now require industries to meet specific water quality standards before releasing wastewater to the environment. As it turns out, the most effective and economical way to comply with these requirements is often to treat and recycle water, thereby discharging less. Pollution control laws have therefore not only helped clean up rivers, lakes, and streams, they have promoted conservation and more efficient water use.

Japan, the United States, and the former West Germany are among the countries that have achieved striking gains in industrial water productivity. After a period of rapid industrialization following World War II, total water use by Japanese industries peaked in 1973 and then dropped 24 percent by 1989. Three industries—chemicals, iron and steel, and pulp and paper manufacturing—account for 60 percent of Japan's industrial water use, and each has boosted its water recycling rate markedly since the early seventies. Industrial output, meanwhile, has been climbing steadily. As a result, in 1989, Japan got $77 worth of output from each cubic meter of water supplied to industries, compared with $21 (in real terms) in 1965. (See Figure 2–2.) In just over two decades, the nation more than tripled its industrial water productivity.[39]

Similarly, U.S. industry's total water use has fallen 36 percent since 1950, while industrial output has risen 3.7-fold (in real terms). And in the former West

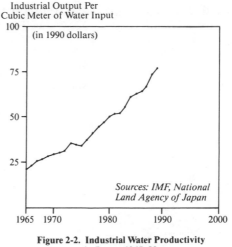

Industrial Output Per
Cubic Meter of Water Input

Figure 2-2. **Industrial Water Productivity in Japan, 1965–89**

Germany, total industrial water use today is at the same level as in 1975, while industrial output has risen 44 percent. State-of-the-art paper manufacturing plants there now use only 7 kilograms of water to produce a kilogram of paper, 1 percent as much as older factories elsewhere.[40]

Although these gains are impressive, achievements by individual companies facing water supply constraints show clearly that further large cuts in industry's water needs are possible. For instance, a detailed look at 15 companies in San Jose, California—including several computer makers, a food processor, and a metal finisher—found that by adopting a diverse set of conservation measures they collectively reduced their annual water use by 5.7 million cubic meters, enough to supply about 9,200 San Jose households. Water savings ranged from 27 to 90 percent, and in most cases the payback period was less than 12 months. (See Table 2–3.)[41]

Indeed, one positive outcome of California's six-year drought is that this state, which has an economy larger than all but seven countries, may now be the world's leader in industrial water recy-

Table 2–3. San Jose, California: Industrial Water Conservation and Cost-Effectiveness, Selected Companies

Company	Water Use		Water Savings	Payback Period on Investment
	Before Conservation	After Conservation		
	(thousand cubic meters per year)		(percent)	(months)
IBM[1]	420	42	90	3.6
California Paper-Board Corp.	2,473	689	72	2.4
Gangi Bros. Food Processing	568	212	63	10.8
Hewlett-Packard[1]	87	42	52	3.6
Advanced Micro Devices	2,098	1,318	37	7.2[2]
Tandem Computers	125	87	30	12.0
Dyna-Craft Metal Finishing	193	140	27	2.4

[1]Water use rates apply only to one or more processes involving conservation measures.   [2]Payback based only on that portion of water savings with which costs could be associated.
SOURCE: Worldwatch Institute, based on City of San Jose, Brown & Caldwell Consultants, and California Department of Water Resources, *Case Studies of Industrial Water Conservation in the San Jose Area* (Sacramento: California Department of Water Resources, 1990).

cling. Manufacturers of all kinds—aircraft, chemicals, computers, and oil refiners—have boosted their water efficiency dramatically in a matter of years. In addition to the typical inducements of strict federal and state water quality regulations, California industries have faced the possibility of large cutbacks in water supply because of the ongoing drought. As a result, many are investing in water conservation well beyond what is normally considered financially justified as an insurance policy against future rationing, which could threaten production.[42]

A 1990–91 survey of 640 manufacturing plants in 12 California counties documented a 19-percent reduction in water use between 1985 and 1989. These savings, which derived from such measures as recycling cooling and process water, reducing flow rates, and fixing leaks, came on top of impressive conservation gains made during the previous 15 years in response to increasingly strict environmental standards. All told, the three largest water-using industry groups in these counties have cut their water demands by nearly two thirds during the last two decades. Moreover, if all California plants came up to the level of the most efficient ones of their type, total water needs in all the industry groups surveyed would drop another 19 percent.[43]

Unfortunately, few developing countries are yet giving industries the incentives they need to adopt more efficient water practices. Most neither charge appropriately for water and wastewater services nor enforce pollution control regulations adequately. Yet where inducements do exist, industries have responded. For example, in the town of Goa, India, about 380 kilometers south of Bombay, a fertilizer plant owned by Zuari Agro-Chemical Limited cut its water use by half over six years in response to high water prices and government pressure to reduce effluent discharges to the sea. And in São Paulo, Brazil, high effluent charges encouraged a dairy factory, a pharmaceutical company, and a food processing plant to reduce their water use per unit of output by 62 percent, 49 percent, and 42 percent, respectively.[44]

Given the proper incentives, industries of many types have shown they can cut their water needs 40–90 percent with available technologies and practices, while at the same time protecting water from pollution. Industrial conservation offers many cities facing shortages a large untapped supply. Ensuring that new factories incorporate conservation and recycling from the outset would help delay costly investments in urban water supplies, reduce overpumping of aquifers, lessen competition for water, and help prevent pollution from reaching levels hazardous to people and wildlife. Closing the industrial water and wastewater cycle is not only technically possible, it increasingly makes good economic and environmental sense.

CONSERVING IN CITIES

Homes, apartments, small businesses, and other municipal enterprises account for less than one tenth of the world's total water use. But their demands are concentrated in relatively small geographic areas, and in many cases are escalating rapidly. As cities expand, they strain the capacity of local water bodies and force engineers to reach out to ever more distant sources.

In addition, the reservoirs, canals, pumping stations, pipes, sewers, and treatment plants that constitute a modern water and wastewater system require huge sums of money to build and maintain. Collecting and treating water and wastewater also takes large amounts of energy and chemicals, adding to environmental pollution and the overall costs of a community's water system. Under such constraints, many cities are having difficulty meeting the water needs of their residents, and large numbers of low-income households in developing countries get no service at all.

Conservation, once viewed as just an emergency response to drought, has been transformed in recent years into a sophisticated package of measures that offers one of the most cost-effective and environmentally sound ways of balancing urban water budgets. Just as energy planners have discovered that it is often cheaper to save energy—for instance, by investing in home insulation and compact fluorescent lights—than to build more power plants, so water planners are realizing that an assortment of water efficiency measures can yield permanent savings and thereby delay or avert the need for expensive new dams and reservoirs, groundwater wells, and treatment plants. Slowly the idea is spreading that managing demand rather than continuously striving to meet it is a surer path to water security while saving money and protecting the environment at the same time. (See Table 2–4.)[45]

In almost every case, successful efforts to curb domestic water use permanently include some combination of economic

Table 2–4. Urban Conservation Initiatives, Selected Cities

City/Region	Activities/Accomplishments
Jerusalem, Israel	Installation of water-saving devices, leak detection and repair, and more efficient irrigation of parks contributed to a 14-percent drop in per capita use between 1989 and 1991.
Mexico City	Replaced 350,000 toilets with six-liter models, saving enough water to meet needs of 250,000 residents; goal of cutting per capita use by one sixth by 1996 through pricing, education, retrofitting, and efficiency standards.
Southern California	Metropolitan Water District pays its member agencies $125 for each 1,000 cubic meters they save. Estimated savings as of June 1992 total nearly 33 million cubic meters/year. Conservation efforts have cut annual demand by 541 million cubic meters, enough to supply about 885,000 households.
Beijing, China	New pricing system links charges to amount of water used; regulations from November 1992 set quotas on consumption and authorize fines for exceeding them.
Greater Boston, Massachusetts	Comprehensive retrofit, water audit, leak detection, and education program reduced total annual demand by 16 percent in five years, bringing it back to the level of the late sixties.
Municipality of Waterloo, Canada	Delayed expansion of regional water supply through higher water rates, distribution of water conservation kits, and public education. Per capita water use has fallen 10 percent during last three years.
Singapore	With water use rising more than twice as fast as population, the island nation cut unaccounted-for water to 10 percent through leak repairs, and promoted conservation with higher prices and public education.
Melbourne, Australia	Since 1982–83 drought, when water use dropped 30 percent, a conservation strategy has kept demand from climbing above the level of 1980, allowing construction of new water works to be postponed and saving $50 million.

SOURCE: Worldwatch Institute, based on sources documented in endnote 45.

incentives, regulations, and public outreach that together promote the use of water-saving technologies and behaviors. These measures are mutually reinforcing, and together form a water supply option as reliable and predictable as a dam and reservoir.

Raising the price of water to better reflect its true cost is one of the most important steps any city can take. Water is consistently undervalued, and as a result is chronically overused. The water rate structures of many utilities actually reward waste by charging less per liter the more that is consumed. Even worse, water charges for most British households are linked to the value of the homes, and have nothing to do with actual consumption.[46]

Many residences in both industrial and Third World cities are not equipped with water meters, making it impossible to charge people appropriately for their water use. Metering is not only a prerequisite to the success of most conservation measures, it encourages savings in and of itself simply by tieing the water bill to the amount used. In Alberta, Canada, the city of Edmonton meters all residential users, and its per capita water use is half that of Calgary, which is only partially metered. The areas of Calgary that are metered, however, register water use rates similar to Edmonton's. Trials in the United Kingdom have shown that metering can cut household use there by 10–15 percent.[47]

Raising water prices can often be politically difficult to do. But if accompanied by public outreach explaining the need for the price hike and the steps consumers can take to keep water bills down, higher prices can have a strong positive effect. When faced with dire water supply conditions in the mid-seventies, for instance, officials in Tucson, Arizona, raised water rates sharply to make them better reflect the true cost of service. At about the same time, they ran a public education campaign called "Beat the Peak" with a goal of curbing water use on hot summer afternoons, when the supply was most in danger of running short. The result was a 16-percent drop in per capita use within a few years, which, along with the lowered peak demand, allowed the Tucson water utility to cut its water supply expansion costs by $75 million.[48]

Pricing was the main tool of a conservation strategy adopted by the water utility serving Bogor, Indonesia, as well. With a proposed new water project estimated to cost twice as much per unit of water as existing supplies, the utility tri-

pled or quadrupled water prices, depending on the amount used, to encourage residents to conserve. Between June 1988 and April 1989, average monthly residential water use dropped nearly 30 percent, which will allow the utility to connect more households to the water system at a lower cost.[49]

Along with economic incentives and public outreach, setting water-efficiency standards for common fixtures—toilets, showerheads, and faucets—can be a critical component of a reliable conservation strategy. Standards establish technological norms that ensure a certain level of efficiency is built into new products and services. Mexico has established nationwide standards, and Ontario, Canada, is including standards in its province-wide conservation strategy as well.[50]

In the United States, there has been a growing movement to mandate the use of water-efficient plumbing fixtures. In 1988, Massachusetts became the first state to require that all new toilets installed use no more than six liters per flush. Since then, 14 other states have followed suit, with most adopting efficiency standards for showerheads and faucets as well.[51]

Legislation setting national standards was signed into law in October 1992 as part of a broad energy bill. It requires that showerheads and faucets manufactured after January 1, 1994, use no more than 2.5 gallons (9.5 liters) per minute; domestic toilets manufactured after that date are to use no more than 1.6 gallons (6 liters) per flush. As all new homes and major remodeling nationwide incorporate these more-efficient fixtures, water savings will build over time, and they will be reliable and predictable. According to estimates by Boston-based water consultant Amy Vickers, the standards will cause average U.S. indoor residential water use to fall gradually from 291 liters per person a day to 204, a 30-percent reduction.[52]

Effective pricing, regulations, and public outreach can also help curb water use outdoors. In many dry regions, the sprinkling of lawns accounts for a third to half of residential water demand. Many communities in the United States have turned to "Xeriscape landscaping," which draws on a wide variety of attractive indigenous and drought-tolerant plants, shrubs, and ground cover to replace the thirsty green lawns found in most suburbs. A Xeriscape yard typically requires 30–80 percent less water than a conventional one, and can reduce fertilizer and herbicide use as well. Just a decade old, the Xeriscape concept has spread rapidly; programs are now in place in at least eight states. And it is making inroads in a handful of other countries as well, including Australia, Canada, and Mexico.[53]

In addition to cutting indoor and outdoor water use, a comprehensive urban conservation effort will curb water losses in the water distribution system itself. As urban water systems deteriorate because of age or lack of maintenance, large amounts of water can be lost through broken pipes and faults in the distribution network. More than half the urban water supply simply disappears in Cairo, Jakarta, Lagos, Lima, and Mexico City. Although some of this water is probably siphoned off by poor residents not served by the system, much of it gets to no one. Moreover, these are costly losses because this "unaccounted-for water" is collected, stored, treated, and distributed, but never reaches a billable customer.[54]

In most cases, finding and fixing leaks rewards a city not only with water savings, but with a quick payback on the investment. At a cost of $2.1 million, the Massachusetts Water Resources Authority's leak detection program cut systemwide demand in the greater Boston area by about 10 percent, making it one of the most cost-effective measures in a successful conservation strategy. Leak repair can be especially beneficial in developing-country cities with very large losses, since the existing water supply system can then serve more people. Reducing Jakarta's "unaccounted-for-water" from 51 to 31 percent, for example, would retrieve some 45 million cubic meters annually, enough to supply 800,000 people.[55]

With a few notable exceptions, such as Mexico City and Bogor, Indonesia, few Third World cities are actively trying to conserve water. Most are preoccupied with the daunting challenge of providing reliable water services to the millions of people now lacking them. Given that average household use in most developing countries is a fraction of that in industrial countries, conservation and efficiency are often viewed as irrelevant or, at best, options to pursue later.

Quite to the contrary, conservation is an integral part of any practical solution to the water supply problems of poorer nations. Constructing water distribution networks, connecting each individual household to water and sewer pipes, and building centralized water and wastewater treatment plants cost $450–700 per person served. By holding down each household's water demand, water-efficient plumbing fixtures and other conservation measures can help lower these costs. They allow expensive new treatment plants and distribution pipes either to be scaled down in size, reducing capital and operating expenditures, or to serve more people. The World Bank, in collaboration with the United Nations Development Programme, has started to work with a number of countries, including Chile, China, India, and South Korea, to identify cities that could serve as useful demonstration sites for urban conservation.[56]

TOWARD WATER SECURITY

Together, the many ways of conserving, recycling, and reusing water constitute the makings of an efficiency revolution. With tools and technologies readily available, enormous savings are possible in agriculture, industries, and cities. Yet we are stuck at the brink of this transformation because of policies and laws that encourage wastefulness and misuse rather than efficiency and conservation.

Many of the water shortages cropping up around the world stem from the widespread failure to value water at anything close to its true worth. Pricing water properly is especially important in agriculture, because wasteful irrigation constitutes the single largest untapped new supply. Unfortunately, water subsidies are larger and more pervasive in agriculture than in any other sector. Governments often build, maintain, and operate irrigation systems with public funds, and then charge farmers next to nothing for these expensive services. Irrigators in Indonesia, Mexico, and Pakistan, for instance, pay on average less than 15 percent of their water's full cost. The situation has been no better in the United States. As of the mid-eighties, irrigators benefiting from California's huge federally built and operated Central Valley Project had repaid only 4 percent of its capital costs: $38 million out of $950 million. U.S. taxpayers footed the bill for the remainder.[57]

Such extreme undercharging not only fosters waste and the planting of water-intensive crops, it also deprives government agencies of the funds needed to maintain canals and other irrigation works adequately. But correcting the situation is easier said than done. It requires bucking deeply entrenched and politically influential special interests, instilling irrigation bureaucracies with a broader sense of mission, and decentralizing water management so that local water suppliers and users have more responsibility and accountability for the performance of their operations.

In the United States, an important step forward was taken with passage of the Central Valley Project Improvement Act in October 1992. Part of a broader water bill, the act establishes a tiered pricing system that should encourage more-efficient water use by California farmers with contracts under the federal project. It also allows irrigators to voluntarily transfer a portion of their supplies to other water users in the state, thereby creating additional market incentives for conservation and wise use.[58]

Many of the water shortages cropping up around the world stem from the widespread failure to value water at anything close to its true worth.

Proposing that farmers in developing countries at least pay for the operation and maintenance of their irrigation systems is often countered with the argument that they cannot afford higher prices. Yet those benefiting from irrigation typically earn far more than farmers who cultivate rainfed lands. Reducing irrigation subsidies would free up funds to invest in the productivity of rainfed farming, which accounts for the bulk of the world's cropland and provides the livelihood of most of the rural poor. Moreover, Third World irrigators have shown time and again that they are willing and able to pay more for water that is reliable and over which they can exercise control. With an assured and timely supply, they can invest in fertilizers, high-yielding seeds, and better management practices, often boosting their crop production and income enough to offset any rise in water prices.[59]

With the pace of water development slowing and supplies no longer expanding in places, new demands must increasingly be met by shifting water among different users—irrigators, industries, cities, and the natural environment. In the western United States, competition for scarce supplies has spawned an active water market. During 1991, 127 water transactions of various kinds were reported in 12 western states. Almost all the water sold or leased came from irrigation, and two thirds of the trades resulted in cities getting more water for immediate or future use. Such transactions will almost certainly increase as a result of the groundbreaking California water reform legislation, since it fosters water transfers.[60]

Exactly how far U.S. water trading ultimately will go in reallocating supplies remains unclear. According to some estimates, redirecting 7 percent of western agriculture's water to cities could meet the growth in urban demand projected for the end of the decade. After that, larger shifts would be needed. Unless cities stabilize their water use through conservation, reuse, and, where necessary, limits on the size of their populations and economies, agriculture ultimately could lose more water—and land—than is socially desirable, given the challenge that lies ahead of feeding a much larger world population.[61]

Wherever pricing and marketing fail to take into account the full social, environmental, and intergenerational costs of water use, some additional correction is needed. In areas with declining groundwater levels, for instance, governments can limit the total amount pumped to the average rate of aquifer recharge. In the case of fossil aquifers, such as the Ogallala in the U.S. High Plains or the deep desert aquifers in Saudi Arabia and Libya, a "depletion tax" might be levied on all groundwater extractions. In this way, those profiting from draining one-time reserves would at least partially compensate society.

Public action is also needed to ensure that ecological systems get the water they need to remain healthy. One option is simply to limit the total amount that can be diverted from a river, lake, or stream. In the western United States, this has become easier now that most states recognize water left "instream" to protect ecological functions as a legitimate beneficial use to which water rights can be attached. Montana, for instance, passed a law in 1973 that allows the state and federal governments to reserve water for instream uses. As a result, about 70 percent of the average annual flow in the upper basin of the Yellowstone River and half to two thirds of the lower basin flow have been reserved to protect aquatic life, water quality, and other ecological services. And the 1992 federal reclamation act mentioned earlier reserves 800,000 acre-feet or about 10 percent of California's Central Valley Project water for protection and restoration of fisheries and wetlands.[62]

Protecting water systems also depends on regulating the use of those critical areas of land that help moderate water's cycling through the environment. Degradation of the watershed—the sloping land that collects, directs, and controls the flow of rainwater in a river basin—is a pervasive problem in rich and poor countries alike. Besides contributing to flash floods and loss of groundwater recharge, which can exacerbate the effects of drought, it leads to soil erosion that prematurely fills downstream reservoirs with silt, shortening the useful life of expensive water projects.

Fortunately, many of the measures that can help safeguard water supplies also enhance crop production in upland areas. Terracing, mulching, agroforestry (the combined production of crops and trees), and planting vegetative barriers on the contour are just a few of the ways soil and water can be conserved while improving agricultural output. On lands not suitable for cultivation, the menu of options for watershed protection includes revegetating deforested slopes, reducing grazing pressures, and altering timber practices. The challenge for local and national governments is to plan the use of watershed lands with soil and water conservation in mind, recognizing that the way uplands are managed greatly affects the livelihoods of people and the integrity of water systems downstream.

Land use planning in and around cities and suburbs can be equally important for the protection of local water supplies. Unplanned development can end up paving over rainwater's main point of entry into a key drinking-water source. Especially in areas dependent on local groundwater, protecting these critical aquifer recharge areas is essential to ensure that water sources get replenished. Suffolk County, Long Island, recently spent $118 million to acquire 3,440 hectares of open space in order to preclude development in recharge zones vital to the region's underground water supply, its sole source of drinking water.[63]

Here and there, pricing, marketing, and regulatory actions are being used effectively to promote conservation, efficiency, and sustainable water use. But nowhere have all the elements been brought together into a strategy ensuring that human use of water remains within ecological bounds and that the integrity of water systems overall is protected.

The challenge now is to put as much human ingenuity into learning to live in balance with water as we have put into controlling and manipulating it. Conservation, efficiency, recycling, and reuse can generate a new supply large enough to get us through many of the shortages on the horizon, buying time to bring consumption and population growth down to sustainable levels. Yet the pace of this transition needs to quicken if we are to avert severe ecological damage, economic setbacks, food shortages, and international conflicts. In the end, the time available to adjust may prove as precious as water itself.

3

Reviving Coral Reefs

Peter Weber

In September of 1987, fishers along the southwest coast of Puerto Rico reported that the reef's normally beige corals had turned bright white. At first, marine scientists Lucy Bunkley-Williams and Ernest Williams, Jr., assumed it was an ordinary case of "bleaching." Corals bleach if stunned by any number of stresses: an extremely low tide, freshwater flood, pollution, abnormally low or high water temperatures. Although corals can die if the strain is not relieved, in the experience of both fishers and scientists, bleaching was normally nothing to worry about.[1]

1987, however, was not a normal year. When the two scientists took a dive to examine the reef, they found that its corals had bleached to greater depths than they had ever seen. They became more concerned as accounts of bleaching arrived from across Puerto Rico's southern coast and the entire Caribbean. Soon, reports from throughout the tropics revealed the most widespread case of coral bleaching in history. Reefs in every major region of the world were touched.[2]

Because many of the reports mentioned higher than usual water temperatures, which can cause bleaching, some people thought that scientists had found the proverbial canary in the coal mine

that would prove that global warming was under way. But this was not the case. Mass bleaching adds to the growing body of evidence—and may be a harbinger of what is to come—but only a long-term trend in global temperatures can definitively confirm that climate change has begun.[3]

Although inconclusive, the debate over mass bleaching and global warming at least drew some needed attention to another global environmental trend, the decline of coral reefs. They were already suffering from a broad array of stresses, including silt from deforestation and coastal pollution from crowded coastlines, which are choking them, and overexploitation by coral miners, fishers, and tourists, who are destroying and depleting them. A study from the World Conservation Union and the U.N. Environment Programme (UNEP) in the mid-eighties found that people had damaged or destroyed significant amounts of reef off the coasts of 93 countries. Reefs, it turns out, are among the most endangered ecosystems on earth.[4]

They are also among the most precious. Coral reefs are underwater marvels of fluorescent colors, fantastic shapes, and improbable creatures: delicate purple sea fans, blood-red sponges, blue-spotted groupers, spiny pufferfish, snorkel-nosed moray, poisonous scorpionfish, giant clams, yellow-lip snakes, and giant manta rays. "The eye struggles to make sense of the confusions of color, motion, and shape that assault it," relates Kenneth Brower, an environmental writer. "Nothing in the temperate zone can prepare the retina, or mind behind, for what goes on under the surface of shallow tropical seas." For their beauty alone, reefs are one of the treasures of the earth.[5]

This showy display, however, merely hints at greater riches. Coral reefs are among the most biologically diverse ecosystems on earth, holding a substantial portion of the biological underpinnings of life on the planet. They form what are thought to be the most species-rich ecosystems in the oceans, the crucible of life some 3 billion years ago. Covering only 0.17 percent of the ocean floor, an area the size of Texas, coral reefs are home to perhaps one quarter of all marine species, earning them the title "the tropical rain forests of the oceans." Only the vast, little-explored deep ocean floor could rival their marine biological diversity.[6]

Globally, coral reefs are thought to be second only to tropical rain forests in terms of the number of species they contain, and, considering other measures of biological diversity, such as broader classifications of species and food chain complexity, coral reefs may be more diverse.

Like the rain forests, reefs hold considerable untapped potential to contribute to science, particularly medicine. The intense crush of life spawns unique chemicals such as kainic acid, collected from reef organisms in Japan and Taiwan. Kainic acid is used as a diagnostic chemical to investigate Huntington's chorea, a rare but fatal disease of the nervous system. Other reef organisms produce chemicals useful for cancer and AIDS research. Corals themselves produce a natural sunscreen, which chemists are developing to market in Australia, and their porous limestone skeletons are promising for bone grafts in humans.[7]

For the 109 countries whose shores are lined with more than 100,000 kilometers of reefs, the ecosystem is a national asset. Reefs provide immeasurable service by protecting coastal lands from the erosive forces of the sea. Already, over two thirds of the world's sandy shorelines are thought to be eroding. The results of losing reefs can be seen in Tanzania, where formerly protected resort beaches are now eroding at a rate of 5 meters per year. The bill for replacing these self-repairing breakwaters can run into the hundreds of millions of dollars, depending on the technology used. In the Maldives, for instance, the government destroyed a reef for a land reclamation project; the replacement seawall cost $12 million for a little more than one kilometer.[8]

Reefs hold considerable untapped potential to contribute to science, particularly medicine.

Besides protecting coastlines, reefs also help form the idyllic white sand beaches and light turquoise lagoons that draw tourists to the tropics. In the Caribbean, the tourist Mecca, coastal tourism is worth over $7 billion annually. Other regions have seen coastal visitors double and triple in numbers over the last decade, and in Southeast Asia, more than 110 existing and planned tourist sites are found along the coasts, many of which are reef-lined. Worldwide, coastal tourism is the largest sector of the $250-billion tourism industry, which is projected to be the number one industry by the turn of the century.[9]

Locally, reefs are saltwater supermarkets of food and raw materials, especially for traditional coastal and island people. Pacific Islanders obtain up to 90 percent of their animal protein from reef fish, and people in Southeast Asia, the Caribbean, and parts of south Asia and east Africa derive a substantial portion of the protein in their diets from the fish that live in these ecosystems.[10]

Small-scale fishers rely heavily on the world's reefs for their livelihoods as well as their daily meals.

Healthy reefs are thought to be among the most productive fisheries in the oceans—10 to 100 times higher per unit area than the open ocean. The total catch from reefs is estimated at 4–8 million tons per year, approximately one tenth of the fish caught for use as human food. According to John McManus, a marine scientist doing research at the University of the Philippines Marine Science Institute in Bolinao, coral reefs may account for up to 20–25 percent of the fish catch of developing countries.[11]

Small-scale fishers, who typically do not have the equipment to work the open ocean, rely heavily on the world's reefs for their livelihoods as well as their daily meals. Some 4 million small-scale fishers—about eight times as many people as work in commercial fishing and a third of all subsistence fishers—haul in their catch from coral reefs.[12]

Beyond their considerable value as a natural resource, reefs have intrinsic worth as living, thriving, awe-inspiring ecosystems. Reefs are the largest structures built on the planet, unsurpassed even by human endeavors such as the Great Wall of China. Australia's Great Barrier Reef, actually composed of some 2,900 individual reefs, is said to be visible from the moon. With 500 million years of history, reefs are among the oldest ecosystems on earth. Yet, we are rapidly extinguishing these intricate works of evolution that we are only beginning to understand.[13]

REEF ECOLOGY

Charles Darwin, the founder of modern biology, wrote the seminal work on reefs in 1842. His famous five-year voyage on the HMS *Beagle* took him to the south Pacific, where he was especially interested in atolls, low islands that form on exposed reef. From their telltale circular shape with a lagoon in the center, Darwin deduced that atolls were reefs that had formed on the shores of islands that had since sunk below the ocean surface. The reefs survived by continuing to build upward. Darwin wrote that "the naturalist will feel this astonishment more deeply after having examined the soft and almost gelatinous bodies of these apparently insignificant creatures, and when he knows that the solid reef increases only on the outer edge, which day and night is lashed by the breakers of an ocean never at rest."[14]

The creatures Darwin referred to are the coral polyps, tiny sedentary relatives of jelly fish that live in colonies on the reefs. Individual coral colonies look like curiously fabricated tables, heads, branches, and leaves randomly arranged along the slope of a reef. A single coral colony can be golfball-sized or, after centuries of growth, 5–10 meters in diameter. Corals build these structures, technically their skeletons, out of limestone that they secrete. They continually build up and expand their skeletons to fight erosion and to compete with each other for sunlight. A coral colony will extend tiny tentacles to fight off other corals that try to over-shadow it.[15]

Although corals are animals, not plants, sunlight is the key to their survival scheme. They need sunlight to power the millions of microscopic algae, called zooxanthellae, that live in their translucent tissues. The zooxanthellae provide the corals with food and oxygen from photosynthesis in return for raw materials and a secure place to exist. This teamwork gives corals a competitive edge in nutrient-poor tropical seas, which are crystal clear because they are low in algae and other microorganisms that cloud more nutrient-rich waters. In hospitable conditions, corals can grow from just below sea level down to about 30 meters, at which point the sunlight is too weak to energize the coral-zooxanthellae symbiosis.

Within their limited habitat of shallow, warm seas, any number of changes in the environment—from clouded waters to extreme water temperatures—can disrupt this relationship and lead to the decline of the reef. Coral bleaching is a common result. When stressed, the polyps expel their generally brownish zooxanthellae, exposing their white limestone skeletons through their translucent tissues. Without the algae, corals cannot grow or reproduce. If the corals die, their skeletons, and eventually the reef, begin to erode away.

Although this symbiotic relationship is the keystone of these ecosystems, a reef is much more than a stand of corals. Coralline red algae, which encrust themselves in lime, cement the actual reef together. Pieces of broken coral, mollusk shell, and other stony particles catch under the coral stands. Coralline algae grow over the top, strengthening the foundation of the reef. Parrot fish and sea urchins help with maintenance by chomping on the limestone with their powerful jaws, scouring off other algae that compete for space. In turn, they and other reef residents find shelter in the reef.

These chains of interdependence extend throughout a reef like a self-perpetuating immune system. Higher levels of coral diversity correspond to greater varieties of fish and other organisms. (See Table 3–1.) Conversely, destruction of coral and other reef species can lead to the decline of both the diversity and the productivity of whole ecosystems. Although one square kilometer of healthy reef might be able to sustainably meet the protein needs of hundreds of people, the same area, if degraded, is likely to support only a fraction of that number.[16]

Table 3–1. Coral Reef Biological Diversity

Location	Coral Species	Fish Species
	(number)	
Philippines	400	1,500
Great Barrier Reef (Australia)	350	1,500
New Caledonia	300	1,000
French Polynesia	168	800
Aqaba	150	400
Toliara (Madagascar)	147	552
Society Islands	120	633
St. Gilles (Réunion)	120	258
Tadjoura (Djibouti)	65	180
Baie Possession (Réunion)	54	109
Tutia Reef (Tanzania)	52	192
Hermitage (Réunion)	30	81
Kuwait	23	85

SOURCES: World Conservation Monitoring Centre, *Global Biodiversity: Status of the Earth's Living Resources* (London: Chapman & Hall, 1992); Philippines from Alan White, Coastal Resources Center, University of Rhode Island, Narragansett, R.I., private communication, October 21, 1992; Wendy Craik, Great Barrier Reef Marine Park Authority, Townsville, Australia, private communication, June 9, 1992.

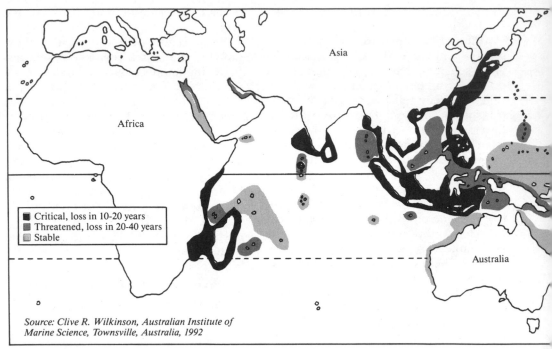

Source: Clive R. Wilkinson, Australian Institute of
Marine Science, Townsville, Australia, 1992

Figure 3-1. Critical and Threatened

Scientists are only beginning to understand the biological intricacies of reefs. No one knows for sure how many species live in coral reefs—or indeed in the oceans. In general, however, shallow waters have more species than deeper waters, rocky areas have more than sandy or muddy ones, and the tropics contain more than colder seas. Coral reefs fall into the richest realm of all three categories. Reef diversity may also increase with occasional disturbances, such as storms that level stands of corals, or plagues of coral-eating predators that clean the reef of living tissue. As the corals recover through various stages of succession, more species may be able to find niches in the reef.[17]

Human disturbances are harder on reefs than most natural disasters. People are thought to reduce reef diversity because they disrupt and destroy reefs too often for the corals to recuperate fully—through frequent visits by tourists, for

example. The effects of pollution can further degrade reefs and inhibit rejuvenation. The reefs off Jamaica's north coast have not begun to recover from hurricanes in 1980 and 1988, as they would be expected to, apparently due to the effects of overfishing and pollution. The once highly diverse, highly intricate reef there is now "flat" and dominated by algae.[18]

REEFS ON THE ROCKS

For the 1992 international symposium on coral reefs, held in Guam, Clive Wilkinson of the Australian Institute of Marine Science pulled together information from around the world on the status of these ecosystems. He estimates that to date people have directly or indirectly caused the death of 5–10 percent of the

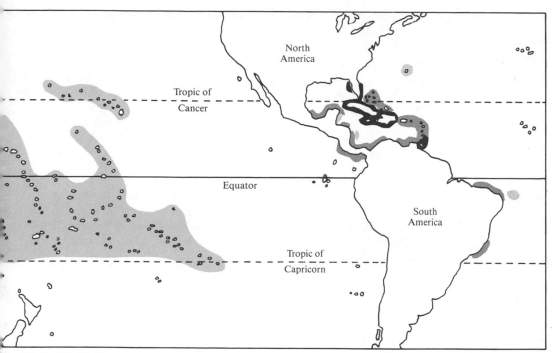

Coral Reefs of the World

world's living reefs, and that at current rates of destruction another 60 percent could be lost in the next 20–40 years. (His assessment did not include the potential effects of global warming and ozone depletion, problems that are discussed later in this chapter.)[19]

Wilkinson's rough assessment plots the general trend that reef scientists have been documenting for more than two decades. The picture he paints is not an encouraging one: only reefs in remote regions are generally healthy. (See Figure 3–1.) Although the combination of stresses and threats varies, reefs usually suffer from a mix of declining water quality, direct destruction, and depletion.[20]

Areas with tracts of particularly devastated reefs include Japan, Taiwan, the Philippines, Indonesia, Singapore, Sri Lanka, and India in Asia; Kenya, Tanzania, Mozambique, and Madagascar in Africa; and the Dominican Republic,

Haiti, Cuba, Jamaica, Trinidad and Tobago, and Florida in the Americas. The causes of degradation vary, but dense coastal populations and heavy coastal development are factors shared by all. (See Table 3–2.)[21]

Topping a long list of abuses against reefs is sedimentation from logging, farming, mining, dredging, and other coastal activities. According to a review of the scientific literature by top experts, "on a global scale, other impacts seem insignificant by contrast."[22]

Sediments that wash over reefs have a number of negative effects on corals. The initial plume blocks out sunlight, reducing zooxanthellae photosynthesis and therefore the quantity of energy available to the coral polyps. If the sediment settles on the reef, the polyps have to work together in waves to attempt to uncover themselves, and they produce extra quantities of mucus to try to wash off the particles. As a result, corals are

Table 3–2. Status of Coral Reefs in the Major Regions of the World

Region (with estimated percent of global total)	Status
Southeast Asia (30 percent)	In the primary countries, including the Philippines and Indonesia, 60–70 percent of the reefs are in poor condition. Deforestation, fishing with dynamite, and coral mining are the most severe causes of reef degradation. Overharvesting of reef species and pollution from coastal development also harm reefs. Over 70 percent of the population lives in the coastal region.
Pacific Ocean (25 percent)	Has largest area of reefs in good condition due to low populations and intensive management—both traditional and modern. Stresses on reefs include fishing with explosives, overharvesting of reef species, coral predators, land-based and coral mining, and pollution from coastal development.
Indian Ocean (24 percent)	Has lost over 20 percent of reefs due to coral mining, fishing with explosives, and coastal pollution. Excepting Australia's west coast and isolated midocean islands, reefs are heavily exploited for fish and other reef species. Coastal erosion is increasing due to degraded reefs. Region has some of the highest coastal population densities in the world.
Caribbean (9 percent)	Pollution from coastal development and deforestation, the primary causes of reef degradation, is exacerbated by low water circulation in the sea. Region has world's highest density of ocean cruises and coastal tourism. Worst damage is off countries with high rates of population growth and poverty, such as Haiti, the Dominican Republic, and Jamaica.
Atlantic Ocean (6 percent)	Coastal development and tourism damage reefs in the northern Atlantic. The notable exception is Bermuda, where reefs are in protected marine reserves and fishing is regulated. In the southern Atlantic, off the coast of Brazil, deforestation, coral mining, and tourism threaten reefs.
Middle East (6 percent)	Low runoff due to low rainfall, low populations, and low tourism have preserved many of the reefs, particularly in the Red Sea. Shipping, oil spills, and water pollution from coastal cities are the notable and growing stresses.

SOURCE: Worldwatch Institute, based on sources cited in endnote 21.

weakened. They have less energy for growing and reproducing, and they are more vulnerable to disease. If the stress is too high, the corals will bleach and perhaps die. Sediments also impede coral larvae from forming new colonies on the reef.[23]

Deforestation is the most common

source of sediments, and mangrove clearing is the most important type of forest loss. Mangroves, which form along coastlines, trap soils that would otherwise wash into the coastal waters onto reefs. When trees are cleared, they can no longer play this protective role. In the watershed of Bacuit Bay in the Philippines, logging increased erosion into the bay by more than 200 times. The sediment plume over the reefs blocked out precious sunlight and smothered corals in a blanket of soil. In 1985, the first year of logging there, 5 percent of the corals in the bay died.[24]

Similar scenarios of deforestation are playing themselves out in most regions where reefs are deteriorating. In the Caribbean, nearly all mangroves are disturbed, and countries such as Haiti, the Dominican Republic, and Jamaica are largely deforested. In the Indian Ocean, Sri Lanka and southern India have lost almost all their primary forest, and Madagascar is expected to have cut down 30 percent of its primary forests by the end of this decade. The Philippines has less than a fifth of its original mangrove forests left, and has lost over half its upland forests since the sixties. Other Southeast Asian countries are rapidly following the same course.[25]

Coastal development, which helps drive this deforestation, is itself a major cause of reef decline. Sewage, industrial pollution, and urban runoff lower coastal water quality and harm reefs. Singapore, one of the economic success stories of Southeast Asia, has built up its coastline rapidly since the sixties. Extensive land reclamation and dredging have resulted in higher levels of suspended sediment in the coastal water. Visibility averages two meters, compared with eight meters prior to 1960. As a result, coral growth below five meters is now minimal. In addition, Singapore has directly filled in some reefs for land reclamation, or removed them to enlarge

channels for shipping. Today, less than 2 percent of Singapore's reefs are in good shape.[26]

Over half the world now lives in coastal regions, and as human numbers continue to grow this proportion is expected to increase. Already, more than 70 percent of the people in parts of Southeast Asia live near the coast. Along the coastlines of India and Sri Lanka, population densities often reach up to 500 people per square kilometer, more than twice the density in the interior of the country. In the island nations of the Philippines and Indonesia, coastal populations are growing by 4 percent or more a year, compared with rates of 3 percent or less for the uplands. Along Africa's east coast, Kenya, Tanzania, Mozambique, and Madagascar are experiencing annual population growth rates of 3–4 percent. Even Pacific Island nations, which traditionally held populations steady, are growing at 2–3 percent a year. As populations continue to grow, both land clearing and development will increase.[27]

Coastal pollution does not always have immediate, obvious effects. But the steady influx of nutrients from soils and sewage, called eutrophication, can gradually cause the health of the reef to deteriorate. Initially, coral productivity increases with rising nutrient supplies. At the same time, however, corals are losing their key advantage over other organisms: their symbiotic self-sufficiency in nutrient-poor seas.

As eutrophication progresses, algae start to win out over corals for newly opened spaces on the reef because they grow more rapidly than corals when fertilized. The normally clear waters cloud as phytoplankton begin to multiply, reducing the intensity of the sunlight reaching the corals, further lowering their ability to compete. At a certain point, nutrients in the surrounding waters begin to overfertilize the corals' own zooxanthellae, which multiply to toxic levels inside the polyps. Eutrophication may also lead to black band and white band disease, two deadly coral disorders thought to be caused by algal infections. Through these stages of eutrophication, the health and diversity of reefs declines, potentially leading to death.[28]

Mounting evidence suggests that the secondary effects of eutrophication may be as bad in some cases. Charles Birkeland, a reef scientist at the University of Guam, believes that nutrient flushes into coastal waters cause the outbreak of crown-of-thorns starfish, a coral predator that has plagued reefs from the Indian to the Pacific Ocean in recent decades.[29]

Historically, these spiny, many-legged starfish are thought to have come and gone in waves every few decades or so. They clean entire reefs of coral polyps and move on. Since the late sixties, however, this self-fashioned natural disaster seems to have occurred more frequently and lasted longer in parts of the Pacific, jeopardizing slower-growing, larger corals and perhaps entire coral communities.[30]

Tracing Japanese agricultural records, Birkeland found that outbreaks of crown-of-thorns starfish occurred two to three years after extremely rainy seasons—which is how long it takes juvenile starfish to grow to become adults. He hypothesizes that heavy soil and nutrient runoff into coastal waters improve the chances that starfish larvae will survive to become adults. Since one female can produce 20–60 million eggs in one year, a one one-thousandth increase in larvae survival can lead to a twenty- to sixty-thousand-fold increase in the population of crown-of-thorns. Experiments with starfish larvae have shown that increased nutrients improve their survival rate.[31]

In addition to prompting these natural threats to reefs, people can also spread them. The crown-of-thorns starfish, now found throughout the Pacific, could spread to the Caribbean via the Panama Canal, especially if it is ever deepened. Black band and white band diseases, which historically had only been found in the Caribbean, have recently been documented in Japan, the Middle East, and parts of the Indian Ocean. Cargo ships discharging ballast water from the Caribbean are a likely cause.[32]

Only reefs that are relatively untouched by human activity are in good shape. Among the better-off ones, Australia's Great Barrier Reef is more than 260 kilometers from shore at its most distant point. Belize also has a generally well preserved barrier reef due to the country's low population density. Elsewhere, reefs are usually healthy along sparsely populated islands—particularly atolls, since soil runoff is limited.[33]

But people are steadily encroaching on reefs. In the Middle East, the lush reefs of the Red Sea contrast starkly with the surrounding desert landscapes. Until recently, this isolation had been the reefs' salvation: settlements along these bodies of water have been scarce, and people living there have not used the reefs extensively for fishing or raw materials. With the oil boom, however, increased commerce has led to the degradation of some of the region's reefs. Oil spills can kill shallow corals outright, interrupt reproduction and metabolism, and smother corals if heavy tars settle. Even worse, detergents used to disperse spills are acutely toxic to corals, although new methods have been developed that avoid this problem.[34]

Shipping is another serious threat to the Middle East reefs. In one case, a ship "virtually eliminated" all life on 500 square meters of reef when it ran aground and released several hundred tons of phosphate. Obviously, reefs at busy ports are the most vulnerable. Since the Iraq-Iran war, shipping through Al 'Aqabah, Jordan, has intensified. The U.N. embargo of Iraq after its invasion of Kuwait resulted in as many as 40 ships anchoring over the reefs at a time, waiting to get into the port. Similar damage from shipping and oil spills is also found in the Caribbean, off the coast of southern India, and in parts of Southeast Asia.[35]

EXPLOITED ECOSYSTEMS

The many assets of reefs are also the source of their decline. They attract people in pursuit of food, exotic species, gift-shop corals, and limestone for building materials, as well as tourists and tourist complexes. Although less insidious than sediment and other pollutants, overexploitation is a pervasive problem for reefs.

Too many fishers chasing too few fish is a nearly ubiquitous problem that can reduce a reef's productivity. Reef fish are prone to overfishing because like many slow-growing, long-lived animals, they have low natural fertility. When depleted, they are slow to repopulate the reef. Overfishing may also have secondary effects on the reef itself. Off the coast of east Africa, depletion of fish stocks has apparently led to the outbreak of rock-boring sea urchin, which undermine the structure of corals and reefs. Researchers in Kenya found that the removal of two species of triggerfish were at the root of the sea urchin infestations. Densities reached as high as 65 sea urchins per square meter. Off Okinawa, Japan, sea urchins and sponges are eating away the reef faster than it can form. Reefs off at least 80 countries are threatened by overfishing.[36]

The combination of overfishing and other strains can create a self-reinforcing cycle of degradation. As incomes fall, fishers are forced to pursue other sources of income, some of which can be destructive to reefs. In the Philippines, where small-scale fishers are among the poorest groups in society, this pressure is particularly acute. The country's reefs, acclaimed as the most biologically diverse in the world, are severely degraded due to a daunting list of stresses. A recent survey showed that only 5 percent of the reefs were in pristine condition, while 30 percent were largely dead and another 39 percent had only a 25–50 percent covering of healthy corals. The poor condition of the reefs reduces their productivity at the same time that increasing numbers of fishers are trying to land as many fish as the reef will yield.[37]

Some fishers earn extra income by collecting turtles, mother of pearl, and other prized reef species that will fetch high prices in foreign markets. These species in particular are overharvested. Giant clams, once common in the reefs of Southeast Asia, have been eliminated from reef after reef because their meat is a delicacy in the region. Other coveted species could suffer a similar fate.[38]

Too many fishers chasing too few fish is a nearly ubiquitous problem that can reduce a reef's productivity.

Cyanide and other poisons are commonly used to collect exotic fish for the world's $4-billion aquarium industry. In the Philippines, where these are the sixth largest fishery export, 80–90 percent of the exotic fish are captured using cyanide. A squirt of the chemical into a hole or crack in the reef causes fish to come reeling out, stunned for easy capture. Repeated application can kill corals as well as fish, eggs, larvae, and mollusks.[39]

Corals themselves are gathered and sold as part of the international trade of reef products. Worldwide, some 1.5 million kilograms of coral are harvested annually. The Philippines accounts for more than a third of this, with Malaysia, Indonesia, New Caledonia, and Fiji supplying another third. Although a portion is sold to tourists domestically, most is exported.[40]

A major destination for this coral and for tropical aquarium fish is the United States, which accounts for more than a third of the world demand for both products. Live corals for elaborate home saltwater aquariums are a small but growing portion of this market. Most corals go to gift shops to replace truncated domestic supplies. Florida was a major supplier of corals until 1989, when the state shut the industry down to protect its reefs. In 1989, the United States also banned the import of coral from the Philippines, where export is illegal, but supplies continue to enter the country from Indonesia, Singapore, and illicit channels.[41]

In Sri Lanka and India, entire sections of reef have been removed to produce cement.

Other forms of exploitation have led to the wholesale destruction of some reefs. Although it is almost universally illegal, blast fishing still occurs in 40 countries throughout the Pacific, Southeast Asia, the Indian Ocean, and, to a lesser extent, the Caribbean. An explosion near a reef kills or stuns fish for divers to gather. In the Pacific Islands, fishers have even used bombs recovered from sunken World War II battleships. Off the coast of Africa, some small coral islands have been entirely demolished in the pursuit of fish. Researchers estimate that about a sixth of the reefs in the Phil-

ippines have been damaged by explosives since 1945.[42]

Another destructive fishing practice in Southeast Asia, *muro-ami*, has left entire tracts of reef in rubble. To scare fish into nets, children are forced to swim through the water pounding the reef with rocks tied to brightly colored streamers. Besides depleting reefs and damaging corals, *muro-ami* is dangerous for these children, who are killed by needlefish, sharks, barracuda, poisonous sea snakes, and disease. In the Philippines, one corporation has been responsible for running 40 *muro-ami* ships that each carry up to 300 boys and collectively could destroy 1 square kilometer of reef per day.[43]

Reefs are also mined for building materials. In Sri Lanka and India, entire sections of reef have been removed to produce cement. Small coral islands in the Philippines and Indonesia have likewise been mined out of existence. People in island regions especially use the reef's limestone for construction, either because they have no other source of rock or because an island's base rock is volcanic, which is not strong or durable. On the South Pacific island of Palau, construction workers mined the area above the island's widely acclaimed reef to build a new airport runway to accommodate increasing numbers of tourists. Besides the direct destruction, removing large sections of reef can alter the water circulation and inhibit regrowth. This is particularly serious when dredged navigation channels allow lagoons to drain with the falling tide, exposing corals to the air.[44]

Tourism is often cited as a motivation for countries to protect their reefs from these various forms of destruction, yet the boom in this industry is also contributing to the degradation of reefs in some areas. In some instances, tourists and divers walk on the reef, killing coral polyps. Ellen McRae, a marine biologist in Belize, reports seeing dead patches of coral exactly the shape of snorkelers' fins. Reckless divers also kick up sediments and break off pieces of corals. Although single incidents may be minor, the cumulative effect in heavily visited tourist centers, like the Florida Keys, can be devastating.[45]

Anchors from both small boats and cruise ships can break off larger chunks of coral. In one instance off Grand Cayman Island in the Caribbean, a 525-foot cruise ship dropped its five-ton anchor and dragged its chain across 150 meters of reef. The anchor crushed corals within a three-meter radius, and the slowly swinging chain cut a swath across the reef, sending corals up to eight meters in diameter tumbling down the reef slope in an effect akin to an avalanche. On a calm day, the anchoring cruise ship destroyed a 3,100-square-meter section, about half the size of a football field. Although this kind of damage is poorly documented, it is thought to be fairly common, especially in the Caribbean—the top cruise ship destination in the world.[46]

Even if tourists stay out of the water, resorts built to serve them contribute to the degradation of coastal water quality. Beachfront development increases sedimentation of reefs, and hotels generally pipe their sewage and wastewater directly into the ocean, polluting nearby reefs. They also attract entrepreneurs who harvest corals and other souvenirs for local sale.[47]

Ultimately, the forces behind reef decline are hard to untangle. Overexploitation and coastal pollution stem from business interests, wealthy consumers, the growing number of coastal poor, and governments trying to balance conflicting development goals. No single group is the cause of reefs' precipitous decline, yet all contribute to the tragedy.

THE CHANGING CLIMATE FOR CORALS

In addition to the immediate threats of pollution and overuse, reefs will have to weather the future consequences of two forms of global environmental change: the gradual warming of the earth due to the accumulation of carbon dioxide and other heat-trapping gases in the atmosphere, and the rising intensity of the sun's harmful ultraviolet rays due to the destruction of the stratospheric ozone layer by long-lived chlorofluorocarbons (CFCs) and other chemicals.

Climatologists project that atmospheric concentrations of the earth's heat-trapping gases will double within the next five decades, primarily due to carbon emissions from fossil fuel burning and deforestation. As a result, global temperatures are expected to rise 0.2–0.5 degrees Celsius a decade during the next century, with greater warming toward the poles than around the equator.[48]

The subsequent warming is likely to cause a number of additional global changes. As the oceans warm and the polar ice caps melt, sea level is expected to rise some 6 centimeters per decade. The changing climate is predicted to alter weather patterns and to lead to stronger storms. The combination of differential warming of the oceans and changed weather patterns could in turn shift the oceans' normally stable circulation patterns.[49]

In addition, scientists expect stratospheric ozone depletion to progress into the early part of the next century, despite international accords to ban production of CFCs and other chemicals that have caused the problem. Ozone depleters could thin the protective layer by 0.5–5 percent over the tropics, increasing the intensity of the ultraviolet radiation that reaches the earth's surface in the equatorial region by 1–10 percent.[50]

Many of these changes are likely to harm coral reefs. (See Table 3–3.) Higher atmospheric carbon dioxide levels alone could chemically inhibit coral-building by the polyps. Stronger, more frequent storms would increasingly damage reefs. Despite general warming, major changes in ocean circulation would imperil reefs where cold or nutrient-laden waters replaced the more hos-pitable waters that now bathe them. Increased ultraviolet radiation may already be damaging corals in the shallow portions of reefs.

Coral bleaching episodes in the past decade could be a preview of what is to come. Scientists have found strong correlations between unusually high water temperatures and bleaching in some areas. One of the most closely studied events occurred during the 1982–83 El Niño. Named for the Christ child, El

Table 3–3. Global Warming, Ozone Depletion, and Coral Reefs

Predicted Change	Potential Effect on Coral Reefs
Doubling of Carbon Dioxide in Atmosphere by 2050	Increased concentration of CO_2 in ocean water raises the pH and possibly inhibits coral-building. Also could fertilize algae that compete with corals.
Rise in Temperature in Tropics of 1-2° Celsius by 2100	Peak summer temperatures can cause bleaching. Corals may be able to adapt to higher temperatures, but the rate of increase could be too rapid to avoid mass death. In long run, higher global temperatures would expand coral habitat out of the tropics.
Rise in Sea Level of 0.6 Meters by 2100	Healthy reefs are capable of up to 1 meter of upward growth in a century. Slower growing or unhealthy reefs could drown over the course of centuries. Increased coastal erosion is likely to deposit sediments on reefs, inhibiting growth.
Altered Weather Patterns	Flooding of nearby land could inundate reefs with deadly levels of fresh water or sediments. Stronger, more frequent storms would damage reefs.
Shifts in Oceanic Circulation Patterns	Dangerously cold and nutrient-rich currents could reach reefs, despite general planetary warming. In long run, surviving corals could colonize new, more hospitable regions.
Ultraviolet Radiation Increase of 1-10 Percent in Tropics	Could damage corals in reef flat and upper reaches of reef, changing coral distribution and decreasing diversity. Could harm coral larvae that drift near the ocean surface in early stages, impairing reproduction.

SOURCES: Intergovernmental Panel on Climate Changes (IPCC), *Climate Change 1992* (Cambridge: Cambridge University Press, 1992); IPCC, *Climate Change: The IPCC Scientific Assessment* (Cambridge: Cambridge University Press, 1990); S.V. Smith and R.W. Buddemeier, "Global Change and Coral Reef Ecosystems," *Annual Review of Ecology and Systematics*, Vol. 23, 1992, pp. 89–118; Robert W. Buddemeier, "Corals, Climate, and Conservation," plenary lecture, Seventh International Coral Reef Symposium, Guam, June 22–26, 1992 (proceedings in press).

Niño is an unusually warm patch of water that arrives on South America's Pacific coast around Christmas every 3–10 years. The 1982–83 El Niño was particularly long and severe, according to University of Miami marine biologist Peter W. Glynn. During its height, corals experienced several bleaching bouts, followed by extensive death two to four weeks later. Up to 70–90 percent of the corals off the Pacific coast of Costa Rica, Panama, and Colombia died, and coral mortality was more than 95 percent off Ecuador's Galápagos Islands.[51]

Glynn's research confirmed what scientists have generally found: corals bleach in response to temperatures that are as little as a degree or two above the normal maximum. Temperatures more than 4 degrees Celsius above normal, even for a few hours, will result in greater than 90 percent mortality.[52]

Although scientists cannot say that this and other mass bleaching events prove that global warming is under way, the evidence is provocative. First, changes in global weather patterns, such as stronger El Niños, are a possible outcome of global warming. Glynn found geologic evidence that no comparable events had occurred in the Galápagos or Panama in the last 200 years. He also reported that the 1982–83 El Niño came in the middle of a decade-long warming period in the Pacific tropics. Second, in global terms, the eighties turned out to be the warmest decade on record. Additional bouts of mass bleaching during this time led the Intergovernmental Panel on Climate Change, a group of scientists assembled by the United Nations, to conclude that coral bleaching is additional evidence that global temperatures are rising.[53]

On their own, not all aspects of global warming would be damaging to corals and reefs. Healthy reefs can grow upward by as much as 10 centimeters per decade, faster than the predicted rate of sea level rise, and higher global temperatures could expand the range of reef-building corals beyond the tropics. In the course of centuries, corals could even adapt to changes in climate by colonizing new regions of the world or evolving to withstand higher water temperatures, as those in the Persian Gulf have done in order to survive summers there. Some scientists hypothesize that bleaching may be the way corals adapt to warmer temperatures.[54]

Acclimation, however, will be difficult for corals because global temperatures are expected to rise 10 to 100 times faster than they have since the height of the last Ice Age. Furthermore, corals' ability to adjust is limited. Even Persian Gulf corals bleach if exposed to temperatures higher than their normal maximum.[55]

As for increasing ultraviolet radiation due to stratospheric ozone depletion, corals in the shallows of a reef produce a natural sunscreen to protect themselves from the intense tropical sun. Ultraviolet radiation, however, can still harm these corals, and in exceptionally calm seas, the harmful rays can reach corals deeper in the reef. Although the exact amount of increased exposure is uncertain, any rise will stress corals.[56]

The outlook for coral reefs is made more dismal by their current situation: rising sea levels alone would be a problem for polluted, abused reefs, which would not be able to grow as quickly as normal, if at all. Rising seas would also increase coastal erosion, potentially clogging the reefs with sediment, and over the course of centuries, the rising tide could "drown" some reefs by blocking out their sunlight.

At a minimum, global warming and ozone depletion are poised to further stress reefs that are already under enormous pressure from pollution and overuse. In addition, they are likely to harm reefs that have been isolated or protected until now.

SETTING PRIORITIES

Coral reefs have surprised scientists with the rate at which they can recover once stress is relieved. When water quality is good, plenty of larvae drift in from healthy reefs, and the reef is sufficiently free of sediment and algae, scientists have found signs of recovery within a year, although it takes centuries to rebuild larger corals and missing sections of reef.[57]

Thus, most coral reefs could begin to recover if governments pursued policies to protect and revive them. Currently, however, only a smattering of pilot projects and a few regional programs exist. The more common response is for a country to enact a few laws, which are not enforced or enforceable, and to designate a marine park or two, which may protect just a small section of reef or, worse yet, offer no funds or personnel for management. Governments rarely attempt to address the more basic problem of controlling land use and coastal development to prevent pollution of reefs.

Out of necessity, traditional cultures established conservation methods to ensure the long-term productivity of reefs.

To avoid continued reef decline in the decades ahead, countries need to pursue two areas of policy. One is the management and protection of reefs themselves, and the other is pollution prevention.

The basic tenants of reef management were developed over thousands of years by traditional cultures in the Pacific and Southeast Asia who relied on reefs for food. Out of necessity, they established conservation methods to ensure the long-term productivity of reefs. Typically, a master fisher regulated use of the resource with closed seasons, restricted areas, size limits, species restrictions, quotas, and equipment regulations, all of which prevented overfishing and allowed reef species to repopulate. Breaking the taboos against these restrictions could have led to expulsion from the community or death.[58]

While still in force in some areas, these traditional management systems, along with traditional cultures, are disappearing under the weight of outside influence. (See Chapter 5.) In the Federated States of Micronesia, periods of rule by Europeans and Japanese initiated these changes. Centralized government subverted the local authority to enforce taboos, and the cash economy led to the exploitation of mother of pearl, giant clams, and other prized species for export. The constant presence of foreign culture has continued to undermine the practices of outlying communities.[59]

Modern centralized governments, however, have failed to protect and manage reefs. The few laws enacted to ban or regulate destructive fishing practices or coral removal are not enforced, due to either the lack of resources or the lack of will. Parks—the classic form of protection for natural habitats—are largely ineffective as traditionally designed. Although 65 countries worldwide have designated some 300 parks that include coral reefs, these are largely "paper parks," without the funds or staff to protect reefs sufficiently. In the Caribbean, which has the highest proportion of marine reserves, less than 30 percent of the designated area is truly protected. Furthermore, in most countries, existing parks include only a small fraction of the reefs.[60]

Australia broke the mold in 1975 when it created the Great Barrier Reef Park. Under the founding legislation, the entire reef complex is part of a 350,000-square-kilometer park. But this is not a park in the traditional sense. The managers split the reef into sectors to satisfy various public demands: some areas are restricted to scientific research, others allow tourists, and still others are open to commercial fishing and harvesting. The park authority monitors and regulates the use of the reef to try to ensure its health over the long term.[61]

Marine scientists generally herald the Great Barrier Reef as the modern success story of reef management. The approach used there, however, does not easily transfer to developing countries. First, Third World governments do not have the resources to manage entire coastlines. Second, central management could conflict with local rights, as it has in the small sections of the Great Barrier Reef that aborigines traditionally used.[62]

Local management holds greater promise in terms of both effectiveness and equity. In one example from the Philippines, university researchers convinced a local community on Sumilon Island to set aside a portion of the reef as an undisturbed breeding ground. The experiment led to a dramatic increase in the number of fish along the reef—so much so that outsiders wanted to fish there. Initially, the mayor of a nearby town overruled the restrictions and allowed commercial fishing, which again depleted the reef. Eventually, however, the national government passed legislation to protect the local community's rights to the reserve.[63]

Numerous communities in other countries have similarly demonstrated the value of locally managed fisheries. This approach draws on the lessons of traditional reef management. Given sufficient knowledge or training, local people are in the best position to manage the resource. If they have exclusive rights to it, they have a strong incentive to manage a reef for long-term sustainability.

As the Sumilon Island story highlights, for this form of management to succeed, governments must provide legal backing for the community. Some Pacific island nations such as the Solomon Islands recognize traditional sea rights either in their constitutions or in practice. An alternative approach is to create a marine reserve in which the local community has control over the resources, as has been done at the Sian Ka'an Biosphere Reserve along the Caribbean coast of the Yucatán peninsula. These reserves are managed for both conservation of the natural habitat and local use. UNESCO's Man and the Biosphere Program has established 10 biosphere reserves worldwide that include coral reefs.[64]

Conservation of the reef itself is vital, but not sufficient. Some of the sections of the Great Barrier Reef, for instance, are threatened by nutrients originating from the shore. Stopping coastal water pollution is thus a vital piece of the policy puzzle.

Protecting coastal waters from pollution would offer many benefits beyond conserving reefs. Halting sedimentation would also protect the land's topsoil, a precious commodity that requires centuries to form and that just one heavy rainstorm can wash away. Besides lowering the future productivity of agricultural and forest lands, soil erosion lowers the value of streams and rivers for drinking, irrigation, and fishing. Indiscriminate land clearing can also increase flooding and endanger people downstream.

When factored together, the economic benefits of conserving soil and reefs would likely outweigh the costs of conservation in many cases. According to one study, a government-granted logging concession in the Bacuit Bay in the Philippines was expected to reduce the economic value of the local reefs for fishing and tourism by $50–75 million while generating only $13 million over the course of a decade. The economic analysis did not factor in lost productivity of the logged land due to erosion.[65]

Tourists and tourist resorts can harm coral reefs, even though the money they attract should be strong motivation to conserve the allure of coasts.

Although attractive to more and more people, coastal living has its own environmental costs. Mangroves and coastal wetlands—which are destroyed for homes, cities, and aquaculture—help protect coastlines from erosion, are important spawning grounds for oceanic fisheries, and are teeming ecosystems in their own right. Coastal developments are also vulnerable to flooding and destruction by storms, which imperil people's lives and can lead to heavy financial liabilities. In the United States, the risks of coastal living have raised the cost of flood insurance so high that homeowners can generally only afford federally subsidized policies.[66]

Where coastal development occurs, cities can regulate industrial and municipal discharge into coastal waters to attempt to prevent damage to reefs. Controlling this form of coastal pollution would benefit not only reefs and other marine ecosystems, but also public health. In some instances, beaches must be closed to tourists and fishers to guard against poisoning or the spread of disease. Insufficient sanitation facilities leads to the transmission of waterborne diseases, which are among the top killers of children in the developing world.[67]

Ideally, sewage treatment would be part of a broader policy to improve soil fertility and conserve water. In the Middle East, Israel treats and recycles wastewater for use on crops because water is in short supply in the country. Farmers receive added benefits of improved soil fertility and lower fertilizer bills. (See Chapter 2.) This approach is particularly important in semienclosed seas such as the Red Sea, the Persian Gulf, and the Caribbean, where nutrients are not readily diluted.[68]

Elsewhere, reefs have been protected from eutrophication by centralizing waste and pumping it beyond the reefs. The classic example is Kaneohe Bay in Hawaii, where the city moved the sewage outfall beyond the reefs in 1979, and the ecosystem was on its way to recovery in a couple of years. This approach, however, is less than ideal—and illegal in some cases—if the waste is not treated.[69]

Controlling dispersed sources of pollution is equally important. A recent survey of Kaneohe Bay indicates that pollution from urban runoff and septic tanks may be inhibiting the reefs' recovery. The city is proceeding with plans to connect to the central system homeowners who still have septic tanks, which will reduce their contribution to the problem. Elsewhere, such as in the Florida Keys, pollutants from septic tanks, city streets, and chemical agriculture continue to stress reefs.[70]

Countries will also have to work with their neighbors to improve coastal water quality, especially in semienclosed seas. A promising forum for cooperation is the Regional Seas Programme set up by UNEP in 1974. Under this initiative, countries establish goals and negotiate legally binding treaties to manage coastal waters. Ten regional programs now exist, encompassing most of the world's reefs, but so far the concept has fallen short of its potential due to lack of funds from member countries.[71]

The role of tourism is a controversial issue because tourists and tourist resorts can harm coral reefs, even though the money they attract should be strong motivation for countries to conserve the allure of their coasts. Australia spends $11 million annually to manage the Great Barrier Reef, which is estimated to generate $800 million in annual revenue. Tourism in parts of Southeast Asia has prompted local authorities to halt blast fishing and other destructive practices.[72]

To begin to make tourism ecologically sound, local managers need to regulate it both in the water and on land and to apply some of their profits to conservation. If divers and tourists are told how to avoid damaging the reef and if their numbers are limited, visitors are less likely to cause serious stress. Permanent moorings on the reef help prevent anchor damage from small boats, and laws and regulations can prohibit cruise ships from anchoring over reefs, as in the U.S. Virgin Islands. U.S. officials have even taken shipowners to court for damage caused by their crafts. Finally, managers need to plan tourist accommodations to minimize coastal pollution.[73]

Especially in developing countries, the role of the local community is crucial. Do local people benefit from tourism? Or are their traditional rights and cultures undermined? Unless the people who have traditionally relied on a section of coastline are part of the overall plan, ecotourism can lead to broader environmental and social problems.

Since the international community has a stake in the biological health of reefs, it too has a role to play in their conservation. Growing recognition of the importance of reefs has prompted trade restrictions on corals under the Convention on International Trade in Endangered Species of Wild Flora and Fauna, and the United Nations now includes seven reefs in its World Heritage Sites. The World Bank plans to put 15–20 percent of its $3-billion biodiversity budget into marine and coastal habitats, and the U.S. Agency for International Development and other national governments are cooperating with Southeast Asian nations on the conservation of their reefs. If ratified and funded, the Convention on Biological Diversity signed by 153 governments at the Earth Summit in Rio would likely supply money for the conservation of reefs as well.[74]

One major contribution industrial countries could make would be to map the world's reefs with satellite and airplane surveillance equipment. NASA, the U.S. space agency, could do this as part of its Mission to Planet Earth program. Currently, countries do not have enough basic information on their total reef area to enable them to monitor the health of these ecosystems.

International donors, however, will have a larger impact on reefs through their support of industrial, agricultural, and forestry projects than through any reef conservation programs. Reefs will continue to decline as long as economic development strategies fail to address fundamental environmental issues such as consumption, population, and biological diversity. Even the domestic policies of industrial countries will likely contribute to the further decline of reefs, given that these nations have contributed disproportionately to the buildup of greenhouse gases and the depletion of the stratospheric ozone layer.

The current rate of global environmental deterioration does not inspire hope that change will proceed rapidly enough to protect a significant portion of the world's reefs. For this reason, many marine scientists have come to think of the problem in terms of battlefield triage. Asked to compare the current conditions to the future threats of global warming, Guam University's Charles Birkeland replied, "It's like walking into a doctor's office with a spear in your chest, and the doctor saying, 'Let's see if you have a fever.' "[75]

This sense of imminent loss has led some scientists to propose that the few remaining undisturbed reefs should be protected before they too are damaged by expanding human activity. Robert Buddemeier, a reef scientist with the Kansas Geological Survey, suggests that island nations should receive compensation for setting aside remote or sparsely inhabited coral reef environments as permanent ecological preserves. He proposes that an international agreement could be developed along the lines of the Antarctic Treaty for the benefit of all.[76]

But protecting only a few reefs for future generations and allowing the rest to continue on their current path of decline would be a crime against nature and would make the world a poorer place—aesthetically, biologically, economically, and culturally. Yet as the general state of the global environment goes, so go the world's reefs. Ultimately, it is as much a question of whether we save or destroy the world as it is a question of whether we save or destroy the world's coral reefs.

4

Closing the Gender Gap in Development

Jodi L. Jacobson

The women of Sikandernagar, a village in the Indian state of Andhra Pradesh, work three shifts per day. Waking at 4:00 a.m., they light fires, milk buffaloes, sweep floors, fetch water, and feed their families. From 8:00 a.m. until 5:00 p.m., they weed crops for a meager wage. In the early evening they forage for branches, twigs, and leaves to fuel their cooking fires, for wild vegetables to nourish their children, and for grass to feed the buffaloes. Finally, they return home to cook dinner and do evening chores. These women spend twice as many hours per week working to support their families as do the men in their village. But they do not own the land on which they labor, and every year, for all their effort, they find themselves poorer and less able to provide what their families need to survive.[1]

As the twentieth century draws to a

An expanded version of this chapter appeared as Worldwatch Paper 110, *Gender Bias: Roadblock to Sustainable Development*.

close, some 3 billion people—more than half the earth's population—live in the subsistence economies of the Third World. The majority of them find themselves trapped in the same downward spiral as the women of Sikandernagar.[2]

In the not-so-distant past, subsistence farmers and forest dwellers were models of ecologically sustainable living, balancing available resources against their numbers. Today, however, the access of subsistence producers to the resources on which they depend for survival is eroding rapidly. As their circumstances grow more and more tenuous, pressures on the forests and croplands that remain within their grasp grow increasingly acute. Yet in an era when sustainable development has become a global rallying cry, most governments and international development agencies seem oblivious to this dilemma.

The reason is brutally simple: women perform the lion's share of work in subsistence economies, toiling longer hours and contributing more to family income than men do. Yet in a world where economic value is computed in monetary terms alone, women's work is not counted as economically productive when no money changes hands.

Women are viewed as "unproductive" by government statisticians, economists, development experts, and even their husbands. A huge proportion of the world's real productivity therefore remains undervalued, and women's essential contributions to the welfare of families and nations remain unrecognized. So while the growing scarcity of resources within subsistence economies increases the burden on women and erodes their productivity, little is being done to reverse the cycle.

Women's essential contributions to the welfare of families and nations remain unrecognized.

Ironically, by failing to address the pervasive gender bias that discounts the contributions of women, development policies and programs intended to alleviate impoverishment—and the environmental degradation that usually follows—actually are making the problem worse.

Gender bias is a worldwide phenomenon, afflicting every social institution from individual families to international development organizations. But it is especially pernicious in the Third World, where most of women's activity takes places in the nonwage economy for the purpose of household consumption. In Sikandernagar, for example, women earn less than half the amount men do for the same work. Because their cash income is not enough to buy adequate supplies of food and other necessities

(which they are responsible for obtaining one way or another), they work additional hours to produce these goods from the surrounding countryside.[3]

In most societies, gender bias compounds—or is compounded by—discrimination based on class, caste, or race. It is especially pervasive in the poorest areas of Africa, Asia, and Latin America, where it ranges from the exclusion of women from development programs to wage discrimination and systemic violence against females. In its most generic form, this prejudice boils down to grossly unequal allocation of resources—whether of food, credit, education, jobs, information, or training.

Gender bias is thus a primary cause of poverty, because in its various forms it prevents hundreds of millions of women from obtaining the education, training, health services, child care, and legal status needed to escape from poverty. It prevents women from transforming their increasingly unstable subsistence economy into one not forced to cannibalize its own declining assets.

And it is also the single most important cause of rapid population growth. Where women have little access to productive resources and little control over family income, they depend on children for social status and economic security. The greater competition for fewer resources among growing numbers of poor people accelerates environmental degradation. Increased pressure on women's time and labor in turn raises the value of children—as a ready labor force and hedge against an uncertain future. The ensuing high rates of population growth become part of a vicious cycle of more people, fewer resources, and increasing poverty. A necessary step in reducing births voluntarily, then, is to increase women's productivity and their control over resources.

THE DIMENSIONS OF GENDER BIAS

Implicit in the theory and practice of conventional economic development are three assumptions that are influenced by sex differences—and that reinforce the biases. One assumption is that within a society, both men and women will benefit equally from economic growth. The second is that raising men's income will improve the welfare of the whole family. The third is that within households, the burdens and benefits of poverty and wealth will be distributed equally regardless of sex. Unfortunately, none of these assumptions holds true.

The first assumption—that economic growth is gender-blind—is rarely challenged. But as economies develop, existing gender gaps in the distribution of wealth and in access to resources usually persist, and in many cases grow worse. From the fifties through the early eighties, for example, worldwide standards of living as measured by widely used basic indicators—including life expectancy, per capita income, and primary school enrollment—rose dramatically. Yet women never achieved parity with men, even in industrial countries.

According to the Human Development Index prepared by the United Nations Development Programme, which gauges the access people have to the resources needed to attain a decent standard of living, women lagged behind men in every country for which data were available. The differences were least pronounced in Sweden, Finland, and France, where measures of women's level of access as a share of men's passed 90 percent. They were most pronounced in Swaziland, South Korea, and Kenya, where women had less than 70 percent the access that men did.[4]

Not only do women not automatically benefit from economic growth; they may even fall further behind. Unless specific steps are taken to redress inequity, gender gaps often increase over time—especially where access to resources is already highly skewed. This has happened, for example, with literacy. In 1985, 60 percent of the adult population worldwide was able to read, compared with about 46 percent in 1970—clearly a significant improvement. Literacy rose faster among men than among women, however, so the existing gender gap actually widened. Between 1970 and 1985, the number of women unable to read rose by 54 million (to 597 million), while that of men increased by only 4 million (to 352 million). These numbers reflect females' much lower access to education in developing countries.[5]

The second assumption—that social strategies to raise men's income by increasing their access to productive resources will lead directly to improvements in total family welfare—is also not supported by the evidence. It may seem reasonable to assume that each dollar of income earned by a poor man in Bangladesh, Bolivia, or Botswana would go toward bettering the lot of his wife and children. Indeed, development programs have been built on the premise that what is good for men is good for the family. But in many areas this is patently not the case, because it is women who effectively meet the largest share of the family's basic needs, and because men often use their income to purchase alcohol, tobacco, or other consumer products.

Generally speaking, men in subsistence economies have fewer responsibilities than women to produce food and other goods solely for household consumption. While a woman labors to produce food for her children and family, her husband may focus his energies on developing a business or pursuing interests that do not include his wife and children.

In much of sub-Saharan Africa, for instance, both men and women plant crops, but they do so with different goals. Husbands and wives maintain separate managerial and financial control over the production, storage, and sale of their crops. Men grow cash crops and keep the income from them—even though their wives still do the weeding and hoeing. Women, by contrast, use their land primarily for subsistence crops to feed their families. They are also expected to provide shelter, clothing, school fees, and medical care for themselves and their children, and so must earn income to cover what they cannot produce or collect from the village commons land. Given adequate acreage, high yields, or both, women do plant and market surplus crops to earn cash. When land is scarce or the soil poor, they sell their labor or put more time into other income-producing activities.[6]

Women use their land primarily for subsistence crops to feed their families.

Because responsibilities for securing the goods needed for household consumption often fall to the woman, even an increase in the income of a male within a household may not mean an increase in total consumption by family members. As subsistence economies become increasingly commercialized, for example, men whose families are below the poverty line often spend any additional cash income to raise the productivity of their own crops, and sometimes to increase their personal consumption. In Africa, according to one World Bank report, "it is not uncommon

for children's nutrition to deteriorate while wrist watches, radios, and bicycles are acquired by the adult male household members." The connection between malnutrition and the diversion of income by males to personal consumption has also been found in Belize, Guatemala, Mexico, and throughout the Indian subcontinent.[7]

In fact, contrary to conventional assumptions, women are the main breadwinners in a large share of families throughout the Third World. They contribute proportionately more of their cash income to family welfare than men do, holding back less for personal consumption. A study in Mexico found that wives accounted for 40 percent or more of the total household income, although their wage rates were far lower than their husbands'. The women contributed 100 percent of their earnings to the family budget, while husbands contributed at most 75 percent of theirs. Similar discrepancies in the amount of money contributed have been found to be virtually universal throughout the developing world.[8]

Moreover, studies in every region of the Third World confirm that it is the mother's rather than the father's income or food production—and the degree of control she maintains over that income—that determines the relative nutrition of children. In Guatemala, for example, the children of women earning independent incomes had better diets than those of women who were not earning their own money or who had little control over how their husbands' earnings were spent. Women who retain control over income and expenditures spend more not only on food but also on health care, school expenses, and clothing for their children. Similar patterns have been found in studies from the Dominican Republic, Ghana, India, Kenya, Peru, and the Philippines.[9]

Differences in the responsibilities and

workloads of men and women within subsistence economies can also affect family welfare. A project in the Indian state of West Bengal, for example, gave villagers conditional access to trees on private land. The "lops and tops" of trees were to be reserved for women's needs, while men were to harvest the timber for cash on a sustainable basis. In response to offers from a contractor, however, the men sold the trees for a lump sum. Women obtained little fuel.[10]

The third assumption—that within poor households resources will be distributed equally regardless of sex—may seem so obvious as to be beyond question. But even when a man's income is used to improve his family's, it may improve the welfare of males at the expense of females. In many cultures, a family's resources are distributed according to the status of household members, rather than according to their need. Men and boys fare far better than women and girls. In India, for instance, studies show that in many states sons consistently receive more and better food and health care than their sisters. Consequently, far more girls than boys die in the critical period between infancy and age five. And with the exception of girls aged 10 to 14, Indian females die from preventable causes at far higher rates than males do through age 35.[11]

Basic indicators of caloric intake and life expectancy measured by the Indian government's 1991 census reveal a growing gender gap in several states since 1980. In fact, contrary to sex ratios found in most countries, the ratio of women to men in India has actually been declining since the early part of the century. There are now only 929 women for every 1,000 men, compared with 972 in 1901. Dr. Veena Mazumdar, director of the Delhi-based Centre for Women's Development Studies, notes that "the declining sex ratio is the final indicator

that registers [that] women are losing out on all fronts—on the job market, in health and nutrition and economic prosperity."[12]

Evidence of similar patterns of discrimination in the allocation of household resources has been found in Bangladesh, Nepal, Pakistan, throughout the Middle East and North Africa, and in parts of sub-Saharan Africa. Harvard economist and philosopher Amartya Sen calculates that 100 million women in the developing world are "missing," having died prematurely from the consequences of such gender bias.[13]

Because of these patterns, argues Bina Agarwal, professor of agricultural economics at the Institute of Economic Growth in Delhi, "existing poverty estimates need revision." The current practice is to first identify poor households by specified criteria and then calculate the total numbers, the assumption being that all members are equally poor. However, Agarwal argues, this reveals little about the relative poverty of men and women. The differences in the distribution of resources within households mean there are poor women in households with cash incomes or consumption levels above the poverty line. Conversely, there are nonpoor men in households below the poverty line.[14]

Globally, much of this discrimination against females in families and societies stems from another form of gender gap—the huge disparity between the real economic and social benefits of women's work and the social perception of women as unproductive.

In every society, women provide critical economic support to their families, alone or in conjunction with spouses and partners, by earning income—in cash or in kind—in agriculture, in formal and informal labor markets, and in emerging international industries, such as the manufacture of semiconductors. U.N. data indicate that, on average, women work longer hours than men in every country except Australia, Canada, and the United States. Hours worked earning wages or producing subsistence goods are rarely offset by a reduction of duties at home. Time allocation studies confirm that women throughout the world maintain almost exclusive responsibility for child care and housework. Moreover, disparities in total hours worked are greatest among the poor: in developing countries, women work an average of 12–18 hours a day—producing food, managing and harvesting resources, and working at a variety of paid and unpaid activities—compared with 8–12 hours on average for men.[15]

In subsistence economies, measuring work in terms of the value of goods produced and time spent shows that women usually contribute as much as or more than men to family welfare. The number of female-headed households is growing. But "even where there is a male earner," notes World Bank consultant Lynn Bennett, "women's earnings form a major part of the income of poor households."[16]

Official definitions of what constitutes "work" often fail to capture a large share of women's labor.

The low valuation of women's work begins with the fact that in developing countries, most of women's activity takes place in the nonwage economy for the purpose of household consumption— producing food crops, collecting firewood, gathering fodder, and so on. "Income generation" of this type is critically important; indeed, the poorer the family, the more vital is the contribution of women and girls to the essential goods that families are unable to buy with cash. But in the increasingly market-oriented economies of the Third World, work that does not produce cash directly is heavily discounted.[17]

Low valuation is further reinforced by women's institutionally enforced lack of control over physical resources. In most subsistence economies, females have few legal rights regarding land tenure, marital relations, income, or social security. In a world where control over land confers power, the value of wives' and mothers' contributions in subsistence economies also is discounted because these are directed mainly at day-to-day sustenance and do not yield such visible assets.

The "invisible" nature of women's contributions feeds into the social perception that they are "dependents" rather than "producers." Indeed, the tendency at every level of society seems to be to play down the importance of female contributions to family income, which anthropologist Joke Schrijvers, cofounder of the Research and Documentation Centre on Women and Autonomy in the Netherlands, attributes to the "ideology of the male breadwinner."[18]

The ideology appears to be universal. And rather than combatting the idea that women's work has low economic value, governments and international development agencies have tacitly condoned it. Thus despite overwhelming evidence to the contrary, these institutions persist in counting women as part of the dependent or "nonproductive" portion of the population.

This bias is then perpetuated by government recordkeeping practices: official definitions of what constitutes "work" often fail to capture a large share of women's labor. In India, conventional measures based on wage labor showed that only 34 percent of Indian females are in the labor force, as opposed to 63 percent of males. But a survey of work patterns by occupational categories including household production and domestic work revealed that 75 percent of females over age five are working, compared with 64 percent of males. In a study of Nepalese villages, estimates of household income based only on wages earned put the value of female contributions at 20 percent. Taking account of subsistence production, however, brought this contribution to 53 percent. And in a study of women in the Philippines, "full income" contributions were found to be twice as high as marketed income.[19]

Given such distorted pictures of their national economies, it is not surprising that policymakers in virtually every country invest far less in female workers than in males. Moreover, international development assistance agencies, staffed mostly by men with a decidedly western view of the world, have based their decisions on the erroneous premise that what is good for men is good for the family. And because most strategists neither integrate women into their schemes nor create projects that truly address women's economic needs, development efforts aimed at raising productivity and income often bypass women altogether.

Ignoring the full value of women's economic contributions cripples efforts to achieve broad development goals. Lack of investment results in lower female productivity. Coupled with persistent occupational and wage discrimination, this prevents women from achieving parity with men in terms of jobs and income, and leads to further devaluation of their work. The omnipresence of this bias is a sign that virtually every country is operating far below its real economic potential.

Current measures of economic development tell little about how the benefits of that development will be distributed. Higher aggregate levels of agricultural production, for example, do not necessarily imply lower levels of malnutrition.

A rising gross national product does not always produce a decline in the incidence of poverty or an improvement in equity. And a real increase in the health budget of a country does not automatically lead to better access to primary health care among those most in need of it. With any project or investment, it is important to ask, Whose income is rising? Whose opportunities are increasing?

SUSTENANCE FROM THE COMMONS

Because women in rural subsistence economies are the main providers of food, fuel, and water and the primary caretakers of their families, they depend heavily on community-owned croplands, grasslands, and forests to meet their families' needs. The widespread depletion and degradation of these resources have led to equally widespread impoverishment of subsistence families throughout Africa, Asia, and Latin America.

In rural areas, both men and women engage in agriculture, but women are the major producers of food for household consumption. In sub-Saharan Africa, women grow 80 percent of the food destined for their households. Women's labor produces 70–80 percent of food crops grown on the Indian subcontinent, and 50 percent of the food domestically consumed in Latin America and the Caribbean. In all regions, roughly half of all cash crops are cultivated by women farmers and agricultural laborers.[20]

By custom, labor contributions are divided by sex. In sub-Saharan Africa, for example, males generally clear and till the land, while females are expected to do the bulk of the hoeing, weeding, and harvesting of crops, the processing of food, and various other subsistence activities. Women, therefore, perform the majority of the work in African agriculture. Similar patterns in the division of labor are found throughout the subsistence economies of Asia and Latin America.[21]

Female subsistence producers appear to be as careful in conserving forests as they are reliant on using them.

Using traditional methods, women farmers have been quite effective in conserving soil. Given access to appropriate resources, they employ managed fallowing (allowing land to rest between plantings), crop rotation, intercropping, mulching, and a variety of other soil conservation and enrichment techniques. And they have played a leading role in maintaining crop diversity. In sub-Saharan Africa, for instance, women cultivate as many as 120 different plants in the spaces alongside men's cash crops. In the Andean regions of Bolivia, Colombia, and Peru, women develop and maintain the seedbanks on which food production depends.[22]

Faced with the endemic insecurity of their situation, women have evolved techniques to make efficient use of all available resources—planting a diverse array of crops, collecting wild fruits and vegetables, maintaining farm animals, and earning whatever cash income they can to ensure a measure of food security. And while cultivating food is obviously difficult or impossible for women in families with little or no land, studies show the land-poor to be highly resourceful in devising ways to meet their families' needs. Solutions used include drawing more heavily on products gathered from commons, expanding their workloads,

and hiring themselves out as laborers in exchange for grain or cash.[23]

Women in subsistence economies also are active managers of forest resources, and traditionally play the leading role in their conservation. Forests provide a multitude of products to households. They are, for example, a major source of fuel, without which none of the food grown and harvested could be cooked, or many other essential tasks be carried out. In fact, lack of fuel to cook available food is itself a cause of malnutrition in some areas. "It's not what's in the pot, but what's under it, that worries you," say women in the fuel-deficit areas of India.[24]

The dependence of subsistence households on biomass—including wood, leaves, and crop residues—as the traditional form of domestic energy remains widespread. Seventy-five percent of all household energy in Africa is derived from biomass, for example. Women also use biomass fuel to support innumerable private enterprises, such as food processing and pottery, from which they gain cash income.[25]

Women depend heavily on the availability of nonwood forest products, too. They collect plant fibers, medicinal plants and herbs, seeds used in condiments, oils, resins, and a host of other materials used to produce goods or income for their families. The fruits, vegetables, and nuts widely gathered as supplements to food crops are important sources of protein, fats, vitamins, and minerals not found in some staple crops. In times of drought, flood, or famine, these gathered foods have often made the difference between life and death.[26]

In most subsistence economies, forest products are key sources of jobs and income. Throughout the Third World, women make up a large share of the labor force in forest industries, from nurseries to plantations and from logging to wood processing. In hard times, landless and underemployed female agricultural laborers often fall back on the collection of nontimber forest products to generate cash.[27]

These nonwood forest products make substantial contributions to local and national economies. Although unrecognized or unrecorded by national statistics, these activities often contribute more to national income than wood-based industries do. A report by World Bank researchers Augusta Molnar and Gotz Schreiber estimates that in India, for example, nontimber products account for two fifths of domestic forest revenues and three fourths of net export earnings from forestry products.[28]

In the true spirit of sustainability, female subsistence producers appear to be as careful in conserving forests as they are reliant on using them. With traditional methods of extraction, women in Africa and Asia obtain their fuel from branches and dead wood (often supplemented with crop residues, dried weeds, or leaves) rather than live trees. Seventy-five percent of domestic fuel collected by women in northern India is in this form. And women are the chief repositories of knowledge about the use and management of trees and other forest products.[29]

In surveys, women have consistently cited the ecosystem services provided by forests, such as their critical role in replenishing freshwater supplies, as reasons for their preservation. In fact, research on communal resource management systems—the "commons" on which women depend so heavily in subsistence economies—shows them to be more effective at protecting and regenerating the environment than management approaches taken by either the state or private landowners.[30]

The reasons are obvious: commons are as indispensable to land-poor women in subsistence economies as these women are to the maintenance of the commons. A study of 12 semiarid districts of India in the early eighties, for instance, showed that 66–84 percent of total domestic fuel needs of both the land-poor (those with less than 2 hectares of dryland equivalent) and the landless were derived from these commons areas, as opposed to 8–32 percent of the nonpoor. The poorest households also relied heavily on these lands for grazing. (See Table 4–1.) Even in the northwest of the country, where Green Revolution technologies have been widely applied, commons land accounted for the bulk of foods used to supplement the cereals bought by the poor or earned in kind.[31]

Commons lands constitute the one resource, apart from their children, that women traditionally have had access to relatively unfettered by the control of men. Unfortunately, women's access to

Table 4–1. Share of Total Income Reaped from Village Commons by Poor and Nonpoor Families in Seven States of India, 1985

	Share of Total Income	
Commodity	Poor Families	Nonpoor Families
	(percent)	
Firewood	91–100	—
Domestic Fuel Supplies	66–84	8–32
Grazing Needs	70–90	11–42
Gathered Food	10	—

SOURCE: N.S. Jodha, "Depletion of Common Property Resources in India: Micro-Level Evidence," in Geoffrey McNicoll and Mead Cain, eds., *Rural Development and Population: Institutions and Policy* (New York: Oxford University Press and the Population Council, 1990).

these lands and the goods they yield is fast diminishing. The results are already evident in declining food security among subsistence households.

CASH CROPS VERSUS FOOD SECURITY

Three interrelated trends, all set in motion or perpetuated by the agricultural strategies of low-income countries since the fifties, have particularly damaged the ability of rural women to produce or procure enough food. All are a product of the increasing emphasis on cash crops.

First, large amounts of land once jointly owned and controlled by villagers—and accessible to women—have shifted into the hands of government agencies and private landowners. Second, the distribution of resources on which cash crop agriculture depends heavily—including land, fertilizers, pesticides, irrigation, and hybrid seeds—has reflected persistent gender bias. Third, the mechanization of agriculture has reduced or replaced the labor traditionally done by men but increased that done by women without raising their income.

The first of these trends has been hastened by development strategies that, as noted earlier, make false assumptions about who benefits from gross economic gains. Thus, while shifting ownership to government agencies and private landowners may improve agricultural output in the aggregate, it fails to address critical differences between men's and women's farming responsibilities.

Despite their major role in food production, women farmers rarely have land of their own. In the patrilineal cultures found in Bangladesh, India, Pakistan, much of sub-Saharan Africa, and Latin America, women gain access to land only through their husbands or sons. In the past, at least, customary laws have afforded women some security of land tenure.[32]

In the "common property" systems of precolonial Africa and Asia, access to the resources needed by men and women to fulfill their respective family obligations were determined by sex. Consequently, while women could rarely "own" land, as members of a community they usually had equal rights to use it in accordance with their family's needs. Under traditional systems operating in parts of southern Ghana, for instance, women had rights to land as members of a lineage; they applied to the male head of their lineage for the acreage needed for food production, which was allocated according to a family's size and needs.[33]

These customary laws and practices have been deteriorating since the beginning of the colonial period. The process accelerated with the independence of African countries as the result of several influences. Declining mortality rates led to rapid population growth and increased demand for cropland. Increasing migration, and governments' policies encouraging the acquisition of land by the state and individual producers, put previously accessible land beyond the reach of impoverished women.[34]

Common property resources traditionally controlled by a community have either been privatized or turned into open access systems over which virtually no one has control. In most regions, privatization of land was an explicit policy: investments by governments, donor agencies, and multinational corporations directly encouraged the shift of land away from subsistence to cash crops.

In a 1992 study, *The Population, Agriculture and Environment Nexus in Sub-Saharan Africa*, World Bank researchers Kevin Cleaver and Gotz Schreiber state that

African governments allowed customary law to guide use of some of the land, "while arbitrarily allocating other land to private investors, political elites, and public projects." In Latin America, there is little commons land left; most of it long ago was privatized and shifted into cash crops. The highly skewed landownership patterns now found in countries like Brazil, where 2 percent of the farmers own 57 percent of the arable land and more than half of all agricultural families own none, are but the most obvious legacies of such shifts.[35]

As a result of privatization favoring male landholders, the amount and quality of land available to women food producers in the Third World is declining. Legal and cultural obstacles prevent women from obtaining title to land and, therefore, from participating in cash crop schemes. Land titles invariably are given to men because governments and international agencies routinely identify them as heads of their households, regardless of whether or not they actually support their families. Women's rights to land are now subject to the wishes of their husbands or the whims of male-dominated courts and community councils.

In Zambia, for example, women continue to be discriminated against in the allocation of land despite the 1975 Land Act guaranteeing women equal access. Researcher Mabel Milimo of the University of Zambia points out that women's access remains limited by the control men have over distributing land. The act vests all land in the president, who in turn delegates his powers of allocation to district councils and other local bodies. Although women farmers outnumber male ones, the councils are made up of men and often require a husband's consent for a married woman to receive land. Milimo points out that "in most cases, the husbands are reluctant . . .

because they prefer the wife to work on their . . . cash crops."[36]

Dianne Rocheleau, a geographer at Clark University in Massachusetts, notes that the erosion of women's customary rights under modern legal reforms is widespread throughout Africa, Asia, and Latin America. In southeast Asia and the Indian subcontinent, for instance, at least 70 percent of the female labor force is engaged in food production—yet fewer than 10 percent of women farmers in India, Nepal, and Thailand now own land. Rocheleau contends that both modern and traditional laws tend to be interpreted in favor of male ownership and control, and that even where reforms have provided for equality in most spheres, "strong gender inequality often exists with respect to [allocating] agricultural land." Either way, a woman's access to land is tied to her marital status and the number of sons she bears.[37]

The amount and quality of land available to women food producers in the Third World is declining.

The second trend—discrimination in the allocation of agricultural resources—follows directly from the first. Agricultural development schemes promoted by governments and development agencies encourage expansion of cash crop operations by offering market incentives, improved agricultural technologies, credit, seeds, and the like—with access to these resources dependent mainly on the use of land as collateral. Without ownership and control over land, women are further disadvantaged because they cannot compete in cash crop schemes, and have fewer resources with which to produce food crops.[38]

The focus of agricultural research and

development, too, has favored cash crops over food ones, to the detriment of women and of family nutrition. This has not only diminished the relative productivity of food crops, it has increased the perception that cash crops are more "valuable." The spread of high-yielding seeds has nearly doubled maize yields in Africa since 1950, for example. But cultivating hybrid maize, a cash crop, is expensive. New seeds must be bought each year, and the crop demands repeated applications of fertilizer. Subsistence farmers who lack credit can afford neither the seeds nor the fertilizer. On the other hand, the development of high-yielding varieties of millet and sorghum has lagged far behind, even though these traditional food crops are considerably more drought-resistant and nutritionally balanced than maize.[39]

Women are the sole breadwinners in one fourth to one third of the world's households.

Vegetables, beans, cassava, and fruit crops, all important to family nutrition in subsistence economies, also have been neglected. These are usually not considered "important" because they are not perceived as being related to food trade. International Labour Organization consultant Ingrid Palmer argues that such policies are shortsighted because growing more of these crops would not only diminish the need for imports, it would provide a chief source of cash to women who sell them in local markets. And, because many of these "minor" crops keep well, they are available to families for a longer part of the year than the grain crops they have no storage space for.[40]

Agricultural extension has also suffered from gender bias. Despite the fact that most of Africa's farmers are female,

for example, the vast majority of extension officers are male and trained to deal primarily with men. A 1981 survey found only 3 percent of all agricultural extension agents in sub-Saharan Africa were female. Not surprisingly, they were paid substantially less than their male colleagues. This pattern, too, is found on every continent; Lynn Bennett of the World Bank notes that agricultural extension services in India largely bypass the 40 percent of the country's farm workers who are female. And studies of extension services in Central and South America find similar biases.[41]

The third trend undermining women's ability to provide food security, beyond the diminishing availability of land and other resources, has been the technological "modernization" of developing countries. Mechanization, like privatization, has tended to benefit men who own land, while only making things harder for women who do not. Scattered introduction of tractors and improved animal-powered equipment in Africa, for instance, has lightened the workload of male landowners, enabling them to expand cultivation of their cash crops. But at the same time it has increased the amount of labor done by their wives, who must spend more time doing the "women's work" on the expanded fields.[42]

Aggravating these three pressures on food security is the fact that the labor available to subsistence households in many countries has become increasingly scarce. Greater migration of males to cities, low wages, abandonment, divorce, widowhood, and—in some cultures—the practice of having more than one wife all have conspired to reduce the amount of labor and of income contributed to families by men. This, in turn, puts increasing pressure on women to make up the labor shortages by carrying out all the traditionally male activities as well as their own. Under these intensifying time and labor pressures, state Cleaver and Schreiber of the World Bank, "[African] women farmers have little choice but to continue to practice [agricultural methods] such as sharply shortened fallow periods, that are neither environmentally sustainable or viable" over the long term.[43]

The growing number of female-headed households—now swelling the ranks of the poor in virtually every country of the Third World—is one indication of how widespread these conditions are. Estimates indicate that women are the sole breadwinners in one fourth to one third of the world's households. And at least one fourth of all other households rely on female earnings for more than 50 percent of total income.[44]

THE LOSS OF FOREST RESOURCES

Just as they are losing their access to farmland, women in subsistence economies are losing their access to forest resources in every region, and for most of the same reasons: privatization, lack of credit and extension services, and male veto power over women's decisions.

In many countries, large areas of communal forestland have been privatized and set aside for agriculture, resulting in widespread deforestation and a decline in women's access to woodland resources. On the island of Zanzibar, for example, commercial clove tree plantations began to replace natural forests in the late nineteenth century. One hundred years later, the spread of commercial agriculture is creating a fuel crisis within subsistence households, which now spend up to 40 percent of their income on fuel. Similarly, in western Kenya communal resources have declined in areas where increases in private landownership have "commercialized" trees.[45]

In India, much of the commons land now disappearing into government and private hands was previously used by village women to secure fuel according to community rules. "Contrary to the popular belief that it is the gathering of wood for fuel that is [primarily] responsible for deforestation and fuelwood shortages," states Bina Agarwal, "existing evidence [in India] points to past and ongoing state policies and schemes as significant causes." In a seven-state survey, village commons areas were shown to have declined 26–58 percent as a result of land grabs by commercial interests and large landowners. Agarwal contends that, if sustained, the widespread appropriation of sacred groves and other communal land by government and private interests for cash crops, dams, and commercial timber will have claimed what remains of India's forests in 45 years.[46]

Within the subsistence economy, differences in the access of men and women to trees are very similar to, and usually linked with, those of land for food crops. In one region of Kenya where women cannot own land, for example, they are also restricted from planting trees. According to custom, control over land is determined by the ownership or planting of trees on it. Not surprisingly, men in the area have opposed women's attempts to increase supplies of biomass. In northern Cameroon, some men only allow their wives to plant papaya trees, which are short-lived and do not confer land rights.[47]

Increasingly, wood and other biomass products are becoming "cash crops" to which men and women have differential access. Both men and women may be interested in raising cash from the harvesting and sale of trees in their control. But studies show that women usually seek to gather wood and other biomass resources on a sustainable basis, balancing their needs for cash with their need for other products and with the ecological services forests provide. Men, lacking the responsibilities for collection of fuel, fodder, and the like, may have different priorities. Yet it is plantation or farm forestry that receives by far the greatest amount of support from governments and donor agencies.[48]

The spread of cash crops has also diminished women's access to biomass resources. In the past, it was common practice for Indian landowners who regularly employed women agricultural laborers to allow them to collect from the land, as part of their "wages," crop residues, grasses, and other biomass for home use. But these sources, too, have dwindled. New crops and harvesting practices leave fewer residues, and so have reduced the total amount of biomass available from lands under cash crops. And landlords themselves are now interested in the increasing value of biomass for sale in the market. The spread of dairy cooperatives in India, for instance, has created a market for grasses on which to feed milk cows, removing a main source of fodder for village women. "Now I have to steal the grass for my buffalo," states a female agricultural worker from Sikandernagar, "and when the landlord catches me he beats me."[49]

Shifting access to this land away from the poor makes it increasingly difficult for women to procure fuel and other products, leading to their further impoverishment. Time allocation studies show that as a result of scarcity, women are spending more hours in such tasks as the collection of fuel, fodder, and water. In severely deforested areas of India, the typical rural woman and her children now spend four to five hours a day to gather enough fuel for the evening meal. For women in Sudan, the average time

required to collect a week's worth of fuelwood has quadrupled since the seventies.[50]

Because of their prominent role as users and managers, including women in the management of forest ecosystems is vital to achieving increases in rural productivity. Still, states Paula Williams, a Forest and Society Fellow with the Institute for Current World Affairs, "most forest policies and most foresters continue to overlook or ignore this." The exclusion of women's needs and expertise has grave implications for the future of forest resources.[51]

In forest management, as in agricultural development, the international community has been of no help in prodding governments to recognize and support the needs of women in subsistence economies. Here, too, women remain curiously invisible to the development community. World Bank consultant Ravinder Kaur concludes that "the importance of other forest products to women and the very active role that women play in forest resource management have remained largely unrecognized and unspecified."[52]

Tree planting campaigns and international investments to stem deforestation have all but ignored women: out of 22 social forestry projects appraised by the World Bank from 1984 through 1987, only one mentioned women as a project beneficiary. And only 4 of 33 integrated rural development programs that involved forestry funded by the Bank over the same period included women in some way.[53]

Williams points out that no African women participated in the World Forestry Congresses of 1978 and 1985. Most national-level forestry plans do not consider women and children as users of these resources, nor how they fare when biomass becomes scarce. Major forestry policies, such as the Tropical Forestry Action Plan prepared by the World Resources Institute in conjunction with multilateral institutions and individual governments, scarcely consider the role of women in forest use and conservation.[54]

Undervaluing women's social and economic contributions hampers efforts to achieve other broad social and environmental goals, such as preserving biodiversity and protecting the role played by forests in water cycles. Women's experience with forest products represents a vast data base on the species scientists regularly lament being unable to catalogue. Tribal women in India, for example, have been found to know medicinal uses for some 300 forest species. "Many people believe," Williams asserts, "that first we should save the world's tropical forests: then we can worry about women and children. Unless we work with women and children, however, it will be impossible to 'save' the humid and dry-land tropical forests. You cannot save the trees when you ignore over half the users and managers of forest resources."[55]

FEMALE POVERTY AND THE POPULATION TRAP

From food production to control over income, indications are that the position of women within subsistence economies is growing increasingly insecure. As women's access to resources continues to dwindle in subsistence economies, their responsibilities—and the demands on their time and physical energy—increase. They are less likely to see the utility of having fewer children, even though population densities in the little land left for subsistence families are rapidly increasing.

These trends extend from rural areas into urban ones. Environmental degradation and impoverishment have driven millions of people into the slums and shantytowns of Third World cities. In these urban subsistence economies, women maintain their heavy burden of labor and responsibility for the production of subsistence goods. And urban women are also discriminated against in the access to resources they require to support their families. "When urban authorities refuse to provide water supply, sanitation, and refuse collection to low-income urban areas," write Diana Lee-Smith and Catalina Hinchey Trujillo of the Women's Shelter Network, "it is the women who have to make up for the lack of such services . . . who have to work out ways of finding and transporting water and fuel and keeping their homes reasonably clean, [all] with inadequate support from urban laws and institutions which usually completely fail to comprehend their situation."[56]

The growing time constraints imposed on women by the longer hours they must work to make ends meet simultaneously lower women's status and keep birth rates high. When they can no longer increase their own labor burdens, women lean more heavily on the contributions of their children—especially girls. In fact, the increasing tendency in many areas of keeping girls out of school to help with their mothers' work virtually ensures that another generation of females will grow up with poorer prospects than their brothers. In Africa, for example, "more and more girls are dropping out of both primary and secondary school or just missing school altogether due to increasing poverty," states Phoebe Asiyo of the United Nations Fund for Women.[57]

Rapid population growth within subsistence economies, in turn, compounds the environmental degradation—the unsustainable escalation of soil erosion, depletion, and deforestation—first put in motion by the increasing separation of poor farmers from the assets that once sustained them. The health of women and girls, most affected by environmental degradation because of the roles they play, declines further. The cycle accelerates.

This is the population trap: many of the policies and programs carried out in the name of development actually increase women's dependence on children as a source of status and security. Moreover, environmental degradation triggered by misguided government policies is itself causing rapid population growth, in part as a result of women's economically rational response to increasing demands on their time caused by resource scarcity. Unless governments move quickly to change the conditions confronting women in subsistence economies, rapid population growth will continue unabated.

The objective of reducing population growth is critical to reversing the deterioration of both human and environmental health. But the myopic divorcing of demographic goals from other development efforts has serious human rights implications for the hundreds of millions of women who lack access to adequate nutrition, education, legal rights, income-earning opportunities, and the promise of increasing personal autonomy.

TOWARD A NEW FRAMEWORK FOR DEVELOPMENT

In the post-Earth Summit era, sustainable development has become a slogan of governments everywhere. But given the abysmal record of conventional development strategies in the realms of equity, poverty, and the environment, it is imperative to ask, Development *for whom*? With input *from whom*?

Failing to ask these questions is a failure in the fundamental purpose of development itself. If women in subsistence

economies are the major suppliers of food, fuel, and water for their families, and yet their access to productive resources is declining, then more people will suffer from hunger, malnutrition, illness, and loss of productivity. If women have learned ecologically sustainable methods of agriculture and acquired extensive knowledge about genetic diversity—as millions have—yet are denied partnership in development, then this wisdom will be lost.

Development strategies that limit the ability of women to achieve their potential also limit the potential of communities and nations.

Without addressing issues of equity and justice, then, development goals that are ostensibly universal—such as the alleviation of poverty, the protection of ecosystems, and the creation of a balance between human activities and environmental resources—simply cannot be achieved.

In short, development strategies that limit the ability of women to achieve their real human potential are also strategies that limit the potential of communities and nations. Only when such strategies recognize and are geared toward reducing gender bias and its consequences can we begin to solve many of those economic and environmental problems that otherwise promise to spin out of control.

Improving the status of women, and thereby the prospects for humanity, will require a complete reorientation of development efforts away from the current overemphasis on limiting women's reproduction. Instead, the focus needs to be on establishing an environment in which women and men together can prosper. This means creating mainstream development programs that seek to expand women's control over income and household resources, improve their productivity, establish their legal and social rights, and increase the social and economic choices they are able to make.

The first step toward achieving these goals—a step that is consistently overlooked—is to ask women themselves which needs should be accorded top priority. Some answers to the question "What do women want?" were provided in a forum on international health held in June 1991. (See Table 4–2.) Among the key needs identified by participants from Africa, Asia, and Latin America were investments in the development and dissemination of appropriate technology to reduce women's work burden and access for women to credit and training programs.

Table 4–2. Some Answers to the Question "What Do Women Want?"

- Durable arrangements for the transfer of resources; reductions in (if not cancellations of) the debt burden; direct investment to meet capital requirements.

- Favorable trading terms and better prices for primary commodities such as coffee, tea, and cocoa.

- Access to credit and training; programs for awareness and confidence-building.

- Small to medium joint ventures to create jobs; continuing investments in sustainable economic growth.

- Investments in the development and dissemination of appropriate technologies to reduce women's work burdens.

- Access to good food, safe water, and education for both girls and boys.

- Sustainable strategies for the use of natural resources.

- Reallocation of financial resources to critical health care needs, including disease control, maternal and child health and family planning, and development of appropriate health systems.

- Cooperation to establish, expand, and strengthen community-based approaches for promotional and educational activities of family planning and family life education.

- Access to information concerning women's bodies.

- The right to choose the number of children born and to plan families without government interference.

- Access to vaccines, medicines, and equipment.

- Universal access to contraceptives for both men and women.

SOURCE: "What do Women Want?" panel discussion held at Women's Health: The Action Agenda for the Nineties, 18th Annual National Council on International Health Conference, Arlington, Va., June 23–26, 1991.

The second step is to act immediately to increase the productivity of subsistence producers, whether in rural or urban areas. Quick gains can be realized by increasing women's access to land, credit, and the tools and technologies to increase their own and their families' welfare.

Land reform and the enforcement of laws guaranteeing gender equity in the distribution of land resources, for example, need to be assigned high priority in every country. Given the intimate connections among women's lack of access to land, their increasing work burden, and their subsequent reliance on children, Third World land distribution and allocation policies should be at the top of the agenda for groups concerned about the environment, human rights, hunger, and population issues. By mounting a concerted campaign, grassroots groups can focus the attention of media, governments, and international agencies on the issue of land reform. Pushing for simultaneous reform of other policies that discriminate against women—such as those limiting access to credit, improved technologies, and farm inputs—is equally important.

The third step is to examine critically the definitions and assumptions made by conventional development policies in order to collect information that creates a real picture of subsistence economies. As the evidence shows, women are responsible for producing an equal or larger share of the goods on which families depend for survival, yet often are denied credit for their contributions either because it is not in the form of cash income or because it is simply assumed their income is relatively less important than that of men. These assumptions need to be changed.

A redefinition of the concepts of "productivity," "value," and "work" to include activities that are indeed productive—such as those that yield family income in goods rather than in cash or that support people without degrading the environment—would dramatically alter the base of relevant information sought by those truly interested in improving the human prospect. This is a necessary precondition to environmentally sound economic systems. As Lee-Smith and Hinchey Trujillo of the Women's Shelter Network point out, "careful management of the local resource base to provide for continued human sustenance is something women have been doing for a long time . . . [and is] what is required of the whole human community to achieve sustainable development at the planetary level."[58]

Following from changes in how work is defined is the need to generate critical new information by redirecting some of the research on the benefits of development. Already, the collecting of gender-disaggregated data on a small scale has helped policymakers recognize the disparate effects on men and women of conventional gender-blind development practices. But for many areas of the economy in which women play important but officially ignored roles, not enough information is available yet to truly inform public policy. Such gender-based data need to be incorporated into all relevant areas of economics, health, and environment.

Research and development in the sciences and in appropriate technologies needs to be far more gender-sensitive, not only to benefit women but to benefit from them, especially in areas of crop production and biodiversity. Focusing research on the needs of women in subsistence economies would dramatically boost food crop and forest production within a decade.

But this cannot be achieved unless women enjoy the same degree of independence and freedom of choice as men. Governments and international agencies also need to be pushed to recognize the effects of their policies on how men and women interact, and on how such resources as money, food, and opportunities for learning are allocated within the household. Instead of increasing the division between men and women, the goal of development should be to seek more cooperation between the sexes in achieving mutual goals of ending hunger and poverty and securing the environment.

And family welfare cannot be improved without increasing women's access to and control over resources that are essential to improving nutrition, lowering infant mortality, reducing fertility, and changing a wide range of other variables including violence against women. These ends can most easily be achieved in the short run by directing resources into the formal education of young girls and the formal and informal education and training of older women. At the same time, policies that increase women's access to information and training as well as credit will improve their employment prospects and enable women entrepeneurs to establish businesses, earn income, and create jobs.

Experience suggests that winning these reforms will not be easy. Gender bias—like that based on race, class, and ethnicity—dies hard. Much of the information regarding women's roles in agriculture and forestry, for example, has been available to governments and development planners for two decades and has yet to provoke real changes in policy. In part, this is due to the lack of support by grassroots women's groups in the wealthy countries for a broad-based, politically charged international movement to combat discriminatory development policies.

Without doubt, many of the cultural and economic obstacles faced by women in countries such as Brazil, India, Thailand, and Zimbabwe are vastly different from those faced by the majority of women in more prosperous countries like the United States and France. But in reality, many of these differences are matters of magnitude rather than substance. A number of trends, including the growth in and disproportionate poverty of female-headed households, are as evident in the urban and rural areas of industrial countries as they are in the Third World. And issues such as equal pay for work of equal value, domestic violence, reproductive health and freedom, and environmental sustainability are universal.

For many areas of the economy in which women play important roles, not enough information is available to truly inform public policy.

Addressing these issues requires closer cooperation between women's movements in the world's North and those in the South. The early signs of a truly international women's movement can already be seen, most recently in the U.N.-sponsored Global Assembly on Women and the Environment and the World Women's Congress, both held in Miami, Florida, in November 1991. And as both the 1994 U.N. Conference on Population and Development and the 1995 Conference on Women draw near, groups concerned about a broad range of gender, environment, and development issues are seeking new ways to harness the power of women everywhere in creating change.

These concerns are not for women only. Indeed, it is in the interest of every person—from the poor farmers of Sikandernagar to the chiefs of industry, from grassroots activists to heads of state—to combat gender bias. Ultimately, the changes needed to make women equal partners in development are the same as those required to sustain life itself. Nothing could be more important to human development than the reform of policies that suppress the productive potential of half the earth's people.

5

Supporting Indigenous Peoples

Alan Thein Durning

In July of 1992, an aged chief of the Lumad people in the Philippines—a man with a price on his head for his opposition to local energy development—sat at the base of the cloud-covered volcano Mount Apo and made a simple plea. "Our Christian brothers are enjoying their life here in the plains," said 86-year-old Chief Tulalang Maway, sweeping his arm toward the provincial town of Kidapawan and the agricultural lands beyond, lands his tribe long ago ceded to immigrants from afar. Turning toward the mountain—a Lumad sacred site that he has vowed to defend "to the last drop of blood"—Maway slowly finished his thought, "We only ask them to leave us our last sanctuary."[1]

Chief Maway's words could have been spoken by almost any tribal Filipino, or, for that matter, any Native American, Australian aborigine, African pygmy, or member of one of the world's thousands

An expanded version of this chapter appeared as Worldwatch Paper 112, *Guardians of the Land: Indigenous Peoples and the Health of the Earth.*

of other distinct indigenous cultures. All have ancient ties to the land, water, and wildlife of their ancestral domains, and all are endangered by onrushing forces of the outside world. They have been decimated by violence and plagues. Their cultures have been eroded by missionaries and exploited by wily entrepreneurs. Their subsistence economies have been dismantled in the pursuit of national development. And their homelands have been invaded by commercial resource extractors and overrun by landless peasants.

Chief Maway's entreaty, in its essence, is the call of indigenous peoples everywhere: the plea that their lands be spared further abuse, that their birthright be returned to them. It is a petition that the world's dominant cultures have long ignored, believing the passing of native peoples and their antiquated ways was an inevitable, if lamentable, cost of progress. That view, never morally defensible, is now demonstrably untenable.

Indigenous peoples are the sole guardians of vast, little-disturbed habitats in remote parts of every continent. These territories, which together encompass an area larger than Australia, provide important ecological services: they regulate hydrological cycles, maintain local and global climatic stability, and harbor a wealth of biological and genetic diversity. Indeed, indigenous homelands may provide safe haven for more endangered plant and animal species than all the world's nature reserves. Native peoples, moreover, often hold the key to these vaults of biological diversity. They possess a body of ecological knowledge—encoded in their languages, customs, and subsistence practices—that rivals the libraries of modern science.[2]

The human rights enshrined in international law have long demanded that states shield indigenous cultures, but instead these cultures have been dismembered. A more self-interested appeal appears to be in order: supporting indigenous survival is an objective necessity, even for those callous to the justice of the cause. As a practical matter, the world's dominant cultures cannot sustain the earth's ecological health—a requisite of human advancement—without the aid of the world's endangered cultures. Biological diversity is inextricably linked to cultural diversity.

Around the globe, indigenous peoples are fighting for their ancestral territories. They are struggling in courts and national parliaments, gaining power through new mass movements and international campaigns, and—as on the slopes of Mount Apo—defending their inheritance with their lives. The question is, Who will stand with them?

STATE OF THE NATIONS

Indigenous peoples (or "native" or "tribal" peoples) are found on every continent and in most countries. (See Table 5–1.) The extreme variations in their ways of life and current circumstances defy ready definition. Indeed, many anthropologists insist that indigenous peoples are defined only by the way they define themselves: they think of themselves as members of a distinct people. Still, many indigenous cultures share a number of characteristics that help describe, if not define, them.[3]

They are typically descendants of the original inhabitants of an area taken over by more powerful outsiders. They are distinct from their country's dominant group in language, culture, or religion. Most have a custodial concept of land and other resources, in part defining themselves in relation to the habitat from which they draw their livelihood. They commonly live in or maintain strong ties to a subsistence economy; many are, or are descendants of, hunter-gatherers, fishers, nomadic or seasonal herders, shifting forest farmers, or subsistence peasant cultivators. And their social relations are often tribal, involving collective management of natural resources, thick networks of bonds between individuals, and group decision making, often by consensus among elders.[4]

Measured by spoken languages, the single best indicator of a distinct culture, all the world's people belong to 6,000 cultures; 4,000–5,000 of these are indigenous ones. Of the 5.5 billion humans on the planet, some 190 million to 625 million are indigenous people. (These ranges are wide because of varying definitions of "indigenous." The higher figures include ethnic nations that lack political autonomy, such as Tibetans, Kurds, and Zulus, while the lower figures count only smaller, subnational societies.) In some countries, especially those settled by Europeans in the past five centuries, indigenous populations are fairly easy to count. (See Table 5–2.) By con-

Table 5–1. Indigenous Peoples of the World, 1992

Region	Indigenous Peoples
Africa and Middle East	Great cultural diversity throughout continent; "indigenous" share hotly contested. Some 25–30 million nomadic herders or pastoralists in East Africa, Sahel, and Arabian peninsula include Bedouin, Dinka, Masai, Turkana. San (Bushmen) of Namibia and Botswana and pygmies of central African rain forest, both traditionally hunter-gatherers, have occupied present homelands for at least 20,000 years. (25–350 million indigenous people overall, depending on definitions; 2,000 languages)
Americas	Native Americans concentrated near centers of ancient civilizations: Aztec in Mexico, Mayan in Central America, and Incan in Andes of Bolivia, Ecuador, and Peru. In Latin America, most Indians farm small plots; in North America, 2 million Indians live in cities and on reservations. (42 million; 900 languages)
Arctic	Inuit (Eskimo) and other Arctic peoples of North America, Greenland, and Siberia traditionally fishers, whalers, and hunters. Sami (Lapp) of northern Scandinavia are traditionally reindeer herders. (2 million; 50 languages)
East Asia	Chinese indigenous peoples, numbering up to 82 million, mostly subsistence farmers such as Bulang of south China or former pastoralists such as ethnic Mongolians of north and west China. Ainu of Japan and aboriginal Taiwanese now largely industrial laborers. (12–84 million; 150 languages)
Oceania	Aborigines of Australia and Maoris of New Zealand, traditionally farmers, fishers, hunters, and gatherers. Many now raise livestock. Islanders of South Pacific continue to fish and harvest marine resources. (3 million; 500 languages)
South Asia	Gond, Bhil, and other adivasis, or tribal peoples, inhabit forest belt of central India. In Bangladesh, adivasis concentrated in Chittagong hills on Burmese border; several million tribal farmers and pastoralists in Afghanistan, Pakistan, Nepal, Iran, and central Asian republics of former Soviet Union. (74–91 million; 700 languages)
Southeast Asia	Tribal Hmong, Karen, and other forest-farming peoples form Asia ethnic mosaic covering uplands. Indigenous population follows distribution of forest: Laos has more forest and tribal peoples, Myanmar and Vietnam have less forest and fewer people, and Thailand and mainland Malaysia have the least. Tribal peoples are concentrated at the extreme ends of the Philippine and Indonesian archipelagos. Island of New Guinea—split politically between Indonesia and Papua New Guinea—populated by indigenous tribes. (32–55 million; 1,950 languages)

SOURCE: Worldwatch Institute, based on sources in endnote 3. Languages include some of nonindigenous peoples.

Table 5–2. Estimated Populations of Indigenous Peoples, Selected Countries, 1992

Country	Population[1]	Share of National Population
	(million)	(percent)
Papua New Guinea	3.0	77
Bolivia	5.6	70
Guatemala	4.6	47
Peru	9.0	40
Ecuador	3.8	38
Myanmar	14.0	33
Laos	1.3	30
Mexico	10.9	12
New Zealand	0.4	12
Chile	1.2	9
Philippines	6.0	9
India	63.0	7
Malaysia	0.8	4
Canada	0.9	4
Australia	0.4	2
Brazil	1.5	1
Bangladesh	1.2	1
Thailand	0.5	1
United States	2.0	1
Former Soviet Union	1.4	< 1

[1]Generally excludes those of mixed ancestry.
SOURCE: Worldwatch Institute, based on sources documented in endnote 5.

trast, lines between indigenous peoples and ethnic minorities are difficult to draw in Asia and Africa, where cultural diversity remains greatest.[5]

Regardless of where lines are drawn, however, human cultures are disappearing at unprecedented rates. Worldwide, the loss of cultural diversity is keeping pace with the global loss of biological diversity. Anthropologist Jason Clay of Cultural Survival in Cambridge, Massachusetts, writes, "there have been more

. . . extinctions of tribal peoples in this century than in any other in history." Brazil alone lost 87 tribes in the first half of the century. One third of North American languages and two thirds of Australian languages have disappeared since 1800—the overwhelming share of them since 1900.[6]

Cultures are dying out even faster than the peoples who belong to them. University of Alaska linguist Michael Krauss projects that half the world's languages—the storehouses of peoples' intellectual heritages—will disappear within a century. These languages, and arguably the cultures they embody, are no longer passed on to sufficient numbers of children to ensure their survival. Krauss likens such cultures to animal species doomed to extinction because their populations are below the threshold needed for adequate reproduction. Only 5 percent of all languages, moreover, enjoy the relative safety of having at least a half-million speakers.[7]

To trace the history of indigenous peoples' subjugation is simply to recast the story of the rise of the world's dominant cultures: the spread of Han Chinese into Central and Southeast Asia, the ascent of Aryan empires on the Indian subcontinent, the southward advance of Bantu cultures across Africa, and the creation of a world economy first through European colonialism and then through industrial development. Surviving indigenous cultures are often but tattered remnants of their predecessors' societies.[8]

When Christopher Columbus reached the New World in 1492, there were perhaps 54 million people in the Americas, almost as many as in Europe at the time; their numbers plummeted, however, as plagues radiated from the landfalls of the conquistadors. Five centuries later, the indigenous peoples of the Americas, numbering some 42 million, have yet to match their earlier population. Similar contractions followed the arrival of Europeans in Australia, New Zealand, and Siberia.[9]

Worldwide, virtually no indigenous peoples remain entirely isolated from national societies. By indoctrination or brute force, nations have assimilated native groups into the cultural mainstream. As a consequence, few follow the ways of their ancestors unchanged. Just one tenth of the Penan hunter-gatherers continue to hunt in the rain forests of Malaysian Borneo. A similar share of the Sami (Lapp) reindeer-herders of northern Scandinavia accompany their herds on the Arctic ranges. Half of North American Indians and many New Zealand Maori dwell in cities.[10]

Tragically, indigenous peoples whose cultures are besieged frequently end up on the bottom of the national economy. They are often the first sent to war for the state, as in Namibia and the Philippines, and the last to go to work: unemployment in Canadian Indian communities averages 50 percent. They are overrepresented among migrant laborers in India, beggars in Mexico, and uranium miners in the United States. They are often drawn into the shadow economy: they grow drug crops in northern Thailand, run gambling casinos in the United States, and sell their daughters into prostitution in Taiwan. Everywhere, racism against them is rampant. India's adivasis, or tribal people, endure hardships comparable to the "untouchables," the most downtrodden caste.[11]

Native peoples' inferior social status is sometimes codified in national law and perpetuated by institutionalized abuse. Many members of the hill tribes in Thailand are denied citizenship, and until 1988 the Brazilian constitution legally classified Indians as minors and wards of the state. In the extreme, nation-states are simply genocidal: Burmese soldiers systemically raped, murdered, and enslaved thousands of Arakanese villagers

in early 1992. Guatemala has exterminated perhaps 100,000 Mayans in its three-decade counterinsurgency. Similar numbers of indigenous people have died in East Timor and Irian Jaya since 1970 at the hands of Indonesian forces intent on solidifying their power.[12]

In much of the world, the oppression that indigenous peoples suffer has indelibly marked their own psyches, manifesting itself in depression and social disintegration. Says Tamara Gliminova of the Khant people of Siberia, "When they spit into your soul for this long, there is little left."[13]

HOMELANDS

Indigenous peoples not yet engulfed in modern societies live mostly in what Mexican anthropologist Gonzalo Aguirre Beltran called "regions of refuge," places so rugged, desolate, or remote that they have been little disturbed by the industrial economy. They remain in these areas for tragic reasons. Peoples in more fertile lands were eradicated outright to make way for settlers and plantations, or they retreated—sometimes at gun point—into these natural havens. Whereas indigenous peoples exercised de facto control over most of the earth's ecosystems as recently as two centuries ago, the territory they now occupy is reduced to an estimated 12–19 percent of the earth's land area—depending, again, on where the line between indigenous peoples and ethnic nations is drawn. And governments recognize their ownership of but a fraction of that area.[14]

Gaining legal protection for the remainder of their subsistence base is most indigenous peoples' highest political priority. If they lose this struggle, their cultures stand little chance of surviving.

As the World Council of Indigenous Peoples, a global federation based in Canada, wrote in 1985, "Next to shooting Indigenous Peoples, the surest way to kill us is to separate us from our part of the Earth." Most native peoples are bound to their land through relationships both practical and spiritual, routine and historical. Tribal Filipino Edtami Mansayagan, attempting to communicate the pain he feels at the destruction of the rivers, valleys, meadows, and hillsides of his people's mountain domain, exclaims, "these are the living pages of our unwritten history." The question of who shall control resources in the regions of refuge is the crux of indigenous survival.[15]

Indigenous homelands are important not only to endangered cultures; they are also of exceptional ecological value. Intact indigenous communities and little-disturbed ecosystems overlap with singular regularity, from the coastal swamps of South America to the shifting sands of the Sahara, from the ice floes of the circumpolar north to the coral reefs of the South Pacific. When, for example, a National Geographic Society team in Washington, D.C., compiled a map of Indian lands and remaining forest cover in Central America in 1992, they confirmed the personal observation of Geodisio Castillo, a Kuna Indian from Panama: "Where there are forests there are indigenous people, and where there are indigenous people there are forests."[16]

Because populations of both indigenous peoples and unique plant and animal species are numerically concentrated in remnant habitats in the tropics—precisely the regions of refuge that Beltran was referring to—the biosphere's most diverse habitats are usually homes to endangered cultures. The persistence of biological diversity in these regions is no accident. In the Philippines and Thailand, both representa-

tive cases, little more than a third of the land officially zoned as forest remains forest-covered; the tracts that do still stand are largely those protected by tribal people.[17]

The relationship between cultural diversity and biological diversity stands out even in global statistics. Just nine countries together account for 60 percent of human languages. Of these nine centers of cultural diversity, six are also on the roster of biological "megadiversity" countries—nations with exceptional numbers of unique plant and animal species. (See Table 5–3.) By the same token, two thirds of all megadiversity countries also rank at the top of the cultural diversity league, with more than 100 languages spoken in each.

Most native peoples are bound to their land through relationships both practical and spiritual, routine and historical.

Everywhere, the world economy now intrudes on what is left of native lands, as it has for centuries. Writes World Bank anthropologist Shelton Davis: "The creation of a . . . global economy . . . has meant the pillage of native peoples' lands, labor and resources and their enforced acculturation and spiritual conquest. Each cycle of global economic expansion—the search for gold and spices in the sixteenth century, the fur trade and sugar estate economics of the seventeenth and eighteenth centuries, the rise of the great coffee, copra and . . . tropical fruit plantations in the late nineteenth and early twentieth centuries, the modern search for petroleum, strategic minerals, and tropical hardwoods—was based upon the exploitation of natural resources or primary commodities and led to the displacement of indigenous

Table 5–3. Cultural Diversity, Circa 1990

Country[1]	Languages Spoken
Papua New Guinea	850
Indonesia	670
Nigeria	410
India	380
Cameroon	270
Australia	250
Mexico	240
Zaire	210
Brazil	210

[1]Countries in italics are biological "megadiversity" nations, with exceptionally high numbers of unique species.
SOURCES: Michael Krauss, "The World's Languages in Crisis," *Language*, March 1992; megadiversity countries from Jeffrey A. McNeely et al., *Conserving the World's Biological Diversity* (Gland, Switzerland, and Washington, D.C.: International Union for Conservation of Nature and Natural Resources et al., 1989).

peoples and the undermining of traditional cultures."[18]

The juggernaut of the money economy has not slowed in the late twentieth century; if anything, it has accelerated. Soaring consumer demand among the world's fortunate and burgeoning populations among the unfortunate fuel the economy's drive into native peoples' territories. Loggers, miners, commercial fishers, small farmers, plantation growers, dam builders, oil drillers—all come to seek their fortunes. Governments that equate progress with export earnings aid them, and military establishments bent on controlling far-flung territories back them.[19]

Logging, in particular, is a menace because so many indigenous peoples dwell in woodlands. Japanese builders, for example, are devouring the ancient hardwood forests of tropical Borneo, home of the Penan and other Dayak peoples, for disposable concrete molds. Most mahogany exported from Latin America is now logged illegally on Indian reserves, and most nonplantation teak cut in Asia currently comes from tribal lands in the war-torn hills of Myanmar.[20]

The consequences of mining on native lands are also ruinous. In the late eighties, for instance, tens of thousands of gold prospectors infiltrated the remote northern Brazilian haven of the Yanomami, the last large, isolated group of indigenous peoples in the Americas. The miners turned streams into sewers, contaminated the environment with the 1,000 tons of toxic mercury they used to purify gold, and precipitated an epidemic of malaria that killed more than a thousand children and elders. Just in time, the Brazilian government recognized and began defending the Yanomami homeland in early 1992, a rare and hopeful precedent in the annals of indigenous history. Still, in Brazil overall, mining concessions overlap 34 percent of Indian lands.[21]

Similarly destructive results follow oil extraction. The swampland range of the reindeer-herding Khant and Mansi peoples of Siberia contains the richest oil deposits in Russia, but the reckless exploitation of those reserves is killing both the wetlands—the largest in the world—and the herders' way of life. Oil derricks there leak as much as one barrel of oil for each barrel they produce, spreading slicks over thousands of square kilometers of swamp grasses. Reindeer, wildlife, fish, and indigenous peoples suffer the consequences. The energy industry and other development pressures have rendered three fourths of the Khant-Mansi lands—and the neighboring Nentsy lands—useless for hunting, fishing, and herding.[22]

Other energy projects, especially large dams, also take their toll on native habitats. In the north of Canada, the provincial electric utility Hydro Quebec completed a massive project called James Bay I in 1985, inundating vast areas of Cree Indian hunting grounds and unexpectedly contaminating fisheries with naturally occurring heavy metals that had previously been locked away in the soil. The Cree and neighboring Inuit tribes have organized against the project's next gigantic phase, James Bay II. The $60-billion project would tame 11 wild rivers, altering a France-sized area to generate 27,000 megawatts of exportable power. As Matthew Coon-Come, Grand Chief of the Cree, says, "The only people who have the right to build dams on our territory are the beavers."[23]

On the seas, the familiar pattern is repeated. Mechanized trawlers and factory fishing fleets have pushed into the coastal ranges of the world's 12 million small-boat fishers, many of whom are indigenous peoples. The modern boats overtax near-shore fisheries and undermine local fishing traditions, which still provide one third of all fish caught worldwide each year. Fleets from Taiwan, for example, regularly work the reefs of the Torres Strait between Australia and Papua New Guinea in violation of both countries' laws and the fishing rights of the aboriginal islanders.[24]

Commercial producers have also taken over indigenous lands for large-scale agriculture. The Barabaig herders of Tanzania have lost more than 400 square kilometers of dry-season range to a mechanized wheat farm. Private ranchers in Botswana have enclosed grazing lands for their own use, and Australian ranchers have usurped aboriginal lands. In peninsular Malaysia, palm and rubber plantations have left the Orang Asli (Original People) with tiny fractions of their ancient tropical forests.[25]

Less dramatic but more pervasive is the ubiquitous invasion of small farmers onto indigenous lands. Sometimes sponsored by the state but ultimately driven by population growth and maldistribution of farmland, poor settlers encroach on native lands everywhere. In In-donesia during the eighties, for example, the government shifted 2 million people from densely populated islands such as Java to 800,000 hectares of newly cleared plots in sparsely populated indigenous provinces such as Irian Jaya, Kalimantan, and Sumatra. Half the area settled was virgin forest—much of it indigenous territory.[26]

Large dams take their toll on native habitats.

The appropriation of indigenous home ranges has been accomplished in part by appeal to specious legal doctrines, such as the now-discredited principle that *terra nullius* (empty or ungoverned territory) is free for the taking. Declaring most of the world beyond Europe "empty," colonial governments—and the independent states that followed them—staked claims to all lands that were not physically occupied or under permanent cultivation. With the stroke of a pen, states reserved for themselves forests, wetlands, drylands, mountain slopes, bodies of water, wildlife, fisheries, and the minerals in the earth. Ever since, states have dispensed these resources to private firms and others as suited their political ends.[27]

For native peoples, the result was summary dispossession. "In law," says attorney Gus Gatmaytan of the Manila-based Legal Rights and Natural Resources Center, "the indigenous peoples of the Philippines are squatters in their own lands," because the Philippine state claims ownership of 62 percent of the country's territory. The story is the same around the world. Indonesia asserts its dominion over 74 percent of the nation's land, along with all waters and offshore fishing rights. The Thai Royal Forestry Department claims 40 percent of Thailand. Cameroon and Tanzania claim all forestland, as do most African states. Even Australia, which has returned large areas to aboriginal peoples since 1970, has kept all mineral rights in the hands of the state.[28]

Few states recognize indigenous peoples' rights over homelands, and where they do, those rights are often partial, qualified, or of ambiguous legal force. Countries may recognize customary rights in theory, but enforce common or statutory law against those rights whenever there is a conflict; or they may sanction indigenous rights but refuse to enforce them. Through this cloud of legal contradictions a few countries stand out as exceptional. Papua New Guinea and Ecuador acknowledge indigenous title to large shares of national territory, and Canada and Australia recognize rights over extensive areas. (See Table 5–4.) Still, across all the earth's climatic and ecological zones—from the Arctic tundra to the temperate and tropical forests to the savannahs and deserts—native peoples control slim shares of their ancestral domains.[29]

Arctic peoples have won rights to more of their resource base than other indigenous peoples have. Native communities in Alaska secured rights to 11 percent of the state in 1971. Negotiations between Canada and the Inuit people resulted in late 1991 in an agreement to create Nunavut, a self-governing region covering one fifth of national territory. Greenland, a self-governing territory of Denmark, is effectively Inuit land because of its overwhelmingly indigenous population, and the Sami have exclusive rights to graze reindeer in about one third of Sweden. In Russia, indigenous peoples of the Arctic lack effective resource rights. There, ethnic autonomous regions created by the Soviet state (encompassing much of Siberia on paper) were powerless against state-

Table 5–4. Areas Legally Controlled by Indigenous Peoples, Selected Countries, 1992

Region	Area Legally Controlled[1]	Share of National Territory
	(thousand square kilometers)	(percent)
Papua New Guinea	449	97
Fiji	15	83
Ecuador	190	41
Nicaragua	59	40
Sweden	137	31
Venezuela	234	26
Colombia	260	23
Canada	2,222	22
Australia	895	12
Panama	15	20
Mexico	160	8
Brazil	573	7
New Zealand	16	6
United States	365	4
Costa Rica	2	4

[1]Figures are in most cases liberal. They include area over which, in principle, indigenous peoples have exclusive rights to use land and water bodies. Does not imply recognized indigenous ownership (many states retain ownership of indigenous reserves), or rights to minerals or petroleum (which states often retain). Does not necessarily imply effective state backing and full enforcement of rights. Some indigenous rights to use resources are limited (for example, Sweden recognizes indigenous peoples' rights only to graze reindeer). Figures generally exclude private, individually owned farms of indigenous peoples, as in Andean countries and Mexico.
SOURCE: Worldwatch Institute, based on sources documented in endnote 29.

sponsored resource exploitation. Prospects appear better in the new Russia and some reforms are under way.[30]

In temperate-zone nations, the indigenous land rights situation is mixed. Aboriginal peoples of Japan and Taiwan have no land rights; in contrast, Indian reservations in the United States cover 3 percent of the country (outside of Alaska)—though most of these refuges are infertile drylands. In southern Canada, where Indian reservations are numerous but tiny, crucial legal rulings have denied Indian claims to broader ancient-forest homes since 1990. Among the southern hemisphere temperate nations of Argentina, Chile, and New Zealand, only the last has recognized substantial indigenous land—and fishery—rights.[31]

The tens of millions of pastoralists who occupy the world's grasslands and drylands have little control over the resources they tap along their ancestral nomadic routes. The pastoralists of the Sahel have extremely few legal guarantees that their seasonal rangelands will remain open to them. In east Africa, the situation is similar, although the Masai have managed to hold on to some of their land base in Kenya and Tanzania by subdividing it into group ranches for registration under national land laws. On the plains of central Asia, pastoralists live in theoretically autonomous regions created for them by China and the former Soviet Union, but only in Mongolia, where herders constitute a majority of the population, have such paper guarantees translated into effective local control over grazing lands.[32]

Among the world's tropical forest peoples, South American Indians have substantial land rights (though enforcement has been lacking), Asian peoples have minimal rights even on paper, and African forest dwellers have none. South American nations seem to be competing in the decisiveness of their actions. In 1989, Colombia recognized Indian rights over much of its Amazon territory. In 1990, Bolivia granted territorial protection to tribes in the jungle region of Beni. In 1991, Venezuela and Brazil reserved lands for the Yanomami—whose home range spans the border of those

countries. Together, the two Yanomami reserves are the size of Uruguay. And in 1992, Ecuador set aside much of the Amazon province of Pastaza for Indians. These legal decrees have yet to be translated into effective indigenous control on the ground, but they are nonetheless salutary achievements for South American Indians.[33]

In Asia, tropical forest peoples have fragmentary protection. On the mainland, only the Orang Asli of peninsular Malaysia and the adivasis of India have legal rights over token aboriginal reserves, and those areas are constantly shrinking. The states of Laos, Cambodia, Thailand, and Vietnam—along with China in its neighboring provinces—claim all forestlands, although Laos reportedly plans to map communal forests for tribal villages. Worst in the region are Bangladesh and, especially, Myanmar. Both are waging war on tribal peoples to deny them control of forested highlands.[34]

In the island nations of Southeast Asia, governments pay lip service to indigenous land rights but disregard them in practice. The Philippine Constitution of 1987 promised swift recognition of indigenous peoples' ancestral domain, for example, but in 1992 the Congress shelved a bill to implement that pledge after five minutes of debate. Indonesia purports to respect *adat*, or customary rights, unless the national interest is at stake; however, the government translates national interest as "economic development," effectively voiding indigenous claims. In the Malaysian province of Sarawak, on the island of Borneo, one fifth of state land is officially classified as Native Customary Rights Land. Yet just one tenth of that is actually titled to communities, and even there the government can unilaterally override customary rights for timber concessions.[35]

The most progressive land policies for forest-dwellers in Asia—in force in India and the Philippines—involve joint management agreements between forest services and indigenous communities. Under these "comanagement" or "stewardship" schemes, ownership remains with the state but local people gain recognition of long-term rights to use forest products and make some resource management decisions. Forest agencies are turning to this approach in desperation, realizing that their few thousand employees will never be able to protect or regenerate remote habitats without the help of the millions who live there. In one region of Irian Jaya, Indonesia, for example, just five government foresters monitor 110,000 square kilometers of lands. Lacking even motorized vehicles, they have never visited most of the forests they are charged with watching over. Across the Pacific, the government of Bolivia so despaired of patrolling public lands that in 1992 it began to deputize Indians as forest guards.[36]

The most progressive land policies for forest-dwellers in Asia involve joint management agreements between forest services and indigenous communities.

Sadly, even such limited recognition of indigenous peoples' rights is scarce in the tropical forests of Africa. The pygmies of central Africa, probably the most ancient of all the world's forest peoples, have absolutely no rights to their forests in Cameroon and neighboring states. Indigenous homelands, like indigenous peoples, are a taboo subject in much of Africa, where leaders anxious to avoid fratricidal civil wars in their multiethnic nations have made discussion of customary land claims taboo.[37]

The only bright spots for African forest dwellers are a handful of experimental programs in the dry forests of southern and eastern Africa. There, embattled conservation agencies overwhelmed by wildlife poachers have turned to local tribes for help in the struggle against game extinctions. Recognizing that indigenous peoples managed elephant and other game long before African states existed, these pilot programs have returned ownership of wildlife to villagers, allowing them to sell quotas of high-priced wildlife products so long as they guard breeding stocks. The results, as in the larger forest stewardship programs in Asia, have been heartening, with ecosystems recuperating and game populations rebounding.[38]

Spreading the joint management approach quickly—and moving beyond it to recognize indigenous land rights—will depend on pressing national governments from all directions. Indigenous movements are doing their part through their grassroots movements, as described later in this chapter. The World Bank and the regional development banks, all of which are committed on paper to supporting endangered peoples and fostering sustainable development, have yet to take a consistent stand on indigenous rights. Simply conditioning new loans on the demarcation of indigenous lands—or on the institution of joint management—might put thousands of square kilometers of imperiled habitat back into the hands of its rightful stewards.

Even without such gains, however, indigenous peoples' role as guardians of nature's bounty merits recognition. Indigenous cultures occupy a substantial share of the world's little-disturbed tropical and boreal forests, mountains, grasslands, tundra, and desert, along with large areas of the world's coasts and near-shore waters. Though they inhabit 12–19 percent of the earth's land surface, they have officially sanctioned rights to use roughly 6 percent. (On paper, native peoples in the Americas—the region for which the best data are available—have exclusive rights to use or have won a degree of autonomous self-governance over 10 percent of land, more than half of it in the Arctic, and are pressing for recognition of rights to 7 percent more.) In effect, indigenous peoples tend more of the earth than do park and nature reserve authorities, which—again, on paper—collectively manage 5 percent of the globe's land.[39]

STEWARDS

Sustainable use of local resources is simple self-preservation for people whose way of life is tied to the fertility and natural abundance of the land. Any community that knows its children and grandchildren will live exactly where it does is more apt to take a longer view than a community without attachments to local places.

Moreover, native peoples frequently aim to preserve not just a standard of living but a way of life rooted in the uniqueness of a local place. Colombian anthropologist Martin von Hildebrand notes, "The Indians often tell me that the difference between a colonist [a non-Indian settler] and an Indian is that the colonist wants to leave money for his children and that the Indians want to leave forests for their children."[40]

Indigenous peoples' unmediated dependence on natural abundance has its parallel in their peerless ecological knowledge. Most forest-dwelling tribes display an utter mastery of botany. One typical group, the Shuar people of Ecuador's Amazonian lowlands, uses 800 species of plants for medicine, food, animal fodder, fuel, construction, fishing, and hunting supplies.[41]

Native peoples commonly know as much about ecological processes that affect the availability of natural resources as they do about those resources' diverse uses. South Pacific islanders can predict to the day and hour the beginning of the annual spawning runs of many fish. Whaling peoples of northern Canada have proved to skeptical western marine biologists that bowhead whales migrate under pack ice. Coastal aborigines in Australia distinguish between 80 different tidal conditions.[42]

Specialists trained in western science often fail to recognize indigenous ecological knowledge because of the cultural and religious ways in which indigenous peoples record and transmit that learning. Ways of life that developed over scores of generations could only thrive by encoding ecological sustainability into the body of practice, myth, and taboo that passes from parent to child.

The most trivial of customs can have ecological significance. Kayapó women in the Brazilian Amazon, for instance, traditionally grind red ants to make their face paint for maize festivals. North American anthropologist Darrell Posey asked them why and was told, "the little red ant is the friend of the manioc [cassava]." Ecological studies confirmed their explanation. Manioc produces a nectar that attracts ants; the ants, trying to get at the nectar, chew through wandering bean vines that otherwise smother manioc stems. The beans, in turn, are left to climb neighboring corn stalks, where they do no harm. Indeed, corn benefits from the nitrogen that beans add to soil. Red ants thus boost yields of Kayapó women's three staple crops—manioc, beans, and corn.[43]

Indigenous peoples use innumerable techniques to husband their forests, grasslands, farms, fisheries, and wildlife. (See Table 5–5.) On Brazil's Rio Negro, for example, flood waters regularly in-

Table 5–5. Selected Traditional Stewardship Techniques of Indigenous Peoples

Resource/Ecosystem	Stewardship Technique
Forest	Tribal peoples of India revere and protect certain trees as holy. Gorowa of Tanzania, like the Gabra of Kenya, reserve ancient forest groves as sacred sites dedicated for coming-of-age rituals, men's and women's meeting places, and burials. Lacondon Maya of southern Mexico plant intricate tree gardens, mimicking the diversity of natural rain forests. Karen tribal elders in Thailand carefully regulate community use of forested watersheds.
Grassland	Sukuma, south of Africa's Lake Victoria, rotate grazing on a 30- to 50-year cycle. Zaghawa of Niger move their camels and sheep north to wet-season Saharan pastures in separate, parallel paths, leaving ungrazed strips for the return trek. Fulani orchestrate the orderly return of thousands of head of livestock to the Niger delta in early dry season to avoid overgrazing.
Waters	Since ancient times, temple priests and rice farmers in Bali have used an efficient water distribution system that also serves to control pests. In mountains of Iran, long-lived gravity-powered quanat system provides irrigation water through elaborate excavations and recharging of groundwater.
Fisheries	In South Pacific, ritual restrictions based on area, season, and species prevent overfishing; religious events often open and close fishing seasons. In Marquesas islands, chieftains forbid the consumption of certain fish and enforce the ban, in extreme cases, by expulsion from island. Wet'suwet'en and Gitksan of Canadian Pacific believe salmon spirits give their bodies to humans for food but punish those who waste fish, catch more than they can use, or disrupt aquatic habitats.

SOURCE: Worldwatch Institute, compiled from sources in endnote 44.

undate low-lying plains, giving fish critical but short-lived access to the forest floor; Tukano Indian tradition there prohibits farming on the flood plain. The Tukano consider these riparian habitats the property of the fish. Tribal law also sets aside broad areas of the watercourse as fish sanctuaries, where fishing is strictly forbidden; the prohibition is backed up by the belief that the ancestors of the fish will kill one Tukano child for each fish caught in a reserved stretch of the river. Around the world, the means of indigenous conservation vary endlessly, and traditional conservation techniques, like modern ones, differ

in their effectiveness. But the end—survival over the long term—is universal.[44]

The quality of native stewardship is also evident in comparisons of the ecological condition of indigenous lands with that of neighboring lands managed by others. The island of New Guinea—divided politically between the Indonesian province of Irian Jaya and the independent country of Papua New Guinea—has more distinct cultures than any comparable land area on earth, with more than one sixth of the world's languages on an island the size of Turkey. Most of Papua New Guinea is controlled by leaders of local tribes under customary land rights, while in Irian Jaya, land management decisions are made exclusively by the state. The consequences for local peoples, natural habitats, and social equity are clear: In Papua New Guinea, although indigenous groups have sold resources from their homelands to loggers and miners, they have done so slowly, without devastating their own cultures, and have received some of the profits. In Irian Jaya, indigenous peoples have had their resources stolen, their cultures devastated, and their subsistence economies gutted.[45]

Ingenious as customary stewardship arrangements are, they are also vulnerable. When the pressures of the cash economy, powerful modern technologies, and encroaching populations—or, occasionally, their own growing populations—come to bear, traditional approaches to management frequently collapse, with catastrophic results for nature. In these circumstances, indigenous peoples—like anyone else—are prone to overuse resources, overhunt game, and sell off timber and minerals to pay for consumer goods. Indeed, some of the worst clear-cuts in the United States are on Alaskan Native lands, and members of the Philippine Manobo tribe now hunt for wild pigs by packing explosives into overripe fruit.[46]

What are the conditions in which traditional systems of ecological management can persist in the modern world? First, indigenous peoples must have secure rights to their subsistence base— rights that are not only recognized but enforced by the state and, ideally, backed by international law. Latin American tribes such as the Shuar of Ecuador, when threatened with losing their land, have cleared their own forests and taken up cattle ranching, because these actions prove ownership in Latin America. Had Ecuador backed up the Shuar's land rights, the ranching would have been unnecessary.[47]

Second, for indigenous ecological stewardship to survive the onslaught of the outside world, indigenous peoples must be organized politically and the state in which they reside must allow democratic initiatives. The Khant and Mansi peoples of Siberia, just as most indigenous people in the former Soviet Union, were nominally autonomous in their customary territories under Soviet law, but political repression precluded the organized defense of that terrain until the end of the eighties. Since then, the peoples of Siberia have begun organizing themselves to turn paper rights into real local control. In neighboring China, in contrast, indigenous homelands remain pure legal fictions because the state crushes all representative organizations.[48]

Third, indigenous communities must have access to information, support, and advice from friendly sources if they are to surmount the obstacles of the outside world. The tribal people of Papua New Guinea know much about their local environments, for example, but they know little about the impacts of large-scale logging and mining. Foreign and domestic investors have often played on this ignorance, assuring remote groups that no lasting harm would result from leasing parts of their land to resource extractors. If the forest peoples of Papua New Guinea could learn from the experience of indigenous peoples elsewhere— through supportive organizations and indigenous peoples' federations—they might be more careful.[49]

A handful of peoples around the world have succeeded in satisfying all three of these conditions, as examples from the United States and Namibia illustrate. In treaty negotiations a century ago, the U.S. government promised the salmon-based cultures of the Pacific Northwest permanent access to their customary fishing grounds both on and off reservations in exchange for territorial concessions. But starting early in this century, non-Indian fishers began to take most of the catch, leaving little for Indians. The Indian fishing industry dwindled and by mid-century had almost died, until Indians organized themselves to demand their rights. Eventually, in a series of landmark legal rulings in the seventies, U.S. courts interpreted the treaties as reserving half of all disputed fish for Indians.[50]

Their rights secured, the tribes have once again become accomplished fishery managers—rejuvenating their traditional reverence for salmon and training themselves in modern approaches with the help of supportive non-Indians. As stipulated under the court rulings, state and federal fisheries regulators have agreed with qualified tribes to manage fish runs jointly. Today, the Lummi, Tulalip, Muckleshoot, and other northwestern tribes are managing the salmon runs that nourished their ancestors.[51]

In Namibia, most of the San—after a century in which their population declined by 80 percent and their land base shrank by 85 percent—are now day laborers on cash-crop plantations. In the eighties, however, some 48 bands of San, totalling about 2,500 individuals, organized themselves to return to the desert homes they had tenuous rights over. There they have created a modified version of their ancient hunting and gathering economy. With the help of anthropologists, they have added livestock and drip-irrigated gardens to the daily foraging trips of their forebears, fashioning a way of life both traditional and modern.[52]

Perhaps because natural resource rights are best recognized in the Americas, indigenous groups there are furthest advanced in adapting traditional resource management arrangements to the modern context. In northern Canada, the Inuvialuit people have created management plans for grizzly and polar bears and for beluga whales. In southern Mexico, the Chinantec Indians are gradually developing their own blend of timber cutting, furniture making, butterfly farming, and forest preservation in their retreat in the Juarez mountains. The Miskito Indians of Nicaragua's Atlantic Coast, meanwhile, are forming local management groups to police the use of forests, wetlands, and reefs in the extensive Miskito Coast Protected Area they helped create in 1991.[53]

As they struggle to adapt their natural resource stewardship to modern pressures, indigenous peoples are beginning to pool their expertise. The Native Fish and Wildlife Service in Colorado, formed by a coalition of North American tribes, serves as an information clearinghouse on sustainable management. The Kuna of Panama—whose tribal regulations on hunting turtles and game, catching lobsters, and felling trees fill thick volumes—have convened international conferences on forest and fisheries management. Such instances are still exceptional, but they blaze a trail for indigenous peoples everywhere.[54]

New approaches to trade and to intellectual property rights—two relatively recent developments—could assist indigenous communities' efforts to sustain their systems of stewardship against outside forces. They also promise native peoples greater control over their interaction with the money economy.

Alternative traders, organizations committed to cultural survival and environmental sustainability, now market millions of dollars worth of indigenous peoples' products in industrial countries. The Mixe Indians of southern Mexico, for example, sell organic coffee through Texas-based Pueblo to People, an alternative trade organization, to consumers in the United States, while the Kayapó sell Brazil-nut oil to the U.K.-based firm The Body Shop for use in hair conditioners.[55]

By eliminating links from the merchandising chain, Pueblo to People, The Body Shop, and other alternative traders keep more of the product value flowing back to indigenous producers. The potential for alternative trade to grow is enormous, given the billion-dollar purchasing power of environmentally conscious consumers worldwide and the abundance of plant products hidden in indigenous lands. Mexico's forests hold an estimated 3,000 useful substances known only to Indians. Among the Quechua of lowland Ecuador, each hectare of forest yields fruits, medicinal plants, and other products worth $1,150 per year in Ecuadorean urban markets. Alternative trade will never make indigenous peoples rich; it can, however, assure them a modest cash income to supplement their subsistence. Admittedly, harvesting wild products for national and international markets has its risks: it can fuel overexploitation of resources and create schisms within communities. Still, in a world where money is power, no group can survive long without some source of revenue.[56]

A newer route to assuring indigenous peoples a basic income traverses the legal terrain of intellectual property rights—proprietary rights to ideas, designs, or information most commonly typified by patents and copyrights. Indigenous peoples have painstakingly studied their environments, and their knowledge has aided billions of people elsewhere, when, for example, traditional medicinal plants became the sources of life-saving drugs. Hundreds of years ago the highland Quechua of Peru revealed to Europeans the antimalarial quinine, the lowland Indians of the Amazon showed them how to make the emetic ipecac, and the peoples of the Guyanas instructed them on extracting from plants the muscle-relaxant curare used in abdominal surgery for a century.[57]

Yet indigenous peoples have rarely received anything of commensurate value in return; indeed, they have sometimes been annihilated for their efforts. One fourth of the coal the Soviet Union dug from the earth during its seven-decade history came from the lands of the Shorish people of Western Siberia. The Shors first disclosed the locations of the minerals, but the destruction that mining unleashed has whittled them down to a few hundred survivors. In Guyana, likewise, the Macushi tribe revealed the ingredients of their blow-dart poison to English naturalist Charles Waterton in 1812. Scientists used that recipe to develop curare. The tribe—dispossessed, uprooted, and alienated from its culture in the intervening period—now lives in misery, not even remembering how to make blow guns.[58]

The Kuna of Panama have convened international conferences on forest and fisheries management.

With the explosive growth in biotechnology since 1980, the demand for new genetic material is burgeoning. Many of the world's genes are in the millions of species in the endangered places inhabited by endangered peoples. Indeed, some indigenous leaders think of the gene rush as the latest in the long history of resource grabs perpetrated against them. Still, supporters of indigenous peoples are developing legal strategies to turn the gene trade to native advantage by demanding recognition that indigenous communities possess intellectual property rights as valid as those of other inventors and discoverers.

Native peoples' cultural ties to their local environments predispose them to guard and conserve the flora and fauna of their ancestral homes, but they need rights to their subsistence base, a degree of political organization, and support from allied segments of the world beyond their borders to translate that cultural predisposition into sustainable development. The world's indigenous peoples devote much of their energy to the first of those conditions: securing resource rights. To date, their successes have been few, but there are ample reasons to hope for better—reasons rooted in advances that have come on the second and third conditions: indigenous political mobilization and support from nonindigenous people.

RISING FROM THE FRONTIER

From the smallest tribal settlements to the U.N. General Assembly, indigenous peoples organizations are making themselves felt. Their grassroots movements have spread rapidly since 1970, gaining strength in numbers and through improvement of their political skills. They have pooled their talents in regional, national, and global federations to broaden their influence. This uprising, which like any movement has its share of internal rivalries, may eventually bring fundamental advances in the status of all endangered cultures.

The nature of the organizing process is evident in the case of Mount Apo. There, Chief Tulalang Maway and his people opposed plans to tap the mountain's internal heat for geothermal energy from the time the Philippine National Oil Company proposed it in the mid-eighties. Geothermal energy is renewable and relatively clean, but developing it on Mount Apo requires clearing primary forests high up the mountain, degrading the habitat of endangered species like the Philippine eagle, and intruding on the nation's oldest national park.[59]

In 1989, when their other protests had failed, Maway and 20 other Lumad elders performed a sacred ritual called D'yandi, committing themselves, their people, and all their Lumad descendants to protecting Mount Apo with their lives. Explaining the motivation for such a firm stance, he quietly recounted the creation myth passed down to him from his great-great-grandfather. In the tale, the creator of the world, Apotio, bids the Lumad farewell and goes to his resting place in Mount Apo after finishing his work: "Apotio told us," said Chief Maway, "'Guard this place, never let anyone destroy or desecrate this place. You may suffer hardships and poverty, but never leave this place because this is where I live . . . .Never give the mountain. It is better for you to die, to die rather than to give this mountain.' "[60]

The D'yandi—and the nonviolent blockades of the construction site that the Lumad periodically carry out—has drawn others to their cause, including Philippine environmentalists and human rights advocates such as the Legal Rights and Natural Resources Center. That organization, a group of young lawyers who have set themselves the task of overturning Philippine law's utter disregard for indigenous land rights, challenged the project's sketchy environmental impact assessment before the Supreme Court, seeking an injunction to halt construction. Despite a meticulously documented case, the Supreme Court dismissed the motion on a technicality.[61]

While legal arguments swirled, a national Save Mount Apo movement was gaining momentum, finding supporters even within municipal, provincial, and national government. Through the Philippine federation of indigenous peoples, the Lumad reached out overseas, hoping to augment their domestic campaign with foreign pressure. Lumad representatives pleaded their case at international conferences in New York, Seattle,

Tokyo, and Santiago, Chile. In a major victory, the Lumad and their allies even convinced the World Bank to refuse to finance the project because of its intrusion onto tribal lands.[62]

In 1992, however, five army and marine battalions encamped themselves around the mountain, ostensibly to ward off attacks from communist guerrillas, but mostly to intimidate the Lumad. Death threats against indigenous leaders began to come at regular intervals—including a widely reported $1,600 reward allegedly put on the head of Chief Maway by unnamed parties associated with the project. The Philippine National Oil Company, sponsor of the project, vehemently denied any involvement in the plot, but a cloud of intimidation and fear nonetheless cloaked the mountain.[63]

Finally, some Lumad broke ranks and accepted the terms of the company. If the plant is completed, the company promised to establish a foundation for supportive Lumad and put more than $250,000 a year into it. Capitalizing on the disarray in the Lumad camp, construction crews high on the flanks of the mountain moved quickly to clear-cut forests and begin drilling wells. In mid-1992, Maway and those loyal to the D'yandi were regrouping for a full-fledged blockade of the construction site. In the quiet before the storm, the chief was steadfast, "I'm old. If they kill me, others will take my place."[64]

As everywhere that indigenous peoples stand between industrial developers and ancestral homelands, the Lumad confront an adversary better equipped, better financed, and better connected with centers of power than they are. All that the Lumad have on their side is the strength of their convictions. Their experience is unusual only in the degree of support they have received from afar. The long odds, the unflagging determination, the intimidation, the threats of violence, the danger of factionalism within the community, and the elusiveness of victory are all par for the course.

Still, victory does sometimes come. Across the Pacific in Ecuador, for example, Indians have mounted a dramatic and effective campaign to claim their due. After centuries of second-class citizenship, the Indians of Ecuador want secure rights to the lands they have worked since time immemorial and constitutional recognition of their distinct cultures. In June 1990, after decades of grassroots organizing, Ecuador's Indian federations called their people to march peacefully on the cities, to blockade the nation's highways, and to refuse to sell food outside their communities. For three days, 1 million Indians brought the country to a standstill; enraged as they were, the ruling classes had no choice but to take heed as the Indians enumerated their priorities. High on the list were 72 land claims languishing in the bureaucracy.[65]

Grassroots movements have spread rapidly since 1970.

Negotiations with the government begun that watershed week in 1990 continued with little progress until a new march began in 1992. This time 2,500 marchers set out from the jungle lowlands of Pastaza province heading for the mountain capital of Quito. As the marchers gained altitude, they gained support, swelling to 10,000 when they reached the seat of government in April. There, with the weight of national opinion behind them, they won rights to 12,000 square kilometers of their forest homeland.[66]

The key to success in Ecuador has been unity among indigenous peoples. For example, as Ecuador's Huaorani, the least assimilated tribe in the nation, have struggled against oil development on their land in the extreme east of the country, other tribes have come to their aid. The Confederation of Indian Nationalities of the Ecuadorean Amazon, using a technique perfected by the Awa people of Ecuador's extreme west, is helping them clear a boundary strip around their territory and post it against trespassers. The Awa, meanwhile, have aided their tribe members in the contiguous zone of neighboring Colombia to demarcate their land, and convinced both national governments to recognize the area as an international ethnic forest reserve.[67]

Without democratic rights to organize and argue their case, indigenous peoples have little prospect of defending themselves.

Grassroots movements, whether nascent as in the Philippines or mature as in Ecuador, are found among most of the world's indigenous peoples. They are most abundant, and most successful, where political systems are democratic and where legal channels for the defense of human rights are open—countries such as Canada, New Zealand, Sweden, and the United States. Democracy is not a sufficient condition for cultural survival, of course. U.S. democracy, for example, has not stopped the government from violating most of the treaties it signed with Indian tribes. Still, without democratic rights to organize and argue their case, indigenous peoples have little prospect of defending themselves.

In undemocratic societies, indigenous peoples movements have a hard time getting off the ground. Cameroon, like most of Africa's autocratic regimes, follows an avowedly assimilationist policy; forest-dwellers there have only the "right" to integrate into modern society. The tens of millions of indigenous peoples in China likewise have few hopes while that country squelches all independent political organizing. With the doors of state closed to them, indigenous peoples under repressive regimes sometimes take up arms, as they have in Myanmar and parts of Indonesia.[68]

At the local level, even indigenous peoples who are not organized into larger movements commonly resist outside encroachment. In Thailand, remote hill tribes have stood up to illegal loggers backed by the military. In India, tribal communities have defended their lands against state-sponsored tea plantations, loggers, and commercial reed collectors, frequently without the benefit of national organizations. When such groups have organized, however, local resistance has greater effect. The hunter-gatherer Penan of Malaysian Borneo have repeatedly blocked logging roads to save their home range. Organizing efforts at home and abroad have transformed their cause from a local nuisance into an international controversy. Mistreatment of the Penan has thrown a pall on Malaysia's reputation.[69]

As grassroots movements advance they sometimes turn to electoral politics, as in Chile, where the Mapuche people have spearheaded efforts by the nation's million native people to form their own political party, called Land and Identity. In Sweden and Norway, the Sami have organized parliaments that present unified policy positions to the legislatures. Elsewhere, indigenous movements set their sights on national constitutions. In Mexico, Indians are calling for an amendment to enshrine land rights, much as Brazilian Indians achieved in that country's constitutional convention of 1988. Colombian Indians won representation in 1991 in the nation's constitutional assembly, and Canadian indigenous peoples may win recognition of the right to self-government.[70]

Some indigenous movements have also mastered use of communications media. Brazil's Kayapó tribe takes video cameras to meetings with politicians to record the promises they make. Aboriginal groups in Australia publish newspapers reflecting their culture. And 2 million Aymara Indians in Bolivia, Peru, and Chile tune in to Radio San Gabriel for Aymara language news, music, and educational programming.[71]

Legal cases play an important part of native movements in places where the rule of law is strong. North American tribes now have a generation of talented lawyers who turn what they call "white man's law" to Indian advantage, winning back ancestral land and water rights. Maori organizations in New Zealand catalyzed the creation of a special tribunal to investigate violations of the century-old Waitangi treaty, which guaranteed Maori land rights. The tribunal is charged with sifting through claims that cover 70 percent of the country.[72]

Regional and global meetings on the rights of indigenous peoples are now commonplace. In June 1992, for example, three separate conferences of indigenous peoples were held in Rio de Janeiro, one preceding and two coinciding with the U.N. Conference on Environment and Development.[73]

The longest-lived series of meetings, and perhaps the most important, has been the annual sessions of the Geneva-based U.N. Working Group on Indigenous Populations. Established by the U.N. Human Rights Commission in 1982, the Working Group is drafting a Universal Declaration on the Rights of Indigenous Peoples. The version of late 1992 stated that: "Indigenous peoples have the collective and individual right to own, control and use the lands and territories they have traditionally occupied or otherwise used. This includes the right to full recognition of their own laws and customs, land tenure systems and institutions for the management of resources, and the right to effective measures by States to prevent any interference with or encroachment on these rights."[74]

The Declaration follows close on the heels of the International Labor Organization's Convention 169, which took effect in September 1991, calling for respect for the cultural integrity of indigenous peoples. Convention 169 marked a considerable improvement upon earlier international documents on native peoples, which encouraged the assimilation and "modernization" of their cultures. The debate advanced remarkably in the eighties, according to attorney Steve Tullberg of the Indian Law Resource Center in Washington, D.C.: "As recently as 1980, any government could stand up in the U.N. and say 'our treatment of our Indians is not your business.' They no longer could." Indeed, the United Nations has declared 1993 the International Year of Indigenous Peoples.[75]

Indigenous peoples' cause is also strengthened by a growing movement of advocacy organizations whose members are not native people themselves. These hundreds of organizations may specialize in recording Indian land claims in Brazil, as does the Ecumenical Center for Documentation and Information in São Paulo, or legal aid in the Philippines, as does the Legal Rights and Natural Resources Center in Manila, or countless other tasks. At the international level, organizations such as Cultural Survival, Survival International in London, and the International Work Group for Indigenous Affairs in Copenhagen rally nonindigenous people to the cause. They press recalcitrant governments, spotlight reckless corporations, and prod stodgy development funders such as the World Bank to halt their transgressions against endangered cultures.

In a world where almost all nations have publicly committed themselves to the goal of sustainable development and most have signed a global treaty for the protection of biological diversity, the questions of cultural survival and indigenous homelands cannot be avoided much longer. As guardians and stewards of remote and fragile ecosystems, indigenous cultures could play a crucial role in safeguarding humanity's planetary home. But they cannot do it alone. They need the support of international law and national policy, and they need the understanding and aid of the world's more numerous peoples.

Giving native peoples power over their own lives raises issues for the world's dominant culture as well—a consumerist and individualist culture born in Europe and bred in the United States. Indeed, indigenous peoples may offer more than a best-bet alternative for preserving the outlying areas where they live. They may offer living examples of cultural patterns that can help revive ancient values within everyone: devotion to future generations, ethical regard for nature, and commitment to community among people. The question may be, then, Are indigenous peoples the past, or are they the future?

6

Providing Energy
in Developing Countries

Nicholas Lenssen

In the small Ecuadorean village of Guamalán lives an elementary school teacher named Marco Coloma. Electricity only reached his isolated village in 1990, but most homes are unable to afford the steep hook-up fee. Tanks of propane are hauled in occasionally over a rough dirt track, though most of the community's energy is firewood culled from the trees that border local cornfields and pastures. Coloma's energy use—directly or in products he consumes—is equivalent to 4.6 barrels of oil each year, assuming he manages to consume the Ecuadorean average.[1]

Five thousand kilometers away, in the U.S. town of Winsted, Connecticut, his brother uses 48 barrels of oil-equivalent annually, 10 times as much energy. Carlos Coloma owns a car and a pickup truck, as well as a home equipped with an electric cooking range, electric lights, a refrigerator, a washing ma-

chine, and two televisions. These are all things that his brother Marco longs for, a dream likely shared by more than 4 billion people in Africa, Asia, and Latin America.

For decades, increasing the use of energy in developing countries has been one aim of planners and institutions around the world, in the belief that expanding energy supplies was an essential step for raising living standards in the Third World, or the South. While developing countries have more than quadrupled their energy use since 1960, the strategies for achieving this have left these nations reeling from oil shocks, struggling under foreign debt, and suffering from serious environmental problems. Persistent energy shortages still plague their economies, as power outages shut down bustling cities and as fuelwood shortages make women's lives even more difficult in the countryside. Developing countries have also become a rapidly growing source of climate-altering greenhouse gases.[2]

If the Marco Colomas of the world are

An expanded version of this chapter appeared as Worldwatch Paper 111, *Empowering Development: The New Energy Equation.*

to achieve the hoped-for gains in living standards, they need affordable and environmentally sound ways to meet their energy needs. A strategy based on more efficient use of energy and the pursuit of less-expensive and less-polluting domestic energy resources, such as natural gas and renewable energy, would allow developing countries to break out of the energy dilemma they now find themselves in: needing to supply more energy but knowing that following the current path may hinder development, not help it. The starting point for such a strategy is understanding that it is the services that energy can provide—such as cooking, lighting, and increased agricultural productivity—and not simply energy supply itself that are at the base of economic and social development.

By embracing improved efficiency and cleaner, domestic energy resources, developing countries can "leapfrog" to the advanced technologies being commercialized in industrial countries today, avoiding billions of dollars of misdirected investments in infrastructure. Such a move would also lead to greater employment—a major benefit in economies that are labor-rich and capital-poor. Finally, and most important for the health of the global environment, an efficient energy system would delay global warming by slowing down the increase in carbon emissions from expanding economies.[3]

Such a change in investment priorities will require major reforms—in developing-country institutions and in the industrial countries that control international financial institutions such as the World Bank. But the alternative to an efficient energy system—capital shortfalls, repeated oil shocks, and ever-growing emissions of global warming gases and air pollutants—would only lead to stagnant development prospects for much of the planet.

THE ENERGY DILEMMA

While some may interpret the swift growth in Third World energy consumption as a sign of progress, at times the opposite may be true—development may be derailed if the energy sector continues on its current trajectory. Imports of energy supplies and equipment are expensive, and their costs contribute to the underlying debt and foreign-exchange problems that plague developing countries. Growth in energy use also increases environmental and health problems. Put simply, the Third World needs more energy to provide goods and services to growing populations, but, for economic and environmental reasons, these nations cannot rely simply on expanding supplies as they have in the past.

It is clear that growth in developing countries' use of oil, coal, and other sources of energy, fuelled largely by speedy industrialization and urbanization, has been rapid. Since 1970 alone, these nations—home to 77 percent of the world's population—have nearly tripled energy use at a time when it increased in industrial countries by only 21 percent. Energy use grew far faster than population, and even more quickly than economic growth. (See Figure 6–1.) By 1991, developing countries used 24 percent of the world's oil, coal, natural gas, and electricity. Including wood and agricultural wastes, which provide more than a third of the energy in these regions, brings the total to some 30 percent of the world's energy use.[4]

Despite the increase, people in developing countries use just one ninth as much commercial energy on average as those in industrial countries do. (See Table 6–1.) And wide disparities exist: Bangladeshis use one tenth the amount of energy of Thais, while South Koreans consume three times as much as Thais. The differences within countries are sim-

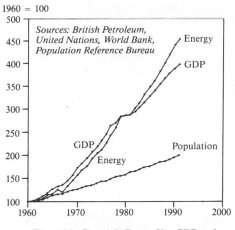

1960 = 100

Sources: British Petroleum, United Nations, World Bank, Population Reference Bureau

Energy

GDP

GDP

Population

Energy

Figure 6-1. Growth in Energy Use, GDP, and Population, Developing Countries, 1960–91

ilar to those between them, with elite minorities devouring as much energy as their rich Northern counterparts while most rural dwellers use little.[5]

Per capita consumption, though, can be a misleading indicator of economic or social well-being: the service that energy provides is important; the actual amount used is not. A better, though still not exact measure is to gauge energy use by the amount of goods and services provided. The typical Indian, for example, uses slightly more energy than a neighboring Pakistani but has only half the income. Prior to unification, the average East German consumed 41 percent more energy than a West German, though the West German was nearly twice as wealthy. Indians and East Germans are thus not getting as many services for each barrel of oil or kilowatt-hour of electricity as their neighbors do.[6]

Energy policies in developing countries have largely been dictated by the choices—and needs—of industrial countries. Foremost is the thirst for oil, which has led multinational companies to search the globe for new supplies and to encourage developing countries to export it for foreign exchange. Due to oil's

convenience in transportation and storage, most developing countries have also followed the path of Northern countries and used oil to fuel industry and transport, as well as for cooking, lighting, and producing electricity. But while a few nations have greatly helped their balance sheets through these exports, most face a continual drain on scarce foreign exchange as they import oil, a drain that siphons resources away from development. Three fourths of developing countries are oil importers. And of the 38 poorest countries, 29 import more than 70 percent of their commercial energy, nearly all of it in the form of oil.[7]

Oil importers are highly vulnerable to the sudden price increases and energy shortages that have rocked the global economy three times in the past 20 years. Following the 1973 Arab oil embargo, oil import bills went from absorbing 10 percent of export earnings to taking more than 20 percent in sub-Saharan Africa; after the Iranian revolution of 1979, oil imports took more than half the export earnings in many poorer countries. Even at today's lower oil prices, nearly a third of sub-Saharan Africa's hard-currency earnings are spent on petroleum imports, stifling investment in other areas.[8]

Foreign debt loads—totalling some $1.35 trillion at the start of 1992—also have an oil connection. During the past decade, India's oil import bill soaked up nearly a third of export receipts and reached $36.8 billion, almost 87 percent of the debt created, according to the International Energy Initiative in Bangalore. When foreign purchases of electric generating equipment are included, energy accounted for more than four fifths of India's export earnings between 1980 and 1986.[9]

In much of the Third World, government-owned power companies are deeply in debt from electric power con-

Table 6–1. World Commercial Energy Consumption, 1970 and 1990

Region	1970		1990	
	Energy Consumption	Per Capita	Energy Consumption	Per Capita
	(exajoules)	(gigajoules per person)	(exajoules)	(gigajoules per person)
Developing Countries[1]	30	12	84	21
Latin America	8	26	16	37
Asia	19	10	59	20
Africa	4	10	9	14
Industrial Countries	129	180	154	185
Centrally Planned Economies	44	120	71	167
World[1]	203	55	310	59

[1]Columns may not add up to totals due to rounding.
SOURCES: British Petroleum, *BP Statistical Review of World Energy* (London: 1992); United Nations, *World Population Prospects 1990* (New York: 1991).

struction programs. An average of 25 percent of the dollars developing-country governments paid to Northern creditors in the eighties went to pay off past energy projects. At the same time, in an effort to boost economic growth, stem inflation, or simply win popular support, governments slashed electricity prices, with tariffs dropping from an average of 5.5¢ a kilowatt-hour in 1983 to 3.8¢ by 1988. Overall, consumers in developing countries pay just 60 percent of the cost of producing electricity. Put simply, many utilities are not earning enough money even to cover their monthly bills, much less pay back foreign banks.[10]

Yet many developing countries still face shortages of electricity. India's shortfall is 22 percent during peak periods, 9 percent generally, and worsening. In China, shortages of electricity and coal result in regular shutdowns of industry, idling one fourth of the country's industrial capacity in 1987. And in Latin America, electricity shortages cost as much as $15 billion annually in lost output.[11]

Such shortfalls have social repercussions, as well. Following a power outage in Calcutta in 1991, citizens attacked utility workers, while Bombay has twice been on the verge of riots over breakdowns in the past three years. Such scenes led S. Rajgopal, then India's secretary to the department of power, to say that "power is no longer just an economic issue. It's a question of law and order."[12]

To close the generating gap, electric utilities throughout the developing world are building power plants as fast as they can. Plans call for spending some $100 billion annually—including $40 billion in foreign exchange—on new power plants and transmission lines through the nineties, according to the World Bank. For many utilities, acting on these plans will be impossible. The inability of utilities to repay their existing debt has reduced the willingness of private banks to lend them more money. Third World utilities will be lucky to borrow half the $40 billion a year the Bank says is needed. And internal capital markets are unlikely to make up the rest, given current financial problems of utilities. Senior World Bank economist John Besant-Jones foresees massive economic disruption in developing countries during the nineties if power sector crises go unresolved.[13]

Cash-strapped utilities that cannot meet present obligations have little prospect of extending power supplies to people without electricity. Some 2.1 billion people in the developing world still fall in this category; for most, the chance of change is slim. The traditional way of providing power to rural communities—extending power lines throughout a country—is too expensive for many governments to keep subsidizing. Building power lines costs up to $15,000 per kilometer. In most countries, utilities manage to hook only 2–3 percent of unserved rural families up to the electric grid each year, a rate that is often below that of population growth.[14]

Rural energy users must cope with a scarcity in biomass energy resources such as wood. At least 2 billion people depend almost exclusively on biomass for their energy supplies, though their total energy consumption is relatively small. The U.N. Food and Agriculture Organization, meanwhile, estimates that the number of people suffering from wood fuel shortages will grow from 100 million in 1980 to more than 350 million by the end of the decade.[15]

Development experts no longer offer fuelwood collection as the driving force behind most deforestation. Land clearance for agriculture ranks as the primary cause. Still, scouring the countryside for fuelwood places severe pressures on the land—and on people. Shortfalls in fuelwood contribute to increased fuel costs for urban biomass users, longer collection times for women and children in the countryside, and a reduction of crop residues and dung returned to agricultural land when these natural fertilizers

are used as fuel to replace ever-diminishing wood supplies.[16]

Environmental and health costs associated with energy use also constrain developing countries from improving their living standard. Burning wood in traditional stoves pollutes the air in Third World kitchens. Some 400–700 million people, primarily women and children, suffer from high levels of carbon monoxide, particulates, and cancer-causing emissions such as benzopyrene. Acute respiratory infections are now the leading killer of children under five, accounting for more than 3.5 million deaths annually, according to the World Health Organization. Urban areas are beset with energy-related air pollution problems, primarily from motor vehicles. Bangkok, Mexico City, Nairobi, Santiago, and São Paulo are among the long list of cities that suffer from lung-damaging air pollution.[17]

Oil and coal burning can result in wide-ranging emissions of sulfur and nitrogen oxides that lead to acidic rainfall, damaging forests, crops, and water ecosystems. Acid rain falls in at least 14 percent of China. In the Philippines, pollution from a Batangas province coal plant is reported to have reduced output of rice and sugar, while increasing respiratory problems among the residents. As in industrial countries, public protest over the environmental effects of energy use has hindered plans to expand supplies; the controversy created in Batangas, for instance, has stalled other Philippine power plants.[18]

Industrial countries have recently shown greater interest in energy use in developing countries partly because of growing recognition that greenhouse gases—from whatever sources—pose a threat to the world as a whole. In its 1992 report to the U.N. Conference on Environment and Development (UNCED), the Intergovernmental Panel on Climate Change reiterated its earlier finding that doubling atmospheric carbon dioxide—generated mainly by the burning of fossil fuels—will warm the planet by 1.5–4.5 degrees Celsius by the end of the next century. Although industrial countries have emitted 79 percent of fossil fuel–derived carbon dioxide since 1950, and still accounted for 69 percent of the total in 1990, future growth is expected to come more from the South than from the North. If recent trends continue, developing-world emissions will increase from 1.8 billion tons of carbon in 1990 to 5.5 billion tons in 2025, boosting global emissions by half at the time when they should be reduced at least 60 percent if the atmospheric concentration is to be stablilized and global warming minimized. A reduction of that magnitude will require major changes in all countries—industrial and developing.[19]

If recent trends continue, developing-world emissions will increase from 1.8 billion tons of carbon in 1990 to 5.5 billion tons in 2025.

Most developing-country governments, however, accept increasing emissions of carbon dioxide as a necessary evil if they are to raise living standards, claiming that since carbon dioxide remains in the atmosphere for well over 100 years, it is largely the North that caused the problem. Yet many in the South are well aware of the risks they run if predictions of climate change come true. Sea level rise, for example, could inundate 33 island nations, as well as low-lying coastal regions of populous countries such as Bangladesh and Egypt, leading to massive dislocations. Research in Indonesia, Kenya, and Malaysia found that agricultural output would decline as a result of global warming. And China's Meteorological Bureau

is concerned that global warming may already be exacerbating a severe drought in the northern part of the country.[20]

Mitigating these environmental impacts will be difficult at best, given that future population growth alone will spur a 70-percent jump in energy use in 30 years even if per capita consumption remains at current levels. Combined with high rates of economic growth, these nations could triple their energy use by 2020, according to conventional projections. This would require massive investments in energy infrastructure to build thousands of new power plants and to meet the expected tripling in oil, natural gas, and coal use. Many expert observers no longer find such plans realistic, given the economic and environmental constraints.[21]

Yet the threat of climate change might be turned to the advantage of developing countries if industrial nations, seeking to slow the process, help the Third World build efficient systems that limit greenhouse gas emissions while meeting energy service needs.

ENERGY EFFICIENCY: THE POTENTIAL REVOLUTION

Since the 1973 oil embargo, industrial countries have made impressive gains in using energy more economically. For the members of the Organisation for Economic Co-operation and Development, energy use rose only one fifth as much as economic growth between 1973 and 1989. These gains have largely bypassed developing countries, where energy use expanded 20 percent faster than economic growth during the same period.[22]

Developing-country economies now require 40 percent more energy than western ones to produce the same value of goods and services. Part of the difference is due to the fact that they are still building energy-intensive infrastructure and related industries, but they often use outdated technologies that squander energy, whether in industry, buildings, transportation, or agriculture. From wood stoves to cement plants, developing countries can limit energy consumption and expenditures while expanding the services energy provides. For example, the U.S. Office of Technology Assessment estimates that nearly half of overall electricity use in the South can be cut cost-effectively.[23]

To compete in increasingly integrated world markets—and meet needs at home—developing countries will need to reap the economic savings that improved energy efficiency offers. But it will take a concerted effort by consumers, businesses, and governments to capture the full potential. Individual consumers, particularly poorer ones, often cannot afford to buy more-efficient appliances, and manufacturers and importers lack incentives to reduce products' energy use even when no additional cost is involved. Meanwhile, governments and international aid institutions usually direct their money and efforts toward expanding supplies while neglecting energy services.

Half of Third World commercial energy consumption goes to industry (see Table 6–2), yet for each ton of steel or cement produced, the typical factory in the South uses far more energy than its Northern counterpart. Steel plants in developing countries, for example, consume roughly one quarter more energy than the average plant in the United States, and about three quarters more than the best plant. Indian fertilizer plants use about twice as much oil to produce a ton of ammonia as a typical British plant does. Such records are often the result of poor maintenance and

Table 6–2. Energy Use in Developing Countries, by Sector, 1985

Sector	Commercial[1]	Biomass	Total
	(percent)		
Residential & Commercial	28	90	44
Industrial[2]	52	10	41
Transportation	20	—	15

[1]Commercial energy refers to coal, oil, natural gas, electricity and other fuels that are widely traded in organized markets. [2]Includes agriculture.

SOURCE: U.S. Congress, Office of Technology Assessment, *Fueling Development* (Washington, D.C.: U.S. Government Printing Office, 1992).

operating procedures, and can be readily improved—given sufficient information and incentive to do so. Indonesian industries, for example, could cut energy use 11 percent without any capital investment simply by changing operating procedures, and a Ghanaian survey found potential savings of at least 30 percent in medium- to large-scale industries.[24]

Older technologies and processes used in developing countries contribute to high rates of energy consumption as well. Cement plants, which are found in 84 of 110 developing countries, are often the major energy-consuming industry; more than two thirds of Kenya's industrial energy use, for instance, goes to making cement. Yet Southern cement plants typically use 50–100 percent more energy than the best ones in industrial countries, partially due to reliance on an antiquated wet process. Prompted by a government program in the eighties, Tunisia reduced by 13 percent the energy needed for each ton of cement produced between 1983 and 1991.[25]

The electric power industry also offers abundant opportunities to save energy and money. Third World power plants typically burn one fifth to two fifths more fuel for each kilowatt-hour generated than those in the North, and they experience far more unplanned shutdowns for repairs, as they are often poorly maintained and operated by inadequately trained staff. Once electricity is generated, 15–20 percent of it disappears to line losses and theft, as industries and individuals hook into power lines without paying for the service. In some countries, the rates are even higher: Bangladesh reportedly loses over 40 percent of its generated power this way.[26]

The developing world has only begun to build its industrial infrastructure, creating an opportunity to base future development on not just highly efficient processes but also products. Building a $7.5-million compact fluorescent light bulb factory, for example, would eliminate the need to build $5.6 billion worth of coal-fired power plants if the bulbs (which need 75 percent less power than incandescent ones) were used domestically. In Pakistan, a switch from incandescent to compact fluorescent bulbs helped Karachi's Aga Khan Hospital cut its total energy consumption 20 percent. Such a strategy would also generate products in high demand internationally; global demand for compact fluorescent bulbs grew by 36 percent over each of the past two years, and exceeds supply.[27]

The emphasis on energy-intensive industrialization often found in developing countries can have unforeseen impacts on economies already burdened by underemployment and debt. In Brazil, for instance, the government subsidizes electricity for energy-intensive industries such as aluminum smelting (which pays just one third the actual cost of producing power) to boost exports that can service its foreign debt. As a result, the government has been stuck with the large bills for hydroelectric dams built to run industry. A move toward lighter industry, such as computers, would create

120 times as many jobs and increase tax receipts twentyfold compared with a similar investment in energy-intensive, export-oriented industries such as aluminum.[28]

Agriculture is also a large consumer of electricity in some developing countries. India's 8 million irrigation pumps, which use nearly one quarter of the country's electricity, employ inefficient motors and pumps and poorly designed belts, and they are plagued by leaky foot valves and high friction losses. Using more-efficient pumps could cut electricity consumption roughly in half at a cost of only 1¢ per kilowatt-hour saved. But tariffs for electricity are so low, often based on an annual fee, that farmers have no incentive to conserve energy. Still, one retrofit program conducted by the Indian Rural Electrification Corporation in the mid-eighties reduced electricity consumption in 23,000 pumps by a quarter, and the improvements paid for themselves in less than six months.[29]

Although industry still consumes most of the commercial energy in developing countries, the urban residential and commercial sectors are growing much faster. In Thailand, some 40 percent of the projected increase in electricity growth is for commercial buildings. Cooking and water heating are still the primary energy uses in urban and rural households, but most of the growth is driven by use of electricity-consuming devices such as lights, televisions, refrigerators, and even air conditioners. In China, only 3 percent of Beijing's households had refrigerators in 1982; six years later, 81 percent did.[30]

Developing countries, however, often rely on outdated technologies that consume more energy than needed. A typical Chinese refrigerator, for example, uses 365 kilowatt-hours of electricity each year. In South Korea, a similarly sized model uses 240 kilowatt-hours, and a Danish one needs less than 100 kilowatt-hours. Yet industrial planners and manufacturers in developing countries are rarely concerned with the energy efficiency of their products—only with producing and selling more of them by keeping the initial cost as low as possible.[31]

The same can be said for architects and civil engineers. Much of the developing world relies on air conditioning in commercial buildings. Improved building designs—including insulation, better windows, and natural ventilation—can cut cooling needs while saving money. For example, Bangkok's large offices typically use windows made of a single sheet of glass. By substituting advanced double-paned windows with a special low-emissivity coating (which filters out infrared rays but allows in visible light), builders would reduce costs since smaller, less expensive air conditioning units could be installed.[32]

Chinese buildings use three times as much energy for heating as U.S. buildings do, even though inside temperatures remain far colder. By making boiler improvements and using insulation and double-glazed windows, building temperatures could be raised from an average of 11 degrees Celsius to 18 degrees—while consuming 40 percent less coal. One study found that such improvements can pay for themselves in 6.5 years in the northern city of Harbin even with subsidized coal; with unsubsidized coal, the payback would be around four years.[33]

Developing countries also stand to gain from efficiency improvements in the use of biomass for cooking, allowing women to spend less time or money acquiring fuel. Traditional cooking stoves operate at an efficiency level of around 10 percent, but improved stoves can convert 20–30 percent of biomass to useful cooking energy. Similar gains in efficiency can be achieved in converting wood to charcoal for urban markets or rural industries.[34]

In the seventies, development organizations put a high priority on improving cooking stoves, yet by the early eighties, no program had resulted in spontaneous, large-scale sales or dissemination. More recently, the situation improved following advocates' efforts to test the new technologies to ensure reliability and affordability before promoting them. In Kenya, more than a half-million improved charcoal stoves, the ceramic jiko, have been sold, with at least 130,-000 being added each year. Kenya's success helped inspire similar programs in 15 other countries in Africa, with some 150,000 improved stoves sold in Niger and 200,000 in Burkina Faso.[35]

Once electricity is generated, 15–20 percent of it disappears to line losses and theft.

Energy consumed in transportation is also growing fast, mainly due to the rapid increase in urbanization and in ownership of cars and two- and three-wheeled motor vehicles. During the past decade, car registrations shot up in Asian developing countries by more than 10 percent annually.[36]

Motor vehicles made in developing countries often fall below the efficiency levels found in the North. New cars manufactured in Brazil, for instance, are 20–30 percent less efficient than comparable cars in Europe and Japan. Meanwhile, prototype vehicles built in the industrial world can quadruple the current level of efficiency. Increasing gridlock in Third World cities can negate even these vast gains, however. Congestion in Bangkok has dropped the average vehicle speed from 12 kilometers per hour in 1980 to an estimated 5 kilometers per hour today. More serious measures are needed to improve transportation of people and goods, including improved traffic management, nonmotorized vehicles, mass transportation such as railways, and better planning for future land use activities. (See Chapter 7.)[37]

In combination, efficiency potentials in industry, buildings, transportation, and agriculture are staggering. By investing $10 billion a year to tap them, developing countries could halve the rate of growth of their energy demand, lighten the burden of pollution on their environments and health, and staunch the flow of export earnings into fuel purchases. Gross annual savings would average $53 billion for 35 years, according to a study prepared by scientists at the U.S. government's Lawrence Berkeley Laboratory.[38]

Efficiency improvements could mean Third World energy consumption would double instead of triple during the next 30 years.

Although such wide-scale savings remain paper prophecies, some countries have had notable successes. In 1980, China launched an ambitious efficiency program to improve energy use in major industries. By directing roughly 10 percent of its energy investment to efficiency over five years, the nation cut its annual growth in overall energy use from 7 percent to 4 percent, without compromising industrial production. Efficiency improvements accounted for more than 90 percent of the energy savings, with shifts toward less energy-intensive industries explaining the remainder. And efficiency gains were found to be one third less expensive than comparable investments in coal supplies. One result was that China's energy consump-

tion expanded at less than half the rate of economic growth from 1980 through 1988.[39]

China achieved this result in the midst of building its infrastructure, a phase of industrialization that in most countries has involved soaring energy consumption. Had the nation failed to make such progress, energy consumption in 1990 would have been 50 percent higher than it actually was. (See Figure 6–2.) Unfortunately, China has poured money into expanding energy supply since the mid-eighties; spending on efficiency has declined to just 6 percent of total investment in the energy sector.[40]

Brazil's National Electricity Conservation Program (PROCEL) has catalyzed impressive savings of energy and money. Between 1985, when it was created, and early 1990, PROCEL spent $20 million on more than 150 efficiency projects and programs, with private industry providing matching funds. This yielded electricity savings worth between $600 million and $1.3 billion in reduced need for power plants and transmission lines. For each $1 invested, roughly $25 was freed up for other, urgently needed uses.[41]

Brazil and China need not be anoma-

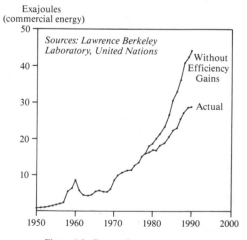

Exajoules
(commercial energy)

Sources: Lawrence Berkeley Laboratory, United Nations

Without Efficiency Gains

Actual

Figure 6-2. Energy Consumption in China, Actual and Without Efficiency Gains, 1950–90

lies, as similar potential exists throughout the developing world. Efficiency improvements could mean Third World energy consumption would double instead of triple during the next 30 years, while reducing future pollution and lessening costly shortages. And billions of dollars would be freed up to make development—and meeting people's basic needs—more affordable and feasible.

OTHER SUPPLY CHOICES

No matter how much waste is squeezed out of the way energy is used in developing countries, over the long term energy supplies must be increased. Unfortunately, government planners and international institutions assume that developing countries have to follow the energy path the North blazed a century ago, a strategy that relies primarily on expanding supplies of coal and oil. These two fossil fuels already provide 51 percent of all energy used in developing countries (see Table 6–3), and more than 75 percent of commercial energy.[42]

Table 6–3. Energy Use in Developing Countries, 1991[1]

Source	Share
	(percent)
Biomass	35
Oil	26
Coal	25
Natural Gas	8
Other Renewables	6
Nuclear	< 1

[1]Primary energy.
SOURCE: Worldwatch Institute, based on British Petroleum, *BP Statistical Review of World Energy* (London: 1992), on United Nations, *1990 Energy Statistics Yearbook* (New York: 1992), and on J.M.O. Scurlock and D.O. Hall, "The Contribution of Biomass to Global Energy Use," *Biomass*, No. 21, 1990.

Over the long haul, the Third World will need to develop its own alternatives to costly oil and polluting coal. Many developing countries have extensive, unexploited reserves of natural gas, which could supplant oil and coal use in buildings, transport, industry, and power generation. And all have enormous potential to rely on solar, wind, biomass, and geothermal energy resources to meet needs in rural and urban areas. Driven by technological advances and cost reductions, western countries are increasingly pursuing these resources. In developing countries the opportunities are even greater. Decisions they make today will determine how readily they tap these resources in the future.

Oil still provides most commercial energy for developing countries, and its use continues to grow. During the past decade oil consumption increased by a third in the developing world, a period when it fell in North America, Europe, and the former Soviet Union. As world oil reserves and production become more concentrated in the volatile Persian Gulf region (now the site of nearly two thirds of the world's proven oil reserves and more than a quarter of its production), the likelihood of disruptive oil cutoffs or rapid price rises will grow.[43]

Other energy resources, notably coal and hydroelectric power, face growing problems of their own, especially since most of the less expensive resources have already been exploited. Coal resources are concentrated in a few countries, so most nations would remain energy importers even if they chose to use coal. Even the big users, China and India, face obstacles. In China, for example, shipping coal from mines in the north to the eastern economic heartland has led to transport gridlock and supply shortfalls; coal shipments already account for 40 percent of railway tonnage. In India, where most coal is of poor quality, public opposition to strip mines and polluting power plants has escalated in recent years. Both countries will need to move toward more efficient, less polluting methods to convert coal to electricity and heat.[44]

Energy planners hold high expectations for hydroelectric power, which currently provides a third of developing-country electricity. Less than 10 percent of its technical potential has been tapped. Yet exploiting the rest has run into roadblocks and declining orders in recent years as the real costs of building large dams have been taken into account. High capital costs put electric utilities deep in debt. (Brazil's and Paraguay's Itaipu Dam, for example, was budgeted at $3.5 billion before construction started in 1975, but recent estimates for the project, which only now is in the final stage toward completion, run to $21 billion, excluding interest.) Dam reservoirs flood vast tracts of land—roughly 10 times as much land as is needed for comparable coal or solar energy projects—forcing people from their homes. Hydroelectric power will continue to be pursued, but countries are likely to design smaller projects with lower economic risk and fewer environmental and social impacts.[45]

Nuclear power, too, has fallen short of its promise to supply cheap electricity in developing countries—just as it has elsewhere. The Third World accounts for only 6 percent of the world's nuclear generating capacity, with many programs—including those of Argentina, Brazil, and India—over budget, behind schedule, and plagued by technical problems. Taiwan and South Korea have better records, though public opposition has frozen Taiwan's expansion plans since 1985, and, along with rising costs, threatens South Korea's as well. Due to its high cost and complex technology, nuclear power is not a viable option for

the vast majority of developing countries.[46]

When oil companies operating in developing countries find natural gas—for which export markets are poorly developed—in their exploratory wells, they usually cap the well and write the venture off as a tax loss. Yet locally, the gas in these so-called noncommercial wells could provide fuel for cooking, produce electricity, and replace coal and oil in factories and motor vehicles. To the oil exporters, a commercial-scale find of natural gas needs to be 100 times larger than a find that could be considered cost-effective for local use. The key is building the infrastructure to bring natural gas to the large markets waiting for it in developing countries.[47]

Petroleum geologists have already found substantial reserves of natural gas in some 50 developing countries, with many others holding high promise. Many of these nations have treated gas as a waste by-product of petroleum production and burned it off without capturing any useful energy. The 21 billion cubic meters of gas Nigeria flared in 1990 represented enough energy to meet all the country's current commercial energy needs, along with those of neighboring Benin, Cameroon, Ghana, Niger, and Togo. But oil exporters are not the only ones who waste natural gas. India burned off more than 5 billion cubic meters of natural gas in 1990, enough energy to save the country nearly $700 million on oil import bills.[48]

Natural gas can be substituted for nearly any energy source used today. According to studies by researchers in India and at the World Bank, compressed natural gas is a cost-effective replacement for gasoline and diesel as a motor vehicle fuel. Gas can also replace oil and coal in industrial processes and be used for cooking and for water and space heating in buildings. Propane, often found along with natural gas, can play an important role in reducing urban use of charcoal and wood for cooking. Producing electricity from natural gas, particularly in advanced combined cycle gas turbines, is usually less expensive than oil- or coal-fired plants in developing countries, according to the World Bank.[49]

Just as North America and Europe have witnessed a gas renaissance in recent years, so too have countries in the South. Government and private engineers have drawn up plans for vast networks of gas pipelines that would connect developing countries. In Latin America, a project to pipe Bolivian gas to southern Brazil and northern Argentina received its initial go-ahead in 1992. And in Southeast Asia, Thailand hopes to build a gas grid with neighboring Malaysia and Myanmar.[50]

Even China is reconsidering natural gas as part of its effort to slow the growth in oil and coal use. In early 1992, the government decided to build a pipeline from a large offshore gas field discovered during an unsuccessful search for oil in 1983. Gas commonly accompanies not only oil but also coal, suggesting that China is well endowed with natural gas too. One Chinese multiagency group estimates the country's gas resource at about half as big as its enormous proven coal reserves. Recent experience appears to indicate this is correct: in one region in north-central China, every well drilled in the first five months of 1991 struck natural gas.[51]

Developing countries also have abundant supplies of renewable energy resources, such as sunlight, wind, biological sources, and heat from deep within the earth, that are increasingly economical sources. The past decade has seen dramatic technological improvement in the use of these renewables, trimming costs for solar and wind energy systems, for example, by 66–90 percent. Electricity sources such as solar thermal power

and photovoltaics could be the least expensive route for developing countries, predicts World Bank economist Dennis Anderson, partly due to the higher insolation found at low latitudes, which allows more energy to be produced by each system installed. (Land availabilty is not a problem: for solar energy to double total current Third World energy consumption, only 0.2 percent of developing-country land area would be needed.) Many renewables are already less expensive than fossil fuels or nuclear power once social and environmental costs—such as air pollution, resource depletion, and government subsidies—are included.[52]

To take advantage of renewable energy's potential quickly, energy planners need to search out uses that are viable today even without including pollution costs. Such investments can develop the in-country expertise, both private and public, and the technological and business infrastructure needed to deploy renewables on a large scale in the future.

Using the sun to heat water is already a cost-effective way for societies to save electricity. Total capital costs for electric water heating are on average nearly one third higher than those for solar hot water when the cost of building power plants is included, according to data collected by the Office of Technology Assessment. Many developing countries have seen solar industries spring up. Residents of Botswana's capital, Gaborone, have purchased and installed more than 3,000 solar water heaters, displacing nearly 15 percent of the residential electricity demand. Colombia, Jordan, and Kenya also have strong domestic solar hot water industries.[53]

For grid-connected power supplies, new wind generators, based on variable-speed turbines, and geothermal power plants can produce electricity at a cost comparable to coal-fired power plants. India leads the developing world in wind energy, with 38 megawatts installed by the beginning of 1992. Aided by a Danish joint venture, the country plans to install 1,000 megawatts of domestically manufactured wind turbines by the end of the decade. Excellent wind resources exist in Central and southern South America, northern Africa, and in parts of South Asia, and could provide more than 10 percent of developing-country electricity.[54]

Geothermal energy produced 21 percent of the electricity in the Philippines, 18 percent in El Salvador, and 11 percent in Kenya in 1990. Yet heat from deep within the earth can play a role in other countries as well, as large, untapped resources exist in Bolivia, Costa Rica, Ethiopia, India, and Thailand. Another two dozen countries appear to have equally good, though less explored, potential.[55]

More than 60,000 photovoltaic lighting units have been installed in recent years in some dozen developing countries.

Rural areas of developing countries are also proving to be ready for renewable energy technologies. In Mexico, the National Solidarity program, a government agency that works to improve economic and social conditions in rural areas, has been deploying wind, photovoltaic, and small hydroelectric power technologies in villages. And the program is converting existing diesel generators to "hybrid" systems that combine diesel with renewable sources. These increase reliability while lowering the amount of fuel that needs to be hauled over long distances.[56]

Villagers are starting to use photovoltaic cells to power lights, radios, and even televisions, needs that are currently met with kerosene lamps and disposable or rechargeable batteries. More than 60,000 photovoltaic lighting units have been installed in recent years in some dozen developing countries, such as Colombia, the Dominican Republic, Mexico, and Sri Lanka. Still, at current prices (roughly $500 for a 50-watt system), only a small minority can afford photovoltaics. One survey in the Dominican Republic estimated that just 20 percent of nonelectrified rural households could afford a system even with a seven-year loan. Price declines would bring in another chunk, as could smaller systems, but governments will need to continue their support to ensure complete rural electrification, while focusing less on line extension and more on dispersed renewables.[57]

Biomass energy sources supply 35 percent of developing-country energy but could contribute more, particularly if existing amounts of agricultural and industrial wastes were better utilized and efforts to increase biomass production met greater success. For example, sugar operations, found in virtually every developing country, can become more profitable by converting into electricity the waste from extracting sugar from cane.[58]

Although this waste, known as bagasse, is often burned in boilers that use the heat to fuel the sugar extracting process, modern combustion systems can make even better use of bagasse. For each ton of bagasse, a typical sugar mill boiler produces enough steam to fuel the plant's operation along with 15–25 kilowatt-hours of electricity. Modern steam turbines, already in use in some Brazilian plants, increase electricity output eightfold while maintaining steam production. Gas turbines designed to run on biomass, which are currently being commercialized, could raise electricity output by more than thirtyfold over today's standard boiler (though steam production would fall slightly). If sugar mills burned all their residues using advanced gas turbines, they would meet more than a third of the total current electricity needs in developing countries.[59]

Hundreds of millions of hectares of degraded lands could be returned to productivity and rural economic development could be promoted by planting fast-growing trees and other crops suitable for energy use, according to the U.N. Solar Energy Group for Environment and Development. Any such attempt to boost biofuels production, however, would require major investments by governments and private companies. Past efforts to entice villagers to plant more trees have failed more often than not, particularly if the undertaking was packaged as an energy project. Villagers are often hesitant to plant trees for energy even if they are suffering from fuelwood shortages, partly due to conflicts over landownership and use. And men, who control land use decisions, want crops that can be sold in markets instead of those needed at home, while it is women who are responsible for obtaining cooking fuel. (See Chapter 4.)[60]

Agroforestry techniques, which combine food and wood production, offer a way to boost both food yields and fuelwood and fodder harvests. Research in Kenya and Nigeria has shown that mixing corn and leucaena trees can increase corn production 39–83 percent over a corn-alone field, while achieving wood yields of at least 5 tons per hectare. Even though agroforestry can supply additional fuel for landholders, the poorest of the poor are landless and will continue to face problems meeting their cooking energy needs. Indeed, it is difficult to divorce rural energy problems and their solutions from landownership, economic equity, and agricultural policy transformations.[61]

Together with efficiency improve-ments on the demand side, an energy system run on renewable energy resources and natural gas has the potential to meet the needs of developing countries, according to Amulya Reddy and his colleagues at the Indian Institute of Science in Bangalore. In a blueprint for what a sustainable, efficient energy economy could look like, they crafted a scenario that could meet the state of Karnataka's electricity needs in the nineties for only $6 billion of investment, rather than the $17.4 billion a government committee had proposed to spend on large hydroelectric, coal-fired, and nuclear power plants.[62]

Among the new supplies in Reddy's plan are natural gas, solar hot water, and the better use of existing sugar mill wastes and other biomass. One key to the proposal is redirecting energy investments toward improving the lot of the poor, while moving away from energy-intensive industrialization. Unlike the state's plan, which foresees continuing power shortages despite the enormous investment, Reddy's proposal would electrify all homes in the state and employ more people, while boosting carbon dioxide emissions by only one fiftieth the amount the government plan envisioned.[63]

ENERGY POLICIES FOR DEVELOPMENT

Even though technologies exist to allow developing countries to build a sustainable energy system, extensive barriers—from entrenched special interests that have a bias toward large supply-side projects, to consumers who are ignorant of or unable to finance alternatives—have prevented their widespread adoption. To overcome these obstacles, governments in both the South and the North will need to change their long-held assumptions and priorities about energy, and the numerous policies that have followed from them.[64]

The conventional approach to energy looks not at maximizing energy services but at increasing supplies. Yet as China learned with its success in cutting energy growth in the eighties, investing in energy efficiency can yield handsome rewards that developing countries can hardly afford to miss. Although policies across the board need reforming, there are four priority areas: charge accurate prices for energy, redirect investments and infrastructure toward energy efficiency and new supplies, refocus international energy assistance, and strengthen energy institutions and expertise in developing countries.

Substantial price hikes may need to be joined by efforts to improve end-use efficiency.

With energy prices of traditional supplies often held down by governments, efficiency improvements and alternative sources become less attractive. Farmers in India, for example, pay a flat fee or extremely low tariffs for electricity used for irrigation; the subsidy costs the central Indian government nearly $3 billion a year, and it removes any incentive to improve efficiency. Estimating that developing countries spend more than $49 billion a year subsidizing energy, the World Bank has given energy price reform its highest priority, believing that once prices convey full economic and environmental costs, optimal levels of efficiency will occur.[65]

This first step of raising prices is a formidable one, however. The political reality in developing countries—where

inexpensive energy, particularly electricity, is often considered a right—means that it is very difficult to raise prices. Indeed, substantial price hikes may need to be joined by efforts to improve end-use efficiency, so that the final cost of the energy service, whether cooking, lighting, or pumping water, remains unchanged or actually declines.

A great deal can be done to improve efficiency and boost alternatives. In India's case, it would be less expensive for the government to retrofit irrigation pumps than to fund the enormous subsidies for wasted electricity; similarly, subsidizing the use of efficient lighting technologies would cost less than providing below-cost electricity to poorer households and building new power plants.[66]

Governments can help move energy-efficient products through a wide range of programs for technology development, testing, information, product labelling, and standards. Although standards for appliances have been adopted in some industrial countries, they do not exist yet in developing ones. Brazil does have a testing program, however, and Thailand and the Philippines are moving toward adopting standards. Publicizing results through labelling requirements can push manufacturers to improve efficiency. Soon after Brazil adopted such a program, the average efficiency level for the standard refrigerator rose to that of the previous year's most efficient model. Similarly, standards for new buildings and motor vehicles can help push improved technologies into the marketplace.[67]

Understanding the energy implications of an industrial project from the beginning is essential to capturing the efficiency potential. One novel proposal that could make many standards obsolete is the Energy Efficiency Impact Statement (EEIS) proposed by Jayant Sathaye and Ashok Gadgil, scientists at the Lawrence Berkeley Laboratory in

California. The EEIS would require builders of new facilities in energy-intensive industries, such as cement and steel, and producers of energy-consuming devices, such as automobiles and appliances, to compare the lifetime energy implications of their projects with those of available alternatives. If a facility has to pay more up front to use or produce an energy-efficient technology that is cost-effective overall, then the utility company, a government body, or an international aid institution could provide the additional capital needed.[68]

The disproportionate investment by electrical utilities in building power plants—and the resulting financial and production crises they are now in—also needs reordering. Utilities could adopt a planning process known as integrated resource planning that has been successfully pioneered by U.S. utilities and regulators. This requires power companies considering new generating capacity to compare improvements in customer energy efficiency to supply options, whether owned by the utility or privately. If efficiency improvements prove less expensive, utilities invest money in obtaining such gains. They also can invest in alternative supply options, such as solar hot water heaters, that cost-effectively reduce electricity use. And if environmental costs are included in the calculations, other renewable supplies may prove economical.[69]

In late 1991, Thailand became one of the first developing countries to adopt a utility-run efficiency program based on the concept of integrated resource planning. By 1997, the country's utilities expect to save 225 megawatts of electricity capacity by investing $183 million in efficiency—less than half what it would cost to build an equal amount of new electric generating capacity. Although the current program is expected to reduce the projected increase in electricity use by only 4 percent, studies show that

Thailand could push that figure to nearly 25 percent over 10 years.[70]

For rural electricity, extension of transmission lines can still be justified in many areas, but decentralized systems, whether small hydropower plants or renewable hybrid facilities, can also play a greater role. And directing more official support to household photovoltaics could help fill the persistent unmet demand for electric lighting. Although it may be impossible for a utility to manage thousands of such dispersed systems, it can assist in financing their purchase. Some rural banks are already offering small loans, and consumer cooperatives have established revolving credit funds for homeowners to purchase photovoltaic lighting kits. A utility-established fund of $10 million could finance 87,000 photovoltaic systems in 10 years.[71]

Sadly, foreign assistance is now doing as much to hinder the needed energy transition in developing countries as to help it. Most important to developing countries are the activities of the multilateral development banks, especially the World Bank. While these agencies provide at most 10 percent of the roughly $60 billion of overall investment annually made in developing countries' energy sectors, they do supply the "seal of approval" that private banks usually require before providing loans.[72]

Based on their loan portfolios, the multilateral development banks appear to equate energy with expanding electric power, to the virtual exclusion of efficiency. Eighty percent of the $54 billion the World Bank lent for energy projects since 1948 has been for power projects, while energy as a whole has accounted for nearly one fifth of total Bank lending. The regional development banks for Africa, Asia, and Latin America dedicate even higher percentages to power and energy. Less than 1 percent of the $67 billion loaned for energy by all the development banks between 1980 and

1990 went to improving end-use energy efficiency. The World Bank even foresees funding for efficiency remaining at only 1 percent of energy lending through 1995.[73]

Changes in priorities are needed, and at the World Bank they may be afoot. Late in 1991, the Bank formed an alternative energy unit in its Asian section to encourage efficiency and renewable investments. And in July 1992, energy staff presented a new policy paper to the Bank's executive directors laying out the strategy it will follow for future lending to electric utilities. Disturbed by the proposal's reliance on old, failed measures, the Bank's directors refused to approve it, requesting that more emphasis be placed on efficiency. By October 1992, the Bank's directors were pleased enough with the redrafted paper to adopt it as Bank policy.[74]

Still lacking in the new strategy, however, is the integration of energy policy with broader development goals. The development banks can only fulfill their mandated responsibilities by giving up their destructive practice of simply providing energy supplies, and moving instead toward a strategy that ties investments in all sectors together. Rather than relying only on politically difficult price hikes to pursue efficiency, the banks could encourage the use of integrated resource planning—as the Asian Development Bank has recently started to do—while investing directly in energy efficiency.[75]

Developing-country government ministries and utility companies are hesitant to request large loans for efficiency or renewables technologies with which they have little experience. So far, the Global Environment Facility (GEF) (an international fund set up in 1990 under the direction of the World Bank, the United Nations Development Programme, and the United Nations Environment Programme) has taken on the role of financing efficiency and renewables projects through making grants designed to slow global warming.[76]

The GEF has supported some promising initiatives, including a $7-million project for household photovoltaics in Zimbabwe and a $3.3-million project for energy from sugarcane residues in Mauritius. And it is considering several other worthy ideas: installing efficient lighting in Mexico, capturing methane from coal mines in China, financing electricity end-use efficiency improvements in Thailand, developing biomass-fueled gas turbines in Brazil, and promoting a variety of renewable energy technologies in India.[77]

But by including them in its portfolio, the GEF sustains the false notion that these projects are not economical on their own, but only as a means to reduce carbon emissions. Also, the GEF's total funds—$1.3 billion for three years, of which only 40–50 percent can be energy-related—are not up to the task of reforming energy development. The multilateral development banks give 30 times as much per year to traditional energy projects. The institution's real impact will be felt once the development banks' entire energy portfolios follow the pattern of today's GEF grants in emphasizing efficiency and renewables.[78]

Each country needs stronger institutions to coordinate sustainable energy activities between different ministries and the private sector, to ensure that sufficient data on energy use and requirements are obtained, and to guarantee that locally based research and development is undertaken. Such national institutions and programs can be financed through a modest tax on fossil fuels, as Ghana funds its independent energy board. In early 1992, the Thai parliament levied a tax on petroleum products and natural gas, equivalent to just over 1¢ per liter of petroleum product, that will provide some $50–60 million annually for investments in efficiency and renewables. Over five years, the Thai government expects the tax, private businesses, utilities, and a proposed GEF project to push total investment in energy efficiency and renewables to $500 million.[79]

Energy taxes set by the carbon content of fuel are another tool for governments to redirect energy investments. Such carbon taxes would encourage research and investment in efficiency and renewables in developing countries. Carbon taxes in the North could provide funds for developing countries to purchase advanced technologies and, more important, domestic manufacturing capability. The Italian government has recommended that European nations dedicate part of the revenue from a proposed European Community carbon tax to sustainable energy investments in the South.[80]

Prompted by the concern in the North over global warming, developing countries are starting to reexamine the connections between energy and sustainable development. Indeed, the signing of the climate change convention by 116 developing countries during UNCED in June 1992 underscores this, committing them to explore ways to mitigate climate change while preparing inventories of their emissions. Northern countries agreed to adopt policies to limit emissions of greenhouse gases, and, through the GEF, to help developing countries slow their emission increases. So far very little new funding has become available,

however, and the world community has made no real commitment to help developing countries blaze a new energy path. It is worth noting that in the eighties, Northern countries failed to supply the resources needed to fulfill promises made at the U.N. Conference on New and Renewable Sources of Energy in Nairobi in 1981.[81]

Yet developing countries desperately need a new energy path—for reasons quite apart from the fate the earth's climate. Simply reducing the cost of energy services, as well as the environmental and health costs of air pollution, would allow developing countries to invest in more pressing areas. In Brazil, to cite just one example, about 30 percent of children are malnourished and 78 percent do not complete primary school. With the technologies of efficiency and renewables now available and with the policies for their dissemination that have proved effective, Brazil could shift $2–3 billion a year out of the power sector and roughly double funding for nutrition, preventive health care, and water and sanitation programs.[82]

Such investments may not be feasible without the savings generated by a more efficient energy system. Indeed, an energy strategy based on efficiency and low-polluting sources is a cornerstone of the sustainable development process—and necessary if developing countries are to improve living standards for everyone. As countries move toward this new approach, their energy economies will shift from obstructing development to enabling it.

7

Rediscovering Rail

Marcia D. Lowe

When the first commercial steam railroad was opened in England in 1825, it sparked a transport revolution across the world. The new iron horse suddenly transformed industry. In a matter of decades, it changed the face of both city and countryside forever. When electric rail systems were introduced at the end of the nineteenth century, people in cities could travel farther and faster than ever before. Columbia University historian Kenneth T. Jackson observes of the immmensely popular electric streetcar that, by comparison, "the automobile, which was invented at about the same time, was a late bloomer."[1]

Once private cars became widely available, however, it was not long before they overtook rail. In the United States, the shift took place in a single generation. Other governments also began spending most of their transport funds on highways after World War II, although the gap between their road and rail investments was not nearly as wide. By the late seventies and eighties, a global race toward automobile ownership was taking place, including in developing nations, where only a tiny elite could afford it.

Combined with a boom in air travel, the steady surge in road transport has left many countries' rail systems carrying fewer passengers and goods than they did when this century began. Even where train service is still frequent and reliable—in Japan and much of Europe—governments have hastened the decline of rail by chronically underinvesting in their networks.

By failing to invest adequately in rail, governments have missed important opportunities to strengthen their economies and protect the environment. In the United States alone, switching 5 percent of highway driving to electrified intercity rail could save more than 160 million barrels of oil each year—one sixth the amount imported from the Middle East. And for every ton of goods switched from roads to rail in the United Kingdom, the amount of carbon emitted per kilometer would drop by 88 percent, reducing the nation's contribution to global warming. Also untapped are the social benefits of this form of transport: quiet, convenient rail service can improve the quality of life in cities and give people who cannot drive a way to get around.[2]

BENEFITS OF RAIL

The term rail encompasses many kinds of trains. For passengers, urban rail includes heavy rail or metro (running largely in tunnels and on overhead structures), light rail (the modern trolley), and commuter rail (sometimes called regional or suburban service). Most intercity rail travel is on national passenger networks. Some of these include high-speed lines, in which powerful, aerodynamic trains race between cities along specially designed tracks. Freight trains operate on conventional tracks, most of which are also used by passenger trains.

Many transport problems of the twentieth century can be addressed by creating a diverse system in which rail plays a major role. All rail options have compelling advantages over highway and air transport. These include several economic and environmental benefits, many of which are linked to rail's efficient use of energy. Others stem from the potential for rail to relieve highway and air traffic congestion. Still others result from the ability of rail corridors to induce optimal use of land. In addition, rail offers the incalculable social value of far lower accident rates than road transport, and of serving people who are otherwise left out of a system that caters overwhelmingly to drivers.

Rail's capacity for saving energy is one of its most important potential contributions to the environment and to national economies. Trains are far more energy-efficient than most other modes of transport. Measured by the energy required to move one passenger one kilometer under U.S. commuting conditions, an intercity train uses 948 kilojoules—one third the energy used by a commercial airplane, and one sixth the energy of an automobile with a sole occupant. Equivalent travel by commuter rail uses some 1,269 kilojoules per passenger-kilometer, and by urban rail, an average of 1,174.[3]

Moving freight by rail is also more energy-efficient than using trucks on highways. In the United States, intercity freight movement by truck requires 2,300 kilojoules per ton per kilometer, more than eight times as much as rail. The advantage of hauling more freight by rail is particularly apparent in developing countries. Older truck models commonly used in the Third World are much less efficient than trucks in industrial countries; they require 1.5–2.5 times as much energy per ton-kilometer, and efficiency is further lost to poor maintenance, bad road conditions, and traffic congestion.[4]

Rail can greatly reduce the portion of a country's oil consumption that goes toward transport.

Dependence on oil to fuel the road transport sector places great strains on a nation's balance of payments and makes economies vulnerable to swings in the world price of petroleum. As an alternative to private cars, rail can greatly reduce the portion of a country's oil consumption that goes toward transport. In industrial countries, transport typically accounts for some 30 percent of total oil use, but in China, where bicycles and rail dominate the transport system, only 8 percent of total energy goes to the transport sector. In Eastern Europe, where rail ridership is high and private car ownership low, the figure is 10 percent. Although inefficient energy use in these countries' industrial, commercial, and residential sectors accounts for some of this difference, reliance on rail is a major factor.[5]

Dramatic oil savings are possible through electrification of diesel rail lines. Western Europe has the highest concentration of electrified rail, ranging from 99 percent of Switzerland's inter-city network to 55 percent of Italy's and 26 percent of the United Kingdom's. Thirty-five percent of Japan's intercity network is electrified, while the United States lags behind with 1 percent. Electrification minimizes oil use by rail since only small portions of national electric grids rely on oil combustion. In the former West Germany, for instance, 38 percent of the railways were electrified by 1987, and only 2 percent of the electricity was generated by oil.[6]

Not only national economies but also regional and local ones are affected by oil dependence. In the United States, the states with the least public transport consume nearly three times as much fuel in transport, per household, as states with extensive rail services. A study by the Los Angeles Regional Transportation Commission shows that 85¢ of every dollar local residents spend on gasoline leaves the regional economy, much of it even going outside the country. Out of each dollar spent on public transport fare, by contrast, an estimated 80¢ goes toward transit workers' wages, which in turn buys more than $3.80 in goods and services in the region.[7]

Because lower energy use translates into less air pollution, an expanded role for rail would help improve air quality. Nitrogen oxides and nonmethane hydrocarbons from transport sources react in the presence of heat and sunlight to form ozone, the main component of smog. Carbon dioxide, nitrous oxide, and methane (released during oil production and processing) are greenhouse gases, and carbon monoxide contributes indirectly to the greenhouse effect by aiding the buildup of methane. Other effects of all these pollutants range from headaches, pneumonia, cancer, and permanent lung damage to added stress for people with heart disease. They also contribute to corrosion of buildings and damage to forests and crops.[8]

Emissions from all forms of transport parallel each mode's use of energy. Accordingly, the most energy-efficient passenger rail mode, electrified intercity rail, emits the least pollution. The only way a person needing to get somewhere can create less air pollution is by walking or biking. Electric rail has an added advantage: the emissions do not come out of a tailpipe but from a power plant, where they are less likely to find their way into people's lungs. Power plant emissions are also easier to monitor and control.

The extensive damage done by air pollution makes it clear that the costs of oil-intensive road transport far exceed the price of obtaining fuel. In the United States, annual damage to human health and the environment from vehicular emissions is estimated as up to $93 billion. A conservative calculation for the European Community puts the costs of transport-related air pollution at an average of 0.5 percent of gross domestic product (GDP). Developing countries, with their fragile economies, can ill afford such costs; without effective controls, by the end of the nineties an estimated 300–400 million people in Third World cities will be exposed to unhealthy and often dangerous levels of air pollution.[9]

Greater reliance on rail would help alleviate traffic congestion on highways and in airports, both of which translate into major economic costs from reduced worker productivity and delays in goods delivery. The Texas Traffic Institute estimates that in 1988 traffic congestion in U.S. urban areas cost more than $400 per vehicle, and $750 per vehicle in cities in the Northeast. According to the U.S. Office of Technology Assessment, some federal experts unofficially estimate that congestion costs are now equal to if not greater than the amount that federal, state, and local governments spend on highways each year.[10]

A calculation by the U.S. General Accounting Office found that at the current rate, traffic congestion on roads will triple in 15 years even if road capacity is increased by 20 percent. International experience suggests it is more cost-effective to relieve highway congestion by developing a comprehensive rail system instead of building more lanes of roadway. The European Conference of Ministers of Transport estimates that the financial return on investment in highways now being built in France is 10 percent and the social return (putting a dollar value on time saved and convenience) is 20 percent. Similar estimates for the TGV—France's two high-speed rail lines—are a financial return of 12–17 percent and a social return of 20–33 percent.[11]

Shifting freight off crowded roads and onto railways would further relieve congestion. More than one third of all U.S. freight already moves by rail, yet at relatively little extra cost many more goods could do so. In 1989, Federal Railroad Administrator Gilbert Carmichael estimated that the U.S. freight rail system was being used at only a quarter of its capacity. Railroads can triple their mainline track capacity by improving their train control technologies, and they can increase it by up to six times by installing a parallel track along a segment of existing track. Unlike highways, which require median strips, shoulders, and buffers, new tracks can usually be fit into existing rights-of-way.[12]

Air traffic congestion is another costly problem that can be addressed affordably by rail. Flight delays from crowded air and runway space cost airlines and businesses at least $5 billion annually in the United States. Electrification of the conventional New York–Washington rail corridor enabled trains to travel up to 200 kilometers an hour, which has resulted in Amtrak, the U.S. national passenger rail service, carrying more passengers than any airline on that route. Using rail to relieve air and highway congestion has a double reward: since large-city rail stations tend to be downtown, passengers are more likely to use public transport to reach hotels, business meetings, and tourist sites.[13]

Rail requires far less physical space than highways or airports do, and so displaces far fewer homes and jobs.

An expanded role for rail could make expensive new airports unnecessary, since so much air space in existing facilities is tied up by flights making short trips that easily could be made by train. Electrification and track improvements now under way on the U.S. Northeast corridor (previously in effect only between Washington, D.C., and New Haven, Connecticut) could do away with the need for Boston's controversial proposed second airport. Amtrak and the Coalition of Northeast Governors estimate that electrifying the Boston–New York corridor will displace 50 flights per day and free up 10 gates at Boston's Logan Airport. The rail improvements will cost an estimated $800 million, about one fifth as much as the proposed airport.[14]

Another environmental and economic benefit that is seldom appreciated is railways' modest appetite for land. Rail requires far less physical space than highways or airports do, and so displaces far fewer homes and jobs. Two railroad tracks can carry the same number of people in an hour as 16 lanes of highway, taking up only 15 meters of right-of-way, compared with roughly 122 meters.

Highways occupy far more space than typically is recognized. In 1989, the Department of Transport in the United Kingdom produced a roadbuilding program requiring construction of 2,557 kilometers of highways and trunk roads. One observer graphically depicted the area needed as equal to a 267-lane highway from London to Edinburgh with a parking lot the size of Berkshire at each end.[15]

Similarly, railways' slim space requirements circumvent many of the environmental hazards posed by airports. The massive expanse of continuous land required by an airport produces excessive stormwater runoff—rainwater that flows over land, often becoming contaminated with chemicals deposited by motor vehicles—from hectare upon hectare of impervious rooftops, runways, roads, and parking lots. The runoff threatens to pollute the water bodies it eventually flows into or, if allowed to reach an excessive level without seeping into unpaved terrain, to flood low-lying areas. To create an immense parcel of land, airport construction projects often rechannel rivers, fill in wetlands, or otherwise disturb fragile natural areas. And they may excavate low-value areas that contain landfills and polluted industrial sites, dredging up contaminants.[16]

Railways hold far greater potential than either airports or highways to encourage sustainable land use patterns in a given region. Construction of an airport or highway often pulls future development out and away from a city. Soon, low-density commercial strips with large parking lots dominate the landscape. As new homes and businesses sprawl, it becomes increasingly difficult to move around without a car. Rail-focused growth, by contrast, lends itself to more valuable economic development than the typical highway offerings of strip malls, motels, and fast food outlets. Moreover, a rail station placed downtown can unify a city instead of competing with it.

Rapidly expanding metropolitan areas can use rail to help give a clear and practical structure to anticipated growth. A long-range planning study for Montgomery County, Maryland (a county of 740,000 people near Washington, D.C.), found that even if growth slowed considerably but continued in the usual auto- and highway-oriented pattern, the resulting traffic congestion would stifle further economic development. In contrast, focusing most new growth in pedestrian- and bicycle-friendly clusters along an expanded rail and bus system—and revising commuter subsidies to discourage the use of cars—would enable the county to double its current number of jobs and households without exacerbating traffic congestion.[17]

Rail's many benefits include several advantages that, though difficult to quantify, are invaluable to society. One of these is safety. Rail's accident record is much better than that of road transport, despite disproportionate public attention given to the occasional railway incident. In the United States, passenger rail is nearly 18 times as safe as private car travel, with 0.4 deaths per 1 billion passenger-kilometers, compared with 7 deaths for private automobiles. The risk of being injured or killed in a road accident is 29 times as great as that for rail in the former West Germany and the Netherlands, and 80 times as great in France.[18]

In addition to incalculable health damage and loss of human life, road accidents impose financial burdens. Measures of these costs vary considerably, but may include lost wages; property damage; medical, legal, and administrative charges; and emergency services. The British Department of Transport puts the cost of each of the country's 5,000–6,000 annual road deaths at $1.3

million. Figured as a percentage of gross national product (GNP), estimates of motor vehicle accident costs range from 1.2 percent for several developing countries to 2.4 percent for France, 2.6 for the former West Germany, and 3 percent for Australia. A recent study for the U.S. Federal Highway Administration included estimates of the monetary worth of pain, suffering, and lost quality of life in its tally of the costs of U.S. road accidents in 1988. It arrived at a total of $358 billion, 8 percent of GNP.[19]

The incidence of freight train accidents in the United States is low and declining; between 1980 and 1987 the accident rate per million kilometers fell from 7.3 to 2.9. This is largely the result of annual investments of $4 billion in renovations and maintenance and $3 billion in upgrading track and equipment. Not only are freight trucks less safe than rail, a study by the Organisation for Economic Co-operation and Development (OECD) found that heavy goods vehicles are more frequently involved than other road vehicles in fatal accidents.[20]

Another of rail's intangible benefits is its potential contribution to the quality of life. For rail passengers, the quiet, rapid ride is a welcome break from chaotic traffic jams. A rail-based transport system also benefits people who do not ride trains; while communities that are dominated by highways and airports risk becoming mere throughways for people and goods in transit, those in which rail plays a major role are less likely to be disrupted. Interurban rail seldom runs right through residential neighborhoods—usually operating at a distance from settled areas—but when it is nearby, it makes a less intrusive neighbor than either highways or airports. And rail traffic is confined to the track and therefore does not bring in congestion that can spill onto nearby arteries, as happens with road traffic.

Rail creates less noise than airports or highways. Aircraft noise draws complaints from communities more than 60 kilometers from an airport. In regions crisscrossed by highways and major roads, traffic noise affects large numbers of people. It is estimated that in 13 OECD countries in Europe, the dominant source of noise is road traffic, which nearly 90 percent of people hear within their homes. Effects of excessive noise on human health include hearing loss, stress, and interference with rest and sleep. Studies comparing the noise generated by rail versus roads have shown that when carrying the same load of freight or passengers at the same speed, rail is on average half to three fourths as loud as road transport. For freight transport, the greater goods-hauling capacity of each locomotive represents a dramatic difference in the amount and distribution of noise; for example, moving 200 containers of a given size across the United States would require three to five locomotives versus 200 trucks.[21]

A final social benefit of rail is that it provides a viable alternative to people who do not or cannot drive. Few people in low-income developing countries own cars (the number of people per car is 55 in Peru, 151 in Nigeria, and 367 in India). Even in the auto-dependent United States, nearly 10 million households are without a motor vehicle. And an estimated 10–14 percent of the population in most countries has some physical disability, often rendering them unable to drive. Children and the elderly, many of whom also cannot drive, dominate the demographics in much of the world. All these nondrivers have inferior access to jobs, education, and vital services in car-dominated transport systems. Urban and interurban rail—along with local and regional bus service—therefore provide the only practical transport open to a significant share of the world's people.[22]

The Downhill Slide of Trains

The twentieth century has witnessed a general shrinking of the role of rail transport in most countries where it had flourished before the advent of the automobile. In the worst cases, rail is no longer a serious option for transport of passengers or goods. Even in the best cases, governments have failed to sustain adequate investment in national rail networks, forcing them to close some lines and reduce the frequency of trains.

Nowhere was the historical shift away from rail more abrupt than in the United States. In the 1890s, U.S. street railways carried 2 billion passengers a year—more than twice the number served in the rest of the world's cities combined. Then, in the first three decades of this century, more than half of U.S. families acquired automobiles. The massive urban rail network was given a swift kick out the door by a group of corporations in the auto, oil, and rubber tire industries. From the mid-thirties through the forties, several large companies—including General Motors, Standard Oil of California, Phillips Petroleum, Mack Manufacturing (of Mack trucks), and Firestone Tire and Rubber—schemed to acquire and junk the trolley systems of U.S. cities and replace them with buses. A federal court in 1949 convicted the companies of criminal antitrust violations, but it was too late; the rail networks were long gone.[23]

When the Interstate Highway System was established in 1956, the federal government was set to make the vast bulk of its surface transport investments in roads. Between 1958 and 1989, federal spending on highways totalled an estimated $213 billion, compared with an estimated $23 billion for railroads. In 1990, the federal government spent $13 billion on highways, 22 times what it spent on rail.[24]

Nowhere was the historical shift away from rail more abrupt than in the United States.

The combination of popular fascination with cars, federal disinvestment in rail, and outright conspiracy dealt a serious blow to U.S. train travel. With the exception of New York, Chicago, and other large cities that rely extensively on metropolitan rail systems, trains now play a small role in urban transport, and the intercity rail network accounts for less than 1 percent of passenger transport between cities. In 1925, rail carried nearly 80 percent of intercity freight; in 1990, its share was 38 percent. (Despite this steep drop, the United States still moves more of its freight by rail than do its economic competitors, which are geographically much more compact; in Japan the share is 4 percent, in the former West Germany, 18 percent, and in France, 20 percent).[25]

West European countries never abandoned their rail systems when the automobile became popular; intercity trains, metros, trolleys, and new light rail systems remain an established part of the landscape and people's life-styles even though car ownership is high. The national railways, the largest employer in several countries, represent some of the most comprehensive rail networks in the world. In recent years, however, West European rails have suffered from an investment bias toward highways. Over the past two decades, 18 European OECD member countries have spent about three times as much on roads as on rail. Yet they are still far more committed to rail than the United States is, devoting on average 1–1.5 percent of GDP to rail compared with the U.S. range of 0.04–0.07 percent.[26]

In Western Europe, freight transport is the area in which the role of rail has diminished most. Between 1970 and 1990, rail's share of freight traffic in 14 countries declined from 31 to 17 percent, while roads increased their share from 55 to 74 percent (with inland waterways accounting for the remainder). The planned European single market threatens to heighten the region's already-extensive reliance on road transport for moving freight. The European Commission estimates that between 1990 and 2010 the volume of road freight will jump by 42 percent. Alarmed about the prospect of "completely unmanageable" highway congestion, the European Community's executive proposes shifting freight movement as much as possible from roads to water and rail.[27]

Compared with the United States and Western Europe, Eastern Europe and the former Soviet Union have surrendered little of their rail capacity to the highway era. Lower consumer buying power, public policies that discouraged private car ownership, and relatively small government investments in highway transport have kept the region's rail systems largely intact. Networks are generally very extensive, though often more run down than in the West. The former Soviet rail network covers some 150,000 kilometers, second only to nearly 200,-000 kilometers of track in the United States. Before the breakup of the Soviet Union, nearly 45 percent of passenger traffic travelled by rail. And almost 80 percent of freight was carried by rail, a higher share than in any other country. (See Table 7–1.)

Unfortunately, the former Soviet Republics and countries of Eastern

Table 7–1. Comparison of Rail Networks, Selected Countries, Circa 1990

Country	Length of Rail Network	Share of Total Freight Traffic	Share of Total Passenger Traffic
	(kilometers)	(percent)	
United States	199,938	38	0.4
Soviet Union	147,359	79	45
India	61,976	52	41
China	54,083	80[1]	56
Japan	42,981	4	35
France	34,322	20	10
West Germany	27,045	18	6
United Kingdom	16,926	6	6
Italy	16,030	10	7
Czechoslovakia	13,106	78	31
Switzerland	5,020	40	13
Netherlands	2,828	2	6

[1]percent of inland freight.
SOURCES: Length of rail network from U.N. Economic Commission for Europe, *Annual Bulletin of Transport Statistics for Europe* (Geneva: 1991), and from International Road Federation, *World Road Statistics 1991* (Washington, D.C.: 1991); China rail network from *Jane's World Railways 1990–91* (London: 1990); percentages of passenger and freight based on International Road Federation, *World Road Statistics 1991*, and on International Civil Aviation Organisation, *Traffic: Commercial Air Carriers, 1986–1990*, Digest of Statistics, No. 379 (Montreal: 1991).

Europe seem eager to shift to road transport. Nearly all railways in Eastern Europe have lost passenger ridership; the average decrease in each country was nearly 14 percent between 1989 and 1990. Popular sentiment toward public transport is tainted by a tendency to associate it with the despised former regimes. There is also a distinct clamor toward car ownership, the icon of success in the West. The *Financial Times* reported in 1991 that twice as many cars were sold in unified Germany as in West Germany the previous year—even though unification increased population only 30 percent.[28]

Moscow's subway system stands out for its well-paid workers and reliable trains.

Eastern Europe and the former Soviet Union stand to benefit from keeping their freight on the rails; interruptions in goods distribution are among the region's most serious problems in this time of economic and political transition, and neither the national transport ministries nor the environment can afford a massive buildup of highways. But just as western countries are concentrating on switching freight from roads back to the rails, Eastern Europe seems to be doing the opposite. Largely because of growth in East-West traffic, goods transport by rail has plummeted in Eastern Europe by 15–31 percent. By the end of the decade, East-West European trade could soar as much as tenfold, predicts Georgios Anastassopoulos, vice president of the European Parliament. He warns, "there is a risk that economic growth in Eastern and Central Europe will be crowded out by traffic congestion."[29]

As for urban rail, more than half the world's estimated 326 light rail and tramway systems are in the former Soviet Union and Eastern Europe. Like the intercity railways, urban networks will be a substantial asset to the region if they survive the current stampede toward private car use. Most of the systems are extensive, though their quality varies. Moscow's subway system stands out for its well-paid workers and reliable trains running at no more than 10 minutes apart. It carries 8 million passengers a day—more than any other subway in the world—although in length of track it is in fourth place behind New York, London, and Tokyo.[30]

Japan is notable for maintaining the important role of rail even as car ownership and use became widespread; the ratio of passenger-kilometers traveled by road versus by rail in Japan—nearly two kilometers by road for every one by train—is by far the lowest of any industrial country. (See Table 7–2.) During the seventies, the government invested roughly 0.6 percent of GDP annually in rail. But in the late eighties, when Japan began privatizing the national network (breaking it up into six regional rail companies and one national freight carrier), investment in rail dropped to between 0.1 and 0.3 percent of GDP.[31]

In contrast to its high passenger train ridership, Japan's use of rail to move goods is very low. Trucks account for 90 percent of all freight transport, an excess that is now backfiring. Costly delays caused by road congestion are undermining Japan's famed "just-in-time" delivery system, in which carefully scheduled trucks make continuous, small deliveries so that industrial and commercial enterprises can avoid keeping large inventories on site. Ironically, this just-in-time delivery system, which auto industry analysts have credited for Japan's efficiency in car manufacturing, threatens to choke off highway capacity for the industry's own products.[32]

Table 7–2. Road Versus Rail Travel, Selected Countries, Late Eighties

Country	Road Travel	Rail Travel	Road Versus Rail Ratio
	(kilometers per person per year)		(road/rail kilometers)
United States	12,475	79	157.9
Canada	5,480	72	76.1
Iraq	1,707	93	18.4
Chile	1,136	90	12.6
West Germany	6,788	639	10.6
United Kingdom	5,723	581	9.9
Netherlands	5,934	637	9.3
Denmark	6,748	935	7.2
Italy	4,840	721	6.7
France	7,125	1,072	6.6
Spain	2,372	396	6.0
Cameroon	222	40	5.6
Hong Kong	1,186	348	3.4
Thailand	591	175	3.4
Japan	4,465	2,739	1.6
Poland	1,450	1,279	1.1
Czechoslovakia	148	1,282	0.1
Soviet Union	175	1,403	0.1

SOURCE: "Riding Rails and Roads," *World Monitor*, April 1991, citing International Road Federation, *World Road Statistics 1989* (Washington, D.C.: 1989) and other sources.

Developing countries have some of the least extensive rail systems in the world. Only China and India have significant rail networks. China rivals the former Soviet Union in transporting 80 percent of its inland freight by rail. And 56 percent of intercity passenger traffic is by rail, a greater share than in any other country. But even in China the role of rail is slipping because of increased emphasis on roads. By the end of the eighties, China was spending less than 0.6 percent of GDP on rail, down from 0.9 percent mid-decade.[33]

India's rail passenger traffic has risen more than fourfold since 1950. In contrast to other parts of the crumbling national infrastructure, the rail system is reliable and well maintained, although much of it uses equipment from the sixties. Both passenger and freight demand on India's railways are expected to swell by more than 150 percent during the nineties. Freight traffic on the rails has grown fivefold in the past four decades, but trucking is increasing so fast that the share of freight by rail is actually waning. In 1987, railways there moved 52 percent of freight, down from 89 percent in 1950.[34]

Most other developing countries have marginal rail service at best, initiated long ago by colonial governments but not adequately maintained since independence. Outdated systems have poor safety records and are often slow and unreliable. Urban rail is uncommon in African cities. Typically, public transport consists of buses, taxis, and informal public transport vehicles run by private operators. Other than Cairo and Tunis, which have modern rail systems, most cities' local rail service is limited to suburban lines that are part of the national railways.

Much of Asia also relies on buses and suburban rail for urban public transport. In some cases, suburban rail plays a major role. In Greater Calcutta, 1.7 million passengers a day use suburban rail (compared with roughly 300,000 in New York and 700,000 in London); in Bombay, suburban rail accounts for about half of all travel by public transport. Among Latin American countries, only Argentina, Brazil, and Mexico have national rail networks with notable passenger or freight movement by rail.[35]

SIGNS OF A RAIL REVIVAL

Passenger and freight rail both are making somewhat of a comeback. Several European governments are planning large railway improvements in the near future. Sweden intends to invest equal amounts in its railways and roads during the nineties, and unified Germany's first transport plan calls for investing more in rail than in roads through the year 2010. Even though many other national networks are still not getting adequate government support to compete with highway and air travel, three types of passenger trains are rapidly gaining official favor. These are light rail in cities, commuter rail (also called suburban rail) linking cities with outlying communities, and high-speed rail modelled after Japan's famed bullet trains.[36]

Freight rail is getting a boost from European governments concerned about worsening environmental damage from extensive reliance on goods movement by truck. In Europe and elsewhere, the recent introduction of intermodal technology—equipment that makes it possible to transfer goods easily from trucks, ships, or barges onto rails—is stimulating a revival of freight transport by rail.

Among the passenger rail technologies, it is not surprising that light rail is particularly popular. It is essentially a smoother, quieter version of the nostalgic trolley. More like sleek trains than streetcars, light rail vehicles are smaller and lighter than rapid rail (metro) cars, and about 20 percent less expensive to build.[37]

Unlike rapid rail, light rail does not require an exclusive, separate right-of-way; it can run down the middle or the side of a road or in auto-free malls, utility corridors, or even back alleys. This flexibility saves on construction costs by avoiding the need for expensive and time-consuming underground tunnels and elevated tracks. Light rail construction can cost as little as $10–15 million per kilometer, on average one fifth to one third as much as a surface metro and one tenth the price of an underground subway.[38]

Ironically, several countries that dismantled their trolley systems decades ago to make way for cars are now adopting light rail to ease the resulting smog and traffic jams. Canada, France, the United Kingdom, and the United States are all joining in this light rail revival. Systems are operating in five British cities, under construction in two others, and being considered in 40 additional cities and towns. The United States has 18 cities with light rail systems and six more that are planning or constructing them. In 1990 Los Angeles, which originally had more than 1,600 kilometers of streetcar tracks, opened its first new light rail line—much of it using abandoned trolley right-of-way. Initially expected to attract 10,000 passengers per day, the Blue Line drew 35,000 daily riders in its first year.[39]

In countries where trolleys survived the early automobile boom, some cities have maintained and improved old networks. Japan has systems in 19 cities, although Tokyo, which once had 41 streetcar lines, has phased out all but one. Many cities in Western Europe gradually improved their old tram systems after World War II. Typically, streetcar lines were upgraded and relocated in several stages, eventually becoming modern light rail. Today, half of Western Europe's cities with 600,000 or more people have light rail. Germany alone has 49 light rail networks and, in the eastern part of the country, six old-style tram systems.[40]

Several large cities in the developing world are finding light rail the most appropriate transport investment given their particular conditions—the need to move a large number of people, but little time for construction, very limited funds, and a small amount of available space. Many cities are either building light rail networks or integrating the technologies with traditional rapid rail systems.

Light rail has been proposed for Abidjan, Côte d'Ivoire; Casablanca and Rabat in Morocco; and Johannesburg, South Africa. Manila's light rail line is so popular—it whisks people 22 kilometers in 15 minutes while the same stretch by highway can take two hours—that the city is planning to build three more lines. Guadalajara and Mexico City have light rail systems, and Monterrey is building one. Three Brazilian cities have light rail, and in six others—including São Paulo and Belo Horizonte—it is either authorized or under construction.[41]

Where governments lack the funds even for the least expensive light rail systems, a promising approach is to refurbish suburban rail and link it to express busways. Dakar in Senegal and Lagos in Nigeria have resuscitated suburban rail systems on existing tracks. In both cases, ridership has increased and the systems are now recovering their operating costs—an unusual achievement for any public transport enterprise.[42]

The revival of suburban rail lines in much of the world stems from the need for commuter routes from outlying areas. Whether affluent suburbs or sprawling shantytowns, these peripheral communities are gaining both residents and jobs faster than urban cores. In the United States, for instance, suburban populations are growing at roughly twice the rate of central cities. Even though the central city usually is the single most common destination for commuters, a growing number of urban work trips worldwide do not involve a city's center. Ring roads, originally meant to speed people around central cities, are now becoming clogged suburb-to-suburb routes.[43]

During the eighties, some 50 large cities undertook commuter rail projects, including Bombay, Chicago, and Paris.

During the eighties, many cities responded to these trends by investing in commuter rail service. This was affordable since it mainly entailed upgrading, expanding, and electrifying existing regional rail lines. Some 50 large cities undertook commuter rail projects, including Bombay, Cairo, Chicago, Jakarta, Melbourne, Montreal, and Paris. In the London area, where abandoned crosstown lines were reopened and existing commuter rail was improved, ridership increased 3 percent a year in the latter half of the decade and the system began operating at a profit. Rio de Janeiro and São Paulo revamped their extensive but run-down suburban rail networks, enabling each to handle more than a million passengers daily.[44]

Until recently, commuter rail in the

United States was important only in a few old metropolitan areas such as New York, Philadelphia, and San Francisco. In fact, the New York City region accounts for 60 percent of the nation's 1.1 million daily commuter rail passengers. But since 1989, nine additional major urban areas, from Miami to Seattle, have planned, begun constructing, or opened commuter rail services. Miami's trains started as a temporary link to West Palm Beach during a highway construction project in 1989, but ridership was so high—1.6 million passengers annually— that transport officials decided to retain and expand the service.[45]

The most ambitious commuter rail revival is in car-dependent southern California, which recently committed itself to a $55-billion new system combining 676 kilometers of commuter rail with 187 kilometers of subway and light rail. Much of it will operate on tracks owned by freight railroads. Expected to take 30 years to complete, the network will be second only to New York's among U.S. metropolitan systems. More than 80 percent of the funding for the project is to come from local sources, including taxes voted in by two 1990 referendums.[46]

Even more powerful than the renewed enthusiasm for trolleys and commuter rail is that for high-speed passenger rail. Distinguished from conventional rail by aerodynamic railcars and powerful electric motors, high-speed rail has captured the imagination of citizens and governments alike. Japan introduced the world's first high-speed rail system, the Shinkansen or "bullet train," in 1964. The 200 kilometer-per-hour train was completed just in time for the Tokyo Olympics and nearly attracted more attention than the games. Daily ridership on the first line, from Tokyo to Osaka, tripled annually for the first five years. Eventually operating on four lines, the bullet trains were carrying 135 million passengers each year by the late eighties.

Today the Tokyo-Osaka route offers 61 trains per hour, and rail officials plan to increase this to 76 trains by decade's end.[47]

In 1981, France launched its first high-speed rail line, the TGV (Train à Grande Vitesse) from Paris to Lyon. The second line, from Paris to Le Mans on the west coast, is the world's fastest train, at more than 300 kilometers per hour on regular runs, with a recent trial speed of 515 kilometers per hour. (For comparison, the top speed of a conventional passenger train is roughly 130 kilometers per hour.) The government plans to expand its TGV network to 4,700 kilometers, at a cost of $35 billion, by 2010.[48]

Several clear benefits help explain the appeal of high-speed rail. Despite their velocity, high-speed trains in France and Japan have never had a passenger fatality in carrying more than 3 billion passengers. Some high-speed technologies, including the one employed by the French TGV, can operate on conventional tracks; this versatility enables the fast trains to integrate well with existing intercity rail networks. Although building new high-speed rail lines is relatively expensive (averaging in the range of $3.3 million per kilometer in favorable topography and $20 million per kilometer in rugged terrain), these costs can be recovered with sufficient ridership. Most of the Japanese bullet trains have been profitable for many years, as has the TGV.[49]

Many high-speed rail trips are fast enough to compete with air travel—especially since they save extra time by delivering passengers directly to the central city instead of an airport on the fringes. The trains are considered ideal for distances of 200 to 1,000 kilometers. Today, 80 percent of former air passengers on the Paris-Lyon route go by train, and the bullet train has almost completely displaced air travel between Nagoya and Tokyo. Interestingly, a few airlines in Europe are now lobbying for more rail in order to relieve their overloaded terminals of short-trip passengers. The German airline Lufthansa even runs its own trains between several large cities and airports.[50]

High-speed rail does have some problems, however. Since the fast trains require straighter tracks than conventional rail, many new routes cannot avoid going through farmland and environmentally sensitive areas. Erosion and siltation during construction threaten water quality, particularly in areas where rough terrain necessitates excessive digging. Tall fences paralleling the tracks for safety may disrupt wildlife migration. In southern France, some residents have opposed TGV extensions based on all these objections plus the noise of speeding trains and the prospect of a sudden influx of tourists.[51]

Although high-speed rail promises to relieve both highway and air traffic congestion, its high cost can deflect needed investment away from a country's basic rail system. In France and Germany, some rail service on which people have long depended has been reduced, and a few lines have even been closed. Critics argue that the new trains will create "hypermobility" for the relatively wealthy while stranding those who cannot afford the high fares. European transport analyst Jonathon Bray also warns against focusing on rapid intercity movement at the expense of other transport needs. He notes that "if rail investment is skewed too far towards high-speed rail, getting between cities can be quicker than getting across them."[52]

Cost issues are of even greater concern with magnetic levitation trains—high-speed vehicles that "fly" on a magnetic cushion no more than a few centimeters above the tracks. Germany and Japan both have invested more than $1 billion during the past 20 years into researching "maglev" technology, which was invented, but never developed, in the United States. To date, no maglev passenger service has been put into operation, but various studies show that building maglev guideways could cost from $5 billion to $39 billion per kilometer. Top speed for the floating trains is 480 kilometers per hour, still trailing the TGV record of 515 kilometers per hour. In addition to doubts about maglev's economic feasibility, uncertainty remains about the possible health effects of electromagnetic fields on passengers. And safety concerns were highlighted in 1991 when a Japanese maglev, in a test run, caught fire and burned to the ground.[53]

For the foreseeable future, the prospects for traditional high-speed rail (steel wheels on steel tracks) are much brighter than for maglev. The world's first maglev service, scheduled to open in 1996, is a proposed 23-kilometer jaunt from Orlando, Florida, to Walt Disney World and other resorts. By contrast, steel-wheel high-speed rail lines are being planned or built between major cities in at least 14 countries, including Australia, Brazil, China, Germany, Spain, and the United States. Most of these systems are created incrementally, by first upgrading existing tracks or vehicles and then introducing special high-speed technologies. Finally, record speeds such as the TGV's are reached only by using both high-speed vehicles and special tracks.[54]

European governments are planning to build a vast high-speed rail network that connects such distant corners as Scandinavia, Eastern Europe, the Baltic States, and the Iberian Peninsula, while a version of the TGV will link Britain via the Channel Tunnel. The scheme aims to put 7,400 kilometers of high-speed rail in place by the end of the nineties and a total of 20,000 kilometers by 2020. Part of the impetus for the project is the specter of a 74-percent increase in air travel expected when Europe becomes a single market. Governments are counting on high-speed trains to relieve congestion at major European airports, 30 of which are expected to reach full capacity by the end of the decade.[55]

At the same time that new passenger rail technologies are enticing people back onto trains, intermodal freight equipment is facilitating a return of goods to the rails. Intermodal systems (also called combined transport) make it possible to combine trucking and rail freight, taking advantage of what each one does best: trucks can make on-site deliveries to widely scattered locations, and environmentally sound and economical trains can transport goods across long distances.

Many governments are realizing it was a mistake to abandon railways for highways.

Intermodal freight is growing quickly in the United States, where long distances favor rail but where businesses have become accustomed to the flexibility of shipping and receiving goods by truck. The railroads' intermodal services let them move goods so efficiently and inexpensively that the trucking companies increasingly are using rail for the long-haul portion of their shipments. In 1990, the number of intermodal trailers and containers shipped by rail reached 6.2 million—more than double the number in 1980.[56]

European transport ministers, expecting at least a 30-percent rise in truck traffic in the first decade of the single European market, have proposed a 10-year, $2.7-billion plan to create a combined transport network for the European Community. France, Austria, and Switzerland are particularly interested in

diverting goods traffic from roads because of their central position in European trade routes. The Alpine road network, the busiest mountain system in the world, bears 15 percent of Western Europe's goods transport. Austria and Switzerland recently announced programs to increase capacity on their trans-alpine rail routes. The Swiss plan sets aside $10.7 billion to build two new rail tunnels under ones that already exist.[57]

INVESTING IN THE FUTURE

After decades of traffic congestion, steep oil bills, and smog, many governments are realizing it was a mistake to abandon railways for highways. Slowly, transport priorities are shifting toward an integrated mix of options instead of strict reliance on motor vehicles. But before truly healthy transport systems can emerge, a much greater commitment to improving and expanding the rail sector has to occur.

When asked to reverse a trend that has been in motion for most of this century, policymakers cannot help but ask some difficult questions. The foremost is inevitably, Where will the money come from? Fiscal constraints are universal, with even the strongest national economies now buckling under the strain of a global recession. It is hard to come up with adequate funding for all infrastructure, including rail. A second question decisionmakers confront is, How can we ensure that investments in rail will pay off? A common fear is that new rail service will not attract enough riders. In too many cases, failure to support rail projects with other sensible policies has turned this worry into a self-fulfilling prophecy.

Fortunately, there are satisfactory answers to both these legitimate policy questions. For funding sources, an analysis of most countries' transport sectors reveals a surprising variety of ways to free up funds. The most promising of these is the billions of dollars in subsidies that currently go to other transport modes, particularly highways.

Contrary to popular belief, drivers do not pay their own way through user fees. In the United States, gasoline taxes and other user fees account for roughly 60 percent of federal, state, and local spending on highways and roads. The remainder, $29 billion in 1989, comes from general funds, property taxes, and other sources. Another cost, "free" parking, has an estimated value of $85 billion per year. Additional expenses not covered by drivers, such as for police and emergency services, traffic management, and routine street maintenance, represent some $68 billion annually. When harder-to-quantify costs such as air pollution, traffic congestion, and road accidents are figured in, the total subsidy to drivers in the United States soars to an estimated $300 billion a year.[58]

National treasuries can recapture some of this financial loss in several ways. The most important one—especially in the United States—is to raise unrealistically low fuel taxes. Nowhere do gasoline and diesel taxes reflect the full cost of driving, but the amounts levied in Western Europe—on average 60–70¢ per liter (about $2.50 per gallon)—at least come close to covering fuel-related costs. Tax laws should no longer reward employers disproportionately for providing car-related benefits. In the United States, the major example of this is that employer-provided parking is favored over travel allowances or public transport passes. In the United Kingdom, company cars account for some 60 percent of all new cars sold.[59]

Making heavy trucks pay for the road damage they do would raise additional funds. According to the U.S. General Accounting Office, one 40-ton truck causes as much wear and tear as 9,600 automobiles do. Heavy trucks are believed to do 95 percent of all damage to highways in the United States. This is not only a drain on government funds and the cause of damage to other vehicles, it represents an unfair advantage to truck freight over rail freight, since railroads pay the full costs of maintaining their own infrastructure. The imbalance can be redressed and costs recovered through an annual charge on trucks based on weight and mileage driven. Eight states have weight-distance taxes, as do several West European countries including Austria, Norway, Portugal, and Sweden.[60]

It makes sense to apply the revenue raised from reducing highway subsidies to expanding and improving railways. The main reason that Western Europe has maintained a relatively high degree of balance among transport modes is that governments historically have allocated only a portion of user fee revenues back to highways. Today, most European countries put about 33 percent of fuel tax revenues into highways; the rest goes into the general fund to support intercity rail, urban public transport, and other transportation options as well as nontransport government programs. Doing so benefits both drivers and nondrivers by providing alternatives. Drivers gain more in saved time and convenience from reduced congestion than they pay in user fees.[61]

Alternatively, establishment of a Rail Trust Fund would guarantee a source of funding for national rail networks. Although a trust fund system is usually based on user fees for each mode going to its own fund, correcting a gross imbalance calls for permitting transfers from one fund to another. The United States could benefit from such a move, since rail is completely left out of the federal funding system of trust funds for highways, aviation, and inland waterways. The national passenger railway is increasingly popular, and steadily improved its financial performance throughout the eighties. But Amtrak needs to upgrade its equipment and expand service to meet rapidly climbing demand. A current legislative proposal to transfer 1¢ per gallon from the federal gas tax to an intercity passenger rail capital trust fund, raising roughly $1 billion per year for Amtrak, is gathering support in Congress.[62]

Rail is completely left out of the U.S. federal funding system of trust funds for highways, aviation, and inland waterways.

Another option is to let privatization play a limited role. Selective participation by the private sector is more appropriate than total privatization; a free-for-all private market cannot be trusted to provide service on unprofitable routes that are vital to the system. Especially since rail must compete with far more flexible highway transport, it is crucial for railways to be as comprehensive as possible. The social value lost when a network is disrupted far outweighs the economic gains achieved. A World Bank study of Pakistan, for instance, found that closing nearly 2,000 kilometers of uneconomical rail lines—22 percent of the entire network's length—would cut operating costs by less than 2 percent.[63]

A wide range of scenarios for private participation can help governments with the costs of rail service. One is for private companies to invest capital in the publicly owned railway. In the state of São Paulo, Brazil, private investments are helping the state-owned railroad build intermodal cargo terminals, en-

abling rail to compete better with truck freight. In addition to supplementing public funds for financing, building, and operating rail projects, the private sector can be tapped for managerial, marketing, and technical skills. Public rail entities can also contract with independent operators to provide rail service—an approach that is most effective if the operators are required to maintain certain standards of safety and quality and to guarantee service on lesser-used lines.[64]

Ensuring that investments in rail provide an adequate economic return can only be accomplished by incorporating environmental and social criteria. Rail's worth to society extends far beyond mere farebox revenues. Public transport services that cover their own costs through passenger fares are extremely rare (San Diego's popular trolley is one recent exception, repaying 92 percent of operating costs through fares). But having rail as an alternative to driving represents an incalculable societal gain: avoiding the high costs of pollution, traffic congestion, oil dependence, and road accidents.[65]

In addition, economists generally agree that infrastructure improvements are a sound investment in the national economy. More specifically, a recent U.S. study looked at the impact of government transport expenditures on worker productivity. A 10-year, $100-billion increase in public transport spending was estimated to boost worker output by $521 billion, compared with $237 billion for the same level of spending on highways. Moreover, public transport investments were found to begin returning net benefits nearly three times as quickly as highway expenditures.[66]

Other research has drawn similar conclusions. In a 1991 study, the Washington-based Urban Institute and Boston-based Cambridge Systematics compared the economic effects of investing in rehabilitation and continued operation of SEPTA (the light rail, subway, and commuter rail system in the Philadelphia metropolitan area) with cutting or even eliminating its services. The study found that for every dollar of public spending on rebuilding and continuing to operate SEPTA, $3 would accrue to the state and the region as a direct result of improved transport. The total economic impact, including increases in business sales, jobs, personal income, population, and the accompanying rise in state and local tax revenues, would be $9 for every dollar.[67]

For governments to maximize their financial return on rail investments, though, rail services need to be used to full capacity. Once subsidies to automobiles have been reduced and drivers have to pay more of the costs of driving, rail travel automatically will gain appeal. But encouraging heavy ridership on trains will require additional supportive policies.

One way to ensure that people will use a rail system is to integrate it thoroughly with other transport modes. In cities, even the most comprehensive rail network cannot reach every neighborhood. Well-placed links with bus feeder routes can extend the rail system's reach enough to be convenient for a large number of riders. Similarly, more passengers are able to use intercity trains if the rail lines are coordinated with existing local and regional bus service. And it is advisable to avoid repeating a mistake often made in U.S. cities—failure to provide direct rail service to airports.

Attracting as many riders as possible also requires easy access to rail stations. Many rail authorities concentrate solely on providing car parking—a strategy severely restricted by the expense and limited availability of land. An often-overlooked alternative is to provide safe bicycle parking and to design stations so that pedestrians can approach the entrances easily. Making it convenient for people to walk or cycle to the station frees up car parking space and accommodates nondrivers. Commuter rail can get an extra boost in ridership by allowing bicycles onto trains; this enables riders to reach the rail system from either the home or the workplace, even if neither one is within walking distance of a station.[68]

For the long term, the most important way to encourage widespread use of rail is to promote compact land use in cities, suburbs, and towns. No amount of investment in rail can overcome automobile dependence in a region marked by sprawl. Although planning future urban growth is best left to local authorities and citizens, national governments can use compact land use criteria as a condition for funding local and regional transport projects.

To qualify for national funds, for example, a local rail project (or any other major transport improvement) would have to be accompanied by measures to ensure compact growth. Zoning codes could steer high-density development to the area around rail stations and along rail lines. Developers can be given incentives to site housing, shops, and offices in key areas. Perhaps most important, rail planners would be required to collaborate closely with the region's land use planners in designing the entire system.

Several large cities have used this approach, turning urban growth to their advantage by investing in rail networks and deliberately concentrating further development along the rail lines. In Paris, Hamburg, Stockholm, and Toronto, rail corridors have helped induce compact, efficient land use. These areas depend far less on automobiles than other cities—fostering not only increased rail ridership, but more cycling and walking as well. They also have maintained their urban appeal and livability by using rail lines as a focal point for pedestrian-friendly commercial development and high-density office and residential areas.[69]

In addition to these strategies for maximizing rail ridership, governments can amplify the economic reward for a commitment to rail by having domestic industries produce the necessary equipment. This is especially important for developing countries trying to support a high-value manufacturing base. Mexico, for instance, has been able to build most of its own subway cars. And in countries where most people cannot afford to buy cars, railcar production is likely to pose fewer economic risks than trying to establish a domestic automobile industry.[70]

The debt-ridden, capital-short countries of Eastern Europe and the former Soviet Union have a large existing capacity to supply rail equipment. The former East Germany has particularly impressive expertise in building railcars, which could be produced for export. Czechoslovakia has a similar economic opportunity in a trolley-car factory located in a suburb of Prague. At least two West European conglomerates are interested in cooperating with the plant—taking advantage of its low wages and skilled workers—to build light rail vehicles.[71]

Industrial countries, too, can benefit from railcar manufacture. The United States, once a leader in building passenger railcars, could reenter the market while employing skilled workers who have lost their jobs in declining heavy industries such as steel production. A plant is to be built in the San Francisco area, for example, to turn out the new "California car," a special double-deck commuter railcar. Some of the necessary manufacturing structure is still in place, ready to be revived. An old Pullman freight-car plant in Chicago soon will reopen to produce 173 double-deck railcars and rebuild 140 existing cars for the Chicago commuter rail authority.[72]

Producing rail equipment also provides an opportunity to make socially productive use of defense industries made redundant by the end of the cold war. The Rosyth Royal Dockyard in Scotland illustrates such a transfer of resources. Workers who traditionally have maintained the Royal Navy's ships and submarines currently are overhauling 738 railcars for the London Underground. Although the dockyard probably will remain largely dependent on defense work for the immediate future, its success in refurbishing rail equipment suggests there is considerable scope for such conversions in the long term.[73]

Now that much of the world has rediscovered trains, it is time to speed up the global revival, and to reap the environmental, social, and economic rewards of using the rails. With a growing number of governments stepping up funding, rail is likely to fare much better in the next century than it did for most of the current one. If these public investments are made with the appropriate accompanying policies—to remove unfair transport subsidies, create a well-integrated transport system, and encourage wiser land use—everyone, not just train riders, will benefit.

8

Preparing for Peace

Michael Renner

Si vis pacem, para bellum: if you want peace, prepare for war. Generation after generation, in nation after nation, leaders have faithfully followed the ancient Romans' maxim. Over time, societies' ability to wage war has become an institutionalized, permanent endeavor, with large resources devoted to armies and arsenals, and technological progress honed to spawn increasingly sophisticated and lethal weapons. Contrary to the famous dictum, however, the accumulation of unprecedented military power has brought not eternal peace but massive destruction during war and high economic and environmental costs in preparing for it.[1]

Sowing the seeds of military prowess in an anarchic international system has yielded a rising harvest of violence. The frequency and intensity of war steadily increased from Roman times onward, and its destructive impact has escalated. Three quarters of all war deaths since the days of Julius Caesar have occurred in this century. The number of war-related deaths has risen from less than 1 million in the fifteenth century to some 110 million so far in this one, far outpacing the rate of population growth.[2]

In view of this record, perhaps the world community should try a different motto: if you want peace, prepare for peace. The end of the cold war provides the opportunity for this new approach. The last few years have witnessed a spate of encouraging developments. Superpower nuclear arsenals and European conventional arms are being slashed, diplomats are putting the finishing touches on a convention outlawing the production and possession of chemical weapons, world military spending has peaked, and arms exports have dropped significantly. U.N. peacekeepers are in rising demand, outstripping the organization's capacity to respond. Finally, there is growing recognition that economic vitality and environmental health are more significant than military strength in determining a nation's fortunes.

Yet a new course is not inevitable: many obstacles remain and dangers loom. Already, the euphoria that swept the world in the wake of the cold war's end has been tempered by the violent Gulf conflict. Although the seemingly unstoppable growth of global military spending has been broken, the cuts made so far are rather limited in view of the historic transformations that have taken place; the staying power of the "military-industrial complex" remains formidable. Many Third World conflicts continue unabated, and in places like

Yugoslavia and along the periphery of the former Soviet Union, long-suppressed but unresolved feuds have erupted with a vengeance. Finally, disputes over resources, migration, environment, and other issues threaten increasingly to replace the East-West confrontation with a North-South standoff.

In short, the cold war may be dead, but the war system is alive and well: the war-making institutions remain in place, the permanent war economy continues to command large-scale resources, and, perhaps most important, the view that military rivalry among states is both rational and inevitable—known in political science as the "realism" school—still enjoys wide allegiance.

The cold war may be dead, but the war system is alive and well.

Human society is highly practiced at making war, but remains inept in the art of making peace. Obviously, the recurrence of violent conflict can only be prevented if its multifaceted roots—the deep social and economic inequities and the ethnic and religious antagonisms within and among societies—are adequately addressed. But although armaments are often only a symptom of unresolved deeper conflicts, they frequently do gain a momentum of their own, creating distrust and thus rendering a rapprochement between adversaries more difficult. And military priorities drain enormous resources from civilian society, potentially causing or aggravating conflicts. Thus, a stable peace presumes a world that is much less heavily armed, one that adopts meaningful barriers against the production, possession, trading, and use of arms.

FROM ARMS CONTROL TO DISARMAMENT

Preparing for peace rather than for war requires a sharp break with past practice. To date, many international treaties have been guided by the philosophy of arms control, which is aimed at managing arms races and allows arsenals to grow as long as "stability" is maintained. Fortunately, recent trends indicate a greater embrace of a disarmament approach, which seeks deep reductions or even the elimination of weapons.

Arms control agreements have been carefully tailored to establish weak limits for aging or redundant weapons systems, thus allowing an unabated buildup. And since many treaties have failed to limit the size of existing arsenals, few contain any provision to destroy even part of the accumulated stockpiles. Even more ominously, these treaties have not tried to constrain qualitative characteristics of weapon systems—the development, that is, of ever more sophisticated technologies.[3]

The few constraints put in place have typically limited the deployment—but not the production—of tanks, missiles, and other military equipment. (See Table 8–1.) None of the existing treaties includes a mandate to dismantle or convert arms factories to civilian use. The soon-to-be-signed convention banning the production and possession of chemical weapons will be the only international agreement to stipulate that production facilities must be demolished.

The agreements that avoid these defects are the ones that establish nuclear weapon-free zones (the Tlatelolco and Rarotonga accords for Latin America and the South Pacific) and that ban weapons of mass destruction on the seabed, in outer space, and in Antarctica. The areas covered were, with few exceptions, already free of such arms before

Table 8–1. Constraints Imposed on Armaments by International Treaties[1]

Treaty (Year Signed)	Constraints					Requirement
	Production	Possession/ Deployment	Exports/ Transfers	Use	Testing	Destruction of Stocks
Nuclear Weapons						
Test treaties[2]					o	
Tlatelolco (1967)	•	•	•	•	•	
Non-Proliferation (1968)[3]	o	o	•			
SALT I/II (1972/79)	o	o			o	o
Rarotonga (1985)	•	•	•	•	•	
INF (1988)	•	•			•	•
START (1991)		o				o
Weapons of Mass Destruction[4]						
Outer Space Treaty (1967)		•			•	
Seabed Treaty (1971)		•		•	•	
Moon Treaty (1979)		•		•	•	
Chemical/Biological Weapons						
Geneva Protocol (1925)				•		
Biological Weapons Convention(1972)	•	•	•	•	•	•
U.S.-Soviet Chemical Weapons Agreement (1990)	•	o				o
Conventional Weapons						
Conventional Forces in Europe (1990)		o				o
Inhumane Weapons Convention (1981)				o/•[5]		
Ballistic Missiles						
Anti-Ballistic Missile Treaty (1972)	o	o	•		o	o
Missile Technology Control Regime (1987)[6]			o			

[1] "•" means a total ban, "o" a partial ban or limitation. The table presents constraints imposed by the treaties, but not how well they are enforced. [2] Partial Test Ban Treaty (1963), Threshold Test Ban Treaty (1974), Peaceful Nuclear Explosions Treaty (1976). [3] The prohibitions against production and possession are partial in the sense that they apply to nonnuclear states, but not to nuclear-weapon states. [4] Includes nuclear and nonnuclear types. [5] Use of certain types of weapons banned altogether, use of others restricted. [6] The MTCR is an export control cartel of western suppliers.

SOURCE: Worldwatch Institute, based on Serge Sur, ed., *Verification of Current Disarmament and Arms Limitation Agreements: Ways, Means and Practices* (Aldershot, U.K.: Dartmouth, 1991), on Stockholm International Peace Research Institute, *SIPRI Yearbook 1991: World Armaments and Disarmament* (Oxford: Oxford University Press, 1991), and on Institute for Defense and Disarmament Studies, *The Arms Control Reporter 1992* (Cambridge, Mass.: 1992).

the treaties entered into force. It has proved much harder to negotiate and implement similar measures in regions where weapons of mass destruction are deployed.

Only with the thawing of the cold war were greater restraints put in place. Whereas the Strategic Arms Limitation Talks (SALT) treaties of the seventies let the superpowers pile up huge quantities of nuclear warheads, the 1991 Strategic Arms Reductions Talks (START) and the 1988 Intermediate-Range Nuclear Forces (INF) accords began to cut them. The Conventional Forces in Europe (CFE) treaty is leading to sizable reductions of tanks and artillery on that continent. And, as noted, the Chemical Weapons Convention will outlaw the production and possession of toxic agents, and require the destruction of existing stockpiles.

In some cases, unilateral measures have brought about much more meaningful restraints. Among the prominent instances are President Nixon's halt to U.S. chemical weapons production in 1969 and President Gorbachev's similar action in 1987, and the nuclear testing moratoriums imposed by Gorbachev in 1985–87 and by Russian and French Presidents Yeltsin and Mitterand in 1992. The most striking examples of the impact of unilateral action are the large reductions in nuclear weapons pledged individually by Presidents Bush, Gorbachev, and Yeltsin in late 1991 and early 1992.[4]

A corollary to the focus on arms control as opposed to disarmament is the western emphasis on nonproliferation of certain weapons and military technologies. This approach is embodied in the 1968 Nuclear Non-Proliferation Treaty (NPT), signed by 140 countries, which prohibits the acquisition of nuclear arms by those nations not already possessing them. Nonproliferation would seem like a commendable goal—the spread of weapons of mass destruction cannot be desirable. Yet unless coupled with unambiguous moves toward disarmament among the world's strongest military powers, the approach suggests that the "haves" are more interested in maintaining a system of global military apartheid—preventing the "have-nots" from acquiring military capabilities others already possess—than in finding a way to make the planet less heavily armed and more secure.

Whereas the NPT represents a multilateral bargain that, on paper at least, commits the nuclear powers to disarmament efforts, nonproliferation measures in other fields, such as the 1987 Missile Technology Control Regime, are no more than unilaterally imposed export controls by a cartel of western supplier nations. These just feed into Third World resentment, not least because the technologies in question often can be used not only for military but also for civilian purposes. Moreover, such efforts may even fail to achieve their stated objective. *Finding Common Ground*, a 1991 U.S. National Academy of Sciences report, found that numerous technical and enforcement problems often render export controls relatively ineffective.[5]

In sum, unilateral nonproliferation efforts may well thwart the chances for a more cooperative approach to international security. Attempts to prevent the spread of advanced military technology will work only if restrictions against their development and application are accepted equally by North and South.

Slashing the Arsenals

The late eighties and early nineties have witnessed some breakthroughs in nuclear, chemical, and conventional disarmament, as well as some precedent-setting agreements on international verification measures. But the world still remains a heavily armed place. The nineties provides an opportunity for the international community to formulate the lasting, binding constraints on armed competition among nations and alliances that, by and large, are still lacking.

After growing seemingly inexorably for more than four decades, nuclear arsenals now are set for a dramatic shrinkage. At its peak in 1988, the global stockpile included almost 25,000 strategic warheads (those capable of flying at least 5,000 kilometers) and close to 35,000 tactical, or shorter-range, warheads. The United States and the Soviet Union controlled more than 95 percent. (See Figure 8–1.) With the demise of the cold war, the rapid growth of these arsenals sputtered to a sudden halt. The INF and START treaties were the first accords to require reductions in U.S. and Soviet arsenals. But fears that the disintegration of the Soviet Union might set off an uncontrolled dispersal of nuclear weapons or expertise quickly led to much deeper cuts proposed outside the realm of formal negotiations.[6]

As a result, the combined stockpiles of the United States and Russia (the principal heir to the Soviet arsenal) are scheduled to decline from 57,000 strategic and tactical warheads in 1988 to an estimated 12,000 over the next decade or so, according to Robert Standish Norris of the Natural Resources Defense Council. The much smaller arsenals of the other self-acknowledged nuclear powers—the United Kingdom, France, and China—by contrast are projected to grow from nearly 1,500 warheads now to 2,000 within a few years.[7]

The warheads slated for withdrawal contain more than 150 tons of plutonium and perhaps as much as 700–800 tons of highly enriched uranium (HEU). Existing arms treaties give no guidance concerning the disposition of these dangerous, long-lived weapons-grade materials. Both the United States and Russia have decided to dismantle most of the withdrawn warheads, but without any international scrutiny. Yet with huge numbers of warheads destined to be removed, the need for a stringent accounting of weapons-grade materials—to prevent them from being "recycled" into new warheads, stolen, or secretly diverted—is self-evident.[8]

Although the global stockpile is set for an impressive reduction, the remaining weapons will still contain enough firepower to annihilate all life on earth. None of the nuclear powers is yet contemplating the eventual abolition of nuclear weapons. It is perhaps understandable that governments and people reared on the notion that nuclear weapons have kept the peace are reluctant to foresake their possession. But arguments for retaining nuclear arms indefinitely are not very convincing. It is difficult, for instance, to assume that Russia needs to be deterred from launching a nuclear attack when its leaders are desperate for western assistance.

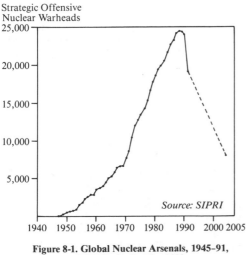

Strategic Offensive
Nuclear Warheads

**Figure 8-1. Global Nuclear Arsenals, 1945-91,
With Projection for 2003**

But what about governments that remain hostile and aggressive? In the wake of Desert Storm, U.N. inspection teams brought to light a clandestine Iraqi nuclear weapons development program of surprising magnitude. The revelations seemed to underscore the need for a residual nuclear arsenal to deter Saddam Hussein or any other aggressive powers. Yet western nations' possession of atomic arms did nothing to deter Hussein from trying to acquire his own; in fact, it may have spurred the Iraqi effort. Without doubt, Iraq was motivated to catch up with its adversary Israel, widely thought to have at least a small nuclear arsenal. Likewise, in other regions of the world, nations locked in intense rivalries with neighbors—among them India, Pakistan, and the two Koreas—seek to cross the nuclear threshold in the belief that such an arsenal might provide insurance against defeat in a conventional battle.[9]

Nuclear weapons do not have to be "uninvented" to be repudiated as a legitimate instrument in the conduct of human affairs.

Continued possession of nuclear weapons by a few "haves" lends legitimacy to other countries' efforts to acquire them. As long as possession of a nuclear arsenal is perceived to have political or military value, and to confer special status and diplomatic leverage, it is not surprising that some governments will attempt to join the club—and may well succeed.

It is often said that the nuclear genie, once out of the bottle, cannot be put back. But nuclear weapons do not have to be "uninvented" to be repudiated as a legitimate instrument in the conduct of human affairs. It is clear what it would

take to ban their possession. The most crucial steps include shutting down test sites; closing the myriad facilities for manufacturing weapons-grade material, warheads, and delivery systems; converting weapons design labs to civilian use; dismantling existing warheads; placing fissile materials under international safeguards; and devising plans for their long-term disposal. At each stage, effective inspection and verification measures to monitor compliance must be established.

Some headway has been made on these issues, but important roadblocks remain. From as many as 58 in 1984, the number of nuclear test explosions has declined considerably—to 14 in 1991 and roughly half that number in 1992. With Russia and France having unilaterally stopped testing, a comprehensive test ban is clearly possible. Yet the continuation of their moratoriums is predicated on the other "haves" joining them. Congressional pressure forced President Bush to accept a nine-month halt, to be followed by complete cessation in 1996 unless other powers continue testing. The United Kingdom wants to continue testing (per year, it conducts one test at the U.S. testing ground in Nevada), but its approach is predicated on U.S. policies. But China, which exploded its largest device ever in 1992, might hold out and give the other governments an excuse to resume tests.[10]

Ending the nuclear era requires a ban not only on testing bombs, but on manufacturing warheads and weapons-grade materials as well. Here, too, there has been some progress. Since July 1990, no nuclear warhead has been manufactured in the United States; production of HEU was halted as early as 1964, and that of plutonium in 1988. In the former Soviet Union, production of HEU ceased in 1990, while plutonium production is to end by 2000. President Yeltsin proposed a binding international agreement to ban any future production, but the Bush administration opposed the idea.[11]

Nuclear arsenals are at last being substantially reduced. The final and most critical disarmament step, moving from small arsenals to their elimination, could be accomplished with the assistance of a transition strategy. A small amount of weapons-grade materials, not assembled in warheads, might temporarily remain under the control of the country that owned it but be placed under international safeguards. Because such a step could be reversed if circumstances warrant it (such as the discovery that another country or group retained a clandestine arsenal), decision makers could grow comfortable with the prospect of complete denuclearization. Once leaders were confident that it could be safely accomplished, the remaining materials could be placed under the full control of an international disarmament organization.[12]

Complementing the changes on nuclear arsenals, long-standing efforts to ban chemical weapons will soon be coming to fruition—in the form of the multilateral Chemical Weapons Convention. The 1925 Geneva Protocol prohibits the use of chemical and biological means of warfare, but not their production and possession. And some 40 states that have signed the Protocol officially interpret that to be a ban on first use only. Following unsuccessful efforts in the thirties, attempts to broaden the ban against chemical weapons resumed in 1968, but languished for the next 20 years. They only gained real momentum in 1989, with U.S.-Soviet rapprochement and the danger (underscored by evidence of repeated Iraqi use of poison gas) that the 1925 Protocol might increasingly be ignored.[13]

In June 1990, the United States and the Soviet Union signed a bilateral agreement that committed them to halt production of chemical warfare agents and to reduce their stocks, by far the largest in the world, from a combined total of about 70,000 metric tons to 5,000 tons each by the year 2002. (Among the Soviet Union's successor states, only Russia has chemical weapons.) The multilateral Chemical Weapons Convention is a more ambitious undertaking. It outlaws the development, production, or acquisition of chemical weapons by any means, prohibits their use, and mandates the destruction of all existing stocks as well as the dismantling of all production facilities within 10 years. The draft treaty is expected to be signed in early 1993 and, if ratified by 65 countries, will come into force two years later.[14]

Unfortunately, no such progress is in sight in the realm of conventional armaments, with only a partial exception in Europe. The 1990 Conventional Forces in Europe Treaty—covering the area from the Atlantic to the Ural Mountains—establishes equal limits on the numbers of battle tanks, armored vehicles, artillery pieces, combat aircraft, and helicopters that the members of the North Atlantic Treaty Organization (NATO) and the Warsaw Treaty Organization (WTO) may deploy. (The WTO is now dissolved but its former members negotiated with each other to set individual limits consistent with the WTO totals.) Since the WTO countries had deployed far more military equipment than the western alliance, they will need to make much greater cuts. By contrast, NATO plans to make only small cuts in its tank and artillery forces, and can even add to its existing arsenals in the other categories. (See Table 8–2.)[15]

Even after the CFE Treaty is implemented, enormous arsenals will remain on the continent. And as the 1991 *SIPRI Yearbook* points out, "it appears that little [surplus] material will be destroyed as states have been rather ingenious in relocating, converting and recategoriz-

Table 8–2. Arms Reductions Under the Conventional Forces in Europe (CFE) Treaty

Weapons Category	Military Alliance	Pre-CFE Arsenals[1]	Treaty Limit[2]	Planned Post-CFE Arsenals	Effective Change
		(number)			(percent)
Tanks	NATO[3]	22,092	20,000	19,142	−13
	WTO[4]	31,713	20,000	20,000	−37
Armored Vehicles	NATO	28,408	30,000	29,822	+ 5
	WTO	41,831	30,000	30,000	−28
Artillery Pieces	NATO	18,604	20,000	18,286	− 2
	WTO	24,756	20,000	20,000	−19
Helicopters	NATO	1,543	2,000	2,000	+30
	WTO	1,662	2,000	2,000	+20
Combat Aircraft	NATO	5,316	6,800	6,662	+25
	WTO	8,368	6,800	6,800	−19

[1]As of November 1990. [2]Maximum numbers allowed by 1995. [3]North Atlantic Treaty Organization [4]Warsaw Treaty Organization.
SOURCE: Adapted from "Data Before and After CFE Reductions," in Institute for Defense and Disarmament Studies, *The Arms Control Reporter 1991* (Cambridge, Mass.: 1991).

ing equipment," all permitted by the treaty. For instance, in the three years before the treaty was signed, the Soviet Union moved a great deal of equipment, including at least 20,000 tanks, east of the Urals—in effect excluding them from treaty limits. And through a "cascading" program, NATO is redistributing the most sophisticated military equipment among its members, ensuring that only older, obsolete tanks and artillery pieces will need to be scrapped. The treaty, in any event, does not erect any hurdles to continued weapons modernization.[16]

For all its shortcomings, however, the CFE Treaty and the confidence-building measures agreed on in 1986 and 1992 represent some progress toward reining in the conventional arms race on the European continent. Unilateral cuts are also leading to sizable troop reductions.[17]

The European experience stands in striking contrast with the situation in many other regions, particularly the Third World, where numerous unresolved conflicts continue to fuel arms races. An important component of defusing these would be to curb the flow of arms across borders (see Table 8–3), since it is the developing countries that are the prime recipients of this deadly trade, accounting for 61 percent of world arms imports. Fewer weapons imports would likely generate at least a modicum of trust among opponents and provide an opening for peaceful settlement.[18]

Throughout the postwar period, attempts to curb the international arms trade have been unsuccessful. The decline in arms exports that did occur since the mid-eighties is a result not of political restraint but of dire economic conditions: many developing countries cannot afford to continue their buying binge.

Table 8–3. Leading Exporters and Importers of Major Conventional Weapons, 1987–91

Exporters	Value	Importers	Value
	(billion dollars)[1]		(billion dollars)[1]
Soviet Union	61.3	India	17.6
United States	60.0	Saudi Arabia	10.6
France	11.2	Iraq	10.3
Britain	9.1	Japan	9.8
China	7.9	Afghanistan	8.4
West Germany	6.1	Turkey	6.4
Czechoslovakia	3.3	Egypt	5.5
Italy	1.9	Spain	5.0
Netherlands	1.8	Czechoslovakia	4.7
Brazil	1.6	North Korea	4.0
Top 10 Exporters	164.1	Top 10 Importers	82.9

[1]In constant 1990 prices; all numbers are rounded.
SOURCE: Adapted from Ian Anthony et al., "The Trade in Major Conventional Weapons," in Stockholm International Peace Research Institute, *SIPRI Yearbook 1992: World Armaments and Disarmament* (Oxford: Oxford University Press, 1992).

Hence, a reversal of economic fortunes could revive the arms market. Although the end of the cold war creates an opportunity to remove the link between arms exports and big-power influence peddling, ideological factors are now often replaced by economic considerations. As domestic military procurement budgets shrink in East and West, many arms producers see their best hope in pursuing export markets. In the absence of adequate programs to convert weapons production facilities to civilian use, this pressure will continue.[19]

The few attempts to curb arms exports remain halfhearted. For instance, the talks among the United States, Russia, China, the United Kingdom, and France on restraining sales to the Middle East produced a vaguely worded statement endorsing transfers "conducted in a responsible manner." Although supplier restraint is crucial, controls are unlikely to work in today's buyer's market without a comparable commitment by recipient nations. On a bilateral or regional basis, they could enforce a quantitative ceiling on weapons imports, agree to prohibit specific weapon systems, or establish weapons-free zones. To date, however, there has been a conspicuous lack of recipient initiatives.[20]

The European situation and approach cannot simply be copied elsewhere, but Susan Willett of the Centre for Defence Studies in London has argued that the CFE model might prove useful in at least one respect: greater transparency about arms imports and other military matters can help build the confidence among governments needed to reduce arms. An encouraging initiative in this regard is the effort to establish an international arms trade register. A December 1991 U.N. General Assembly resolution asked all governments to voluntarily submit, by April 1993, information concerning transfers of major weapons systems for calendar year 1992. Initially at least, the register will include only a small number of items and the reporting requirements are not highly detailed. No distinctions will be made, for example, about the technical sophistication of weapons.[21]

Over time, however, these shortcomings may be corrected; the resolution expressly refers to the possibility of expanding the register's scope. Furthermore, a group of government experts recommended to the U.N. Secretary-General that the register also include arms production, an idea favored by many developing countries. To make the register truly useful, national reporting would need to be made mandatory, with international inspectors verifying data submitted. Eventually, the register could become a tool not just to monitor arms flows but to curb and perhaps eliminate them.[22]

Even where governments have agreed to disarmament measures, the actual elimination of weapons stocks is bound to be a long, costly, difficult process. No country, for example, seems to be in a position to comply, in a safe and environmentally sound manner, with the Chemical Weapons Convention's mandate that all stocks be destroyed within 10 years. In the nuclear arena, too, adequate methods need to be developed to "dispose" of long-lived fissile materials in an acceptable manner. The destruction of conventional equipment and ammunition no doubt presents similar difficulties. The hard work of disarmament has only just begun.[23]

TRUST AND VERIFY

True demilitarization can only occur with international agreements that impose strict limits on military arsenals. Such treaties, in turn, can only be concluded and implemented if there is confidence that all nations will adhere to the terms. And the necessary trust requires the existence of a solid, comprehensive verification and inspection regime.

Throughout the cold war years, on-site inspections of military facilities were generally unacceptable to governments, particularly Soviet leaders, intent on maintaining military secrets. Instead, verification of superpower accords relied heavily on satellites and other remote surveillance technologies. For more far-reaching disarmament treaties, however, such techniques would be inadequate. During the Gorbachev years, the Soviet Union became much more accommodating to on-site inspections. The INF, START, and CFE accords all incorporate extensive and detailed arrangements for such monitoring and verification activities.

Technological advances and greater political acceptance of intrusive measures have combined to boost the role of verification, and the experience to date shows that it is a workable proposition, thereby enhancing future prospects. The important exception to this pattern—Iraq's ability to conceal its nuclear weapons program from inspectors of the International Atomic Energy Agency—revealed substantial flaws in that agency's safeguards system but also led to efforts to strengthen it.[24]

Due to arms treaties concluded in recent years, the NATO states and the former members of the Warsaw Pact all have pools of qualified verification personnel. Yet for future accords, it would be useful to establish a well-endowed and competently staffed international agency. First, inspectors accountable to an international organization tend to be more acceptable than those employed by a national government. Second, many developing countries would be hard-pressed to marshal the trained personnel and sophisticated technologies needed for this purpose. Although the role of such an inspectorate could be spelled out in a founding document, its rights and responsibilities might also be anchored in individual disarmament treaties.

A verification system for nuclear disarmament would have several tasks. The first is to establish a detailed inventory of the quantities, types, and specific locations of all weapons-grade materials, whether deployed or in storage, and of all production reactors, reprocessing facilities, uranium enrichment plants, and other nuclear fuel–cycle facilities. (The precise number of warheads and amounts of fissile materials held by the nuclear powers remain tightly guarded secrets.) The second job would be to dismantle warheads under international monitoring. Ideally, weapons-grade materials would be brought under the control of the international disarmament agency to prevent their clandestine diversion. Meanwhile, inspectors would ensure that the manufacturing of nuclear arms is not resumed through continuous on-site monitoring of declared weapons facilities and challenge inspections at any suspect sites.

Whereas nuclear warhead dismantlement proceeds to date without an adequate international framework, the impending Chemical Weapons Convention contains detailed instructions for weapons destruction and verification and sets up an elaborate institutional structure—including a scientific advisory board, review conferences in five-year intervals, an Executive Council, and a Technical Secretariat to conduct inspections. The Secretariat will have a staff of up to 1,000 and an annual budget of $150–180 million.[25]

The draft calls for systematic on-site inspections to verify the quantities of existing chemical warfare agents and production facilities declared by each signatory, with ongoing monitoring to ensure that no weapons are removed and hidden. International inspectors are also to verify the destruction of weapons and facilities, and to ensure that no civilian facility produces any substances of military value, since any pesticide, fertilizer, or other chemical plant can theoretically be converted to serve that purpose. The draft specifies a list of toxic chemicals and their precursors; facilities producing a minimum amount of these substances are subject to routine inspections.

The proposed convention has considerably weaker provisions for challenge inspections against suspected covert weapon sites than were proposed earlier during the negotiations. China, Pakistan, and other developing nations favored less intrusive verification measures, but the decisive turnabout came in 1991, when President Bush retreated from his earlier proposal that inspections should be allowed any time, any place, without the right of refusal. Opinion on whether full compliance with the convention's provisions can be ensured appears to be divided.[26]

It is crucial that the world's nations gain experience with far-reaching verification measures. For arsenals to be slashed deeply or eliminated altogether, governments need to develop confidence that such measures will enhance, not undermine, security. That confidence often hinges on intrusive, short-notice, nonrefusable inspections to guard against and deter potential treaty violations.

WAGING PEACE

A less violent and ultimately warless world need not be a utopia. More than 30 years ago, Adlai Stevenson explained in a speech at the United Nations: "We do not hold the vision of a world without conflict. We do hold the vision of a world without war—and this inevitably requires an alternative system for coping with conflict." A truly new world order can arise if nonviolent change, both within and among nations, is made possible.[27]

Curbing the world's arsenals is a prerequisite to making nonviolent dispute settlement work. In a world armed to the teeth, each government in an adversarial relationship is likely to see the opponent's capabilities and intentions through the lens of worst-case scenarios and therefore be more willing to build up and rely on its own military prowess. In the absence of a minimum of trust between adversaries, the mediating, negotiating, and peacekeeping services that an impartial go-between such as the U.N. can offer will go unused, and far-reaching disarmament will remain a dream.

The end of the East-West confrontation and the growing demand for peacekeeping services have given new life to the hope that the United Nations may finally play the role its founders envisioned: an organization at the center of a collective security system. But these developments have also revealed the deficiencies of the current ad hoc approach. If the U.N. is to fulfill its designated role, its members need to institutionalize peacekeeping, put greater emphasis on preventive diplomacy—defusing conflicts before they erupt violently—and strengthen the organization's financial backbone.

When U.N. peacekeepers were awarded the Nobel Peace Prize in 1988, Secretary-General Javier Perez de Cuéllar noted that it marked the first time in history that "military forces have been employed internationally not to wage war, not to establish domination and not to serve the interests of any power or group of powers." In the first four decades of U.N. peacekeeping, only 13 operations were undertaken. In recent years, however, the Blue Helmets have been inundated with requests for their services.[28]

The past five years have registered as many new operations as during the previous four decades—including two of the three largest ever undertaken. (See Table 8–4.) Two factors explain this heightened demand. Stalemate, exhaustion, and war weariness have driven many combatants to embrace the U.N. as a peacemaker. Also, with the end of the cold war the superpowers applied pressure on governments they had been supporting to make concessions in order to settle long-standing disputes.[29]

Reflecting operations that are both larger in number and more ambitious in nature, annual U.N. peacekeeping outlays have risen sharply—from less than $300 million in the mid-eighties to some $2.7 billion in 1992. From 1948 to 1992, the United Nations spent about $8.3 billion on peacekeeping—a trifling amount compared with roughly $30 trillion (in constant 1990 dollars) spent for traditional military purposes since World War II. Between 1990 and 1992, the number of people participating in peacekeeping operations rose from 10,500 to a record 50,000. Since 1948, some 70 nations have provided the U.N. with more than a half-million people—military, police, and civilian personnel—for peacekeeping service at one time or another.[30]

Traditionally, U.N. peacekeeping operations focused narrowly on conflict containment—monitoring borders and buffer zones after cease-fires have been signed, and preventing armed incursions or illegal arms flows across borders. But now they are moving beyond these tasks. Missions are more complex and ambitious, and are increasingly engaged not just in keeping the peace but in making it: supervising the disarming or disbanding of armed factions, establishing protected areas, monitoring elections and human rights records, repatriating refugees, and even—in the case of Cambodia—temporarily taking over

Table 8–4. Budgets and Personnel of Recent and Ongoing U.N. Peacekeeping Operations

Location of U.N. Operation	Dates	Budget[1]	Personnel[2]
		(million dollars)	
Israel/Jordan	since 1948	31	300
India/Pakistan	since 1949	5	39
Cyprus	since 1964	91	2,195
Golan Heights	since 1974	43	1,332
Lebanon	since 1978	157	5,823
Afghanistan/Pakistan	1988–90	7	50
Iran/Iraq	1988–91	9	750
Namibia	1989–90	410	6,150
Nicaragua	1989–90	2	494
Angola	1989–92	52[3]	440
Central America	1989–92	26	625
Haiti	1990	5	312
El Salvador	1991–92	13[4]	1,149
Iraq/Kuwait	since 1991	67	540
Western Sahara	since 1991	141	2,700[5]
Cambodia	since 1991	1,000[6]	22,000[5]
Croatia/Bosnia	since 1992	634	20,000[7]
Somalia	since 1992	130[8]	3,550[9]

[1]U.N. peacekeeping operations are not budgeted on a fiscal- or calendar-year basis but for a period that can be shorter than a full year or stretch from one year into the next; the figures here represent assessed budgets during 1991/1992 for ongoing operations; for operations terminated in earlier years, the value for roughly the last active year is given.   [2]Including soldiers, military observers, police, election monitors, civilian experts (composition differs from operation to operation).   [3]Total cost was $128 million.   [4]Total cost was $70 million.   [5]Eventual full strength.   [6]Cost estimate for first full year; $1.9 billion estimated for first 15 months.   [7]Approximately 12,500 in Croatia and 7,500 in Bosnia.   [8]Unofficial six-month estimate.   [9]50 unarmed cease-fire observers and 3,500 soldiers to protect and escort emergency food deliveries, of which 500 had arrived by late September 1992.
SOURCE: Worldwatch Institute, based on various sources.

the administration of an entire nation torn by war in order to facilitate the rebuilding of institutions and infrastructures, and thus the rebirth of civilian society.

The United Nations finds itself increasingly drawn into mediating and conciliating not only international but also internal conflicts and facilitating political transitions. Ten of the 13 missions begun since 1988, including those in El Salvador, Namibia, and Cambodia, were charged with helping resolve domestic conflicts and the transition to more democratic political systems.[31]

Although Article 2 of the U.N. Charter specifies that the United Nations is not authorized "to intervene in matters which are essentially within the domestic jurisdiction of any state," the distinction between internal and international affairs is being blurred for at least two reasons. First, civil strife within a country may have repercussions beyond its borders, either because outside powers are drawn into the conflict or because streams of refugees threaten to destabilize neighboring countries. Second, television images beamed around the world of massive human suffering caused by savage fighting or government repression in places like Iraq, Somalia, and Bosnia have fed the demand for humanitarian intervention. One argument gaining support is that the protection of human rights in such cases should supersede the principle of national sovereignty.[32]

The international community will need to consider establishing a permanent peacekeeping force under direct U.N. authority.

The future may bring even greater U.N. involvement in supervising the settlement of internal conflicts, because the vast majority of violent disputes today are not conventional wars between nations but domestic ethnic and political conflicts. Furthermore, it is likely that at least some of these interventions will go forward even without the consent of some disputants, as measures to protect Kurds in northern Iraq against the central government in Baghdad indicate.[33]

Although important precedents are being set, the involvement of the United Nations in internal affairs raises difficult issues. Keeping the peace inside a country wracked by ethnic conflict, with competing factions and irregular armed groups, can make the monitoring of international borders look like child's play. And such domestic involvement is far from universally accepted. Eager to guard their hard-won sovereignty, many Third World governments suspect that humanitarian relief efforts may simply be a convenient pretext for old-style in-

tervention. China and India have been particularly vocal in their opposition. To avoid abuse and double standards, Edward Luck and Tobi Trister Gati of the private United Nations Association of the United States (UNA-USA) suggest that "over time, it may be useful to try to develop generally applicable rules of intervention. . . . For example, specific kinds of events, threats, or situations might automatically trigger Security Council action."[34]

Having evolved through improvisation, the current system is handicapped in a number of ways. Peacekeeping forces are created for specific missions only, financed on an ad hoc basis, and composed of contingents of national armed forces made available by governments voluntarily. Governments may be unwilling or slow to provide contingents or, if they do provide them, they might decide to withdraw their troops on short notice. Thus, the U.N.'s ability to assemble and dispatch a force swiftly—to prevent a smoldering conflict from erupting into hostilities—is severely compromised.[35]

If these obstacles are to be overcome, the international community will need to consider establishing a permanent peacekeeping force under direct U.N. authority. The impartiality of such a force—and therefore its acceptability—could be emphasized by directly recruiting, from a broad variety of countries, individuals whose loyalty to the United Nations is not in question, rather than forces drawn from sometimes reluctant governments.

Establishing a standing force would bring several benefits. Logistical and financial arrangements could be standardized, and the diverse tasks of civilian and military personnel better coordinated. A standing force would also avoid the perennial problem of familiarizing new peacekeepers with U.N. procedures and practices.

To be effective, peacekeepers need to be somewhat knowledgeable about the history, politics, culture, and language of the countries and regions they serve in. Hence, training is critical. The Nordic countries have established joint centers to train volunteers for peacekeeping missions. Their approach has been emulated by Austria, Canada, Malaysia, Poland, Switzerland, and the former Yugoslavia. A peacekeeping curriculum is now being introduced at U.S. military academies as well.[36]

But personnel from many other countries have no special peacekeeping expertise. To assure that it has a sufficient reservoir of competence, the international community would be well advised to set up training programs to impart the many unique skills that successful peacekeeping operations demand. In fact, the implementation of such programs would be prudent even before a standing peacekeeping force is established.

The early deployment of a standing U.N. force could discourage acts of aggression by underscoring the international community's determination to oppose them. In the future, its existence might permit the establishment of "U.N.-protected countries": any nation seeking to safeguard itself from outside interference would be able to ask the United Nations to send a force to patrol its borders. National governments would then be under less pressure to maintain sizable armed forces and arsenals and to divert large-scale resources from civilian programs. The European Community cautiously endorsed this idea in late 1992, although it is unclear whether its members are prepared to provide material support to make this a reality.[37]

Calls for a standing U.N. force, albeit one of a different nature, are growing more insistent. *An Agenda for Peace*, Secretary-General Boutros Boutros-Ghali's June 1992 report to the Security Council, urged that U.N. member states make contingents of their national armed forces available on a permanent basis, an action spelled out in Article 43 of the U.N. Charter but never implemented. Boutros-Ghali wants as many countries as possible to make available up to 1,000 troops each on 24 hours' notice for peacekeeping operations. Russia, France, and a number of other European countries support the idea, but the United States and China have been much less enthusiastic.[38]

Following this route, however, would seem to imply that the troops earmarked for U.N. duty will remain under the direction of their national military establishments until called on by the United Nations. They would thus not assume the separate identity of a U.N. force. It is also unclear whether the governments supplying the troops would retain any influence over their use, affecting the carefully nurtured impartiality of U.N. peacekeeping forces.[39]

Another crucial question is whether a standing force would continue to be committed to the principle of nonviolence. U.N. peacekeepers to date have succeeded by adhering to nonviolent principles, thereby helping the growth of norms against the use of force. Brian Urquhart, formerly the top U.N. official responsible for peacekeeping, explains that "the principle of nonviolence sets the peacekeeping forces above the conflict they are dealing with: violation of the principle almost invariably leads to the peacekeepers becoming part of the conflict and therefore part of the problem." In fact, peacekeepers have only been dispatched after combatants agreed to their presence and ceased hostilities.[40]

The experiences of the Iraq-Kuwait crisis and the devastation wrought by civil wars in the former Yugoslavia, Somalia, and other places have led a number of observers to conclude that only international military intervention could end these tragedies. The troop contingents that Boutros-Ghali wants U.N. member states to make available would deal militarily with acts of aggression; in addition, *Agenda for Peace* proposes the creation of heavily armed "peace-enforcement units" to enforce cease-fires.[41]

But there are other options short of creating simply an international army. F.T. Liu, a former U.N. Assistant Secretary-General with responsibility for peacekeeping operations, has suggested a two-tier force that preserves the commitment to nonviolence but in addition to lightly armed or unarmed peacekeepers incorporates a militarily more significant backup force to deter those who might resort to violence. It may well be that in some circumstances nonviolent means are unable to halt the fighting and that limited use of force results in the loss of fewer lives than if the international community simply let civil wars continue. If anything, the events in Sarajevo and Mogadishu demonstrate the importance of early U.N. involvement in crises to defuse disputes before they erupt violently.[42]

Although the U.N. is now taking on an astonishing variety of tasks, it is still reacting to crises rather than seeking to prevent them. Change may be afoot, however. When the leaders of the nations represented in the Security Council gathered for a historic post–cold war meeting in January 1992, they asked the Secretary-General to assess the U.N.'s role in "identifying potential crises and areas of instability." In his response, Boutros-Ghali stressed the importance of "early warning based on information gathering and informal or formal fact-finding" and of preventive deployment of U.N. personnel.[43]

Indeed, U.N. fact-finding and dispute resolution capacities will need to be enhanced dramatically if the organization is to have a fair chance of preventing the outbreak of violent conflict in the future. Robert Johansen, director of the Institute for International Peace Studies at Notre Dame University, has made a series of innovative suggestions. For example, he proposes that the Security Council "establish standing conflict resolution committees for each region of the world." He also argues that the Secretary-General should be given authority to send unarmed observers, or even peacekeeping forces, to any international border at any time, and perhaps to any area where heightened tensions threaten to explode.[44]

In addition to on-the-ground fact-finding missions, a U.N. satellite monitoring agency could provide impartial information to support preventive diplomacy—to warn against surprise attacks, for instance, or to confirm or deny alleged border violations or illicit flows of weapons—and hence to mitigate disputes and help build confidence between opposing parties. It could also play a crucial role in monitoring cease-fires, verifying disarmament treaties, and assisting peacekeeping missions. Start-up and operating costs would come to about $1 billion, as calculated by a U.N. study committee. The concept of such a monitoring agency originated 30 years ago and was formally introduced by France in 1978, but has consistently been opposed by the United States and, until the Gorbachev era, the Soviet Union.[45]

If the United Nations is to play a much expanded role in this area, it must be given a strong financial base. U.N. peacekeeping and peacemaking are the bargain of the century when compared with the enormous resources absorbed by the world's military machines. Yet many member governments fail to pay their fair share for this service. "It's a great irony," Secretary-General Perez de Cuéllar commented before leaving office in early 1992, "that the UN is on the brink of insolvency at the very time the world community has entrusted the organization with new and unprecedented responsibilities."[46]

U.N. members have accumulated sizable arrears on their dues, both for the regular budget and for peacekeeping missions (most of which are separately assessed). Total unpaid peacekeeping assessments stood at $859 million in January 1992. Of the five permanent Security Council members, only China has paid its full dues. And of all (then) 159 member states, only 28 owed no money. Given this destitute financial situation, the U.N. is forced to scramble for start-up funds every time a new mission is initiated, and frequently unable to dispatch peacekeepers in a timely manner.[47]

There is no shortage of ideas on how to solidify U.N. finances. Among them are giving the Secretary-General authority to borrow in commercial markets, to charge interest on overdue assessments, and to issue bonds. Military budgets would be a good source of funding. Various proposals have been made—among others, by the Brandt Commission in 1980—to levy a tax on military spending, on the profits of arms manufacturers, or on international arms transfers.[48]

Assessing member states for peacekeeping expenses is done on a mission-by-mission basis, frequently conflicting with members' national budget cycles. William Durch and Barry Blechman of the Washington-based Henry Stimson Center propose establishing a single Peacekeeping Fund, stocked and replenished by regular annual contributions. To cover start-up expenses, they suggest that the Secretary-General be permitted to obligate up to one third of a new mission's proposed budget as soon as it has been authorized, but before the funds have actually been approved. Both Boutros-Ghali and his predecessor, Perez de

Cuéllar, proposed such advanced funding authority. And both have called for the establishment of a $1-billion peacekeeping endowment and a $50-million start-up fund to give the United Nations greater financial flexibility.[49]

A U.N. satellite monitoring agency could provide impartial information to support preventive diplomacy.

Will a strengthened U.N. peacekeeping system be a viable alternative to the use of force by national governments? The two types of conflict that any security system will need to cope with are transborder attacks like Iraq's invasion of Kuwait and civil wars like those raging in the former Yugoslavia and in Somalia.

In the Gulf case, there is good reason to conclude that the conflict would have taken a different course had the U.N.'s peacekeeping and peacemaking capabilities already been strengthened in some of the ways outlined. Iraq's invasion was preceded by clear signs of a gathering storm. Once troops began massing near the border, the Secretary-General could have quickly dispatched a peacekeeping force. While not a militarily significant counterweight, it would have underscored the international community's determination to oppose the takeover of Kuwait. Greater attention to preventive diplomacy would not have ignored the Iraqi-Kuwaiti dispute over oil production and prices that was a key factor leading to the invasion. Even after the invasion, U.N. mediation could have played a much greater role than it did.

In the category of internal conflicts, there is considerably less certainty. Because civil wars are often highly complex, they defy easy solution once they have turned violent. The only alternative to waiting until exhaustion drives the combatants to accept outside mediation is to get the U.N. involved as early as possible to prevent the outbreak of hostilities. At the moment, the international community is clearly ill prepared for this, lacking even the most rudimentary tools and mechanisms for preventive diplomacy.

REFORMING THE UNITED NATIONS

If the United Nations is to move toward a more activist and interventionist stance, it needs not only greater financial backbone but all the political legitimacy it can muster. This concerns in particular the Security Council—which has "primary responsibility for the maintenance of international peace and security," according to the U.N. Charter, and is the only U.N. body invested with the authority to make decisions that are binding on all member states. Currently, the exclusive club of permanent Council members, equipped with veto privileges, consists of the countries that emerged victorious from World War II and that are in possession of nuclear arsenals— the United States, Russia, China, France, and the United Kingdom. Large parts of the world, containing two thirds of humanity, have only temporary representation in the Council, in 10 seats rotated among 174 countries.[50]

Leaving decision making relating to international peace and security exclusively to the Security Council will always carry with it a certain danger of usurpation by great powers, as the Gulf War demonstrated when the coalition led by the United States was given a blank check for driving Iraq out of Kuwait. In contravention of the U.N. Charter, the coalition did not seek a solution by negotiation, mediation, or arbitration, as spelled out by Article 33. Nor was there a determination of whether economic sanctions "would be inadequate or have proved to be inadequate," as required under Article 42. The United States favored using military force and never showed any intention of placing the coalition's military operations under control of the Security Council and its Military Staff Committee, as called for by Articles 46 and 47. In short, instead of nurturing the growth of international norms constraining the use of force, the episode helped relegitimize war as an arbiter of conflict.[51]

Instead of nurturing the growth of international norms constraining the use of force, the Gulf War helped relegitimize war as an arbiter of conflict.

Making the Security Council more representative and democratic may help curb such abuse. The current permanent members' veto privilege is a thorn in the side of many countries, particularly those of the Third World. Because the veto is widely seen as undemocratic, any serious reform of the Council would need to consider its eventual abolition. Meanwhile, there is a growing discussion about expanding the number of permanent seats. Japan and Germany have expressed a desire to become permanent members. Brazil has proposed that in addition to these two countries, permanent seats without veto be created for itself and the other largest regional Third World powers—Egypt, India, and Nigeria. It has also been suggested that the French and British seats be merged into one seat for the European Community.[52]

Jeff Laurenti of UNA-USA has suggested that the permanent seats "should not be assigned in perpetuity to named countries but, rather, made subject to periodic renewal based on criteria that might be written into the Charter." Laurenti does not spell out what the criteria for permanent membership ought to be, but in addition to traditional "big power" factors like military prowess and economic muscle, consideration could be given to population size and financial and other support for the U.N., perhaps with the stipulation that permanent members jointly represent at least 50 percent of the world total in these categories. Unlike today, the composition of the Council could also be made to represent the world's regions in a more balanced manner. And if peaceful conduct of foreign policy is to be given due value, it would be worth considering including at least one country that has been at peace for a long time and shows few signs of militarization.[53]

Accomplishing any changes would require amending the U.N. Charter, which in turn requires a two-thirds majority in the General Assembly and the backing of all five permanent Security Council members. No doubt, the "veto powers" will be loath to relinquish their special status, for some because it is the last vestige of being a great power. In any dilution of the strength of the present permanent members, there is a trade-off. If the big powers feel too constrained by the U.N., they might be more tempted to act unilaterally, in defiance of U.N. Charter norms. At the same time, as the Iraq-Kuwait crisis has shown, even militarily powerful states seek the mantle of legitimacy that the United Nations confers. If enough countries feel that only a more representative Security Council can legitimately exercise its mandate to maintain international peace and security, the big powers will need to allow some change.

Building a peace system undoubtedly presents a challenge of tremendous scope. It requires far-reaching political, social, economic, cultural, and educational change. In particular, the perception that national interests collide with a strengthened United Nations may still preclude rapid movement toward reform. Yet in region after region, the benefits of peacekeeping are becoming clear. The aftermath of destructive and exhaustive wars that fail to achieve combatants' original objectives proves the point. The question is whether the nations of the world are prepared to transform the United Nations from a peacekeeper of last resort to a peacemaker of first, and routine, recourse.

The fact that human history is replete with instances of violent conflict leads many people to assume that war is part of human nature and is therefore an unavoidable evil. At the same time that humans have strived to perfect technologies of death, however, they have also struggled, with halting success, to define acceptable behavior during war and to establish norms against the use of force. Just because war is a social institution does not mean it is inevitable: created by humans, it can also be abolished by them—given sufficient will and perseverance.

9

Reconciling Trade and the Environment

Hilary F. French

Low-cost tropical timber harvested from the rain forest in Malaysia is shipped to Japan, where it is made into plywood that is, among other things, used in construction where plantation-grown softwoods could well have sufficed. Lead car batteries are exported from the United States to a recycling plant on the outskirts of São Paulo, which has health and environmental controls so inadequate that 25 out of 29 workers tested have lead concentrations in their blood that exceed the U.S. recommended limit. A dam built on the La Grande River in northern Quebec in part to generate electricity for export to New England floods an area half the size of Belgium, displacing the Cree Indians who called the land home and poisoning their fishing grounds with the release of naturally occurring mercury. In these and thousands of other cases, world trade is spurring environmental degradation and transferring it around the world.[1]

But the growing integration of the world economy has some positive environmental effects as well. For instance,

villagers in the Dominican Republic use photovoltaic cells shipped in from the United States to light their homes. As recently as 1990, *Greenpeace* magazine imported paper from a Swedish mill because no U.S. facility could supply paper produced with a chlorine-free bleaching system. And fuel-efficient Japanese cars reduced air emissions in the United States and forced U.S. manufacturers to develop more-fuel-efficient models during the seventies.[2]

International merchandise trade, now tallied at $3.5 trillion, has grown 5.4 percent annually since 1950 (see Figure 9–1), regularly outpacing the expansion of global output as a whole. This includes both "primary" goods such as food, raw materials, minerals, and energy, as well as manufactured products. (See Table 9–1.) Trade in services, now worth $810 billion, is also growing fast, as is direct investment in foreign countries. These trends mean that international commerce, for better or for worse, is shaping global environmental trends in various ways more and more each day.[3]

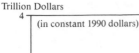

Figure 9-1. World Exports, 1950–91

First, trade magnifies the environmental effects of production by expanding the market for commodities beyond national boundaries. Second, trade allows countries that have depleted their own resource bases, or that have passed strict laws protecting them, to reach past their borders for desired products, effectively shifting the environmental impacts of consumption to someone else's backyard. Finally, national environmental laws and even some international environmental treaties are coming under attack as "nontariff barriers to trade," jeopardizing efforts to restore environmental quality within countries and to protect the global commons, such as the atmosphere and the oceans.[4]

As with transboundary and global pollution, national governments acting alone are unable to control the environmental effects of trade, making international cooperation essential. Yet despite the many interactions between them, trade and environment have traditionally been seen as entirely separate domains in the international arena. When the General Agreement on Tariffs and Trade (GATT) was created in 1948, its main task was lowering the tariff barriers erected in the thirties, which were widely blamed for the global depression. The

environment was scarcely a national concern then, let alone an international one.

Now, however, as environmental issues achieve a new prominence on the international agenda and increasingly bump up against trade agreements, the world is beginning to take note of the connections. Environmental issues have become a major feature of several ongoing trade negotiations—the talks on expanding GATT through the Uruguay Round of negotiations; the debate over Europe's single market set to come into being at the end of 1992 and over the Maastricht Treaty, the next step toward a European Union; and the negotiations and consideration of the North American Free Trade Agreement (NAFTA) between Canada, Mexico, and the United States. In these and other forums, governments are struggling to reconcile antiquated trade rules with present-day environmental realities.

In the postwar era, free trade has sometimes been pursued as an end in itself, rather than as a means to an end. This approach is beginning to give way, however, to the view that trade can be a tool for shaping a world that is ecologically sustainable and socially just. In a number of forums, governments are recognizing sustainable development as an overriding goal of the world community. Now policymakers must get on with the task of determining how the rules of trade can be revised to help achieve it.[5]

TRADE AND THE GLOBAL RESOURCE BASE

More than a quarter of world merchandise trade involves goods derived directly from the natural resource base that underpins the global economy— "primary products" such as timber, fish,

Table 9–1. Value of World Trade, With Breakdown of Trade in Goods, 1990

Trade	Value	Share
	(billion dollars)	(percent)
World Trade in Goods and Services		
Primary Products	927	22
Manufactured Products	2,445	57
Other Goods[1]	113	3
Commercial Services[2]	810	19
Total World Trade[3]	4,295	100
World Trade in Goods		
Primary Products		
Food	329	9
Fuels	369	11
Raw Materials	105	3
Nonferrous Metals	71	2
Ores and Minerals	53	2
Subtotal[3]	927	27
Manufactured Products		
Machinery and Transport	1,237	35
Other Consumer Goods	312	9
Chemicals	298	9
Other Semimanufactures	264	8
Clothing	113	3
Textiles	111	3
Iron and Steel	109	3
Subtotal[3]	2,445	70
Other Goods[1]	113	3
Total Trade in Goods[3]	3,485	100

[1]Includes gold, arms and ammunition, and other goods not classified elsewhere.   [2]Service data are less precise than merchandise data and are likely to be understated.   [3]Columns may not add up to totals due to rounding.
SOURCE: General Agreement on Tariffs and Trade, *International Trade 90–91, Vol. II* (Geneva: 1992).

and copper. For the world as a whole, production for the export market adds up to a significant share of the total for a number of these commodities (see Table 9–2), meaning that trade exerts a strong influence on the health of the global resource base. And for some commodities in some countries, the impact of trade is far greater.[6]

As with international trade overall, much of the commerce in primary products takes place between industrial countries. But developing countries are net exporters of food, raw materials, minerals, and fuels to the industrial world. And, unlike in major industrial countries, in the Third World primary products tend to dominate total exports.

Table 9–2. Trade in Selected Primary Products, 1990

Product	World Production	Exports	Exports as Share of World Production
	(million tons)	(million tons)	(percent)[1]
Plywood	32	11	33
Logs[2]	1,171	85	7
Coffee	6	5	84
Fish[3]	99	38	38
Grain	1,955	224	11
Beef	51	4	9
Bauxite and Alumina	112	52[4]	47
Iron Ore	980	395	40
Crude Oil	3,019	1,386	46
Natural Gas[5]	1,746	267	15
Coal[6]	3,316	358	11

[1]Percentages may differ from the data because of rounding. [2]Technically, "industrial round-wood." [3]1989 data. [4]Reflects only seaborne trade but comprises the vast majority of total exports. [5]In tons of oil equivalent (from terajoules). [6]Also includes trace amounts of peat and wood.
SOURCE: Worldwatch Institute, based on sources documented in endnote 6.

More than 98 percent of the total exports of Bolivia, Ethiopia, Ghana, and Nigeria fall into this category, for instance, compared with 24 percent of U.S. exports and only 2 percent of Japan's. Many developing countries are thus particularly vulnerable to trade-inflicted damage to their natural resource bases, yet many also depend heavily on the foreign exchange these exports can generate, making policies that promote sustainable production over the long run especially important.[7]

The tropical timber trade demonstrates many of the pitfalls of natural resource-based exports. Tallied at $6 billion in 1991, the value of trade in tropical timber has begun to fall as commercially valuable forests are decimated in country after country to please consumers in Europe, Japan, and North America. In Nigeria, exports have fallen precipitously over the past decade in response to overlogging, and Thailand and the Philippines—once wood exporters—have now become net importers due to the ravaging of their forests. Several other countries, including Côte d'Ivoire and Ghana, will soon make the same transition.[8]

Of course, the timber trade is not the only cause of deforestation in the tropics. Fuelwood gathering and the clearing of land for agriculture and grazing are also major contributors, as is timber felled for domestic use. Still, the timber trade is a more important factor than it might appear from numbers alone, as commercial logging sets in motion destruction of a far larger area by spurring road construction, which brings with it miners, farmers, and other forms of economic activity.[9]

The impact of timber trade is particularly great in parts of the world where production is heavily geared to the export market. Just a handful of countries now account for the bulk of all exports of tropical timber. In 1988 (the most recent year for which comprehensive data are available), Malaysia alone provided 89 percent of all tropical log exports. Liberia, Cameroon, the Congo, Ghana, and Côte d'Ivoire accounted for the vast majority of the rest. For plywood, one form of processed wood, Indonesia is the leading supplier, with 75 percent of tropical exports.[10]

In Malaysia, at least half the trees felled for timber are exported, which brings in $1.5 billion in foreign exchange. The East Malaysian states of Sarawak and Sabah, which supply Japan with more than 90 percent of its tropical imports, have been particularly hard hit. In Sarawak, environmentalists predict that there will be no trees left to cut in as little as five years, causing the destruction of the homeland of the local Penan people, who are aggressively fighting to save it. (See Chapter 5.)[11]

In 1985, the International Tropical Timber Organization (ITTO) became the first commodity organization with an explicit conservation mandate, when its 48 members—both producer and consumer nations—granted it the task of seeing that trade in tropical timber shifted to a more sustainable footing. Four years later, however, the ITTO itself concluded that less than 0.1 percent of tropical logging was being done sustainably. In 1990, the members decided to set a target date of the year 2000 for the entire trade to be based on sustainable production. So far, progress toward this goal has been slow.[12]

One of the victims of deforestation induced by the tropical timber trade and other forces is the earth's biological wealth, as plants and animals in the forest are driven to extinction. Biodiversity suffers from another type of trade as well: commerce in wildlife and wildlife parts. For some species that are particularly prized on the international market, such as the Orinoco crocodile and the Sumatran rhinoceros, trade is a leading threat. For others, it is an added pressure that can push to extinction a species already threatened by habitat loss and other forces.[13]

Global wildlife trade is valued at $5–8 billion annually, some 70 percent of which is legal. Each year, 30,000 monkeys and other primates are shipped across international borders, along with 20–30 million pelts, 500,000 parrots, 400–500 million ornamental fish, 1,000–2,000 raw tons of corals, 7–10 million cacti, and 1–2 million orchids. Nations have had some success, through the Convention on International Trade in Endangered Species of Wild Flora and Fauna (CITES), in controlling trade in products from certain particularly well known species, such as the African elephant and the snow lion. However, trade in many other threatened species continues apace.[14]

Regional trade pacts may exacerbate the difficulties in controlling the trade in wildlife. For instance, all border controls between European Community (EC) countries will be eliminated under the single market. An EC task force created to study the environmental impact of the "1992" program warned that this may impede efforts to monitor wildlife trade. In North America, a World Wildlife Fund study projects that the increased tourism and transport likely to result from NAFTA—as well as tariff reductions it mandates—will lead to more trade, both legal and illicit, in furs, exotic leather goods, parrots, stuffed birds of prey, sea turtle products, and other valuable and endangered species.[15]

Freer trade in food products, which account for 10 percent of the value of world trade, would have mixed environmental results. While buying grain is essential to meeting food needs in many parts of the world, massive imports can undermine local agriculture. For instance, reductions on trade barriers mandated under NAFTA on subsidized corn from the U.S. Midwest could force hundreds of thousands of rural Mexicans from their lands. Landless peasants may have little choice but to migrate into forests or overcrowded, polluted cities— or to head for the border.[16]

On the other hand, the agricultural subsidy reductions sought under the Uruguay Round of GATT could help reduce the overproduction that is partially to blame for world markets being flooded with cheap grain. This could raise the price that farmers in developing countries receive, helping to increase production and self-sufficiency. Cutting subsidies would also reduce the inappropriate use of pesticides and fertilizers in the industrial world, as well as overproduction on marginal lands. But numerous small and medium-sized farmers in industrial countries who benefit from those subsidies, some of whom grow more diverse crops better suited to sustainable agriculture than the more typical commodities, could be put out of business if farm programs are not tailored to protect them.[17]

By one count, developing countries lose some $100 billion annually in agricultural sales as a result of quotas, tariffs, and other trade barriers. The Uruguay Round negotiations will improve this situation somewhat by reducing tariffs on several agricultural products commonly grown in the Third World, such as tea, coffee, pepper, oil and coconut palms, cassava, and natural rubber. This will create jobs and generate revenues for these countries, which, if properly channelled, could make investments in environmental sustainability more feasible. But the removal of these barriers in the absence of careful policy reforms could also have negative environmental and

social effects, such as the expansion of agricultural land into the rain forest and the promotion of cash crops over subsistence agriculture. Women and the poor are often the victims of such shifts. (See Chapter 4.)[18]

By one count, developing countries lose some $100 billion annually in agricultural sales as a result of quotas, tariffs, and other trade barriers.

Many other agricultural exports also have important environmental implications. In Costa Rica, for instance, the lure of the export market encouraged people to clear the rain forest for cattle ranching. During the sixties and seventies, the nation's rain forest was reduced to just 17 percent of its original size through agriculture and grazing. The country exported between one third and two thirds of its beef then, in part to whet the almost insatiable demand for hamburgers in the United States. In Botswana, land degradation from overgrazing is partially attributed to special trading arrangements with the European Community: nearly half of Botswana's beef production is exported, much of it bound for the European market.[19]

Overfishing is also being spurred by trade. A staggering 38 percent of all fish caught are exported. In Iceland, which relies on fish exports for more than half its foreign exchange, a 40-percent quota cut thought necessary to restore the health of the local cod fishery would have caused the country's gross national product (GNP) to decline by as much as 4–5 percent. Faced with this, the government decided to cut the quota by only 27 percent for 1993. As stocks are depleted in industrial-country waters, and as world fish prices rise as a consequence, northern consumers are turning increasingly to developing countries to help meet the rapidly growing demand for fish. Between 1974 and 1987, the volume of fish exported from these nations increased nearly fourfold.[20]

Shrimp farming in Asia and Latin America for the export market has led to the clearing of large areas of coastal mangrove swamps, which help protect coastlines, provide sustenance for local people, and serve as spawning grounds for oceanic fisheries. In the Philippines, mangroves are projected to be completely destroyed by prawn farming within a decade.[21]

The production of ores, minerals, and metals for export is also responsible for large amounts of environmental degradation around the world. Mining and mineral processing have a variety of environmental impacts, ranging from the destruction of huge tracts of land to the generation of prodigious quantities of wastes and the creation of large amounts of air and water pollution. Many developing countries rely heavily on mining to earn foreign exchange. But the economic gains come with heavy environmental costs. A single copper mine in Papua New Guinea, for example, yielded 40 percent of the country's export earnings, but it also dumped 130,000 tons of metal-contaminated tailings into the Kawerong River a day. The mine was finally closed in 1989, but only after a civil war ignited at least in part by local people's anger over the environmental damage from the mine forced the government from power.[22]

Most unexploited mineral reserves are in developing countries, meaning these nations will account for a growing share of the total damage from mineral extraction in the years ahead. Metal processing is also on the rise in the Third World. Refined copper production grew by 33 percent during the eighties in developing countries, while increasing by only 13 percent in the industrial world. The share of world aluminum production centered in developing countries increased from 14 percent in 1980 to 35 percent in 1990, and is projected to climb to 44 percent by 1995.[23]

Like most commerce, trade in energy has a considerable impact on environmental quality. Large quantities of oil, gas, coal, and electricity are shipped around the world: energy exports totalled 3.5 billion tons of coal equivalent in 1990, 32 percent of total supply. Some energy trade can have beneficial environmental effects. For instance, natural gas use produces fewer air pollutants than coal or oil do. Transporting it internationally by pipeline could allow gas to be substituted for these more polluting alternatives. The Organisation for Economic Co-operation and Development (OECD) estimates that using gas (much of it from northern Africa and the Commonwealth of Independent States) instead of coal in 20 percent of Western Europe's power plants would cut carbon emissions from the utility sector by 8 percent, sulfur dioxide emissions by 20 percent, and nitrogen oxides by 8 percent.[24]

On the negative side of the ledger, however, the damage wreaked by oil and gas exploration and by coal mining is experienced in the exporting country, while the importer gains the economic benefit of using the fuel without suffering many of the environmental consequences. For example, the Soviet Union long supplied large quantities of oil and gas to Eastern and Western Europe. This provided a key source of foreign exchange, but also left a ruinous environmental legacy. Only recently has the extent of the destruction from this industry in the former Soviet Union begun to come to light.[25]

Many developing countries are trying to expand their exports beyond narrow dependence on a few commodities, largely to insulate themselves from the effect of stagnant or falling prices for them. It is time to realize that diversification is needed for ecological reasons as well as economic ones, if trade is not to exact an unacceptable environmental penalty.

THE GLOBAL FACTORY

Trade and investment in manufactured goods also play an integral role in global environmental management. In this case, it is the environmental issues associated with industrialization that are at stake—energy use, air and water pollution, toxic chemical production, and waste disposal. The global marketplace means that environmentally harmful goods and processes can follow the path of least resistance to countries most willing to accept environmental degradation in order to reap a temporary economic reward. On the other hand, it can also be the means by which technologies that are needed in the shift to an environmentally sustainable world are disseminated.

The export of waste is perhaps the most celebrated example of the world economy serving as a purveyor of hazard. World attention focused on this "toxic trade" in 1989, when several attempts to dump waste in developing countries seized headlines. Since then, the trade has been less well publicized, but no less real. According to Greenpeace, at least 10 million tons of waste of all types have been exported over the last several years, more than half of which have gone to Eastern Europe or developing countries, where regulation has tended to be lax.[26]

In 1989, the international community endorsed the Basel Convention on waste export, which regulates this trade by requiring exporters to notify the recipient nation of a shipment and to receive approval for it before proceeding. After languishing for three years awaiting approval, the treaty came into effect in May 1992 when it received the necessary 20 ratifications. Many found this little cause for celebration, however, believing that the Basel accord legitimizes a trade that should be banned outright.[27]

Some energy trade can have beneficial environmental effects.

There is some reason for concern that trade agreements will make it more difficult to control the trade in waste. For one thing, as with the trade in wildlife, the removal of border controls in Europe and the greater traffic across borders in North America and elsewhere could make it difficult to control illicit traffic. Second, these agreements could dictate that waste is a "good" not dissimilar to others in international commerce, making it difficult for nations to unilaterally ban exports or imports.[28]

This concern is more than hypothetical in the European Community. Under pressure from Dutch waste exporters, the European Commission recently challenged a ban on hazardous waste imports passed in the Belgian province of Wallonia in response to a public uproar over a waste import scandal in the town of Mellery. The European Court of Justice issued an ambiguous ruling in May 1992 that prohibited blanket bans on hazardous waste imports under existing EC law, yet allowed for restrictions on specific shipments. Notably, the ruling did support the idea that free trade should give some ground to environmental concerns in this case, ruling that waste is not an ordinary good and should be disposed of as near its source as possible. The fate of Wallonia's law, as well as of waste import bans being considered by France, Portugal, and the United Kingdom, hinges on the outcome of an ongoing debate within the EC on waste trade legislation.[29]

In 1989, 25 percent of the pesticides exported from the United States were unregistered there.

Many other hazardous goods are commonly sold on the world market. For instance, faced with declining markets for asbestos at home in response to health concerns, the Canadian asbestos industry has joined forces with the government to actively promote sales abroad. Ninety-five percent of the asbestos Canada produces is exported, more than half of it to the Third World. In the past, the government has been known to offer free samples to targetted countries, such as Thailand and India, in order to entice them to buy Canadian-produced asbestos. Export of pesticides banned or restricted for domestic use is also big business in many countries: the U.S. General Accounting Office (GAO) estimated in 1989 that 25 percent of the pesticides exported from the United States were unregistered there. The banned pesticides sometimes return on imported food, a phenomenon known as the "circle of poison."[30]

Freer trade and investment also influence where products are manufactured, and thus where the pollution burden associated with production is located. Some forms of manufacturing are increasingly concentrating in developing countries, including textiles, leather, iron and steel production, and chemicals. These nations accounted for only 19 percent of global textiles production in 1975, for instance, but for 26 percent by 1991. Their share of iron and steel production doubled over the same period, climbing to 20 percent. Altogether, developing countries' share of world exports of manufactured goods increased from 4 to 19 percent between 1955 and 1989. Of course, these numbers mask great variation in individual circumstances. The newly industrialized countries of Southeast Asia have been expanding exports of manufactured goods rapidly, while many developing countries remain highly dependent on primary goods.[31]

The growth in manufacturing in developing countries has a number of explanations. For one thing, development planners have touted manufacturing as the route to prosperity in these countries. Other factors that come into play include cheaper labor or energy, accessibility of raw materials, and the shift toward services and high-tech industries in the industrial world.

The extent to which environmental regulations in industrial countries might be affecting these trends has been the subject of considerable debate over the years. In the seventies, when the United States and other industrial countries were beginning to pass stricter environmental legislation, industries claimed that these laws would disadvantage domestic companies in foreign competition and cause the loss of many jobs as polluting industries moved elsewhere to escape regulation. Some feared that poorer countries would deliberately keep environmental standards lax in order to attract investment by becoming pollution havens.[32]

Most studies suggest that neither of these scenarios has materialized on a large scale, mostly because pollution control expenses alone are generally not a large enough share of total costs to make it worth a company's while to relocate. The U.S. Census Bureau estimates that these costs average just over 1 percent of value added for more than 400 industries, though they are significantly higher for some, including copper smelting, oil refining, and steel production.[33]

Studies do indicate, however, that in certain instances environmental rules can be a decisive factor in industry location decisions. H. Jeffrey Leonard documented in a 1988 book several cases in which particularly hazardous operations relocated, including those producing asbestos, benzidine dyes, and a few pesticides, along with some mineral processing industries. He also found that some countries deliberately set themselves up as pollution havens in the past, such as Ireland, Mexico, Romania, and Spain, though they have since backed away from this policy in the face of growing public concern over the environment.[34]

More recently, researchers found that in Mexicali, along the U.S.-Mexico border, more than a quarter of the factory operators said that Mexico's lax environmental enforcement influenced their decision to locate there. A GAO study found that 1–3 percent of Los Angeles's furniture manufacturers (11–28 firms) relocated to Mexico between 1988 and 1990. More than three quarters of them cited California's more stringent air pollution regulations as a major factor in their decision to move.[35]

Whatever the reason, it is clear that manufacturing, some of it hazardous, is on the rise in much of the Third World. Some of the manufacturing in developing countries is foreign-owned, some is not. In either case, there is a danger that old technologies and the lack of adequate environmental laws and enforcement in many developing countries could mean that this investment causes considerable harm.

The debate over the North American Free Trade Agreement is focusing attention on one area where these forces are readily apparent. The border region between the United States and Mexico is home to nearly 2,000 manufacturing plants known as maquiladoras— branches of companies that are allowed to import duty-free components for processing in Mexico on the condition that the final product be exported back. Almost all the plants are foreign-owned, drawn there by wages as low as 7 percent of what is paid for comparable work in the United States, as well as by the preferential tariff treatment and proximity to markets. More than half the 100 largest U.S. companies operate assembly plants in Mexico.[36]

On the books, Mexico's environmental laws are roughly comparable and in some cases stricter than U.S. ones, but enforcement has been lax. An official with Mexico's environment ministry estimated in 1991 that only 35 percent of the U.S.-owned factories along the border comply with Mexican toxic waste laws. Though maquiladoras are required to return to the United States any waste they generate, compliance with this mandate is believed to be the exception rather than the rule. Even with the intensive focus on Mexico's environmental record in light of the negotiations over NAFTA, a GAO spot survey of six U.S.-owned maquiladoras conducted recently found that none had obtained the environment permit that Mexican law requires.[37]

Investigations by a number of groups have revealed alarming conditions in the area. At three quarters of the maquiladoras sampled in 1991, the U.S. National Toxics Campaign found toxic discharges, including chemicals that cause cancer, birth defects, and brain damage, being emptied into open ditches running through settlements near the factories. The American Medical Association describes the border area as "a virtual cesspool and breeding ground for infectious diseases," in no small measure due to the fact that the population there has swelled to twice its former size in the last two decades, while sewage treatment remains practically nonexistent. Investigations by medical teams on both sides of the border have revealed alarming public health conditions, including elevated rates of hepatitis A and tuberculosis, in part because some of the pollution drifts or flows back and forth across the national boundary.[38]

Mexico has announced its intention to tighten enforcement and explicitly ruled out becoming a "pollution haven" under the North American Free Trade Agreement—a promise environmentalists will try to hold the government to. Under the pact, it will be considered a violation to relax environmental standards or enforcement in order to encourage investment.[39]

Despite the threats, international markets also help diffuse many environmentally helpful products around the world.

Though the maquiladoras have been the focus of particular attention because of the debate over NAFTA, in countless other places around the world companies locating overseas are causing environmental harm. For instance, Japan has come in for heavy criticism from environmentalists in Southeast Asia for allegedly locating extremely harmful processes abroad because they can no longer pass environmental muster at home. A Malaysian subsidiary of the Mitsubishi Kasei Corporation was recently forced by court order to close after years of protests by local residents that the plant's dumping of radioactive thorium was to blame for unusually high leukemia rates in the region. Several multinational corporations operating in South Africa, including local subsidiaries of the Bayer pharmaceuticals concern and a Duracell battery plant, have been implicated by local environmentalists in toxic catastrophes that they believe have caused cancer and other severe health problems among workers.[40]

Despite the threats, international markets also help diffuse many environmentally helpful products around the world. Trade in pollution control technologies is on the rise, particularly as environmental laws are strengthened in developing countries. European countries (mainly France, Germany, and the United Kingdom), Japan, and the United States among them exported $20 billion worth of pollution control devices worldwide in 1990, 10 percent of the value of the industry. Some renewable energy industries are also increasingly aiming at international markets. In 1985, for instance, which was a particularly strong year for the wind energy industry, 553 megawatts' worth of wind turbines were exported, valued at $720 million. In 1992, $200 million worth of photovoltaic cells were exported, more than half of total production. Direct investment is another route by which these technologies make their way around the world: General Electric has entered into a joint venture with the Tungstrum Corporation to build a plant to produce efficient compact fluorescent light bulbs in Hungary.[41]

International trade also can put pressure on companies to match the environmental innovations of their international competitors, as in the U.S. car industry's response to Japan's advances in fuel efficiency. Other examples include the early success of Swedish industries in developing low-flow toilets, which have now been replicated around the world, and a U.S. lead in some air pollution control technologies that has now been overtaken by the Japanese and the Germans.[42]

Though the studies done to date are

by no means conclusive, there are some indications that, contrary to some people's expectations, being open to trade and foreign investment can help prevent the creation of pollution havens, rather than cause them. A study by Nancy Birdsall and David Wheeler of the World Bank found that dirty industries developed faster in relatively closed Latin American economies than in open ones. Another World Bank study looked at the rates at which 60 different countries around the world adopted a cleaner pulping technology, and concluded that the new technology made its way to countries open to trade and foreign investment far more rapidly than to those closed to them.[43]

The authors of these studies suggest several possible explanations for these trends. For one, closed economies might protect capital-intensive, pollution-intensive industries in situations where low-cost labor would otherwise have been a draw to less polluting industries. Second, industries trying to sell their goods in industrial-country markets need to please the growing number of "green consumers" there. Finally, the equipment used by multinationals tends on balance to be newer, and therefore cleaner, than that employed by locally owned firms.[44]

A QUESTION OF SCALE

Whether it be trade in primary products or sales of manufactured goods, trade spurs more economic activity. This can be both positive and negative from an environmental standpoint, depending on whether the policies and incentives are in place to point development in a sustainable direction.

To start with, more trade means that more goods are transported around the world, which means more energy use and pollution. Transporting just the 4 billion tons of freight sent by ship in 1991 required 8.1 exajoules of energy, as much as was used in Brazil and Turkey combined. The 17 million tons sent by plane used 0.6 exajoules, equal to the total annual energy consumption of the Philippines. Though far more goods are sent by ship than by air, it takes 47 times as much energy to carry a ton of goods a kilometer by air as it does by boat. Trucks and trains used to transport internationally traded goods are additional major contributors to trade's total energy bill.[45]

Trade agreements will likely encourage growth in transport. For instance, the EC task force on the single market predicts that crossborder truck traffic—and the air pollution and noise that accompany it—will grow by 30–50 percent when Europe's borders are opened at the end of 1992, and air traffic by even more. Similar problems await North America. Crossborder trucking between the United States and Mexico has doubled in the last five years, reaching at least 1.8 million crossings—a period when trade barriers between the two countries have been slashed—and could increase another fourfold by the end of the decade even if NAFTA is not implemented. And if it is, an environmental review of the agreement by the U.S. government predicts that more than 12 million trucks could cross the border in both directions each year by the end of the decade. Besides causing greater air pollution, this increased traffic in both Europe and North America could lead to more accidents involving trucks carrying hazardous cargoes.[46]

In both areas, the increased volume of goods being shipped may be offset somewhat by a reduction in the number of trucks that have to dump their cargoes at the border and return empty to their home bases due to trade barriers against the trucking industry. Currently, about a third of all trucks on EC roads are empty for this reason, though this will end when the single market comes into effect at the end of 1992. Under NAFTA, as well, trucking restrictions will be lifted. In both Europe and North America, governments also hope to head off some of the growth in road traffic by encouraging the use of rail. (See Chapter 7.)[47]

In general, more trade tends to mean more economic growth. All things being equal, increased growth will lead to increased energy use, materials consumption, and therefore pollution and waste generation. For instance, the EC task force report concluded that, in the absence of technological change, the economic growth likely to result from the single market would increase sulfur dioxide emissions by 8–9 percent and those of nitrogen oxides by 12–14 percent by the year 2010. A study by Princeton economists Gene Grossman and Alan Krueger found that the trade and investment liberalization envisioned under NAFTA would increase annual toxic emissions from all industries to air, water, and land by 10.5 million pounds in Mexico, 13 million in the United States, and 8 million in Canada. The combined total surpasses toxic releases in the state of New Jersey in 1990.[48]

But if the proper policies are put in place, technological change inspired by regulation and economic incentives can at least partially delink these problems from economic growth. Between 1970 and 1989, for instance, energy use per unit of GNP decreased by 30 percent in OECD countries. Though this was due partially to structural changes in the economy away from manufacturing and toward services, and possibly to some transfer overseas of energy-intensive manufacturing, improvement in the energy efficiency of technologies was a key factor. On a more limited scale, bleached pulp production in Sweden grew by 5 percent between 1986 and 1991 while the industry cut its use of environmentally harmful chlorine in the production process by 78 percent.[49]

While economic growth can bring environmental harm, it can also help generate income that might make investments in pollution control more likely. Grossman and Krueger also looked at levels of sulfur dioxide and particulate pollution in cities at different stages of development around the world. They found that once countries reach a certain level of national income, about $5,000 per capita, the levels of these air pollutants tend to decline, presumably because countries find they have the revenue—and the political will—to invest in controls. Estimates of the added income the successful conclusion of the Uruguay Round would likely generate for developing countries are varied, with one estimate as low as $12 billion and another as high as $90 billion. Whatever the actual figure, this is money that could be invested in environmental programs. But in the absence of major policy changes, there is no guarantee that it would be put to that purpose in most countries.[50]

ENVIRONMENTAL TRADE BARRIERS?

If environmentalists fear that free trade will damage natural resources, free trade enthusiasts worry that stricter environmental policies around the world bring with them the potential for sizable disruptions to trade. They raise the specter of hard-won trade reforms being undermined as governments use import restrictions, export constraints, and subsidies to meet environmental goals. In response, environmentalists emphasize the need to sometimes use trade-restrictive tools to meet important environmental goals, particularly given the global nature of the economy and the environment.

Clearly, in some cases environmental policies and free trade goals collide, at least in the short term. Under what circumstances are environmental goals legitimate grounds for suspending the usual trade rules? And are there cases in which trade considerations should override environmental ones? Who makes these difficult decisions? These are some of the vexing questions making their way into the trade arenas with growing frequency.

National environmental rules that involve restrictions on imports are one type of policy that could be threatened by freer trade. Countries commonly restrict the entry of products that do not meet domestic environmental, health, and safety laws. Otherwise, the laws' effectiveness would be quickly undermined. For example, automobile manufacturers aiming at the U.S. market must make cars that meet U.S. emissions standards. Farmers growing produce for export must ensure that pesticide residues are within the allowable limits of the importing country. And beer companies selling abroad must make sure that their bottles are refillable, if that is the national law. Current trade agreements generally protect the right of countries to hold foreign manufacturers to certain rules for products sold in their markets, so long as the same conditions apply to domestic producers.[51]

But sometimes qualifications are attached that are troubling from an environmental standpoint. For one thing, trade agreements seek assurance that a given measure was motivated by genuine environmental concerns and is not just by a disguised form of protectionism. Governments often suspect each other of wrapping protectionism in an environmental mantle. For instance, the United States has long maintained that a ban in the European Community on beef produced using bovine growth hormone is really an attempt to protect EC cattle producers from U.S. competition. And in a dispute with Ontario, the United States claims that a recently imposed Ontario tax on all alcoholic beverages sold in nonrefillable containers was established not for environmental reasons but to keep out U.S. beer, which is mostly sold in cans. Similarly, Mexican citrus growers are convinced that a U.S. requirement that imported limes undergo a treatment for "citrus canker" is a disguised trade barrier, as they say that the disease has long been eradicated.[52]

Environmentalists emphasize the need to sometimes use trade-restrictive tools to meet important environmental goals.

It can be difficult to distinguish between a legitimate environmental measure and protectionism in disguise. For this reason, both NAFTA and the Uruguay Round of GATT would subject some laws to a science test. NAFTA would require that standards designed to protect human, plant, or animal health, such as pesticide residue limits, be "based on scientific principles" as well as on "risk assessment, as appropriate to the circumstances." The Uruguay Round proposal takes it a step further, requiring "scientific justification" as the basis of any such laws deviating from international norms. Because scientists often disagree on these matters, environmentalists are concerned that the domestic environmental laws of some countries could be subject to challenge.[53]

Even if a policy is genuinely aimed at protecting the environment, it can still have the effect of impeding international trade. A bill requiring that bottles be refillable, for instance, might work to the disadvantage of foreign bottlers who would find it costly to pick up the empties. In such situations, which goal—trade or environment—should take precedence?

One of the first prominent tests of this question arose in the late eighties, when foreign bottlers charged that a Danish law forbidding the selling of beer and soft drinks in cans and requiring that bottles be refillable was a disguised restraint on trade, and thus a violation of EC law. To resolve the matter, the European Commission ultimately turned to the European Court of Justice, which decided mostly in Denmark's favor. In a landmark ruling, the Court found that while the Danish law did disadvantage foreign bottlers, the environmental benefits of most aspects of the law outweighed the constraint on trade. The Court did find one relatively minor aspect of the Danish law (requiring bottle types to be officially approved) to be "disproportionate" to the goal at hand, a ruling some feared would impede actual refilling rather than merely recycling bottles, though in practice this has not happened to any appreciable degree.[54]

This ruling implied that, under EC law, for an environmental law that constrains trade to be allowed its environmental benefit must be deemed "proportional" to the restraint on trade—that is, of great enough value to be worth the lost trade. To date, this subjective balancing act has not been part of GATT law or its accompanying code on standards, which has generally required only that a given measure not be a disguised restriction on trade. Some provisions in the Uruguay Round would move GATT in the EC's direction, however, requiring in certain instances that a measure not have the "effect of" creating obstacles to trade, whether or not this was the intent. To this end, members are expected to choose the least trade-restrictive option available to meet a chosen environmental goal. NAFTA also contains some troubling language requiring that certain environmental policies be proved "necessary" to achieving a country's chosen level of enviromental protection. "Necessity," too, can be subjective, and trade dispute resolution panels have tended to interpret trade agreements in a way that would rule out a number of legitimate environmental policies.[55]

Another concern of environmentalists is that trade agreements generally do not accept the notion that product standards can include an evaluation of how something was produced. This became clear in the tuna-dolphin decision of September 1991, when a GATT panel ruled that the U.S. Marine Mammal Protection Act was inconsistent with GATT when it forced an embargo against Mexican tuna because they were caught in a manner that kills more dolphins "incidentally" than U.S. fishers are allowed to. The reasons for the provisions of the U.S. law were clear: if the United States had only restricted tuna caught by its own fishers, then foreign-caught tuna might simply have replaced U.S. fish, subverting the purpose of the law. Indeed, there was considerable evidence that, before the law was amended to prevent it, many U.S. fishers were simply reflagging their vessels and carrying on as usual, further undermining the goal of saving dolphins.[56]

By one interpretation, the embargo on tuna from Mexico amounted to a product standard—a national law defining conditions for tuna sold in the United States. The dispute panel saw it differently, however. It decreed that the GATT rules, which allow for national product standards, did not apply to this case because it was the process by which the tuna was produced rather than the tuna itself that was being rejected by the United States. Though GATT explicitly permits import bans on products made with prison labor, another "process standard," the judges interpreted the agreement to contain no similar provision for environmental standards.[57]

Also, the judges ruled that the environmental exceptions currently written into GATT only pertained to the environment within domestic borders. Particularly because it was done unilaterally rather than through an international treaty, the panel viewed the U.S. action as an attempt to foist one country's environmental laws on another sovereign country. Regrettably, the judges failed to distinguish between environmental issues of purely national concern and those designed to protect the global commons, such as the oceans and the atmosphere. Dolphins, after all, do not know whose waters they are swimming in.[58]

If future dispute resolution panels apply similar logic, several existing or contemplated import bans could be overruled. For instance, U.S. laws ban the import of shrimp from countries whose fishers do not use the turtle exclusion devices required of U.S. fishers. The United States has also threatened to embargo fish from countries using drift-nets or killing whales. The European Community recently passed a measure banning the import of furs after 1994 from countries where painful "leghold" traps are permitted, such as the United States. In addition, in line with what several communities have done and what many countries are considering, the government of the Netherlands recently approved an import ban on unsustainably logged timber to take effect at the beginning of 1995. All these measures would be potentially open to challenge under GATT.[59]

The use of environmentally related export controls can also be restricted by trade agreements. In the face of scarce resources—be they energy, minerals, timber, or water—countries sometimes want to reserve supplies for their own people. This can allow for conservation while still leaving room for domestic consumption. But treating domestic and overseas markets differently runs counter to free trade principles. As a result, such restrictions are discouraged by some trade bodies.

For instance, one tool governments sometimes turn to for environmental reasons are bans on the export of unprocessed goods. These aim to create jobs in value-added industries to maintain domestic employment while reducing resource depletion, making it politically easier to pass resource controls. Such policies are under attack, however, as trade restrictions. Several countries, including Ghana, Indonesia, the Philippines, Thailand, Uganda, and the United States, have banned the export of raw logs in some circumstances. But the European Community has charged that the Indonesian ban violates GATT, and Japan has questioned the U.S. measures. Environmentalists fear it may be only a matter of time before such arguments prevail.[60]

One tool governments sometimes turn to for environmental reasons are bans on the export of unprocessed goods.

Similarly, British Columbia had a policy that restricted the export of unprocessed fish in order to enable local fishers, many of them Native Americans, to continue to earn a livelihood while limiting fishing. A dispute resolution panel convened under the U.S.-Canada free trade agreement declared Canada's policy inconsistent with the agreement. When British Columbia then tried to impose more-limited restrictions, a GATT panel ruled against the province yet again, arguing that the primary goal of the policy was not protecting fish.[61]

There is no doubt that export restraints contradict free trade notions. In some cases, they may not be the most desirable policy from an environmental perspective either. For instance, the wood processing technologies available in developing countries may be older, and therefore more wasteful and polluting, than technologies available elsewhere. And without regulation, the lure of greater profits through processing could cause more resource extraction, not less. On the other hand, there can be more incentive to protect a natural resource that is yielding a high economic return. And politically, export restraints are often the most effective way to preserve resources, as they can make restrictions on resource extraction possible without undermining the economic base of entire communities.[62]

Resort to these second-best policies might not be necessary if industrial countries did not impose higher tariffs on value-added goods than on primary ones in order to protect their own processing industries. For instance, Japan levies a tariff of 9 percent on plywood imports, but allows logs to enter duty-free. Nations also tend to set import tariffs higher on more processed forms of other commodities, such as cocoa, fish, minerals, and rubber. Without these barriers, developing countries would in some cases acquire their own processing industries in response to comparative advantage, perhaps making it easier for them to pass laws to protect their resource bases.[63]

In the wake of the tuna-dolphin ruling and its failure to recognize the global commons, fear is growing that even international environmental treaties with import or export restrictions are not immune from challenge by international trade bodies. At least 17 international environmental treaties fall into this category. In the Basel Convention on hazardous waste export and in CITES, restricting trade is integral to the agreement. In other cases, such as the Montreal Protocol on depletion of the ozone layer, restrictions are used to try to prevent countries that do not sign the treaty from undermining its effectiveness, or to enforce compliance.[64]

This poses a difficult legal issue, as different international agreements are in conflict with one another—GATT, which precludes most restrictions on trade, and these environmental treaties, which require them. Which treaty should take precedence? Under international law, if both parties to the dispute are members of both agreements, the most recent treaty generally holds sway, which would tend to protect most environmental treaties. But problems could develop if a country not party to the environmental treaty were to argue that GATT should rule. So far, no such cases have arisen. NAFTA explicitly states that in cases where the agreement conflicts with the Basel, Montreal, and CITES conventions, the environmental treaty shall prevail. Still, countries are to use the approach that is "least inconsistent" with NAFTA to meet these treaties' terms. If NAFTA members wish to add any other treaties to this list, all three countries must agree, so conflicts over future treaties could arise.[65]

One added policy instrument that could be challenged as a violation of free trade rules is the use of subsidies for environmental goals. Trade agreements generally discourage subsidies, and provide for countervailing duties in some cases to compensate for their continued use. On balance, this should benefit the environment if subsidies are removed for environmentally damaging activities such as unsustainable forestry, energy megaprojects, mines, and intensive farming. However, some subsidies that are aimed at financing environmental protection could also be vulnerable. For instance, the U.S.-Canada agreement forbids subsidies for renewables and efficiency. Ironically, however, it allows those for oil and gas exploration and production to continue. Amendments being considered in the Uruguay Round talks would make GATT a bit more environmentally friendly than NAFTA in this regard. Agricultural land set-aside programs such as the U.S. Conservation Reserve Program and some research and development expenditures for environmental purposes would be exempt from the threat of countervailing duties. Still, a large number of other more general environmental subsidies would be vulnerable under the latest draft of GATT revisions.[66]

Whether the issue is import restrictions, export restraints, or subsidies, disagreements are bound to emerge over whether or not a given measure is indeed motivated by environmental concern rather than protectionism, and if it is consistent with the trade agreement at hand. The dispute resolution processes embedded in trade bodies are thus of critical importance.

The tuna-dolphin decision awoke environmentalists to the power of the GATT dispute resolution process. Its antidemocratic nature was one of their primary complaints: a national environmental law arrived at through the usual political process in the United States was subject to overturn by three international judges through highly secretive proceedings, without any opportunity for public comment. Indeed, even the reports of GATT panels are not routinely released to the public. Alarmingly, a new Multilateral Trade Organization to be created by the Uruguay Round would have even greater powers to overturn domestic laws.[67]

NAFTA will be a modest improvement over GATT when it comes to environmental dispute resolution. For one thing, the burden of proof will rest with a country challenging a given law as a violation of trade, rather than with the country defending an environmental standard. Second, an expert advisory panel to be created for the dispute resolution proceedings may include environmental advisers. A NAFTA member defending an environmental standard can choose whether to have the dispute heard under GATT or NAFTA provisions, meaning that it can ensure that these somewhat more favorable conditions apply. Still, there is no requirement that expert panels include environmentalists or that parties to a dispute consult with them, and there are no provisions to open the dispute resolution process to the public.[68]

The tuna-dolphin decision awoke environmentalists to the power of the GATT dispute resolution process.

Most important, trade agreements themselves need to be more explicit in recognizing the need for exceptions based on environmental concerns if these interests are to emerge victorious in future disputes. GATT, in particular, has a long way to go. As things now stand in that forum, the decks are stacked against the environmental cause, given the pro-trade bent of the organization and the extremely limited nature of the exceptions to its rules that are granted to preserve human health and natural resources. The word "environment" does not even appear anywhere in the lengthy GATT text.

There have been calls for the negotiation of a GATT environmental code, perhaps through a "green round" of GATT to clarify what to do in cases where trade and the environment collide. If the length of the interminable Uruguay Round is any guide, however, revised rules could be quite some time in coming.[69]

TOWARD GREENER TRADE

In a remarkably short period of time, environmental issues have become a prominent element in world trade negotiations. Both the EC's Maastricht Treaty and the North American Free Trade Agreement recognize the pursuit of sustainable development and strengthened environmental policies to be key goals of the agreements, on a par with expanding trade. This is a significant achievement that has yet to be matched by GATT. Though these developments are promising, the next step—actually putting in place the policies to reconcile trade and the environment—will be a far greater challenge.[70]

Economists and environmentalists are in general agreement that one key to making trade environmentally sustainable is seeing that production reflects its full environmental cost. If these costs were internalized by all countries, then trade would be an efficient means of distributing resources around the world. No country would be able to realize a comparative advantage in pollution or environmental degradation.

One of the primary ways to achieve this cost internalization is through environmental taxation. A tax on energy, for instance, would help limit the environmental costs of trade by encouraging the use of the least energy-intensive transport option, and in some cases by making a homegrown product more economical than an imported one. A tax on wood from primary forests would encourage the use of plantation-produced timber, reducing the impact of the timber trade on deforestation.

Although economists prefer economic incentives such as taxation because they are generally more economically efficient, regulations can also help internalize costs. For instance, strong air quality regulations require industry to pay for pollution controls, thereby internalizing some of the costs of damage to human health and infrastructure as well as reducing the environmental impact of manufacturing for export.

Another route to greener trade is through environmental labelling programs that help harness consumer pressure for change, such as Germany's Blue Angel program and the Green Seal effort in the United States. The choice of taxation, regulation, or consumer pressure depends on the circumstances. (See Chapter 10.) Whichever it is, the important point is that strong domestic environmental policies around the world are necessary for trading patterns to contribute to sustainable development.[71]

Yet so long as countries choose dramatically different levels of environmental protection and make varying commitments to enforcement, industries can be handicapped by having to meet tougher regulations than their competitors, and there will be incentives for industries to seek out pollution havens. As things now stand, if one country tries to internalize costs, it can find itself at a competitive disadvantage, at least in the short term. This can be a considerable disincentive to implementing progressive new policies. For instance, the EC's plans to adopt a carbon tax are being slowed by fears of a competitive disadvantage if Japan and the United States do not enact similar measures.[72]

In response to these concerns, as early

as 1972 members of the OECD agreed to a set of "Guiding Principles Concerning the International Economic Aspects of Environmental Policies." In these guidelines, which governments are now trying to update, OECD members committed themselves—in theory at least—to the "polluter pays principle," which encourages cost internalization as a means of avoiding trade distortions, as well as to a number of other precepts. The Earth Summit's Rio Declaration affirmed the polluter pays principle at the international level. But the polluter does not yet pay in most cases, as is amply demonstrated by the high levels of air and water pollution and waste generation around the world, and by the continued destruction of the earth's natural resource base.[73]

Perhaps the fairest way to encourage more widespread cost internalization is through the negotiation of comparable environmental policies. The European Community has taken this route, in effect recognizing that economic integration requires a measure of political integration as well. It now has hundreds of common minimum environmental standards on products and production alike that member countries are in general free to exceed if they wish. These have helped improve environmental conditions across the continent, while making it difficult for any member to derive unfair competitive advantage through lax environmental laws.[74]

EC "directives" are enforceable at the European Court of Justice. Nongovernmental groups play an active role in the process: they can and do submit charges of noncompliance. The number of such complaints rose from 11 in 1984 to 480 in 1990. Though the European Court has no fining or penalty power, the public shaming that results from a ruling against a country can be enough to turn the situation around. Also, in some limited cases EC laws may be enforceable in national courts. Still, many analysts argue that the EC enforcement process needs more teeth.[75]

A North American Environmental Commission has been created under NAFTA that may serve some of these same functions. Though the Commission is as yet just a vision for the future, the three governments have said that they want the new body to oversee implementation of NAFTA's environmental provisions and help encourage stronger environmental policies in all three countries. Justin Ward of the Washington office of the Natural Resources Defense Council argues that "a leading goal of the commission's efforts [should] be to raise environmental standards and enforcement practices to the highest levels within the free trade area." Like the EC, the new Commission will probably rely on the shaming function to try to induce changes in national practices. It remains to be seen if it will be granted the powers it needs to be able to do this effectively.[76]

At the international level, achieving the necessary consensus on environmental issues will of course be more difficult. Yet the more than 170 international environmental treaties that governments have already negotiated represent a first step in this direction. There are sure to be many more such agreements in the future.[77]

Some argue that comparable environmental standards around the world are not worth pursuing, as countries have different levels of "assimilative capacity," and value environmental quality differently. Yet this view overlooks the extent to which nearly all environmental problems affect other countries in one way or another, given the propensity for pollution to cross borders, as well as the desirability of creating a "level playing field" for business.

In addition, it reflects a view that weak environmental regulations are a legitimate source of comparative advantage rather than a form of exploitation similar to disregarding internationally recognized human rights and labor standards. As President Franklin Roosevelt told the U.S. Congress in 1937, "Goods produced under conditions which do not meet a rudimentary standard of decency should be regarded as contraband and not allowed to pollute the channels of international commerce." Complete harmonization of environmental policies is not practical, and is not sought in any existing trade agreements. Still, common minimum standards or taxes can move the world in the direction of environmental parity, thereby minimizing some of the dangers of trade.[78]

Common minimum standards or taxes can move the world in the direction of environmental parity, thereby minimizing some of the dangers of trade.

In the absence of common environmental policies, some environmental groups and legislators argue that lax laws should be treated as a subsidy under GATT, making countries who reap a competitive advantage through environmental neglect vulnerable to countervailing duties. Lower standards do add up to a sizable trade advantage. I. Walter and J.H. Loudon estimate that developing countries exporting to the OECD countries in 1980 would have incurred pollution control costs of at least $5.5 billion if they had been required to meet the requirements then prevailing in the United States. Allowing countervailing duties for environmental subsidies would mean that countries internalizing environmental costs are not unfairly penalized. And it would promote a convergence of environmental

practices around the world. Developing countries, however, fear environmental concerns will be used as an excuse to discriminate against their products.[79]

Countervailing duties could also be a means of raising funds for investment in environmental protection in poorer countries, if the funds raised were channelled back into the country with inadequate laws. This might help allay developing countries' concerns. Another variation, and one that might be more acceptable to the Third World and less likely to contradict GATT, would be for exporters of primary commodities to impose an environmental export tariff on their goods, the proceeds of which would be funnelled to environmental programs in their country. This would partially compensate for persistently low commodity prices. Importers could require the imposition of such a tariff as a condition of market access, in order to prevent a country that adopted one from being unfairly disadvantaged.[80]

To raise funds to mitigate the environmental impact of NAFTA, some are advocating that a portion of tariff earnings from crossborder transactions go into a fund for environmental and social adjustment that would be phased out gradually as tariffs are eliminated. The Mexican government is considering levying a "user fee" on imports and exports to raise money for environmental enforcement and cleanup.[81]

Of course, funding can be generated via more traditional routes as well. The EC has created a multibillion-dollar "adjustment fund" for its southern members (such as Spain and Portugal) that includes some environmental projects, as well as a $552-million fund (to be dispersed over three years) dedicated specifically to financing the development and implementation of EC environmental policy. And the U.S. and Mexican governments have agreed to a border cleanup plan of at least $850 million over four years that will fund a number of pollution control initiatives and cooperative programs in the region. Much of the money has not yet been appropriated, however.[82]

From the heads of Chambers of Commerce to the heads of environmental groups, it is now commonly heard that environment will be the trade issue of the nineties, and that trade will be one of the preeminent environmental issues of the decade. Meanwhile, regional trade agreements are proliferating, and trade is widely peddled as the answer to domestic woes in country after country. Trade is thus sure to have growing impacts on the environment in the years ahead, and trade agreements are certain to become ever stronger instruments dictating policies both within and between nations.[83]

Though a failure to consider the environmental impacts of trade agreements could have dire consequences, integrating environmental considerations into their fabric would yield sizable environmental returns. Trade must become a vehicle for promoting products and technologies that will help ensure ecological health, not those that undermine the prospects for an environmentally sustainable future.

10

Shaping the Next Industrial Revolution

Christopher Flavin and John E. Young

The need to achieve an environmentally sustainable world is now shaping the evolution of the global economy. During the nineties, ecological pressures will increasingly influence economic decisions, making some industries obsolete while opening up a host of new investment opportunities. Companies and nations that fail to invest strategically in the new technologies, products, and processes will fall behind economically—and will miss out on the jobs that these new industries provide.

On its own terms, the modern industrial system is extraordinarily successful. The size of the world economy has quintupled since 1950, bringing unprecedented though unevenly distributed prosperity to many nations. But much of the affluence has been borrowed from future generations. Destruction and degradation of natural assets—air, land, water, forests, plant and animal species—has subsidized the profits of many businesses in the late twentieth century. For industries around the world, the debts are coming due.[1]

Sulfur dioxide, hydrocarbons, and other pollutants flow in immense quantity from the world's smokestacks, fouling the air and shortening lives. Billions of tons of greenhouse gases enter the atmosphere each year, which is expected to make the earth warmer during the next century than it has been for the last 5,000 years. Thousands of chemicals find their way into rivers, lakes, and seas, while chlorofluorocarbons (CFCs) have damaged the protective layer of ozone in the earth's upper atmosphere. The relentless search for new sources of timber, fuels, and minerals is bringing destructive development to the far corners of the earth, disturbing the remaining storehouses of biological and cultural diversity.

Laws enacted by some countries to address these environmental threats have already yielded many gains, from lower sulfur emissions to reduced water pollution levels. But the challenge ahead is more fundamental—going beyond pollution controls and better management to reshape industries in order to make them environmentally sustainable. Responding to problems such as global warming and the loss of biological diversity will require the revamping of today's enterprises—such as chemicals and paper—and the growth of new industries, such as fish farming and solar energy.

Primary responsibility for creating an environmentally sustainable economic system lies with elected governments, which represent the interests of society as a whole. Governments set the rules for environmental improvement, while consumers and local communities create the pressure for change. The challenge is to adopt policies that make economic and ecological imperatives converge, redirecting market forces to achieve environmental goals. Since private businesses are by their nature focused on earning profits, it is up to governments to ensure that the most profitable investments are the ones that are environmentally sustainable. Policies ranging from well-crafted regulations to environmental taxes can be used to achieve these goals.

Still, in a world in which private industry controls the bulk of capital investment, accounts for the preponderance of jobs, and provides trillions of dollars worth of goods and services each year, the role of industry in damaging the environment—or ultimately in sustaining it—is central. In the end, it is industry that has the technological capacity, management skills, and investment capital to achieve an environmentally sustainable economy. Large, diversified corporations—some with annual revenues that exceed the gross national products of many nations—now have the power to shift investments between continents as well as industries, and to determine, in large part, the health of the environment. Small businesses also play a big role: many now have worse environmental records than large corporations do,

but they also contribute disproportionately to technical innovation in many industries.

Without the active participation of businesses of all sizes, there is little hope of achieving a sustainable global economy. This is particularly true in developing countries, where environmental laws and institutions are still woefully inadequate. But in order to move forward, businesses will have to embark on extensive internal reforms that better equip them to respond to fast-moving environmental problems and opportunities. In a competitive global economy, corporations that allow themselves to fall behind will face serious financial risks. In short, companies that fail to invest in the future may find they do not have one.

THE SECOND INDUSTRIAL REVOLUTION

As the number of environmental problems has multiplied in recent years, it has become clear that no corner of the earth is unscathed and no industry free of responsibility for the dilemma that we and future generations face. Gradually the focus has broadened from air and water pollution to sweeping problems of land use such as deforestation and soil erosion, and then to the long-range threats of ozone depletion and global warming. In the seventies it seemed that environmental problems could be solved one at a time through simple, focused solutions mandated by governments. Today, fundamental changes are inarguably necessary—and in some cases, are already being pursued.

Once seen as a distraction to the real business of business, environmental concerns are becoming an engine of the next Industrial Revolution. They are now pervasive in traditional "dirty" industries, such as chemical production and metals processing, and also in high-tech and service industries, such as computer manufacturing and fast food. Businesses are likely to prosper in the future not by selling massive quantities of identical products—the traditional route to economic success—but by meeting consumer needs in the most efficient way possible: supplying energy "services" rather than electricity, "information" rather than a newspaper, and crop protection rather than pesticides. At the same time, many industies are likely to become more decentralized, reversing the massive centralization that has marked recent decades. The challenge of the coming environmental revolution is likely to include alterations in manufacturing processes, the adoption of new agricultural techniques, and the development of alternatives to fossil fuels. Hardly an industry will go untouched.

Environmental protection is already a major industry. The Organisation for Economic Co-operation and Development estimates that the worldwide market for environmental goods and services was some $200 billion in 1990—nearly equivalent to the gross national product of Belgium. The organization projects it will grow 50 percent by 2000, making environmental protection one of the world's fastest growing industries. Some 80–90 percent of this burgeoning environmental industry, which includes an estimated 30,000 U.S., 20,000 European, and 9,000 Japanese firms, is in industrial nations, though it is now growing rapidly in the Third World as well.[2]

But these figures are narrowly defined, only including such items as the market for sewage treatment equipment and the cost of cleaning up toxic wastes. The much larger demands of redesigning basic industrial equipment or creating new industries will likely be measured in the trillions of dollars. The biggest centers of potential business growth lie in the most fundamental areas: finding alternatives to the internal combustion engine, substituting light-weight synthetics for steel, making solar electricity competitive with coal-fired power, substituting aquaculture for deep-sea fishing, and so on.

The far-reaching economic consequences of environmental problems are apparent even for relatively simple issues like air pollution. In the early seventies, scientists and policymakers believed that the solution lay in putting pollution control devices on factories and automobiles. Two decades of this approach have created a multibillion-dollar market for catalytic converters and flue gas scrubbers. Although these efforts have improved air quality in countries like Japan and the United States, few cities yet have genuinely clean air, and some have worse air pollution than ever. In the United States, some 86 million people are still breathing unhealthy air two decades after the first national air pollution laws were passed, while in places such as Bangkok and Mexico City, pollution levels are often several times the U.S. standard. These failures are partly due to inadequate or poorly maintained control devices, but they are also due to increases in the numbers of cars and factories, as well as the complex nature of air pollution—involving many chemicals that interact in ways that scientists are still struggling to understand.[3]

In the late eighties, policymakers in California—which for three decades has led efforts to tackle air pollution—adopted a plan that includes more radical solutions. These ranged from phasing out many industries and promoting public transportation to altering the paints and solvents used, changing the chemicals used by dry cleaners, and developing zero-emission cars. New air standards for the Los Angeles area announced in 1990 have already spurred a wave of technological innovation by industries in several nations that either want to operate in California or that see the state as a bellwether for requirements elsewhere.[4]

The impact of environmental rules in California, which if it were a nation would be the eighth largest economy, has already ricochetted through the global automotive industry. Since 1990, prototype electric cars have been developed by General Motors and BMW, and work on hydrogen-powered cars has been announced by Mercedes and Mazda. Some of these models will be on the market by the late nineties. Indeed, it now appears that the automotive industry is about to undergo some of the most rapid change since Henry Ford introduced the Model T. The gasoline-powered internal combustion engine, which has dominated transportation for most of this century and which survived the oil crises of the seventies unscathed, may finally be on the way out. Nissan and several European automakers are addressing another environmental issue: wasted materials. They have announced plans to build cars that will be nearly 100 percent recyclable—signalling further change in the world's largest manufacturing industry.[5]

But in a sustainable global economy, automobile production may not be the dominant industry it is today. As environmental constraints tighten, a more diverse transportation system is likely to develop, and with it a host of growing industries. The construction, maintenance, and servicing of public transportation systems may become even more important sources of business and jobs in the years ahead (see Chapter 7), and paving contractors may increasingly find themselves building bike paths. The annual production of bicycles, which grew rapidly in the eighties, already exceeds that of cars by nearly three to one.[6]

Among the industries slated for rapid change, basic extractive and material processing enterprises are near the top of the list. Operations such as mining and logging are among the most ecologically destructive human activities, playing important roles in the rapid loss of old-growth forests and wetlands. Such losses of often-irreplaceable habitats are diminishing the earth's storehouse of biological diversity. Scientists estimate that at least 50,000 species per year— 140 each day—are condemned to extinction. Mining and logging also contribute to the demise of the earth's remaining indigenous peoples. (See Chapter 5.)[7]

Automotive technology is about to undergo some of the most rapid change since Henry Ford introduced the Model T.

The logging industry is already under heavy pressure to clean up its act. Government regulations have pushed foresters in the northwestern United States to develop techniques known as New Forestry, which are intended to cut valuable trees selectively while maintaining the integrity and diversity of the forest ecosystem. In addition, many trees are being grown as an agricultural product—on managed plantations—although such practices are sustainable only if sufficient diversity is maintained to prevent serious blights and other problems.[8]

Improved management can cut the environmental impacts of raw materials production, but even greater benefits will be gained through basic changes in other industries that reduce needs for timber and virgin minerals. The efficient use of recycled materials is likely to substantially reduce the size of the mining and logging industries, while repair, remanufacturing, and recycling industries grow rapidly. Already, the per capita use of some virgin materials appears to have peaked in wealthy nations—which have built most of their materials-intensive infrastructure—while recycling is increasing at double-digit rates. There are enormous opportunities for more efficient use of wood: U.S. consumption could be cut in half through increased recycling and reduced waste in wood processing, consumer products, and construction. In Southeast Asia, 40 percent of raw wood now makes its way into finished products, a figure that could be greatly increased. And it is important that practices such as using valuable old-growth hardwoods to make low-value plywood be phased out.[9]

The paper industry is now changing rapidly, beginning in Europe, where government has pushed industry the hardest. Government mandates, consumer pressure, and the rapid proliferation of recycling programs have recently caused paper manufacturers to convert a number of mills to the use of recycled pulp, and at the same time to eliminate the use of dioxin-producing chlorine bleaches. Manufacturers that once claimed recycled paper was only good for low-grade paper products are now making high-grade magazine stock at least partially from recycled fibers. Such developments have set off a technology race that could help determine winners and losers in the paper industry in the next decade. Over time, the industry may move away from the forested areas where it is now centered to the outskirts of large cities, where its major future resource—discarded paper—and its markets lie.[10]

The steel industry is undergoing a similar transformation. Under pressure of higher energy prices, declining grades of iron ore, and environmental concerns, the world steel industry has been replacing its older, less efficient, more polluting mills since the seventies. The

most rapid area of growth is in modular minimills that rely on electric arc furnaces. They are far more energy-efficient, and rely heavily on scrap steel rather than iron ore. Because they do not need to be near iron and coal resources, minimills are likely to be decentralized, and can be a center of economic development even in a small city. Such plants are likely to proliferate in the years ahead. The nations of Eastern Europe and the former Soviet Union, relying on 50-year-old steel technology, may be well placed to leapfrog to the kind of state-of-the-art equipment now being deployed.[11]

The chemical industry is among those most affected by environmental concerns. Chemical manufacturing has grown at a staggering pace in recent decades, as has the number of its products. Complex organic compounds, many of them toxic, now find their way into virtually every product and production process. For example, detergents typically contain three types of chemicals—surfactants, builders, and additives—and for surfactants alone, more than 400 different synthetic chemicals are in use. Government figures show that more than 700,000 tons of toxic pollutants are released each year by the U.S. chemical industry. Many of these chemicals are long-lived and find their way into lakes, groundwater, and the air people breathe.[12]

Concerns over toxic emissions mushroomed after the catastrophic release of methyl isocyanate gas from a Union Carbide plant in India in 1984, killing 2,000–5,000 people and injuring 200,000 more. The Indian government has since assessed Union Carbide $470 million in penalties ($270 million in excess of the company's insurance coverage), has ordered the confiscation of the U.S. firm's 50.9-percent share of its Indian subsidiary, and is still pursuing the U.S.-

based chief executive officer (CEO) on criminal charges.[13]

Governments have gradually cracked down on toxic releases—first into water, then onto land, and finally to the air. Many companies have been faced with the costly cleanup of decades' worth of negligent waste disposal. Others have been hit with costly lawsuits filed by those injured by exposure to toxic materials.

Early on, it became clear that end-of-pipe pollution controls were not always the most cost-effective way to deal with toxic chemicals. The U.S. firm 3M pioneered a different approach. Its "Pollution Prevention Pays" program, established in 1975, encourages employees to find ways to reduce or eliminate use of problem chemicals—and save money—through redesign of products and manufacturing processes. 3M estimates it has prevented more than 1 billion pounds of emissions since then and saved over $500 million. The company plans to cut its releases to the air another 70 percent by the end of 1993.[14]

Many other firms began to emulate the 3M approach in the eighties. Dow Chemical reports that its pollution reduction program has cut its U.S. air emissions in half since 1985. The British chemical giant ICI has built a new terephthalic acid plant in Taiwan that it claims produces virtually no chemical wastes. The new, redesigned production processes are often simpler and cheaper, quickly repaying investments. Some chemical companies have made process redesign an important part of corporate strategy. Ecover, which produces soaps and detergents in Belgium, opened a closed-cycle factory in 1992, with emissions that are near zero.[15]

An even greater challenge is to find substitutes for products that are themselves hazardous or that cannot be manufactured without using dangerous chemicals. The agricultural chemical business is one industry in which cleanup efforts extend well beyond the factory wall. Agriculture has been transformed in recent decades by the massive use of chemical herbicides and insecticides intended to boost yields. Pests have become immune to many chemicals, however, and toxic substances have made their way into groundwater. A number of farmers are turning to alternative forms of pest control, including integrated pest management (IPM). Combining small, targetted applications of pesticides with careful monitoring of field conditions and protection of predator insects, IPM often saves farmers money through reduced chemical bills. It is likely to have far-reaching consequences for agribusiness, giving rise to new firms offering IPM services. Companies may find they do better marketing "pest management" than pesticides alone.[16]

Improving the efficiency of water use will rely on a diverse array of manufacturing and service companies.

Water conservation is another growing enterprise. In contrast to the large dams and diversion projects of the past, improving the efficiency of water use will rely on a diverse array of manufacturing and service companies. The engine of growth is the emergence of water shortages in many regions, which has led to a range of conservation programs. Already, the market for low-flow toilets and showerheads is burgeoning, and many industries are altering their production processes to cut water use by 75 percent or more. Agriculture, the largest user, is turning to drip irrigation and other forms of water management to deliver water more efficiently. (See Chapter 2.)[17]

Depletion of natural resources may also help create entirely new industries—providing for profit what nature once provided for free. Fish is a good example. Growth in the world fish catch, which has proceeded steadily for most of this century, is slowing and may not increase much more in the years ahead. With the world's population surging upward and demand for protein increasing apace, it is not surprising that fish prices are up. One response lies in fish farming, also known as aquaculture. Although aquaculture—like fishing—is constrained by the availability of natural resources, such as clean water, energy, and space, commercial fish farming is a growing industry, having increased from 10.5 million tons in 1984 to 14.5 million in 1988. Currently contributing 10–15 percent of the world's fish, the business ranges from the high-cost salmon farming practiced in the fjords of Norway to the prolific carp and tilapia farms now common in China.[18]

GLOBAL CHALLENGES

Industry's reactions to two international environmental concerns—depletion of the ozone layer and global warming—illustrate the pressures and opportunities arising from a host of worldwide problems, ranging from population growth and the loss of biological diversity to protection of the global commons.

When scientific evidence first surfaced in the early seventies that chlorofluorocarbon chemicals threatened the protective ozone shield in the earth's upper atmosphere, industry was quick to challenge the new studies and to argue that the world simply could not manage without CFCs. These were wonder chemicals, they claimed—inert, nontoxic, and rapidly becoming ubiquitous in everything from refrigerators to foam insulation and silicon chip production. Following difficult political fights, governments in the United States and Scandinavia approved limits on some CFCs—but only for the least valuable uses, in aerosol spray cans. Worldwide, CFC production continued to climb, rising by nearly half between 1975 and 1988.[19]

In the early eighties, growing proof of CFCs' damage to the ozone layer and of the crop degradation and potential epidemic of skin cancer that could result brought ozone depletion back to the attention of policymakers. This time the case was even stronger, and the discovery of an alarming "hole" in the ozone layer over Antarctica made this into a public issue widely discussed in the press. By the mid-eighties, the international community was at work on an ozone agreement—leading to the landmark Montreal Protocol of 1987, which required industrial nations to cut CFC production in half by 1999. Toward the end of the negotiations, many companies eased their opposition. Du Pont, the leading manufacturer of CFCs and a major opponent of restrictions, announced in 1988 that it would totally eliminate production of the most damaging CFCs. It turned out that Du Pont was well on the way to developing CFC substitutes, which would be at least as profitable as the chemicals being phased out.[20]

Reacting to still more alarming scientific evidence, another international agreement was reached in London in 1990, committing industrial nations to halt the use of the most ozone-damaging CFCs by the year 2000. By 1991, world production of CFCs had fallen 46 percent from its peak in 1988. This has created a steep challenge for the hundreds of companies that produce automobiles, computers, and other products that in some way use CFCs. Products and processes that collectively represent a market of tens of billions of dollars must now be revamped. Cooling devices—both refrigerators and air-conditioners—are particularly dependent on CFCs, both as a heat-transfer fluid and for insulation. Although manufacturers once dismissed the feasibility of living without CFCs, major redesign efforts are under way that show promise of yielding even better products. New CFC-free, gas-fired air-conditioners, for example, may be more economical than current models.[21]

Global warming presents a more fundamental challenge—calling into question the fossil-fuel-powered energy systems that are the engine of today's economies. These systems are already under assault. Oil production is falling in many regions, and although coal is abundant, it has contributed to land degradation, air pollution, and acid rain, so its use is constrained. Global climate change presents additional restrictions, however. Scientific studies suggest that the equivalent of a doubling of atmospheric concentrations of carbon dioxide will raise the global average temperature between 1.5 and 4.5 degrees Celsius, putting life-support systems at risk. Current trends would commit the world to that much warming by the latter part of the twenty-first century, a heating that would take centuries to reverse. Even if we were to allow such a doubling but decide not to exceed it, most of the fossil fuels will have to be left in the ground.[22]

Although the climate treaty signed at the Earth Summit in 1992 does not include a timetable for cutting carbon emissions, it does commit industrial nations to the principle of freezing them in the short run and reducing them later. Already, some 23 nations have established national targets for reducing carbon emissions, and new policies—from renewable energy tax incentives to lighting efficiency standards—are being enacted. This suggests major changes ahead in the world's energy industries, ranging from petroleum to coal mining, power generation, and, most important, all forms of energy use. Reliance on coal is already falling in several industrial nations.[23]

The fastest, least expensive way to reduce carbon emissions is to improve energy efficiency. Automobiles, jet aircraft, buildings, home appliances, industrial motors, copper smelters, and virtually everything else that uses energy can be made much more efficient—by amounts that range from 30 percent to more than 90 percent. Even greater benefits may come from structural changes in economies and infrastructures—more compact communities built around efficient public transportation systems, or substitution of recycled for virgin materials—that reduce energy needs. The market in more energy-efficient equipment may reach hundreds of billions of dollars annually. A 1992 study found that a major effort to boost energy efficiency in the United States could lead to a net increase of 1 million jobs by the year 2010.[24]

The market in more energy-efficient equipment may reach hundreds of billions of dollars annually.

The incandescent light bulb pioneered by Thomas Edison more than a century ago is a good example of an old technology that is ripe for replacement. In the early eighties, lighting manufacturers developed a far more efficient compact fluorescent bulb. Although they were bulky and expensive at first, the market for these bulbs has surged, efficiencies have continued to improve, and the cost is coming down. It is now possible to cut lighting energy needs by 75 percent simply by changing a bulb. Compact fluorescent technology has been licensed to lighting companies from the Netherlands to Taiwan. As is frequently the case with new technologies, the companies that had the vision and resources to stick with the compact fluorescent when the cost was high and consumer demand low will reap the big rewards in the future.[25]

As the world seeks to stabilize the global climate, the mix of fossil fuels is also likely to change. Since burning natural gas produces roughly half as much carbon dioxide per unit of energy as burning coal, the role of gas is sure to expand. New technologies already allow gas to be used efficiently to produce electricity, to heat and cool buildings, and even to run cars, allowing the fuel to play a role in every sector of the energy economy. Although fuel cells—a decentralized technology that allows the efficient conversion of gas to electricity inside buildings—were originally developed in U.S. research labs, Japanese companies are now leading the effort to commercialize them.[26]

The oil and gas industries are intertwined in most countries, and with their sunk investment in oil tankers, refineries, and service stations, they have shown minimal interest in gas. But a few companies have begun to consider natural gas as a replacement for oil and coal and a bridge to reliance on hydrogen derived from renewable resources. If this transition is to occur, it will require major investments—particularly in pipeline infrastructure—in the many countries that do not yet rely heavily on natural gas. A consortium of Japanese companies is considering a $20-billion plan to build a gas trunkline that would run the length of Japan and connect under water to Korea in the south and eastern Siberia in the north.[27]

Preparing the world for reliance on re-newable energy will require even more changes. The industries of the next Industrial Revolution—wind turbine manufacturing, solar cell production, biomass gasification, geothermal equipment manufacturing, hydrogen production and storage—are still fledglings. The global energy industry generates more than $1 trillion worth of revenues each year, but renewables account for less than 1 percent of the total. Supported by small, isolated markets from California to Israel, the use of renewable energy is now expanding, spurred by government efforts to remove market barriers and to provide incentives for cleaner energy technologies.[28]

Some $3 billion worth of wind machines have been installed in California in the past decade, and northern Europe has plans to at least match that figure by 2000. By 1992, Germany had nearly 1,000 turbines in place and was installing them faster than any other country. Solar water heating, an even simpler technology, has caught on in countries such as Japan, Jordan, and Israel already, and with some government encouragement could become a major industry. Another solar technology—photovoltaic cells, which turn sunlight into electricity—is expanding rapidly, largely due to the investments of major electrical and electronics companies such as Siemens, Sanyo, and Kyocera. The market for solar cells passed $500 million in 1992 and is expected to double in the next few years. At such growth rates, it will not take renewables long to become major industries.[29]

The ultimate transition to hydrogen, a clean-burning and carbon-free fuel, as a substitute for oil and natural gas will have much broader industrial implications—requiring a gradual rebuilding of much of the world's energy infrastructure. The gas lines that now link North Africa and Western Europe might be altered to carry hydrogen produced in desert-based solar power plants. Developing such a system will require extensive investments in solar power stations, in electrolysis plants for the production of hydrogen fuel, and in new automotive technologies and home energy systems that use hydrogen. For construction industries, the task may be similar in scale to the building of the U.S. interstate highway system in the fifties and sixties.[30]

The advent of these newer, smaller-scale technologies has accelerated a major shift in the power generation industry. In the past, virtually all power plants were built by large utility companies either owned by governments or granted a regional monopoly by them. But in recent years an aggressive independent power industry has sprung up in the United States, and is building over half the new generating plants. Other countries, from the United Kingdom to Pakistan, are following the U.S. lead. Two decades from now, it is quite likely that independent, competitive companies will dominate the power plant construction and operation business, limiting utilities to what they do best—distribution of electricity and investment in more-efficient equipment in buildings and factories.[31]

NEW ROLES FOR GOVERNMENT

If there is a single motivating force for private business, it is to make money for the owners—in the case of the modern corporation, for the shareholders. While well-run companies will pursue profitable investments in environmental remedies, businesses on their own are unlikely to take responsibility for addressing society's broader environmen-

tal problems. It is up to governments to set the conditions that will impel business to do the right thing—to meld the imperatives of short-term profits with the long-term concerns of society. If sustainable development becomes profitable, most companies will pursue it.

If sustainable development becomes profitable, most companies will pursue it.

Governments have in effect been trying to balance this equation since the sixties—setting standards that make pollution and other forms of environmental degradation more costly. Hundreds of environmental laws have been passed in the last three decades, and the resulting regulations fill thousands of pages. Most of these consist of prescriptive regulations—mandating, for example, that cities build sewage treatment facilities or that fly ash precipitators be added to power plants. There is no arguing the extensive changes many of these laws have led to. In the United States, for example, curtailing the use of lead in gasoline cut average levels of the metal in children's blood by 37 percent between 1976 and 1980—sparing many from permanent mental impairment. And tight restrictions on asbestos cut its commercial use from 560,000 tons in 1979 to 85,000 tons in 1988. Robert Bringer, a Vice-President at 3M, calls regulation "a market force of substantial proportion."[32]

As the complexity of environmental ills has grown, however, one-problem-at-a-time regulatory tools have proved blunt and at times ineffective. Such laws often exchange one problem for another; the ash removed from smokestacks, for instance, contains toxic materials that are hard to dispose of. When governments focused on reducing carbon monoxide and hydrocarbon emissions from cars, nitrogen oxide emissions grew—worsening urban smog. Concern has now expanded to include carbon dioxide, which spews in even larger quantities from tailpipes, forcing automakers to serve a series of masters. In addition, prescriptive rules rarely stretch the limits of technology. If a company is required to cut a pollutant by 50 percent but discovers a way to achieve a 90-percent reduction, there is no incentive to go the extra mile.[33]

Prescriptive rules rarely stretch the limits of technology.

It is too early to declare the obsolescence of environmental regulations, many of which need to be strengthened. Often, environmental agencies are overburdened with rules and starved for funds, leaving the laws inadequately enforced. Even when violators are caught, penalties are rarely commensurate with the proceeds, making it more profitable to pay the fines than to clean up. In the United States, breaking environmental laws is now commonplace. The General Accounting Office found that at least 41 percent of firms disposing of toxic wastes in sewer systems were in violation of discharge permits. In the United States and elsewhere, regulations need to be streamlined, monitoring stepped up, and violators held responsible—through criminal penalties if necessary.[34]

Yet prescriptive regulations, no matter how well-designed and enforced, are unlikely to spur the breadth of changes needed to make today's economy sustainable. For example, U.S. automobile emissions restrictions—the tightest in the world—have failed to achieve lasting improvements in air quality in many cities, in part because there are now many more vehicles on the road. Broader changes are likely to occur only if governments reform their fiscal policies to eliminate subsidies for—or tax—environmentally destructive activities. Since such measures change cost and price signals to companies, they can dramatically shift investment decisions. Some governments and business groups have implicitly endorsed "green taxes" by embracing the principle that polluters should be required to pay for their actions. In the United Kingdom, the Advisory Council on Business and the Environment, composed of top business leaders, has proposed a series of environmental taxes and other fiscal incentives.[35]

Ironically, subsidies for environmental destruction are now far more common than taxes on such activities. Current subsidies for the production of virgin materials, for example, put recycling industries at a disadvantage. U.S. mining companies now receive about $500 million each year in special tax exemptions and are allowed to buy federal lands for mining at bargain-basement prices. Their timber counterparts get about $600 million in tax write-offs and are able to buy trees from national forests at prices that fail to cover even the government's administrative expenses—a practice that cost taxpayers an estimated $300 million in 1991. The aluminum industry—the world's largest industrial consumer of electricity—gets special, low prices for power in Canada, Brazil, Australia, France, Ghana, and other nations, and the German coal industry is heavily subsidized.[36]

Powerful political constituencies that benefit from these subsidies, such as the German mining unions and the U.S. timber industry, have blocked attempts to remove them. More progress has been made in enacting green taxes and pollution fees—ranging from small levies on beverage containers and pesticides to broader energy taxes. Such taxes are common in Europe, including many that have been added in recent years. In France, for example, the air emissions of some 870 industrial plants are taxed, as is the discharge of industrial waste into sewage systems. In Sweden, taxes on sulfur and nitrogen oxide emissions are slated to go into effect in the mid-nineties. And in Germany, environmental taxes already in place include federal charges on toxic waste disposal, state charges for cutting trees from certain forests, and municipal fees on the use of packaging.[37]

Environmental taxes began to catch on in the United States in the eighties. The Superfund hazardous-waste cleanup program, for instance, was funded primarily through a tax on chemical feedstocks. An innovative approach to reducing the use of CFCs was also taken in the United States. Rather than mandating what products can and cannot use these chemicals, the Environmental Protection Agency set an overall cap on production and levied a CFC tax that discourages their use and at the same time captures some of the windfall profits that producers earn as CFCs become scarce. Starting at about twice the current price of CFCs, the tax has already helped cut U.S. production of the chemicals by 42 percent from the 1986 level. Such a tariff encourages the most efficient market response: less valuable uses of CFCs are eliminated first.[38]

A carbon tax—a levy on fossil fuels based on the carbon content—is the big-ticket item that many governments are now examining. It would encourage a gradual shift away from the use of oil and coal and toward greater energy efficiency. The European Commission has proposed an energy/carbon tax on fossil fuels in order to meet its pledge to stabilize European emissions of carbon. Al-

though the tax faces strong opposition from energy-intensive industries that want Japan and the United States to match it, Denmark, Finland, the Netherlands, and Sweden have already adopted modest carbon taxes.[39]

A commitment to carbon taxes would likely spur business to invest in technologies such as efficient electric motors, solar power plants, and wind energy generators. Such taxes could also be part of a broader effort to diversify and rationalize tax codes—reducing taxes on desirable items, such as personal income and capital investment, and increasing them on environmentally destructive activities. Studies in Germany and the United States show that if gradually implemented and offset by reductions in other taxes, a carbon tax could spur job and capital formation. In the United States, a tax of $110 per ton of carbon by the year 2000 would yield $120 billion per year, equal to 30 percent of personal income taxes in 1988.[40]

Market forces can be put to work in other ways—mixing regulations and price signals. The U.S. Clean Air Act amendments of 1990, which set a national cap on sulfur dioxide emissions, also established a market for tradable emission permits: companies that reduce pollution can sell their emission rights to firms facing higher cleanup costs. Several well-publicized trades took place in 1992, at roughly half the price that the buyer would have had to pay to install pollution controls. It is hoped that this program will encourage companies to find innovative ways of meeting pollution targets—using efficient light bulbs or wind turbines to eliminate the need for coal-fired power generating stations, instead of installing additional pollution controls on those plants, for example. Also, the Southern California Air Quality Management District announced plans in 1992 to use a similar trading system to achieve its ambitious pollution targets as efficiently as possible.[41]

At times, governments need to step in to remove institutional roadblocks to economically efficient solutions to environmental problems. In the United States, many electric utilities—whose prices and profit margins are set by state regulators—have been reluctant to invest in energy efficiency improvements out of concern that energy savings would reduce electricity sales and thus profits. After extensive consultations, the companies in several states agreed to step up their efficiency spending in return for a pledge by regulators to make the investments at least as profitable as traditional ones in power plants. The result: the utilities' shareholders will make more money, consumers will have lower bills, and the air will be cleaner.[42]

Governments can also close the economic loop by making companies responsible for the fate of the items they sell, and then working closely with industry to make the new system work. Germany now requires that retailers and manufacturers collect and recycle packaging for a wide range of products. By 1995, firms will be required to recycle 80 percent of what they collect—creating a powerful incentive for packaging reductions and use of recycled materials. In response, some 600 German companies have formed the Duales System Deutschland, a private consortium that works with local governments and recyclers to collect and recycle materials. Similarly, German auto manufacturers have agreed, under pressure from the federal government, to redesign cars so they are easier to dismantle and recycle—reducing the number of parts and materials. The government is helping organize a network of licensed recyclers that take back the cars, break them down, and return the materials to the steel, plastics, and glass industries. Carl Hahn, the Chairman of Volkswagen,

says, "We must adopt the cyclical processes on which the whole of nature is based."[43]

The U.S. government is also beginning to work with industry in new ways. The Environmental Protection Agency (EPA) created a Green Lights program in 1991 that encourages private companies to invest in efficient lighting with a payback period of five years or less. By November 1992, more than 300 companies had enrolled; each expected to reduce lighting energy needs by at least 60 percent. This program will prevent pollution and help spur the market for more efficient lights. Impressed with the effectiveness of Green Lights, EPA has initiated a Golden Carrot program, which provides a $27.5-million guaranteed market to the company that designs the most efficient CFC-free refrigerator, and an Energy Star program that encourages major U.S. manufacturers to cut the energy requirements of their desktop computers by more than 50 percent.[44]

REFORMING THE CORPORATION

The era of environmental reforms began with grassroots activism in the sixties, and was joined by active government policymaking in the seventies and eighties. Now industry itself is being swept up in the process. During the past few years, business environmental policies and practices have begun to undergo extensive reforms that in the end may yield not only a cleaner environment but also a different kind of company. Industry as a whole, however, has only taken the first steps in a long journey. In the years ahead business executives will need to spur the process of reform, and governments will need to cooperate in making the new approaches work.

A broad spectrum of environmental philosophies and practices exists among businesses today. At the most primitive level, some companies are still in "attack mode"—lobbying tooth and nail against new environmental legislation, and telling the public that such laws will cost jobs and add to the price of consumer goods. It is clear, for example, that top executives at auto companies such as Ford and General Motors devote more effort to fighting new fuel economy standards than to developing more fuel-efficient engines. Such attitudes not only slow the evolution of public policy, they poison the corporate atmosphere—giving employees the notion that environmental improvement is something to be feared rather than invested in.

Another strategy popular among companies looking to resist change is to run glossy ads that exaggerate their environmental achievements. Mitsubishi, a major cutter of old-growth forests in Southeast Asia, claims it practices "sustainable forestry"; Solvay, a leading European manufacturer of plastics, has taken credit for "recycling" chlorinated wastes that it actually incinerates. Other companies allow industry groups to do their "greenwashing" for them. Sometimes the group's name provides all the distortion needed: the U.S. Council for Energy Awareness represents the nuclear industry, while the Global Climate Coalition is a coal-industry-led group that fought the climate treaty signed in Rio and opposes efforts to reduce dependence on fossil fuels.[45]

The contradictory signals stem not merely from hypocrisy, but from ongoing struggles within companies and industries over environmental issues. A growing number of executives now see that such efforts can backfire—both in the form of attacks from groups such as Greenpeace, and by slowing the internal process of reform. But they still often face stiff in-house opposition from those who vainly yearn for "the way things used to be."

For companies ready to change, it usually begins with better management—an area in which Japanese companies have lessons to offer. Their corporate culture of "quality management," in which waste is avoided, materials are managed as carefully as possible, and processes are constantly improved, is a key ingredient of the Japanese economic miracle. Beginning in the seventies, Japanese companies effectively turned this philosophy to environmental cleanup, which allowed them to make steady gains. Although these concepts are not easy to transfer to western corporate culture, many European and American firms are working to adapt them. In some industries, better management alone can yield rich environmental rewards while adding to profits.[46]

Unless environmental issues are addressed at the highest levels of a company, and diffused throughout, progress is slow.

Effective environmental reform also hinges on changes in management structure and hierarchy. Corporations are controlled by boards of directors, which are supposed to represent the interests of shareholders and, to a lesser extent, employees. In most cases, however, day-to-day control is exercised by CEOs and their top subordinates. Unless environmental issues are addressed at the highest levels of a company, and diffused throughout, progress is slow.

A growing number of companies have established board of directors' committees to deal with environmental issues; some have appointed "outside" directors to represent environmental interests. The Sony Corporation established

a high-level Global Environmental
Council in 1990 that coordinates policy
throughout the company. Many firms
have designated senior vice-presidents
to be responsible for environmental performance. In over a third of major U.S.
corporations, the senior environmental
official reports directly to the CEO, and
in many cases the CEO has taken a personal and public interest in environmental matters. At the BankAmerica Corporation, for example, the largest U.S.
financial company, the CEO personally
announced the company's new environmental strategy in 1990 and has actively
led it since.[47]

As businesses are run by human be-
ings, motivated by the usual mixtures of
ambition, fear, compassion, and greed,
there are often psychological reasons for
a company's performance. Beyond their
concern about the bottom line, executives have an obvious interest in their
personal reputations—which are sometimes sullied by environmental disasters.
Some report that criticism over the dinner table from their spouses or children
has spurred them to action. And as environmental issues have gained public attention, many businesses report a
change in the corporate culture—toward
heightened sensitivity. Often this occurs
as part of a generational shift, as
younger executives inherit the reins of
power. New leadership often leads to
changes in a company's culture and
opens new opportunities for reform.[48]

Another essential element of corporate environmental reform is refocusing
on the long run. It is easier to be concerned about the environment if a company is not obsessed with quarterly
profit figures, as many are today, particularly in North America. In 1985, for example, Wall Street raider Charles Hurwitz gained control of Pacific Lumber
Company, a California firm with a policy
of cutting its forests no faster than they
could grow back. To pay off his takeover

debts, Hurwitz doubled the company's
cutting rates—selling off centuries-old
trees for quick cash. German and Japanese firms are less susceptible to pressures for short-term profit. In Japan, for
instance, the boards of most companies
are controlled by executives, most of
whom rise through the company's ranks
and are more loyal to other employees
than to the firm's shareholders. Free of
the tyranny of the stock market, Japanese executives are able to focus more
on the long-term prospects of the company—and are in a better position to
consider environmental concerns.[49]

The ability of managers and workers
to make sound environmental decisions
also depends on how well they understand the relationships between environmental quality and company operations.
To address this gap, the Ecological Management Foundation in the Netherlands,
for example, now offers a four-day
course on "sustainable business" for
senior executives. The program is held
at company headquarters and is opened
by a statement of support from the CEO,
to ensure that the management team
gives the course its full attention. For
future managers, the National Wildlife
Federation's Corporate Conservation
Council has developed a casebook on
environmental issues in management
that is now being used in some U.S. business schools, which until recently devoted little attention to them.[50]

Employees deliver better environmental results when they know their
company will reward them for doing so.
Today's most successful corporate pol-
lution-prevention programs share several principles, among them formal recognition of employee environmental
achievements, high-level responsibility
for environmental issues, and a strong
commitment from top management.
Linking environmental performance
with pay and promotion can offer strong
incentives for employee innovation. 3M,

for example, includes such considerations in employee performance reviews. Unlike some other firms, however, the company avoids giving cash awards for environmental ideas to individual employees, in the belief that this would discourage cooperation.[51]

One of the keys to corporate environmental progress is to develop systems for routine measurement of performance—so-called environmental auditing. Until recently, companies rarely collected the comprehensive information needed for such evaluations, such as materials and energy consumption, water use, emissions levels, and studies of the impacts of company products. Increasingly, however, companies are tracking emissions, and several accounting firms are offering assistance in identifying and monitoring environmental performance. British Petroleum now audits its compliance with regulations, its record at individual plant sites, and its overall corporate performance.[52]

Environmental auditing is growing in popularity, and the information it yields often spurs companies to make changes that go beyond legal requirements. But while practices are evolving, lack of standardization and public access limit the value of many auditing programs. Audits are usually done by company personnel according to their own criteria—and often for management's eyes only. Sometimes even the board of directors is denied access. To be most effective, environmental audits will need to be conducted by outside auditors, with the results made available to shareholders and the public at large. Standardized, public audits would provide real accountability, and could lead to far-reaching changes in performance. The Valdez Principles, an environmental code of conduct for corporations developed by environmental and investment groups in the late eighties, includes strong auditing requirements, but so far only a handful of small companies have signed up.[53]

Governments may one day wish to require comprehensive annual environmental audits. Several European countries are moving in this direction. The British Standards Institution, for example, which certifies corporate management practices, is developing a new set of environmental management standards. Certification will involve some degree of environmental auditing, and the results are likely to be scrutinized both by corporate executives and by investors, insurers, and financiers. The European Community as a whole is considering a similar program. The state of California now certifies environmental auditors, who are then deemed qualified to determine if firms are complying with state environmental disclosure requirements.[54]

Linking environmental performance with pay and promotion can offer strong incentives for employee innovation.

Comprehensive tracking of materials and energy use can also help companies get a handle on the economic and environmental implications of their production processes. Energy audits are becoming common practice in many firms, and some are moving toward accounting for the inputs and fate of all materials used in company operations—allowing managers to identify inefficiencies quickly. The state of Massachusetts now requires companies to report information on inputs of toxic materials as well as emissions, which is likely to spur closer examination of industrial processes and of alternatives for cleaner production.[55]

The U.S. government does not yet require environmental audits, but it has established the world's most advanced pollution reporting system—the Toxics Release Inventory (TRI). Set up in 1986, TRI collects information on toxic chemicals released from about 24,000 U.S. industrial facilities each year. When first proposed, the inventory was assailed by industry groups as a paperwork nightmare. In practice, it has provided a powerful stimulus for emissions reduction. The CEO of Monsanto "reacted with shock," according to a company case history, when presented with the firm's first report to TRI. He then set an ambitious goal for emissions reduction. In addition, environmental groups have used TRI data to put pressure on major polluters, assembling more than 150 reports on local, state, and national pollution problems in the last three years.[56]

Consumers are often a potent source of pressure.

Armed with such evidence, other groups with a stake in corporate environmental performance are exerting pressure for change. It is increasingly difficult for firms to borrow money, obtain insurance, negotiate labor contracts, offer new stock, site new facilities, or sell products without first demonstrating that their operations are environmentally sound. Many of these parties—who recall the precipitous stock decline that followed Union Carbide's Bhopal accident, or the nearly 17,000 lawsuits by asbestos disease victims that led to Manville Corporation's bankruptcy—are concerned not just with the direct cost of environmental problems but also with the risk of unexpected financial burdens. The liability clause in the U.S. hazardous-waste cleanup law, for example, has spurred lenders and in-

surers to insist on site audits prior to virtually all industrial real estate transactions—so as to preclude the purchase of an expensive waste disposal problem.[57]

A growing number of investors now seek out "green investments"—motivated by the potential financial rewards of such a portfolio and by the desire not to fund morally objectionable activities. This movement includes many pension funds, universities, and other institutional investors. Some are choosing to invest only in firms they believe are environmentally progressive; others use their position as stockholders to demand reform, using information provided by groups such as the Council on Economic Priorities in New York, the Investor Responsibility Research Center in Washington, and Environmental Data Services in London. In addition, environmentally focused investment firms and funds have emerged to serve the individual investor, including the Calvert Group mutual funds and the Global Environment Fund in the United States, British unit trusts such as the Merlin Ecology Fund, and Sweden's Enskilda Environment Fund. By 1990, about $1 billion was invested in such funds in the United States and about half that amount in the United Kingdom. These funds generally performed well through the eighties, but have lagged behind broader stock indices in the nineties.[58]

Although banks have somewhat less at risk in the companies they lend to, some have established environmental policies in recent years. At the simplest level, these include scrutinizing borrowers for potential environmental problems that could make it difficult to repay loans. Deutsche Bank, the largest German bank, has gone further: it has established a European environmental data base that is available to its borrowers—most of whom are small businesses—in order to help them clean up their acts. For Deutsche Bank, this service appears to be in part intended as a way to attract business. Recently, a sizable consortium of mainly European-based banks came together to establish a Banking Charter for Sustainable Development—a code of conduct for financial institutions.[59]

Several companies have found that another way to provoke change is to work "with the enemy." In the late eighties, the fast-food company McDonald's found itself under growing pressure from consumers and environmental groups to reduce its massive use of plastic packaging materials. After first trying to get by with cosmetic recycling, McDonald's entered into an agreement with the Environmental Defense Fund (EDF) in New York to fully assess the potential for packaging reduction, giving EDF experts access to company files. The task force set up for the project was able to identify potential savings—both in front of and behind the counter—that surprised both parties. In 1991, McDonald's and EDF signed an agreement committing the company to reduce its packaging waste in the United States by 80 percent. A year later, EDF announced that it had begun a similar consultation with General Motors.[60]

Consumers are often a potent source of pressure. According to John Elkington, coauthor of *The Green Consumer Guide*—which rose to the top of the British best-seller lists in 1988—demands for environmentally sound consumer products have sent a shock wave through European industry. In Germany, a monthly magazine, *Ökotest*, serves as an independent arbiter for 90,000 environmentally minded shoppers, conducting product tests and evaluating companies' environmental claims—the results of which are often publicized by the media. Shoppers have pushed stores to demand green products—from toilet paper made from recycled fiber to organic produce—from distributors, who have in turn pressured manufacturers to offer such

goods. A host of new companies have sprung up to serve the new markets, including The Body Shop, a U.K.-based chain that sells environmentally friendly beauty products, and Ecover in Belgium, which produces nonpolluting cleaning products. Several nations, including Germany, Japan, and Canada, have instituted "eco-labelling" programs. These have often been hampered, however, by the difficulty of developing criteria for evaluating various products.[61]

Although the process of corporate reform is still in its early stages, there can be little doubt about the sweeping nature of the transition that lies ahead for many companies. The necessary changes will reach deep into business management and culture. The cornerstones of more environmentally responsible corporate practice—openness, accountability, taking a longer-term view—potentially offer companies, and the societies in which they function, far-reaching benefits.

A GREEN INDUSTRIAL STRATEGY

Among the thousands of diplomats, environmentalists, journalists, and indigenous peoples in Rio de Janeiro in June 1992 was a new group that has worked its way onto the environmental stage: business leaders. They came to Rio from around the world, but mainly from nations like Japan and Germany that have targeted environmental progress as one of the great investment opportunities of the coming decades. Although some of the CEOs may have been drawn by the good publicity they would gain, their presence marked a clear break with business as usual. The Business Council for Sustainable Development, composed of the CEOs of 48 multinational corporations, gathered in Rio to promote their book, *Changing Course*. Among its conclusions: "Continued economic development now depends on radical improvement in the interactions between business and the environment."[62]

If radical change is needed (and perhaps inevitable), new business strategies will be essential to cope with the shifting conditions, and new government policies will be needed to accelerate and smooth the transition. Beyond the array of new fiscal and regulatory measures suggested earlier, policymakers will have to think more boldly about how to accelerate the evolution of entirely new industries. Achieving an environmentally sustainable economy will require a "green" industrial strategy—a new partnership between business and government that is aimed at developing new technologies, spurring their commercialization, and channelling investment into new areas.

For developing countries, the economic challenge of the green industrial revolution is particularly severe.

"Industrial policy" is rapidly becoming a catchphrase for the nineties. In the wake of the cold war, Western Europe, Japan, and the United States are battling hard for economic supremacy. In Japan, the Ministry of International Trade and Industry (MITI) has worked closely with business in developing national economic strategies throughout the postwar period. Some West European nations are similarly involved in planning and nurturing their economies, particularly in Germany and France. In the United States—where a de facto industrial policy was until recently driven by national security concerns—the Clinton adminis-

tration is already laying plans for a new era of cooperation between government and industry.[63]

Industrial policy has always had environmental implications—though the links are rarely made explicit. Subsidies and demonstration projects have provided life support for industries, often with unfortunate environmental effects. The challenge now is to develop an explicitly "green" industrial strategy. Japan is the furthest along: it has begun work on a 100-year blueprint for ecological sustainability called New Earth 21, and has created a government research institute to focus specifically on environmental technologies. The Federation of Japanese Industries, Keidanren, has worked with MITI in developing this plan, and has published an environmental charter calling for major changes in Japanese corporate practices. The Dutch government meanwhile has signed a series of covenants with various industries that commit them to making specific environmental improvements. The United States lags badly in this area, though in 1993, 10 percent—$10 million—of the federal contribution to Sematech, a government-industry semiconductor consortium, is earmarked for development of clean computer-chip production technology.[64]

A critical challenge in developing a green industrial strategy is to find ways to support the efforts of small firms, which historically have been responsible for a disproportionate share of industrial innovation. Since smaller firms have less access to capital than large corporations do, it can be more difficult for them to develop and commercialize new technologies. Government assistance can provide much-needed help. For instance, the German government's network of Fraunhofer institutes helps small companies develop new technologies and assemble existing ones into marketable products. Directing such technical support toward green technologies, such as efficient lighting or integrated pest management, could help ensure that small businesses are part of the solution.[65]

For developing countries, the economic challenge of the green industrial revolution is particularly severe. Like generals planning for the last war, many are still industrializing along the lines followed in the West in the fifties and sixties—and paying the environmental price. Massive copper mines, steel plants, and chemical factories can cause enormous damage—particularly when regulated as loosely as they are in many developing countries—and may in the end fail to deliver the economic rewards they promise. As the fastest areas of economic growth are likely to be in cleaner production technologies and in new industries such as solar energy and recycled materials processing, countries that focus their development on resource extraction and smokestacks will be big losers. If the Third World is to join the next Industrial Revolution, basic changes in development plans will be essential, as well as international programs to facilitate the spread of green technologies. A step in the right direction was taken with the 1990 ozone treaty, which established a $240-million fund to help developing countries make the transition to CFC substitutes.[66]

Countries that fail to develop a green industrial policy are likely to lose out economically as well as environmentally. Japanese business leaders have argued that environmentally related products and processes will be among the largest and fastest growing markets in the coming decades. Both executives and government officials have gone so far as to call on all Japanese companies to operate according to the highest environmental standards wherever they operate—regardless of how stringent the local law is. These officials appear to agree with Harvard economist Michael Porter, who argues that industry will ultimately be strengthened in international markets if it is pushed to improve its environmental performance.[67]

The transition to an environmentally sound economy is as great a challenge as business has ever faced. But while the costs may be high, and the danger of missteps real, most companies will face greater risks if they ignore the need for change. Businesses that do not learn how to earn profits in an ecologically sound way may find they have no profits to worry about. And at the national level, those that try to force a false choice between jobs and a healthy environment may end up with neither. In the end, the health of the global economy will depend on the health of the global environmental base on which it stands.

Notes

Chapter 1. A New Era Unfolds

1. Royal Society of London and the U.S. National Academy of Sciences, *Population Growth, Resource Consumption, and a Sustainable World* (London and Washington, D.C.: 1992).

2. Participants at both events from "Twelve Days of UNCED," U.S. Citizens Network on UNCED, San Francisco, Calif., July 2, 1992; heads of states and journalists from U.N. Environment Programme (UNEP), New York Office, private communication, October 26, 1992.

3. UNCED Secretariat, "154 Signatures on Climate Convention in Rio," press release, June 14, 1992; Charles Dickson, press officer, Intergovernmental Negotiating Committee, UNCED Secretariat, private communication, November 6, 1992.

4. Soil erosion figure from Lester R. Brown and Edward C. Wolf, *Soil Erosion: Quiet Crisis In the World Economy*, Worldwatch Paper 60 (Washington, D.C.: Worldwatch Institute, September 1984); Population Reference Bureau (PRB), *World Population Data Sheets* (Washington, D.C.: various years); carbon dioxide concentrations from Charles D. Keeling and Timothy P. Whorf, "Atmospheric CO_2—Modern Record, Mauna Loa," in Thomas A. Boden et al., *Trends '91: A Compendium of Data on Global Change* (Oak Ridge, Tenn.: Oak Ridge National Laboratory, 1991), and from Timothy P. Whorf, Scripps Institution of Oceanography, La Jolla, Calif., private communication, April 2, 1992.

5. World Bank, *World Development Report 1992* (New York: Oxford University Press, 1992).

6. Gross world product in 1950 from Herbert R. Block, *The Planetary Product in 1980: A Creative Pause?* (Washington, D.C.: U.S. Department of State, 1981); world product in 1992 from International Monetary Fund (IMF), *World Economic Outlook October 1992* (Washington, D.C.: 1992); population data from PRB, *World Population Data Sheets*.

7. Annual deforestation figure from "New Deforestation Rate Figures Announced," *Tropical Forest Programme* (IUCN Newsletter), August 1990.

8. Government of Canada, *The State of Canada's Environment* (Ottawa: 1991); Tom Brokaw, "Save the Taiga," *New York Times*, October 22, 1992.

9. "The Price of Pollution," *Options* (International Institute for Applied Systems Analysis), September 1990.

10. Ibid.

11. Ibid.

12. U.S. Department of Agriculture (USDA), *Agricultural Statistics 1990* (Washington, D.C.: U.S. Government Printing Office, 1990).

13. H. Dregne et al., "A New Assessment of the World Status of Desertification," *Desertification Control Bulletin*, No. 20, 1991.

14. U.N. Food and Agriculture Organization (FAO) cited in World Resources Insti-

tute (WRI), *World Resources 1992–93* (New York: Oxford University Press, 1992); bluefin tuna figure from Donella Meadows et al., *Beyond the Limits* (Post Mills, Vt.: Chelsea Green Publishing Company, 1992).

15. Bernard Simon, "Canada Set to Impose Ban on Atlantic Cod Fishing," *Financial Times*, July 2, 1992.

16. Mike Griffin, "Some Very Fishy Business," *South*, August 1991; "Minister Says Fishing Policies Beginning To Show Results," *Environmental Issues*, May 22, 1992.

17. Lester Brown, "The Aral Sea: Going, Going . . .," *World Watch*, January/February 1991; Government of Pakistan and IUCN Pakistan, *Pakistan National Conservation Strategy* (Karachi: 1992); dead lakes in Canada from Government of Canada, *The State of Canada's Environment*.

18. Tom Horton and William M. Eichbaum, *Turning the Tide: Saving the Chesapeake Bay* (Washington, D.C.: Island Press, 1991); Government of Canada, *The State of Canada's Environment*.

19. UNEP and World Health Organization, *Assessment of Urban Air Quality* (Nairobi: Global Environment Monitoring System, 1988); $40 billion figure from Thomas Crocker of the University of Wyoming, as described in James S. Cannon, *The Health Costs of Air Pollution* (New York: American Lung Association, 1985).

20. Josh Friedman, "Bulgaria's Deadly Secret," *Newsday*, April 22, 1990.

21. Chrystia Freeland, "Russians 'Doomed for Next 25 Years,'" *Financial Times*, October 8, 1992.

22. William K. Reilly, "Statement on Ozone Depletion," U.S. Environmental Protection Agency, Washington, D.C., April 4, 1991.

23. Milton Russell et al., "The U.S. Hazardous Waste Legacy," *Environment*, July/Au-gust 1992; Norway figures from Meadows et al., *Beyond the Limits*.

24. One million tons of hazardous waste for the world from Meadows et al., *Beyond the Limits*.

25. Estimate is by Senator John Glenn, cited in "A Hundred Billion Here . . . The Nuclear Mess," *The Economist*, January 14, 1989.

26. USDA, Economic Research Service (ERS), *World Grain Database* (unpublished printouts) (Washington, D.C.: 1991).

27. Derived from FAO, *Production Yearbook* (Rome: various years); Bill Quimby, USDA, ERS, Washington, D.C., private communication, March 20, 1992.

28. FAO, *Fertilizer Yearbook* (Rome: various years); The Fertilizer Institute, *Fertilizer Facts and Figures, 1990* (Washington, D.C.: 1990).

29. U.S. figures from FAO, *Fertilizer Yearbook*, and from USDA, ERS, *World Grain Database*; European information from Lester R. Brown, "Reexamining the World Food Prospect," in Lester R. Brown et al., *State of the World 1989* (New York: W.W. Norton & Co., 1989); Soviet figures from K.F. Isherwood and K.G. Soh, "The Medium Term Supply and Demand Prospects for Fertilizer Materials," International Fertilizer Industry Association, Paris, June 1991; World Bank subsidies from Elliot Berg, "Fertilizer Subsidies" (draft), World Bank, Washington, D.C., December 1985.

30. FAO, *Production Yearbook: Fisheries Statistics, Commodities* (Rome: various years); FAO, Rome, private communication, February 1992; maximum sustainable yield from WRI, *World Resources 1988–89* (New York: Basic Books, 1988).

31. Annual soil erosion figure from Brown and Wolf, *Soil Erosion: Quiet Crisis In the World Economy*; China from USDA, *World Grain Database*; studies from Leon Lyles, "Possible Effects of Wind Erosion on Soil Productiv-

ity," *Journal of Soil and Water Conservation*, November/December 1975.

32. World Bank, *World Development Report 1992*.

33. "Forests, Crops Suffering Ozone Damage," *Dagens Nyheter*, July 5 1990, as reprinted in *JPRS Report: Environmental Issues*, October 12, 1990; Dr. Jan Cerovsky, "Environmental Status Report 1988/89: Czechoslovakia," in World Conservation Union—IUCN, *Environmental Status Reports: 1988/1989, Vol. 1: Czechoslovakia, Hungary, Poland* (Thatcham, U.K.: Thatcham Printers, 1990).

34. James J. MacKenzie and Mohamed T. El-Ashry, *Ill Winds: Airborne Pollution's Toll on Trees and Crops* (Washington, D.C.: WRI, 1988); National Acid Precipitation Assessment Program, *Interim Assessment: The Causes and Effects of Acid Deposition*, Vol. IV (Washington, D.C.: U.S. Government Printing Office, 1987); economic loss estimated by Walter W. Heck, chairman, Research Committee, National Crop Loss Assessment Network, cited in MacKenzie and El-Ashry, *Ill Winds*.

35. "Increased Ultraviolet Radiation Stunts Rice Plant Growth," International Rice Research Institute, News Release, Manila, Philippines, December 1991; "Scientists Say Ozone Depletion Could Affect Productivity of Plants," *International Environment Reporter*, April 22, 1992; Alan H. Teramura, Professor and Chairman, Department of Botany, University of Mayland, College Park, Md., testimony before the U.S. Senate Committee on Commerce, Science, and Transportation, Washington, D.C., November 15, 1991.

36. Grain output from USDA, ERS, *World Grain Database*.

37. Ibid.

38. Government of Pakistan and IUCN Pakistan, *Pakistan National Conservation Strategy*.

39. John Ryan and Sandra Postel, "Reforming Forestry," in Lester R. Brown et al., *State of the World 1991* (New York: W.W. Norton & Co., 1991); "Environment, Growth, and Development," prepared by World Bank staff for consideration by the Development Committee, World Bank, Washington, D.C., April 10, 1987.

40. USDA, *Agricultural Statistics 1988* (Washington, D.C.: U.S. Government Printing Office, 1988).

41. Sandra Postel, *Last Oasis: Facing Water Scarcity* (New York: W.W. Norton & Co., 1992).

42. Russell et al., "The U.S. Hazardous Waste Legacy"; Meadows et al., *Beyond the Limits*.

43. Hilary F. French, *Clearing the Air: A Global Agenda*, Worldwatch Paper 94 (Washington, D.C.: Worldwatch Institute, January 1990); Freeland, "Russians 'Doomed for Next 25 Years' "; Celestine Bohlen, "In the New Russia, Children Are Born Fighting the Odds," *New York Times*, October 4, 1992.

44. World Bank, Department of Socio-Economic Data, unpublished printout; IMF, *World Economic Outlook October 1992*.

45. For details of the effort needed to build an environmentally sustainable global economy, see Lester R. Brown et al., *Saving the Planet* (New York: W.W. Norton & Co., 1991).

46. Ashok Gadgil et al., "Advanced Lighting and Window Technologies for Reducing Electricity Consumption and Peak Demand: Overseas Manufacturing and Marketing Opportunities," Lawrence Berkeley Laboratory, Berkely, Calif., March 1991.

47. Christopher Flavin and Nicholas Lenssen, *Beyond the Petroleum Age: Designing a Solar Economy*, Worldwatch Paper 100 (Washington, D.C.: December 1990).

48. Ibid.

49. Steel minimill information from Robert Garino, Institute of Scrap Recycling Industries, Washington, D.C., private communication, November 6, 1992.

50. Government of Pakistan and IUCN Pakistan, *Pakistan National Conservation Strategy*.

51. Women without access to family planning from Beverly Winikoff et al., "Medical Services to Save Mother's Lives: Feasible Approaches to Reducing Maternal Mortality," presented at the Safe Motherhood International Conference, Nairobi, Kenya, 1987; share of births unwanted from J. Bongaarts, "The Measurement of Wanted Fertility," *Population and Development Review*, Vol. 16, No. 3, 1990.

52. American Wind Energy Association, "1992 Wind Technology Status Report—U.S. Sets New Wind Energy Record as Domestic Market Stagnates," Washington, D.C., undated; WRI, *World Resources 1990–91* (New York: Oxford University Press, 1990).

53. PRB, *World Population Data Sheets*; USDA, ERS, *Agricultural Resources: Cropland, Water and Conservation Situation Outlook Report*, Washington, D.C., September 1990; Ferdinand Protzman, "A Nation's Recycling Law Puts Businesses on the Spot," *New York Times*, July 12, 1992; John Clark, "The Danish Bottles Case: Commission of the European Communities v. Kingdom of Denmark" (draft), London Business School, undated.

54. Incomes from World Bank, *World Development Report 1992*.

55. "EC's Energy/Carbon Tax Proposal Runs into Pre-summit Vacillation," *European Energy Report*, May 29, 1992; Japanese consideration of carbon tax from "Decision on Environment Tax Postponed Until After Earth Summit," Kyodo News Service, April 15, 1992, as reprinted in *JPRS Report: Environmental Issues*, May 22, 1992.

Chapter 2. Facing Water Scarcity

1. World water use and Figure 2–1 from I.A. Shiklomanov, "Global Water Resources," *Nature & Resources*, Vol. 26, No. 3, 1990; Mississippi River flow from Frits van der Leeden et al., *The Water Encyclopedia* (Chelsea, Mich.: Lewis Publishers, Inc., 1990); World Resources Institute (WRI), *World Resources 1992–93* (New York: Oxford University Press, 1992); Population Reference Bureau (PRB), *1992 World Population Data Sheet* (Washington, D.C.: 1992); historical population data from U.N. Department of International Economic and Social Affairs (UNDIESA), *World Population Prospects 1990* (New York: 1991).

2. "Large" dams are those over 15 meters high. Number of dams and rate of dam construction from WRI, *World Resources 1992–93*, and from data from the International Commission on Large Dams and the *International Water Power and Dam Construction Handbook* as presented in van der Leeden et al., *The Water Encyclopedia*.

3. Van der Leeden et al., *The Water Encyclopedia*; WRI, *World Resources 1992–93*; Bradford Morse and Thomas R. Berger, *Sardar Sarovar*, Report of the Independent Review (Ottawa, Ont.: Resource Futures International, Inc., 1992).

4. UNDIESA, *World Population Prospects 1990*; WRI, *World Resources 1992–93*.

5. Swedish hydrologist Malin Falkenmark has put forth these definitions, which have gradually gained wider use. See, for example, Malin Falkenmark, "The Massive Water Scarcity Now Threatening Africa—Why Isn't it Being Addressed?" *Ambio*, Vol. 18, No. 2, 1989.

6. PRB, *1992 World Population Data Sheet*; WRI, *World Resources 1992–93*.

7. Population projections from PRB, *1992 World Population Data Sheet*.

8. For details of the problems in these areas, see Sandra Postel, *Last Oasis: Facing*

Water Scarcity (New York: W.W. Norton & Co, 1992).

9. Fossil groundwater dependence from Abdulla Ali Al-Ibrahim, "Excessive Use of Groundwater Resources in Saudi Arabia: Impacts and Policy Options," *Ambio*, Vol. 20, No. 1, 1991; Mark Nicholson, "Subsidised Security," *Financial Times*, January 30, 1992; Mark Nicholson, "Saudis Reap Bumper Wheat Subsidy," *Financial Times*, January 21, 1992; International Monetary Fund (IMF), *International Financial Statistics* (Washington, D.C.: April 1992).

10. Depletion rates from Al-Ibrahim, "Excessive Use of Groundwater Resources in Saudi Arabia."

11. Texas depletion figure from tables supplied by the High Plains Underground Water Conservation District No. 1, Lubbock, Tex., dated May 3, 1991; Li Hong, "Beijing Set to Tackle Water Thirst," *China Daily*, October 17, 1989; overpumping rate in Mexico from Juan Manuel Martinez Garcia, Director General of Hydraulic Construction and Operation, Mexico City, private communication, October 21, 1991; slumping of cathedral from author's observation during visit to Mexico City, October 1991.

12. People's Republic of China, State Science and Technology Commission, *Beijing-Tianjin Water Resources Study: Final Report* (Beijing: 1991); Thomas Naff, "The Jordan Basin: Political, Economic, and Institutional Issues," prepared for World Bank International Workshop on Comprehensive Water Resources Management Policies, Washington, D.C., June 24–28, 1991.

13. Details of the destruction in these areas can be found in Postel, *Last Oasis*.

14. Damien Lewis, "Will Botswana Put Diamonds Before the Environment?" *New African*, July 1991; Neil Henry, "Arid Botswana Keeps Its Democracy Afloat," *Washington Post*, March 21, 1991.

15. Henry, "Arid Botswana Keeps Its Democracy Afloat"; "Okavango Delta Threatened by Boro River Diversion," *World Rivers Review*, March/April 1991, as reprinted in *Ecoafrica*, June 1991; Lewis, "Will Botswana Put Diamonds Before the Environment?"; Gwenda Brophy, Botswana country profile in *New Internationalist*, October 1991; David B. Ottaway, "A Second Look Saves a Great Delta," *Washington Post*, June 18, 1992.

16. Jack E. Williams et al., "Fishes of North America Endangered, Threatened, or of Special Concern: 1989," *Fisheries*, November/December 1989; continental fish, crayfish, and mussel figures from Larry Master, "Aquatic Animals: Endangerment Alert," *Nature Conservancy*, March/April 1991.

17. Willa Nehlsen et al., "Pacific Salmon at the Crossroads: Stocks at Risk from California, Oregon, Idaho, and Washington," *Fisheries*, March/April 1991; decline in Sacramento River salmon from Marc Reisner, "Can Anyone Win This Water War?" *National Wildlife*, June/July 1991; John Davies, "Columbia River Barges Spared in Latest Fish Rescue Proposal," *Journal of Commerce*, November 26, 1991; Rocky Barker, "U.S. Fish Agency Takes the Slow Road," *High Country News*, July 1, 1991; expected listing of Snake River chinook as endangered from Jay M. Sheppard, Division of Endangered Species, U.S. Fish and Wildlife Service, Washington, D.C., July 2, 1992.

18. Water use estimates from Shiklomanov, "Global Water Resources."

19. "District Salutes Water Savings By Area Irrigators," *The Cross Section* (High Plains Underground Water Conservation District No. 1, Lubbock, Tex.), November 1989; payback from Ken Carver, High Plains Underground Water Conservation District No. 1, private communication, May 29, 1992. For other surge results, see Richard Bartholomay, "USDI Funds Study: Surge Irrigation Lowers Salt Loading in Colorado

River," *Irrigation Journal*, September/October 1991.

20. Donald H. Negri and John J. Hanchar, *Water Conservation Through Irrigation Technology* (Washington, D.C.: U.S. Department of Agriculture (USDA), Economic Research Service (ERS), 1989); retrofit costs and payback periods from Carver, private communication, May 24, 1992. For more on LEPA, see William M. Lyle and James P. Bordovsky,"LEPA: Low Energy Precision Application," *Irrigation Journal*, April 1991.

21. Depletion chart of the Ogallala aquifer from Wayne Wyatt, Manager, High Plains Underground Water Conservation District No. 1, "Water Management—Southern High Plains of Texas," unpublished, May 1991; "District Salutes Water Savings by Area Irrigators"; Texas Water Development Board, *Surveys of Irrigation in Texas—1958, 1964, 1969, 1974, 1979, 1984, and 1989* (Austin, Tex.: 1991); the actual time periods for comparing the depletion rate were 1966–71 and 1986–91.

22. Quote from Meir Ben-Meir, Director General, Ministry of Agriculture of Israel, "Irrigation—Establishing Research Priorities," Address, April 1988. See also "Israel's Water Policy: A National Commitment," in U.S. Congress, Office of Technology Assessment, *Water-Related Technologies for Sustainable Agriculture in Arid/Semi-Arid Lands: Selected Foreign Experience* (Washington, D.C.: U.S. Government Printing Office, 1983).

23. 1974 estimate from Don Gustafson, "Drip Irrigation in the World—State of the Art," in *Israqua '78: Proceedings of the International Conference on Water Systems and Applications* (Tel Aviv: Israel Centre of Waterworks Appliances, 1978); J.S. Abbott, "Micro Irrigation—World Wide Usage," *ICID Bulletin*, January 1984; costs from David Melamed, "Technological Developments in Irrigation: The Israeli Experience," unpublished paper, and from Paul Wilson et al., *Drip Irrigation for Cotton: Implications for Farm Profits* (Washing-

ton, D.C.: USDA, 1984); 130,000 figure and Israel's drip area from Dale Bucks, Microirrigation Working Group, International Commission on Irrigation and Drainage (ICID), Beltsville, Md., private communication, June 22, 1992; Israel's total irrigated area from U.N. Food and Agriculture Organization (FAO), *1990 Production Yearbook* (Rome: 1991); water efficiency gain from Jehoshua Schwarz, "Israel Water Sector Review: Past Achievements, Current Problems and Future Options," prepared for the World Bank by Tahal Consulting Engineers Ltd., Tel Aviv, December 1990. For general background and basic features of drip irrigation, see Kobe Shoji, "Drip Irrigation," *Scientific American*, November 1977, and Sterling Davis and Dale Bucks, "Drip Irrigation," in Claude H. Pair et al., eds., *Irrigation* (Silver Spring, Md.: The Irrigation Association, 1983).

24. Robert Chambers, *Managing Canal Irrigation: Practical Analysis from South Asia* (Cambridge: Cambridge University Press, 1988).

25. Ibid.

26. Montague Keen, "Clearer Thoughts Flow on Irrigation," *Ceres*, May/June 1988. See also Romana P. de los Reyes and Sylvia Ma. G. Jopillo, *An Evaluation of the Philippine Participatory Communal Irrigation Program* (Quezon City: Institute of Philippine Culture, Ateneo de Manila University, 1986).

27. C.R. Bartone and S. Arlosoroff, "Irrigation Reuse of Pond Effluents in Developing Countries," *Water Science Technology*, Vol. 19, No. 12, 1987.

28. Shaul Streit, Project Director, Israel Sewerage Project, Tel Aviv, private communication, March 5, 1992; Schwarz, "Israel Water Sector Review: Past Achievements, Current Problems and Future Options."

29. Hillel I. Shuval et al., *Wastewater Irrigation in Developing Countries: Health Effects and Technical Solutions* (Washington, D.C.: World Bank, 1986); Bartone and Arlosoroff, "Irrigation Reuse of Pond Effluents in Develop-

ing Countries." A project to treat the sewage flows is now under construction, according to Saul Arlosoroff, Project Manager, Water and Sanitation, World Bank, Washington, D.C., private communication, May 27, 1992.

30. Bartone and Arlosoroff, "Irrigation Reuse of Pond Effluents in Developing Countries."

31. Herman Bouwer, "Agricultural and Municipal Use of Wastewater," prepared for meeting of the International Association of Water Pollution Research and Control, Washington, D.C., May 1992; Hillel I. Shuval, *Wastewater Irrigation in Developing Countries: Health Effects and Technical Solutions* (Washington, D.C.: World Bank, 1990). See also Asit K. Biswas and Abdullah Arar, eds., *Treatment and Reuse of Wastewater* (London: Butterworths, 1988).

32. Percentage of cropland irrigated from FAO, *1990 Production Yearbook*, with adjustments from USDA, ERS; figures on arid and semiarid lands and their inhabitants from H.M. Lovenstein et al., "Runoff Agroforestry in Arid Lands," *Forest Ecology and Management*, Vol. 45, 1991.

33. Will Critchley, *Looking After Our Land: Soil and Water Conservation in Dryland Africa* (Oxford: Oxfam, 1991).

34. Ibid.

35. Shawki Barghouti and Guy Le Moigne, *Irrigation in Sub-Saharan Africa: The Development of Public and Private Systems* (Washington, D.C.: World Bank, 1990).

36. Roy Opie, "Prevention Is Not Always Better Than Cure," *World Water and Environmental Engineer*, October 1990; Gary Allie, American Iron and Steel Institute, Washington, D.C., private communication, April 27, 1992.

37. Shiklomanov, "Global Water Resources"; WRI, *World Resources 1992–93*. Hydropower is not included in these industrial use figures, since it does not require removing water from a river or lake, but it does compete with the protection of fisheries, aquatic habitat, and recreational values.

38. Wayne Solley et al., "Preliminary Water Use Estimates in the United States During 1990," U.S. Geological Survey, Open File Report 92–63, Washington, D.C., July 1992; Allie, private communication.

39. Figure 2–2 from National Land Agency, Water Resources Department, *Water Resources in Japan: Present State of Water Resources Development, Conservation and Utilization* (Tokyo: various years), from IMF, *1991 Yearbook* (Washington, D.C.: 1991), from IMF, *International Financial Statistics* (Washington, D.C.: June 1992), and from World Bank, *World Develoment Report 1992* (New York: Oxford University Press, 1992).

40. 1950 figure from Wayne Solley et al., *Estimated Use of Water in the United States in 1985* (Washington, D.C.: U.S. Government Printing Office, 1988); Solley et al., "Preliminary Water Use Estimates"; IMF, *International Financial Statistics* (Washington, D.C.: various years); Roy Opie, "Germany's Double Bill," *World Water and Environmental Engineer*, April 1991; Opie, "Prevention Is Not Always Better Than Cure."

41. Mark Manzione et al., "California Industries Cut Water Use," *Journal of the AWWA*, October 1991; calculation of households served assumes 1 acre-foot (1,234 cubic meters) meets the annual needs of two average households. For more examples, see Maggie Murphy, "Industrial Water Conservation is Feasible," *Water Conservation News* (California Department of Water Resources), April 1991.

42. William W. Wade et al., *Cost of Industrial Water Shortages*, prepared by Spectrum Economics, Inc., for the California Urban Water Agencies (San Francisco, Calif.: 1991); California's economic ranking from U.S. Central Intelligence Agency, *Handbook of Economic Statistics, 1991* (Washington, D.C.: 1991).

43. Wade et al., *Cost of Industrial Water Shortages*.

44. Ramesh Bhatia and Malin Falkenmark, "Water Resource Policies and the Urban Poor: Innovative Approaches and Policy Imperatives," prepared for the International Conference on Water and the Environment: Development Issues for the 21st Century, Dublin, Ireland, January 26–31, 1992.

45. Table 2–4 is from Worldwatch Institute, based on the following: Jerusalem from A.D. Rosenberg, Deputy Manager, Department of Water Supply and Sewerage, Municipality of Jerusalem, private written communication, Jerusalem, Israel, May 18, 1992; Mexico City from Juan Manuel Martinez Garcia, *Program de Uso Eficiente del Agua en la Ciudad de México* (Mexico City: Ciudad de México DDF, 1991), and from Martinez Garcia, private communication; Southern California from Matthew Puffer, Metropolitan Water District, Los Angeles, Calif., private communication, June 8, 1992; Beijing from "Beijing Water Shortages Prompt Introduction of Regulations," *China Daily*, October 30, 1991, as reprinted in *JPRS Report: Environmental Issues*, January 13, 1992; Boston from Paul F. Levy and William A. Brutsch, *MWRA Long Range Water Supply Program* (Boston: Massachusetts Water Resources Authority (MWRA), 1990), and from Marcis Kempe, MWRA, Boston, Mass., private communication, June 4, 1992; Waterloo from Jim Robertson, University of Waterloo, Waterloo, Ont., private communication, March 25, 1992, and from Ralph Luhowy, Regional Municipality of Waterloo, Waterloo, Ont., private communication, May 1, 1992; Singapore from World Health Organization, Regional Working Group on Water Supply Management, *Country Report: Singapore* (Kuala Lumpur, Malaysia: 1990); Melbourne from Melbourne Water Resources Review, "Water for Our Future," Issues Paper, June 1991.

46. British example from "Water, Water—at a Price," *The Economist*, April 13, 1991. For a general discussion of pricing, see Roger McNeill and Donald Tate, *Guidelines for Municipal Water Pricing*, Social Science Series No. 25 (Ottawa, Canada: 1991).

47. Edmonton-Calgary example from David B. Brooks et al., "Pricing: A Neglected Tool for Managing Water Demand," *Alternatives*, Vol. 17, No. 3, 1990; U.K. figure from "Water, Water—at a Price."

48. William E. Martin et al., *Saving Water in a Desert City* (Washington, D.C.: Resources for the Future, 1984); $75 million figure from Linda Smith, "Tucson: A Water Ethic in the Desert," *U.S. Water News*, July 1990.

49. Bhatia and Falkenmark, "Water Resource Policies and the Urban Poor."

50. Mexico's standards from Martinez Garcia, *Program de Uso Eficiente del Agua en la Ciudad de México*; Departamento del Distrito Federal, *Reglamento del Servicio de Agua y Drenaje para el Distrito Federal* (Mexico City: 1990); Martinez Garcia, private communication; Ontario's standards from "Regulations to Amend Ontario's Regulation 815/84 Made Under the Ontario Water Resources Act," *The Ontario Gazette*, O. Reg. 134/92; Ministry of Natural Resources, "Ontario Announces Strategy to Reduce Water Consumption and Use Water Wisely," News Release, Toronto, Ont., Canada, August 19, 1991.

51. "Mass. Mandates Low-Flow," *U.S. Water News*, March 1989; states that have adopted the six-liter toilet standard from Amy Vickers, Amy Vickers & Associates, Boston, Mass., private communication, June 16, 1992. The 15 states are California, Connecticut, Delaware, Georgia, Maryland, Massachusetts, Nevada, New Jersey, New York, North Carolina, Oregon, Rhode Island, Texas, Utah, and Washington. Colorado has adopted standards for showerheads and faucets, but not the six-liter toilet standard.

52. "Energy Conservation Requirements for Certain Lamps and Plumbing Products,"

Congressional Record, No. 142—Part V, October 5, 1992; Amy Vickers, "Water-Use Efficiency Standards for Plumbing Fixtures: Benefits of National Legislation," *Journal of the AWWA*, May 1990.

53. Conserv 90, "Xeriscape: A Growing Idea in Water Conservation," News Release, Dublin, Ohio, February 27, 1990; Patricia Wellingham-Jones, "The Dry Garden Comes of Age," *Garden*, July/August 1986; John Olaf Nelson, "Water Conserving Landscapes Show Impressive Savings," in *Proceedings of CONSERV 90: The National Conference and Exposition Offering Water Supply Options for the 1990s* (Columbus, Ohio: National Ground Water Association, 1990); number of U.S. states with programs and mention of other countries from Raymond Uecker, Executive Director, National Xeriscape Council, Roswell, Ga., private communication, April 1, 1992.

54. Lagos figure from Peter Rogers, "Integrated Urban Water Resources Management," Keynote Paper, International Conference on Water and the Environment: Development Issues for the 21st Century, Dublin, Ireland, January 26–31, 1992; other cities from Bhatia and Falkenmark, "Water Resource Policies and the Urban Poor."

55. MWRA, *MWRA at Work: Massachusetts Water Resources Authority Annual Report 1990* (Boston, Mass.: 1991); "Leak Detectives Boost Manila Supply," *World Water*, November 1983; Jakarta example from Bhatia and Falkenmark, "Water Resource Policies and the Urban Poor."

56. Cost estimate and World Bank programs from Arlosoroff, private communication.

57. Ronald Cummings et al., *Waterworks: Improving Irrigation Management in Mexican Agriculture*, WRI Paper 5 (Washington, D.C.: WRI, December 1989); World Bank, *Indonesia: Sustainable Development of Forests, Land, and Water* (Washington, D.C.: 1990); Pakistan example from Robert Repetto, *Skimming the Water: Rent-Seeking and the Performance of Public Irrigation Systems*, WRI Paper 4 (Washington, D.C.: WRI, December 1986); U.S. example from Richard W. Wahl, *Markets for Federal Water: Subsidies, Property Rights, and the Bureau of Reclamation* (Washington, D.C.: Resources for the Future, 1989).

58. Environmental Defense Fund, "The Central Valley Project Improvement Act—General Summary," Oakland, Calif., October 12, 1992; Keith Schneider, "California Gets Pro-Environment Water Law," *New York Times*, November 1, 1992.

59. Keen, "Clearer Thoughts Flow on Irrigation."

60. Rodney T. Smith and Roger Vaughan, eds., "1991 Annual Transaction Review: Water Comes to Town," *Water Strategist* (Stratecon, Inc., Claremont, Calif.), January 1992.

61. Seven percent figure from Deborah Moore and Zach Willey, "Water in the American West: Institutional Evolution and Environmental Restoration in the 21st Century," *Colorado Law Review*, Vol. 62, No. 4, 1991.

62. Ibid.; Matthew J. McKinney et al., "The Protection of Instream Flows in Montana: A Legal-Institutional Perspective," in Lawrence J. MacDonnell et al., eds., *Instream Flow Protection in the West* (Boulder, Colo.: University of Colorado School of Law, 1989); Robert Reinhold, "New Age for Western Water Policy: Less for the Farm, More for the City," *New York Times*, October 11, 1992.

63. "New York's Suburbs Urged to Plan for Their Groundwater Future," *The Groundwater Newsletter* (Water Information Center, Inc., Plainview, N.Y.), February 28, 1991; Sarah Meyland, Executive Director, Citizens Campaign for the Environment, Massapequa, N.Y., private communication, April 20, 1992. See also Sarah J. Meyland, "Watershed Management Advances Using State-of-the-Art Technologies and Strategies," in *Proceedings of CONSERV 90*.

Chapter 3. Reviving Coral Reefs

1. Lucy Bunkley-Williams and Ernest H. Williams, Jr., "Global Assault on Coral Reefs," *Natural History*, April 1990.

2. Ibid.

3. Ibid.; John R. Ware and Marjorie L. Reaka-Kudla, "Coral Bleaching in the Caribbean as a Detection Mechanism for Global Temperature Change: Preliminary Results," presented at the Seventh International Coral Reef Symposium, Guam, 1992 (hereinafter International Symposium) (proceedings in press); S.V. Smith and R.W. Buddemeier, "Global Change and Coral Reef Ecosystems," *Annual Review of Ecology and Systemetics*, Vol. 23, 1992, pp. 89–118.

4. Susan M. Wells, *Coral Reefs of the World, Vol. III: Central and Western Pacific* (Cambridge: International Union for Conservation of Nature and Natural Resources and U.N. Environment Programme, 1988); Susan M. Wells, "Coral Reefs: Undersea Gardens Lose Their Sheen," *International Wildlife*, March/April 1990.

5. Kenneth Brower, "State of the Reef," *Audubon*, March 1989. For a general text on coral reefs see Charles R.C. Sheppard, *A Natural History of the Coral Reef* (Poole, U.K.: Blandford Press, 1983).

6. S.V. Smith, "Coral-Reef Area and the Contributions of Reefs to Processes and Resources of the World's Oceans," *Nature*, May 18, 1978; World Conservation Monitoring Centre, *Global Biodiversity: Status of the Earth's Living Resources* (London: Chapman & Hall, 1992); Sheppard, *A Natural History of the Coral Reef*; Boyce Thorne-Miller and John Catena, *The Living Ocean: Understanding and Protecting Marine Biodiversity* (Washington, D.C.: Island Press, 1991).

7. Gregor Hodgson, "Drugs from the Sea," *Far Eastern Economic Review*, April 11, 1991; "O.K. Coral," *The Economist*, June 13, 1992.

8. Reef length from Geoffrey Lean et al., *World Wildlife Fund Atlas of the Environment* (New York: Prentice Hall Press, 1990); F. Gable, "Caribbean Coastal and Marine Tourism: Coping with Climate Change and its Associated Effects," in Marc L. Miller and Jan Auyong, *Proceedings of the 1990 Congress on Coastal and Marine Tourism*, Vol. I (Newport, Oreg.: National Coastal Resources Research & Development Institute, 1991); Brower, "State of the Reef"; Wells, "Undersea Gardens Lose Their Sheen"; Don E. McAllister, "What is a Coral Reef Worth?" *Sea Wind* (Ocean Voice, Ontario, Canada), Vol. 5, No. 1, 1991.

9. Sirikul Bunpapong and Apiradee Ngernvijit, "Coral Reef Management Plan for the Islands of Ban Don Bay, Thailand," in Loke Ming Chou et al., eds., *Towards an Integrated Management of Tropical Coastal Resources*, Proceedings of the ASEAN/US Technical Workshop on Integrated Tropical Coastal Zone Management, October 28–31, 1988 (Singapore: National University of Singapore, 1991); P.P. Wong, *Coastal Tourism in Southeast Asia*, Education Series No. 8 (Manila: Association of Southeast Asian Nations, 1991); Enzo Paci, World Tourism Organization, private communication, October 21, 1992; Gable, "Caribbean Coastal and Marine Tourism"; M.T. Agardy, "Integrating Tourism in Multiple Use Planning for Coastal and Marine Protected Areas," in Miller and Auyong, *Proceedings of the 1990 Congress on Coastal and Marine Tourism*.

10. Wells, *Coral Reefs*; Carlos Goenaga, "The State of Coral Reefs in the Wider Caribbean," *Interciencia*, January/February 1991; McAllister, "What is a Coral Reef Worth?"; Don Hinrichsen, "Coastal People on Edge of Survival," *People*, Vol. 17, No. 1, 1990.

11. International Center for Living Aquatic Resources Management (ICLARM), *ICLARM's Strategy For International Research on Living Aquatic Resources Management* (Manila, Philippines: 1992); J. Caddy, Fisheries De-

partment, U.N. Food and Agriculture Organization (FAO), Rome, private communication, September 25, 1992; FAO, *FAO Production Yearbook: Fishery Statistics, Commodities, 1989* (Rome: 1990); Don E. McAllister, "Environmental, Economic and Social Costs of Coral Reef Destruction in the Philippines," *Galaxea* (Sesoko Marine Science Center, Nishihara, Japan), Vol. 7, 1988, pp. 161–78; McManus from "Fisheries Cooperative Research Support Program (CRSP) in the Philippines," in University of Rhode Island International Center for Marine Resource Development (ICMRD) Newsletter, Winter 1988.

12. ICLARM, *ICLARM's Strategy*; R.E. Johannes, CSIRO Marine Laboratories, Hobart, Australia, "Small-Scale Fisheries: A Storehouse of Knowledge for Managing Coastal Marine Resources," presented at the Ocean Management Symposium, Smithsonian Institution, Washington, D.C., November 20, 1991; Thia-Eng Chua and Louise Fallon Scura, eds., *Managing ASEAN's Coastal Resources for Sustainable Development: Role of Policymakers, Scientists, Donors, Media and Communities*, Proceedings of the ASEAN/US Policy Conference on Managing ASEAN's Coastal Resources for Sustainable Development, Manila and Bagio, Philippines, March 4–7, 1990 (Manila: Departments of Science and Technology, Agriculture, Environment and Natural Resources, and Tourism of the Philippine Government, and ICLARM, 1991).

13. Sheppard, *A Natural History of the Coral Reef*; Wendy Craik, Great Barrier Reef Marine Park Authority, "The Great Barrier Reef Marine Park: Its Establishment, Development and Current Status" (draft), June 9, 1992; Clive R. Wilkinson, Australian Institute of Marine Science, Townsville, Australia, private communications, August and October 1992; B.G. Hatcher et al., "Review of Research Relevant to the Conservation of Shallow Tropical Marine Ecosystems," *Oceanography and Marine Biology Annual Review*, Vol. 27, 1989, pp. 337–414.

14. Charles Darwin, *The Structure and Distribution of Coral Reefs* (Berkeley: University of California Press, 1962).

15. Jeremy B.C. Jackson, "Adaptation and Diversity of Reef Corals," *BioScience*, July/August 1991.

16. U.S. Department of Agriculture recommended daily allowance for protein is 50 grams; healthy reefs yield 8-35 tons per square kilometer per year, from ICLARM, *ICLARM's Strategy*.

17. Sheppard, *A Natural History of the Coral Reef*; Thorne-Miller and Catena, *The Living Ocean*; Jackson, "Adaptation and Diversity of Reef Corals."

18. R.C. Bales, "Hydrology Sessions at the 1990 Fall AGU Meeting," *EOS*, Vol. 72, 1991, p. 243, cited in Smith and Buddemeier, "Global Change"; W. David Liddell and Sharon L. Ohlhorst, "Ten Years of Disturbance and Change on a Jamaican Fringing Reef," presented at International Symposium.

19. Clive R. Wilkinson, "Coral Reefs are Facing Widespread Extinctions: Can We Prevent These Through Sustainable Management Practices?" presented at International Symposium; Wilkinson, private communications.

20. Past reviews include R.E. Johannes, "Pollution and Degradation of Coral Reef Communities," in E.J. Ferguson Wood and R.E. Johannes, *Tropical Marine Pollution* (New York: Elsevier, 1975), B.E. Brown and L.S. Howard, "Assessing the Effects of 'Stress' on Reef Corals," *Advances in Marine Biology*, Vol. 22, 1985, pp. 1–63, Wells, *Coral Reefs*, and Hatcher et al., "Review of Research."

21. Area in Table 3–2 from Smith, "Coral-Reef Area and the Contributions of Reefs to Processes and Resources of the World's Oceans." Status in Table from Wilkinson, "Coral Reefs are Facing Widespread Extinctions"; Wilkinson, private communications;

Wells, *Coral Reefs*; World Conservation Monitoring Centre, *Biodiversity*; "The Status of Living Coastal Resources of ASEAN Countries: Reports Presented at the 4th Management Committee Meeting of the ASEAN-Australia Marine Science Project: Living Coastal Resources, Bali, January 29-February 1, 1992," *ASEAN Marine Science* (Newsletter of the ASEAN-Australia Marine Science Project, Townsville, Australia), April 1992; Thia-Eng Chua and Daniel Pauly, eds., *Coastal Area Management in Southeast Asia: Policies, Management Strategies and Case Studies*, Proceedings of the ASEAN/US Policy Workshop on Coastal Area Management, Johore Bahru, Malaysia, October 25–27, 1988 (Manila, Philippines: ICLARM, 1989); Charles Birkeland, "Caribbean and Pacific Coastal Marine Systems: Similarities and Differences," *Nature & Resources*, Vol. 26, No. 2, 1990; North Rohan Gunasekera, "Threat to Sri Lanka's Coral Reefs," *Panoscope*, September 1990; "Coastal Belt Coral Reefs Threatened," Colombo Sri Lanka Broadcasting Corporation International Service, July 28, 1991, in *JPRS Report: Environmental Issues*, August 22, 1991; Paul Dutton, "WWF Master Plan to Preserve Bazaruto Archipelago," *World Wildlife Fund News*, January/February 1991; Tim MacClanahan, "Triggerfish: Coral Reef Keystone Predator," *Swara* (East African Wildlife Society, Nairobi, Kenya), May/June 1992; "Corals in Death Throes," *Down to Earth*, June 30, 1992; Brower, "State of the Reef"; Goenaga, "The State of Coral Reefs in the Wider Caribbean"; Gable, "Caribbean Coastal and Marine Tourism"; Zvy Dubinsky, Bar-Ilan University, Ramat Gan, Israel, private communication, September 18, 1992.

22. Hatcher et al., "Review of Research."

23. Ibid.

24. Ibid.; Gregor Hodgson and John A. Dixon, *Logging Versus Fisheries and Tourism in Palawan: An Environmental and Economic Analysis*, Occasional Paper No. 7 (Honolulu, Hawaii: East-West Environmental and Policy Institute, 1988).

25. Chua and Scura, *Managing ASEAN's Coastal Resources for Sustainable Development*; "The Status of Living Coastal Resources of ASEAN Countries," *ASEAN Marine Science*; World Resources Institute (WRI), *World Resources 1992–93* (New York: Oxford University Press, 1992); Wells, *Coral Reefs*; Lean et al., *Atlas of the Environment*.

26. Alan T. White, "Coral Reef Management in the ASEAN/US Coast Resources Management Project," in Chou et al., *Towards an Integrated Management of Tropical Coastal Resources*; L.M. Chou, "Singapore," *ASEAN Marine Science* (Newsletter of the ASEAN-Australia Marine Science Project, Townsville, Australia), April 1992.

27. WRI, *World Resources 1992–93*; Chua and Pauly, *Coastal Area Management in Southeast Asia*; Don Hinrichsen, *Our Common Seas: Coasts in Crisis* (London: Earthscan Publications Ltd., 1990); Population Reference Bureau, *1992 World Population Data Sheet* (Washington, D.C.: 1992).

28. Hatcher et al., "Review of Research"; Dubinsky, private communication; Peter R.F. Bell, "Importance of Small Scale and Large Scale Eutrophication of Coral Reef Regions—Examples in the Great Barrier Reef (GBR) and Caribbean," presented at International Symposium.

29. Charles Birkeland, University of Guam, private communication, August 6, 1992; Birkeland, "Caribbean and Pacific Coastal Marine Systems"; C. Birkeland and V.S. Lucas, *Acanthaster planci: Major Management Problems of Coral Reefs* (Boca Raton, Fla.: CRC Press, 1990).

30. Birkeland, private communication; Birkeland, "Caribbean and Pacific Coastal Marine Systems"; Birkeland and Lucas, *Acanthaster planci*.

31. Birkeland, private communication; Birkeland, "Caribbean and Pacific Coastal Marine Systems"; Birkeland and Lucas, *Acan-*

thaster planci; Bell, "Importance of Small Scale and Large Scale Eutrophication of Coral Reef Regions."

32. Wells, *Coral Reefs*; Elliot A. Norse, ed., *Global Marine Biological Diversity Strategy: Building Conservation into Decisionmaking* (fourth draft), Center for Marine Conservation, Washington, D.C., May 27, 1992.

33. Wilkinson, private communications; Kathy Twine, Great Barrier Marine Park Authority, Townsville, Australia, private communication, October 22, 1992.

34. Dubinsky, private communication; Wells, *Coral Reefs*.

35. Dubinsky, private communication; J.P. Hawkins et al., "Effects of a Phosphate Ship Grounding on a Red Sea Coral Reef," *Marine Pollution Bulletin*, Vol. 22, No. 11, 1991; WRI, *World Resources 1990–91* (New York: Oxford University Press, 1990); R.P.M. Bak, "Effects of Chronic Oil Pollution on a Caribbean Coral Reef," *Marine Pollution Bulletin*, Vol. 18, No. 10, 1987; Héctor M. Guzmán et al., "Short-term Ecological Consequences of a Major Oil Spill on Panamanian Subtidal Reef Corals," *Coral Reefs*, Vol. 10, 1991, pp. 1–12.

36. James A. Bohnsack, "Reef Resource Habitat Protection: The Forgotten Factor," in Richard H. Stroud, ed., *Stemming the Tide of Coastal Fish Habitat Loss* (Savannah, Ga.: National Coalition for Marine Conservation, Inc., 1992); MacClanahan, "Triggerfish"; Okinawa from Wilkinson, private communications; Wells, "Undersea Gardens Lose Their Sheen."

37. P.M. Alino and H.T. Yap, "Philippines: Coral Reef Resources," *ASEAN Marine Science* (Newsletter of the ASEAN-Australia Marine Science Project, Townsville, Australia), April 1992; Chua and Scura, *Managing ASEAN's Coastal Resources for Sustainable Development*.

38. Brower, "State of the Reef"; Wells, *Coral Reefs*; J.W. Copland and J.S. Lucas, eds.,

Giant Clams in Asia and the Pacific (Canberra: Australian Centre for International Agricultural Research, 1988).

39. Mark Derr, "Raiders of the Reef," *Audubon*, March/April 1992; Therese Gladys Hingco and Rebecca Rivera, "Aquarium Fish Industry in the Philippines: Toward Development or Destruction?" in Chou et al., *Integrated Management of Tropical Coastal Resources*.

40. FAO, *FAO Production Yearbook*; Derr, "Raiders of the Reef."

41. Derr, "Raiders of the Reef"; "U.S. Halts Philippine Coral Imports," *Traffic (USA)*, June 1989.

42. Michael Gawel, Territorial Planning Office of Guam, private communication, August 20, 1992; Wells, *Coral Reefs*; Goenaga, "The State of Coral Reefs in the Wider Caribbean"; Alejandro C. Ansula and Don E. McAllister, "Fishing with Explosives in the Philippines," *Sea Wind* (Ocean Voice, Ontario, Canada), Vol. 6, No. 2, 1992.

43. Gregor Hodgson, "Bubble Bath for Coral," *Far Eastern Economic Review*, March 7, 1991; Wells, *Coral Reefs*.

44. Wells, *Coral Reefs*; Wilkinson, private communications; Kevin McManus, civil engineer, Wellington, New Zealand, private communication, August 17, 1992; Hatcher et al., "Review of Research."

45. Goenaga, "The State of Coral Reefs in the Wider Caribbean"; John C. Ryan, "Belize's Reefs on the Rocks," *World Watch*, November/December 1991.

46. William H. Allen, "Increased Dangers to Caribbean Marine Ecosystems: Cruise Ship Anchors and Intensified Tourism Threaten Reefs," *BioScience*, May 1992.

47. Robert J. Dobias, "Management of Coastal Tourism Resources at Ban Don Bay, Surat Thani Province, Thailand," in Chou et al., *Integrated Management of Tropical Coastal Resources*; Bunpapong and Ngernvijit, "Coral

Reef Management Plan"; Wells, *Coral Reefs*; Hatcher et al., "Review of Research."

48. Intergovernmental Panel on Climate Change (IPCC), Working Group I, *Climate Change 1992* (Cambridge: Cambridge University Press, 1992); IPCC, *Climate Change: The IPCC Scientific Assessment* (Cambridge: Cambridge University Press, 1990); Smith and Buddemeier, "Global Change."

49. IPCC, *Climate Change 1992*; IPCC, *Climate Change*; Smith and Buddemeier, "Global Change."

50. Smith and Buddemeier, "Global Change."

51. *Workshop on Coral Bleaching, Coral Reef Ecosystems and Global Change: Report of Proceedings* (College Park, Md.: Maryland Sea Grant College, 1991); Smith and Buddemeier, "Global Change"; P.W. Glynn, "Coral Mortality and Disturbances to Coral Reefs in the Tropical Eastern Pacific," in P.W. Glynn, ed., *Global Ecological Consequences of the 1982–83 El Niño–Southern Oscillation* (Amsterdam: Elsevier, 1990).

52. Glynn, "Coral Mortality and Disturbances to Coral Reefs"; Smith and Buddemeier, "Global Change"; Steve Neudecker, "Growth and Survival of Scleractinian Corals Exposed to Thermal Effluents at Guam," *Proceedings of the Fourth International Coral Reef Symposium* (Manila: 1981).

53. Ware and Reaka-Kudla, "Coral Bleaching in the Caribbean as a Detection Mechanism for Global Temperature Change"; IPCC, *Climate Change*; Glynn, "Coral Mortality and Disturbances to Coral Reefs"; J. Hansen and S. Lebedeff, "Global Surface Air Temperatures: Update through 1987," *Geophysical Research Letters*, Vol. 15, No. 4, 1988, updated by Helene Wilson, NASA Goddard Institute for Space Studies, New York, private communication, March 23, 1992; IPCC, *Climate Change 1992*.

54. Normal temperature range for corals, between 18 and 30 degrees Celsius, from Sheppard, *A Natural History of the Coral Reef*. For most corals, the maximum tolerated temperature ranges from 27 degrees in Hawaii to 31 degrees in Enewetak; in the Persian Gulf, 33–34 degrees is tolerated by healthy communities, and some species can survive 36–38 degrees Celsius, according to Smith and Buddemeier, "Global Change." R.W. Buddemeier and D.G. Fautin, "Coral Bleaching as an Adaptive Mechanism: A Testable Hypothesis," *Bioscience*, 1993 (in press).

55. Stephan H. Schneider, *Global Warming: Are We Entering the Greenhouse Century?* (San Francisco: Sierra Club Books, 1989); Smith and Buddemeier, "Global Change."

56. D.F. Gleason and G.M. Wellington, "The Intensities of Ultraviolet Radiation That Induce Bleaching of Caribbean Coral," presented at International Symposium; Smith and Buddemeier, "Global Change."

57. Eugene A. Shinn, "Coral Reef Recovery in Florida and the Persian Gulf," *Environmental Geology*, Vol. 1, 1976, pp. 241–45; Mitchell W. Colgan, "Coral Reef Recovery on Guam," *Ecology*, Vol. 68, No. 6, 1987; D.P. Fenner, "Effects of Hurricane Gilbert on Coral Reefs, Fishes and Sponges at Cozumel, Mexico," *Bulletin of Marine Science*, Vol. 48, No. 3, 1991; Stephan V. Smith et al., "Kaneohe Bay Sewage Diversion Experiment: Perspectives on Ecosystem Responses to Nutritional Perturbation," *Pacific Science*, Vol. 35, No. 4, 1981; Héctor M. Guzmán, "Restoration of Coral Reefs in Pacific Costa Rica," *Conservation Biology*, June 1991; Hatcher et al., "Review of Research."

58. Gary A. Klee, "Oceania," in Gary A. Klee, ed., *World Systems of Traditional Resource Management* (New York: John Wiley & Sons, 1980); R.E. Johannes, CSIRO Marine Laboratories, Australia, "Small-Scale Fisheries: A Storehouse of Knowledge for Managing Coastal Marine Resources," presented at Ocean Management Symposium, Smith-

sonian Institution, Washington, D.C., November 20, 1991; Conner Bailey, Auburn University, Auburn, Ala., and Charles Zerner, Woodrow Wilson Institution, Washington, D.C., "Role of Traditional Fisheries Resource Management Systems for Sustainable Resource Utilization," presented at Perikanan Dalam Pembangunan Jangka Panjang Tahap II: Tantangan dan Peluang, Sukabumi, West Java, June 18–21, 1991.

59. Gawel, private communication.

60. Wells, *Coral Reefs*; Wells, "Undersea Gardens Lose Their Sheen"; "Living Marine Resources: Background Paper for the U.S. Response to the 1991 Geneva PrepCom," U.S. Government paper submitted to Second Preparatory Committee meeting, U.N. Conference on Environment and Development, Geneva, March 18, 1991.

61. Craik, "Great Barrier Reef Marine Park."

62. Bruce Rigsby and Nancy Williams, "Reestablishing a Home on Eastern Cape York Peninsula," *Cultural Survival Quarterly*, Vol, 15, No. 2, 1991.

63. Bailey and Zerner, "Role of Traditional Fisheries Resource Management Systems"; Susan Wells, "'Successful' Coral Reef Management Programmes," *Intercoast Network* (Coastal Resources Center, University of Rhode Island, Narragansett, R.I.), September 1992.

64. Graham B.K. Baines, "Asserting Traditional Rights: Community Conservation in Solomon Islands," *Cultural Survival Quarterly*, Vol. 15, No. 2, 1991; Norse, *Global Marine Biological Diversity Strategy*; Jane Robertson, UNESCO, Paris, private communication, October 20, 1992.

65. Hodgson and Dixon, *Logging Versus Fisheries and Tourism in Palawan*.

66. Dan Ashe, Merchant Marine and Fisheries Committee, U.S. House of Representatives, Washington, D.C., private communication, October 21, 1992.

67. UNICEF, *The State of the World's Children 1992* (New York: Oxford University Press, 1992).

68. Israeli wastewater use from Jehoshua Schwarz, "Israel Water Sector Review: Past Achievements, Current Problems and Future Options," prepared for the World Bank by Tahal Consulting Engineers Ltd., Tel Aviv, December 1990.

69. Smith et al., "Kaneohe Bay Sewage Diversion Experiment."

70. Cindy Hunter, Hawaii Institute of Marine Biology, University of Hawaii, private communication, September 21, 1992; Paul Jokiel, Hawaii Institute of Biology, private communication, September 21, 1992; Maureen Eldredge, Center for Marine Conservation, Washington, D.C., private communication, October 16, 1992.

71. Hinrichsen, *Our Common Seas*.

72. Craik, "Great Barrier Reef Marine Park"; Dobias, "Management of Coastal Tourism Resources at Ban Don Bay."

73. Anita van Breda and Kristina Gjerde, *The Use of Mooring Buoys as a Management Tool* (Washington, D.C.: Center for Marine Conservation, 1992); *Protecting Jamaica's Coral Reefs: Final Report of the Negrils Reef Mooring Buoy Workshop & Installation Project* (Key West, Fla.: Reef Relief, 1991); Allen, "Increased Dangers to Caribbean Marine Ecosystems"; McAllister, "What is a Coral Reef Worth?"

74. Derr, "Raiders of the Reef"; Wells, "'Successful' Coral Reef Management Programmes"; Robertson, private communication; Jan Post, World Bank, Washington, D.C., private communication, October 19, 1992; Chua and Pauly, *Coastal Area Management in Southeast Asia*; "ASEAN-Australia Marine Science Project: Living Coastal Resources," brochure, Australian Marine Science and Technology Limited, Curtin,

ACT, Australia; Kenton Miller and Charles Barber, "Biodiversity After the Earth Summit: Prospects for the Convention on Biodiversity," *Network '92* (Centre for Our Common Future, Geneva), June/July 1992.

75. Birkeland, private communication.

76. Robert W. Buddemeier, "Corals, Climate, and Conservation," plenary lecture, International Symposium.

Chapter 4. Closing the Gender Gap in Development

1. Information on women in Sikandernagar from Maria Mies, *Indian Women in Subsistence and Agricultural Labour*, Women, Work and Development Paper 12 (Geneva: International Labour Organization (ILO), 1986).

2. Some 1.2 billion people live in "absolute poverty," and more than 2 billion others—including the land-poor, sharecroppers, wage laborers, village artisans, and street hawkers—have cash incomes insufficient to meet more than their most immediate needs. Urban or rural, all are subsistence producers because they must rely wholly or in part on their own labor to produce, gather, or scavenge goods they cannot purchase. Number of poor worldwide from Alan B. Durning, *Poverty and the Environment: Reversing the Downward Spiral*, Worldwatch Paper 92 (Washington, D.C.: Worldwatch Institute, November 1989), and from U.N. Development Programme (UNDP), *Human Development Report 1991* (New York: Oxford University Press, 1991).

3. Mies, *Indian Women*.

4. UNDP, *Human Development Report 1991*.

5. United Nations Department of International Economic and Social Affairs (UNDIESA), *The World's Women: Trends and Statistics 1970–1990* (New York: United Nations, 1991).

6. See, for example, Kevin Cleaver and Gotz Schreiber, *The Population, Agriculture, and*

Environment Nexus in Sub-Saharan Africa (Washington, D.C.: World Bank, 1992), Jean Davison, ed., *Agriculture, Women, and Land: The African Experience* (Boulder, Colo.: Westview Press, 1988), and ILO, *Rural Development and Women in Africa* (Geneva: 1984).

7. Cleaver and Schreiber, *The Population, Agriculture, and Environment Nexus in Sub-Saharan Africa*; Marilyn Carr, "Technologies for Rural Women: Impact and Dissemination," in Iftikhar Ahmed, ed., *Technology and Rural Women: Conceptual and Empirical Issues* (London: George Allen and Unwin, 1985); Rae Lesser Blumberg, "Gender Matters: Involving Women in Development in Latin America and the Caribbean," prepared for the Agency for International Development Bureau for Latin America and the Caribbean, Washington, D.C., November 1990; George Acsadi and Gwendolyn Johnson-Acsadi, "Safe Motherhood in South Asia: Sociocultural and Demographic Aspects of Maternal Health," background paper prepared for the Safe Motherhood Conference, Pakistan, 1987.

8. Blumberg, "Gender Matters."

9. Ibid.; Bina Agarwal et al. *Engendering Adjustment for the 1990s: Report of a Commonwealth Expert Group on Women and Structural Adjustment* (London: Commonwealth Secretariat, 1990); Acsadi and Johnson-Acsadi, "Safe Motherhood in South Asia."

10. Augusta Molnar and Gotz Schreiber, "Women and Forestry: Operational Issues," Women in Development Working Papers, World Bank, May 1989.

11. Meera Chatterjee, *Indian Women: Their Health and Productivity* (Washington, D.C.: World Bank, 1991); Arun Ghosh, "Eighth Plan: Challenges and Opportunities—XII, Health, Maternity and Child Care: Key to Restraining Population Growth," *Economic and Political Weekly*, April 20, 1991.

12. Chatterjee, *Indian Women: Their Health and Productivity*; Government of India, Cen-

sus Commissioner, Registrar General, *Census of India, Provisional Population Totals, Paper One of 1991* (New Delhi: 1991); Mazumdar quoted in Aisha Ram, "Women's Health: The Cost of Development in India," status report from Rajasthan to Panos Institute, Washington, D.C., 1991.

13. Acsadi and Johnson-Acsadi, "Safe Motherhood in South Asia"; Jodi L. Jacobson, *Challenge of Survival: Safe Motherhood in the SADCC Region* (New York: Family Care International, 1991); Amartya Sen, "More Than 100 Million Women Are Missing," *New York Review of Books*, December 20, 1990.

14. Bina Agarwal, "Neither Sustenance Nor Sustainability: Agricultural Strategies, Ecological Degradation and Indian Women in Poverty," in Bina Agarwal, ed., *Structures of Patriarchy: State, Community, and Household in Modernising Asia* (London: Zed Books, Ltd., 1988).

15. UNDIESA, *The World's Women*; Agarwal et al. *Engendering Adjustment for the 1990s*.

16. Lynn Bennett, "Gender and Poverty in India: Issues and Opportunities Concerning Women in the Indian Economy," World Bank internal document, 1989.

17. Ibid.; Agarwal et al. *Engendering Adjustment for the 1990s*; Acsadi and Johnson-Acsadi, "Safe Motherhood in South Asia."

18. Joke Schrijvers, "Blueprint for Undernourishment: The Mahaweli River Development Scheme in Sri Lanka," in Agarwal, *Structures of Patriarchy*.

19. Bennett, "Gender and Poverty in India"; Chatterjee, *Indian Women: Their Health and Productivity*; Nepal and Philippines from UNDIESA, *The World's Women*.

20. Share of crops grown by women in different regions from Jodi L. Jacobson, "The Forgotten Resource," *World Watch*, May/June 1988; J. Price Gittinger, *Household Food Security and the Role of Women*, World Bank Discussion Paper 96 (Washington, D.C.: World Bank, 1990); Sandra Russo et al., *Gender Issues in Agriculture and Natural Resource Management* (Washington, D.C.: U.S. Agency for International Development, 1989); Chatterjee, *Indian Women: Their Health and Productivity*.

21. ILO, *Rural Development and Women in Africa*; Carmen Diana Deere and Magdalena Leon de Leal, *Women in Andean Agriculture*, Women Work and Development Paper 4, (Geneva: ILO, 1982); Susan V. Poats et al., *Gender Issues in Farming Systems Research and Extension* (Boulder, Colo.: Westview Press, 1988).

22. Janet Abramovitz and Roberta Nichols, "Women and Biodiversity: Ancient Reality, Modern Imperative," *Development*, No. 2, 1992; Deere and Leon de Leal, *Women in Andean Agriculture*.

23. Price Gittinger, *Household Food Security*; Dianne Rocheleau, "Women, Trees, and Tenure: Implications for Agroforestry," in Louise Fortmann and John W. Bruce, eds., *Whose Trees? Proprietary Dimensions of Forestry* (Boulder, Colo.: Westview Press, 1988); Paula J. Williams, "Women's Participation in Forestry Activities in Africa: Preliminary Findings and Issues Emerging from Case Studies," prepared for the Institute for Current World Affairs, Hanover, N.H., October 1991.

24. Rocheleau, "Women, Trees, and Tenure"; Williams, "Women's Participation in Foresty"; Molnar and Schreiber, "Women and Forestry"; Indian women quoted in Agarwal, "Neither Sustenance Nor Sustainability".

25. Paula Williams, "Women, Children, and Forest Resources in Africa, Case Studies and Issues," prepared for Women and Children First, symposium on the impact of environmental degradation and poverty on women and children, U.N. Conference on Environment and Development, Geneva, 27–30, May 1991.

26. Agarwal, "Neither Sustenance Nor Sustainability"; Molnar and Schreiber, "Women and Forestry"; Williams, "Women, Children, and Forest Resources."

27. Molnar and Schreiber, "Women and Forestry."

28. Ibid.

29. Williams, "Women, Children, and Forest Resources."

30. Bina Agarwal, *Engendering the Environment Debate: Lessons from the Indian Subcontinent*, Distinguished Speaker Series, Paper 8, Center for Advanced Study of International Development, Michigan State University, East Lansing, Mich., January 1991; Anil Agarwal and Sunita Narain, *Strategies for the Involvement of the Landless and Women in Afforestation: Five Case Studies from India* (Geneva: ILO, 1990).

31. Trends in northwest India from Agarwal, *Engendering the Environment Debate*.

32. Agarwal, *Engendering the Environment Debate*; Davison, *Agriculture, Women, and Land*; Poats et al., *Gender Issues in Farming Systems*.

33. Cleaver and Schreiber, *The Population, Agriculture, and Environment Nexus in Sub-Saharan Africa*.

34. Ibid.

35. Ibid.; for information on land tenure in Brazil and other Latin American countries, see Roy L. Prosterman and Jeffrey M. Riedinger, *Land Reform and Democratic Development* (Baltimore, Md.: Johns Hopkins University Press, 1987).

36. Mabel C. Milimo, "Women, Population, and Food in Africa: The Zambian Case," *Development: Seeds of Change*, Vol. 2, No. 3, 1987.

37. Rocheleau, "Women, Trees, and Tenure"; female agricultural labor and ownership data from Agarwal, "Neither Sustenance Nor Sustainability."

38. Cleaver and Schreiber, *The Population, Agriculture, and Environment Nexus in Sub-Saharan Africa*; Davison, *Agriculture, Women, and Land*.

39. Jennie Dey, *Women in Food Production and Food Security in Africa*, Women in Agriculture Paper 3 (Rome: U.N. Food and Agriculture Organization, 1984).

40. Ingrid Palmer, "The Impact of Agricultural Development Schemes on Women's Roles in Food Supply," in L'Institut Français de Recherche Scientifique pour le Développement en Cooperation, *Femmes et Politiques Alimentaires* (Paris: Editions de L'OR-STOM, 1985).

41. Katrine Saito and C. Jean Weidemann, *Agricultural Extension for Women Farmers in Africa*, World Bank Discussion Paper 3 (Washington, D.C.: World Bank, 1990); Bennett, "Gender and Poverty in India"; Poats et al., *Gender Issues in Farming Systems Research*.

42. See, for example, Cleaver and Schreiber, *The Population, Agriculture, and Environment Nexus in Sub-Saharan Africa*.

43. Ibid.

44. Agarwal et al., *Engendering Adjustment for the 1990s*.

45. Williams, "Women, Children, and Forest Resources."

46. Agarwal, *Engendering the Environment Debate*.

47. Molnar and Schreiber, "Women and Forestry"; Williams, "Women, Children, and Forest Resources."

48. Molnar and Schreiber, "Women and Forestry"; Williams, "Women, Children, and Forest Resources"; Agarwal and Narain, *Strategies for the Involvement of the Landless and Women in Afforestation*.

49. Mies, *Indian Women*.

50. Agarwal, "Neither Sustenance Nor Sustainability"; Bina Agarwal, as cited in

Cleaver and Schreiber, *The Population, Agriculture, and Environment Nexus in Sub-Saharan Africa*; Mayra Buvinic and Rekha Mehra, *Women in Agriculture: What Development Can Do* (Washington, D.C.: International Center for Research on Women, 1990).

51. Williams, "Women, Children, and Forest Resources."

52. Ravinder Kaur, "Women in Forestry in India," background paper prepared for World Bank review on women and development in India, unpublished, October 20, 1990.

53. Molnar and Schreiber, "Women and Forestry."

54. Williams, "Women, Children, and Forest Resources."

55. Abramovitz and Nichols, "Women and Biodiversity"; Williams, "Women, Children, and Forest Resources."

56. Diana Lee-Smith and Catalina Hinchey Trujillo, "The Struggle to Legitimize Subsistence Women and Sustainable Development," *Environment and Urbanization*, April 1992.

57. Phoebe Asiyo, "What We Want: Voices from the South," presented at Women's Health: The Action Agenda for the Nineties, 18th Annual National Council on International Health Conference, Arlington, Va., June 23–26, 1991.

58. Lee-Smith and Hinchey Trujillo, "The Struggle to Legitimize Subsistence Women."

Chapter 5. Supporting Indigenous Peoples

1. Tulalang Maway, Kidapawan, Philippines, private communication, July 9, 1992.

2. Combined area of indigenous homelands is Worldwatch Institute estimate, as described in endnote 29.

3. The terms indigenous, native, and tribal are used interchangeably in this chapter for the sake of variety, despite the slight differences in their anthropological meanings. Some indigenous people, as the Hmong of northern Thailand or displaced North American tribes, are not native to their current homes; others—such as the loose bands of pygmies in the Central African rain forest or the vast multitudes of Zhuang of China—are not tribal in the anthropological sense. Table 5–1 compiled from sources cited throughout this chapter. Population figures are Worldwatch Institute estimates, based on close comparison of best available data for each country, from scores of official and independent sources, including those cited as sources for Table 5–2 in endnote 5. Languages from Barbara F. Grimes, ed., *Ethnologue: Languages of the World*, 11th ed. (Dallas, Tex.: The Summer Institute of Linguistics, Inc., 1988).

4. Definition and descriptions of indigenous peoples from Julian Burger, ed., *Indigenous Peoples, A Global Quest for Justice*, a report for the Independent Commission on International Humanitarian Issues (London: Zed Books Ltd., 1987), from Robert Goodland, "Tribal Peoples and Economic Development," World Bank, Washington, D.C., 1982, from Jason W. Clay, "World Bank Policy on Tribal People, Application to Africa," World Bank, Washington, D.C., July 1991, and from Robert K. Hitchcock, "Indigenous Peoples: Working Definitions," in Barbara Johnston, ed., *Human Rights and the Environment* (preliminary draft), Society for Applied Anthropology, Oklahoma City, Okla., May 1992.

5. Language as marker of culture from David Harmon, George Wright Society, Hancock, Mich., "Indicators of the World's Cultural Diversity," presented at Fourth World Congress on National Parks and Protected Areas, Caracas, Venezuela, February 1992. Languages of the world from Michael Krauss, "The World's Languages in Crisis," *Lan-*

guage, March 1992. Number of indigenous cultures is Worldwatch Institute estimate based on Jason Clay, "Resource Wars: Nation and State Conflicts of the Twentieth Century," in Johnston, Human Rights and the Environment, on Julian Burger, The Gaia Atlas of First Peoples (London: Gaia Books Ltd., 1990), on Julian Burger, Report from the Frontier, The State of the World's Indigenous Peoples (London: Zed Books Ltd., 1987), and on Grimes, Ethnologue. Population of indigenous peoples is Worldwatch Institute estimate based on comparison of best available data for each country—from scores of sources—extrapolated to 1992 assuming indigenous populations have kept pace with national population growth, as reported in Population Reference Bureau, World Population Data Sheet (Washington, D.C.: various years). Table 5–2 from Worldwatch Institute estimates based on the following sources: Papua New Guinea, Peru, Chile, Malaysia, Brazil, and former Soviet Union from Burger, Gaia Atlas of First Peoples; Bolivia, Ecuador, and Mexico from Stefano Varese, "Think Locally, Act Globally," Report on the Americas, December 1991; Guatemala from Richard N. Adams and Charles Hale, "Sociedad y Etnia: 1930–79," in Edelberto Torres-Rivas, ed., Historia General de Centroamerica (Madrid: FLASCO, forthcoming), cited in Anthony R. De Souza, ed., "The Coexistence of Indigenous Peoples and the Natural Environment in Central America," special map supplement to Research and Exploration (National Geographic Society, Washington, D.C.), Spring 1992; Myanmar from Martin Smith, independent researcher, London, private communication, June 22, 1992; Laos from Charles F. Keyes, "Tribal Peoples and the Nation-State in Mainland Southeast Asia," in Cultural Survival, Southeast Asian Tribal Groups and Ethnic Minorities (Cambridge, Mass.: 1987); New Zealand from 1986 national census cited in Colin James, "Maori Back in the Fold," Far Eastern Economic Review, February 15, 1990; Philippines from Ponciano L. Bennagen, Center for Holistic Community, Quezon City, Philippines, private communication,

July 15, 1992; India from Moonis Raza and Aijazuddin Ahmad, An Atlas of Tribal India (New Delhi: Concept Publishing Company, 1990); Canada from Kimberly Thompson, senior technical officer, Department of Indian and Northern Affairs (INA), Statistics Canada, private communication, July 31, 1992; Australia and Thailand from Burger, Report from the Frontier; Bangladesh from 1981 official estimate from Minority Rights Group, "Adivasis of Bangladesh," London, December 1991; United States from Evelyn Pickett, public information specialist, U.S. Bureau of Indian Affairs, private communication, October 9, 1992.

6. Clay quoted in Elaine Briere and Dan Devaney, "East Timor: The Slaughter of a Tribal Nation," Canadian Dimension, October 1990; Brazilian tribes lost from Darcy Ribeiro, Os Indios e a Civilização (Rio de Janeiro: Editora Civilização Brasileira, 1970); North American and Australian languages lost from Michael Krauss, professor, Alaska Native Language Center, University of Alaska, Fairbanks, private communication, September 13, 1992.

7. Michael Krauss, "The World's Languages in Crisis," Language, March 1992, and Michael Krauss, Alaska Native Language Center, University of Alaska, Fairbanks, "The Language Extinction Catastrophe Just Ahead: Should Linguists Care?" presented at 15th International Congress of Linguists, Quebec City, Que., Canada, August 10, 1992.

8. Eric R. Wolf, Europe and the People Without History (Berkeley: University of California Press, 1982); Alfred W. Crosby, Ecological Imperialism: The Biological Expansion of Europe, 900–1900 (Cambridge: Cambridge University Press, 1986).

9. William Denevan, ed., The Native American Population of the Americas in 1492, 2nd ed. (Madison: University of Wisconsin Press, 1992); population of Europe from Alfred W. Crosby, The Columbian Exchange, Biological and

Cultural Consequences of 1492 (Westport, Conn.: Greenwood Press, 1972); 1992 indigenous population of Americas from Worldwatch Institute estimate based on numerous sources, many but not all of them cited in endnote 5 as sources for Table 5–2; Australia from J.M. Roberts, *The Pelican History of the World*, rev. ed. (London: Penguin Books Ltd., 1987); New Zealand population contraction from Minority Rights Group, "The Maori of Aotearoa-New Zealand," London, February 1990; Siberia from Demetri B. Shimkin and Edith M. Shimkin, "Population Dynamics in Northeastern Siberia, 1650/1700 to 1970," *Muskox*, Vol. 16, 1975, pp. 6–23.

10. Penan and North American Indians from Burger, *Report from the Frontier*; Sami from Hugh Beach, "The Saami of Lapland," Minority Rights Group, London, September 1988; Maori from Robert K. Hitchcock, "Indigenous Peoples: Working Definitions," in Johnston, *Human Rights and the Environment*.

11. Namibia from Gina Bari Kolata, "!Kung Bushmen Join South African Army," in Robert Gordon, ed., *The San in Transition, Vol. II* (Cambridge, Mass.: Cultural Survival, 1989); Asia Watch, "Bad Blood: Militia Abuses in Mindanao, The Philippines," Human Rights Watch, New York, April 1992; Canadian unemployment from Burger, *Report from the Frontier*, and from Stephen Maly, "Indian Summer," Institute of Current World Affairs (Hanover, N.H.), November 4, 1990; Indian migrant laborers from Brinda Singh, chairperson, Mobile Creches, Delhi, India, private communication, August 8, 1991; Mexican beggars from José Matos Mar, director, Inter-American Indian Institute, Mexico City, private communication, May 14, 1992; uranium miners from Bill Lambrecht, "Poisoned Lands," *St. Louis Post-Dispatch*, November 19, 1991; Cornelia Ann Kammerer, "Of Labels and Laws: Thailand's Resettlement and Repatriation Policies," *Cultural Survival Quarterly*, Vol. 12, No. 4, 1988; U.S. gambling from Robert W. Venables, "More Than A Game," *Northwest Indian Quar-*

terly, Fall 1989, and from Edward Walsh, "Rise of Casino Gambling on Indian Land Sparks Controversy," *Washington Post*, June 16, 1992; "Child Prostitution in Taiwan—A National Shame," *Taiwan Church News*, June 1992; adivasis from Alan Whittaker, "Tribal Children: The Superexploited," *Cultural Survival Quarterly*, Vol. 10, No. 4, 1986.

12. Kammerer, "Of Labels and Laws: Thailand's Resettlement and Repatriation Policies"; Brazilian Indians legal status from Burger, *Report from the Frontier*; Asia Watch, "Burma: Rape, Forced Labor and Religious Persecution in Northern Arakan," New York, May 7, 1992; Guatemala from Nina M. Serafino, "Latin American Indigenous Peoples and Consideration for U.S. Assistance," Congressional Research Service, Library of Congress, Washington, D.C., August 31, 1991; East Timor from Ruth Leger Sivard, *World Military and Social Expenditures 1991* (Washington D.C.: World Priorities, 1991); Irian Jaya from Anti-Slavery Society, *West Papua, Plunder in Paradise* (London: 1990).

13. Quoted in Frederick Kempe, *Siberian Odyssey: A Voyage into the Russian Soul* (New York: G.P. Putnam's Sons, 1992).

14. Gonzalo Aguirre Beltran, *Regiones de Refugio* (Mexico City: Instituto Indigenista Americano, 1967); areas legally controlled and occupied by indigenous peoples are Worldwatch Institute estimates, based on scores of sources, including but not limited to the sources for Table 5–4 in endnote 29. Area legally controlled is liberal estimate, as detailed in Table 5–4.

15. World Council of Indigenous Peoples, "Rights of Indigenous Peoples to the Earth," presented to Working Group on Indigenous Populations, U.N. Commission on Human Rights, Geneva, July 30, 1985; Edtami Mansayagan, secretary general, Alliance of Lumad of Southern Mindanao for Democracy, Kidapawan, Philippines, private communication, July 8, 1992; land rights struggles generally from Roger Plant, "Land

Rights for Indigenous and Tribal Peoples in Developing Countries" (draft), World Employment Programme, International Labour Organisation, Geneva, November 1991, from Alan Thein Durning, "Native Americans Stand Their Ground," *World Watch*, November/December 1991, and from Alan Thein Durning, "Last Sanctuary," *World Watch*, November/December 1992.

16. De Souza, "The Coexistence of Indigenous Peoples and the Natural Environment in Central America"; Geodisio Castillo, president, Fundación Dobbo Yala, presentation at American Association for Advancement of Science Annual Meeting, Washington, D.C., February 1991.

17. Owen J. Lynch, Jr., and Kirk Talbott, "Legal Responses to the Philippine Deforestation Crisis," *New York University Journal of International Law and Politics*, Spring 1988; Therese Desiree Perez, "Philippine Forests: A Case of Disappearance," *Philippine Natural Resources Law Journal*, December 1990; Janis B. Alcorn and Owen J. Lynch, "Empowering Local Forest Managers: Toward More Effective Recognition of the Rights, Contributions and Capacities of People Occupying 'Public' Forest Reserves in the Kingdom of Thailand" (draft), Biodiversity Support Program/World Resources Institute, Washington, D.C., August 1992.

18. Shelton Davis, "Globalization and Traditional Cultures," *Northeast Indian Quarterly*, Spring 1991.

19. Intrusions on indigenous lands from Burger, *Report from the Frontier*, and from Burger, *A Global Quest for Justice*.

20. Borneo from Wade Davis and Thom Henley, *Penan, Voice for the Borneo Rainforest* (Vancouver: Western Canada Wilderness Committee, 1990); Latin America from Cathy Fogel, associate international representative, Sierra Club, Washington, D.C., private communication, October 12, 1992; Myanmar from Robert Birsel, "Few Winners in Burma's Teak War," *Cultural Survival Quar-*terly, Vol. 13, No. 4, 1989, and from Crystal Ashley, human rights consultant to Asia Watch, New York, private communication, June 4, 1992.

21. American Anthropological Association, "Report of the Special Commission to Investigate the Situation of the Brazilian Yanomami," Washington, D.C., June 1991; Julia Preston, "Gold Rush Brings Mercury Poisoning to Amazon," *Washington Post*, February 17, 1992; demarcation from Vikram Akula, "Drawing the Line," *World Watch*, November/December 1992; mining concessions and Indian lands from Ecumenical Center for Documentation and Information cited in Barbara J. Cummings, *Dam the Rivers, Damn the People* (London: Earthscan Publications Ltd., 1990).

22. Effects of petroleum production generally from Kempe, *Siberian Odyssey*, and from Z.P. Sokolova, "Peoples of the North of the U.S.S.R.: Past, Present, and Future," *Sovetskaya Ethnografiya*, Vol. 6, 1990, as cited by Gail Fondahl, professor, Middlebury College, Middlebury, Vt., private communication, October 1, 1992; lands useless for subsistence from Gail Fondahl, "The Invasion of Siberia," *Cultural Survival Quarterly*, Fall 1992.

23. James Bay projects from Catherine Foster, "Canadian Hydro Project Opposed," *Christian Science Monitor*, March 21, 1991; Coon-Come quoted in Jeffrey Wollock, "James Bay: Down to the Wires," *Native Nations*, January 1991.

24. Estimated number of small-boat fishers from R. E. Johannes, "Small-Scale Fisheries: A Storehouse of Knowledge for Managing Coast Marine Resources," presented at Ocean Management Symposium, Smithsonian Institution, Washington, D.C., November 20, 1991; estimated share of fish catch by small-boat fishers from John Cordell, "Introduction: Sea Tenure," in John Cordell, ed., *A Sea of Small Boats* (Cambridge, Mass.: Cultural Survival, 1989); Bernard

Nietschmann, "Traditional Sea Territories, Resources and Rights in Torres Strait," in ibid.

25. Charles Lane, "Barabaig Natural Resource Management: Sustainable Land Use Under Threat of Destruction," U.N. Research Institute for Social Development, Geneva, June 1990; Louis A. Picard, *The Politics of Development in Botswana: A Model for Success?* (Boulder, Colo.: Lynne Reinner Publishers, 1987); Australian ranches from Robert Hitchcock, professor, University of Nebraska, Lincoln, private communication, October 2, 1992; Orang Asli from Barbara S. Nowak, "Can the Partnership Last," *Cultural Survival*, Vol. 8, No. 2, 1984.

26. Gloria Davis, "The Indonesian Transmigrants," in Judith Sloan Denslow and Christine Padoch, eds., *People of the Tropical Rain Forest* (Berkeley: University of California Press, 1988); Anti-Slavery Society, *West Papua: Plunder in Paradise*.

27. *Terra nullius* from Olive P. Dickason, "Concepts of Sovereignty at the Time of First Contacts," in *The Law of Nations and the New World* (Edmonton: University of Alberta, 1989), and from Willion H. Scott, "Demythologizing the Papal Bull 'Inter Caetera,'" *Philippine Studies*, Vol. 35, 1987, pp. 348–56.

28. Gus Gatmaytan, chief of direct legal services, Legal Rights and Natural Resources Center, Quezon City, Philippines, private communication, July 7, 1992; share of Philippines in public domain from Perez, "Philippine Forests: A Case of Disappearance"; Indonesia from Mark Poffenberger, ed., *Keepers of the Forest: Land Management Alternatives in Southeast Asia* (West Hartford, Conn.: Kumarian Press, 1990); Thailand from Alcorn and Lynch, "Empowering Local Forest Managers"; Cameroon from Elizabeth A. Halpin, "Indigenous Peoples and the Tropical Forestry Action Plan," World Resources Institute, Washington, D.C., June 1990, and from Kirk Talbott, World Resources Institute, "Nation States and Forest Peoples: Tenurial Control and the Squandering of the Central African Rainforest," presented to Second Annual Meeting of the International Association for the Study of Common Property, Winnipeg, Man., Canada, September 26–29, 1991; Tanzania from Owen J. Lynch, "Whither the People? Demographic and Tenurial Aspects of the Tropical Forestry Action Plan," World Resources Institute, Washington, D.C., September 1990; Australia from Burger, *Report from the Frontier*, and from Ronald T. Libby, *Hawke's Law: The Politics of Mining and Aboriginal Land Rights in Australia* (University Park: Pennsylvania State University Press, 1989).

29. Legal ambiguities regarding indigenous peoples' rights to their homelands from Plant, "Land Rights for Indigenous and Tribal Peoples in Developing Countries," and from Ronald Wixman, "Manipulating Territory, Undermining Rights," *Cultural Survival Quarterly*, Winter 1992. Table 5–4 assembled from scores of sources, including: Papua New Guinea from Owen J. Lynch, "Towards Conservation Partnerships in Papua New Guinea" (draft), World Resources Institute, Washington, D.C., July 1992; Fiji from Brij Lal, "Politics and Society in Post-Coup Fiji," *Cultural Survival Quarterly*, Vol. 15, No. 2, 1991; Ecuador from Plant, "Land Rights for Indigenous and Tribal Peoples in Developing Countries," and from Douglas Farah, "Ecuador Cedes Amazon Lands to Indians," *Washington Post*, May, 4, 1992; Sweden from Beach, "Saami of Lapland"; Colombia from Peter Bunyard, *The Colombian Amazon: Policies for the Protection of its Indigenous Peoples and Their Environment* (Cornwall, U.K.: Ecological Press, 1989); Canada from INA, *Schedule of Indian Bands, Reserves, and Settlements* (Ottawa: 1990), from INA, "Information Sheet No. 9," Ottawa, February 1992, and from INA, "Comprehensive Land Claims in Canada," Ottawa, December 1991; Australia from Libby, *Hawke's Law*, and from Burger, *Report from the Frontier*; Panama from Mac Chapin, program director of resource management, Cultural Survival, Ar-

lington, Va., private communication, June 22, 1992; Mexico from Stefano Varese, professor, University of California, Davis, private communication, September 22, 1992; Brazil from Carlos Alberta Ricardo, Ecumenical Center for Documentation, São Paulo, Brazil, private communication, February 25, 1992; New Zealand from *Asiaweek*, December 23–30, 1988; Nicaragua from Barry Nietschmann, professor, University of California, Berkeley, private communication, September 15, 1992; United States from Pickett, private communication; Costa Rica from Marcos Guevara Berger and Rubén Chacón Castro, "Territorios Indios en Costa Rica: Origenes, Situacion y Perspectivas," unpublished, January 1992; Venezuela from John Frechione, "The Yekuana of Southern Venezuela," *Cultural Survival Quarterly*, Vol. 8, No. 4, 1984, from Nelly Arvelo-Jimenez and Andrew L. Cousins, "False Promises," *Cultural Survival Quarterly*, Winter 1992, and from APPEN Features, "Venezuela: Yanomami Indians Demand Their Land," Asia-Pacific People's Environment Network, Penang, Malaysia, 1990.

30. Thomas R. Berger, *Village Journey: The Report of the Alaska Native Review Commission* (New York: Hill and Wang, 1985); Government of Canada, "Nunavut Political Accord Initialled," news release, Ottawa, April 27, 1992; Greenland from Burger, *Report from the Frontier*; Sweden from Beach, "Saami of Lapland"; Russia from "After the Breakup," *Cultural Survival Quarterly*, Winter 1992, from International Workgroup for Indigenous Affairs, *Indigenous Peoples of the Soviet North* (Copenhagen: 1990), and from Fondhal, private communication.

31. "Taiwan Church News," June 1992; *Japan Environment Monitor*, May 30, 1991; United States from Pickett, private communication; Canadian reservations from INA, *Schedule of Indian Bands, Reserves, and Settlements;* Canadian Indian legal setbacks from Stephen Maly, "Indian Summer," Institute of Current World Affairs, Hanover, N.H., No-

vember 4, 1990, from *Cultural Survival Quarterly*, Vol. 15, No. 2, 1991, and from William Claiborne, "The Fight Over Ontario Pine Forest," *Washington Post*, April 22, 1990; German Pollitzer, honorary president, Fundacion Cruzado Patagonica, Buenos Aires, Argentina, private communication, July 16, 1992; Chile from Burger, *Report from the Frontier*; New Zealand from W.H. Oliver, *Claims to the Waitangi Tribunal* (Wellington: Department of Justice, Waitangi Tribunal Division, 1991).

32. Pastoralists' land rights in general from Paul A. Olson, ed., *The Struggle for the Land* (Lincoln: University of Nebraska Press, 1990); Sahel from H.N. Le Houerou, *The Grazing Land Ecosystems of the African Sahel* (Berlin: Springer Verlag, 1989); Masai from Lee M. Talbot, "Demographic Factors in Resource Depletion and Environmental Degradation in East African Rangeland," *Population and Development Review*, September 1986, and from Solomon Bekure and Ishmael Ole Pasha, "The Response of the Kenya Maasai to Changing Land Policies," in Olson, *The Struggle for the Land*; Russia from Anatoly Khazanov, "Pastoral Nomads in the Past, Present, and Future: A Comparative View," in ibid.; China from Thomas Heberer, *China and Its National Minorities: Autonomy or Assimilation* (New York: M.E. Sharp Inc., 1989); Mongolia from J. Swift and R. Mearns, *The Mongolian Pastoral Economy: Report of an International Workshop* (Rome: U.N. Food and Agriculture Organization (FAO), 1991).

33. Land rights in Americas from Durning, "Native Americans Stand Their Ground"; lax enforcement from internal World Bank reports; Bunyard, *Colombian Amazon*; Ramiro López, "Bolivia: Indigenous Win a Battle Over Land," *Latinamerica Press*, September 27, 1990; James Jones, "The March for Dignity: Rationale and Responses for a Native Movement in Eastern Bolivia," *Hunger Notes*, Spring 1991; Venezuela from Nelly Arvelo-Jiminez and Andrew L. Cousins, "False Promises," *Cultural Survival Quar-*

terly, Winter 1992; Brazil from Akula, "Drawing the Line"; Douglas Farah, "Ecuador Cedes Amazon Land To Indians," *Washington Post*, May 15, 1992.

34. Orang Asli from Nowak, "Can the Partnership Last?"; adivasis from Christoph von Furer-Haimendorf, *Tribes of India: The Struggle for Survival* (Berkeley: University of California Press, 1982), and from Council for Advancement of People's Action and Rural Technology, "People's Action," July 1990; Kirk Talbott, "Trip Report: Vientiane, Laos, and Hanoi, Vietnam," World Resources Institute, Washington, D.C., December 1991; "Cambodia," *Cultural Survival Quarterly*, Vol. 14, No. 3, 1990; Thailand from Alcorn and Lynch, "Empowering Local Forest Managers"; Thomas Heberer, *China and Its National Minorities, Autonomy or Assimilation* (New York: M.E. Sharp Inc., 1989); Minority Rights Group, "Adivasis of Bangladesh"; Martin Smith, *Burma: Insurgency and the Politics of Ethnicity* (London: Zed Books, 1991).

35. Ponciano L. Bennagen, "Tribal Filipinos," in Shelton H. Davis, ed., *Indigenous Views of Land and the Environment* (Washington, D.C.: World Bank, 1991); Ed Legaspi, deputy secretary general, Alliance of Indigenous Peoples Rights Advocates, Quezon City, Philippines, private communication, July 3, 1992; Indonesia from Nancy Peluso, University of California, Berkeley, "Forest Policy—Forest Politics: The Criminalization of Customary Kalimantan," presented at Culture and the Question of Rights in Southeast Asian Environments: Forests, Coasts, and Seas, Woodrow Wilson Center, Washington, D.C., June 3, 1992, and from Sandra Moniaga, WALHI, Jakarta, "Towards Community-Based Forestry and Recognition of Adat Property Rights in the Outer Islands of Indonesia: A Legal and Policy Analysis," presented at Workshop on Legal Issues in Social Forestry, Bali, November 4–6, 1991; Sahabat Alam Malaysia, "Native Customary Rights in Sarawak," *Cultural Survival Quarterly*, Vol. 10, No. 2, 1987; Evelyne Hong, *Natives of Sarawak: Survival in Borneo's Vanishing Forest* (Penang: Institut Masyarakat, 1987).

36. India from Mark Poffenberger, "Joint Management for Forest Lands: Experiences from South Asia," Ford Foundation, New York, January 1990; Philippines from Poffenberger, *Keepers of the Forest*; Irian Jaya from Chip Barber, World Resources Institute, Washington, D.C., private communication, September 21, 1992; Bolivian Indians example from Shelton Davis, anthropologist, World Bank, Washington, D.C., private communication, April 22, 1992.

37. Cameroon from Talbott, "Nation States and Forest Peoples."

38. Jonathan S. Adams and Thomas O. McShane, *Myth of Wild Africa: Conservation Without Illusion* (New York: W.W. Norton & Co., 1992).

39. Indigenous peoples' total world territory is Worldwatch Institute estimate as described in endnote 14; Indian lands in Americas is Worldwatch Institute estimate based on numerous sources including but not limited to sources for Table 5–4 in endnote 29; global extent of national parks, nature preserves, and protected areas of similar stature from International Union for Conservation of Nature and Natural Resources, *1990 United Nations List of National Parks and Protected Areas* (Gland, Switzerland, and Cambridge, U.K.: 1990), and from FAO, *Production Yearbook 1989* (Rome: 1990).

40. Hildebrand quoted in James Brooke, "Tribes Get Right to 50% of Colombian Amazon," *New York Times*, February 4, 1990.

41. Indigenous ecological knowledge generally from D.M. Warren, ed., "Indigenous Agricultural Knowledge Systems and Development," *Agriculture and Human Values*, Winter/Spring 1991, and from D. A. Posey and W. Balee, eds., "Resource Management in Amazonia: Indigenous and Folk Strategies," *Advances in Economic Botany* (New York Botanical Garden), Vol. 7, 1989; Shuar from Brad

Bennett, "Plants and People of Ecuador's Amazonian Rainforests: Lessons and Needs for Sustainable Development," presented at Can Nuts Save the Rain Forest? Symposium, Smithsonian Institution, Washington, D.C., March 25, 1992.

42. South Pacific from Johannes, "Small-Scale Fisheries"; Canadian whalers from Peter Poole, resource management consultant, Alcove, Que., Canada, private communication, May 14, 1992; Australia from Nietschmann, "Traditional Sea Territories, Resources and Rights in Torres Strait."

43. Darrell A. Posey, "Indigenous Ecological Knowledge and Development of the Amazon," in E. Moran, ed., *The Dilemma of Amazonian Development* (Boulder, Colo.: Westview Press, 1983).

44. Tukano from Janet M. Chernela, "Managing Rivers of Hunger: The Tukano of Brazil," *Advances in Economic Botany* (New York Botanical Garden), Vol. 7, 1989. Table 5–5 sources: Indian tribal tree protection from Burger, *Gaia Atlas of First Peoples*; Gorowa sacred groves from C.A. Gerden and S. Mtallo, "Traditional Forest Reserves in Babati District, Tanzania," Swedish University of Agricultural Sciences, International Rural Development Center, Uppsala, 1990; Gabra sacred groves from Maryam Niamir, "Traditional Woodland Management Techniques of African Pastoralists," *Unasylva*, No. 1, 1990; Lacandon tree gardens from James D. Nations, "The Lacandon Maya," in Denslow and Padoch, *People of the Tropical Rain Forest*; Karen watershed protection from Alcorn and Lynch, "Empowering Local Forest Managers"; all grasslands examples from Niamir, "Traditional Woodland Management Techniques of African Pastoralists"; Bali water temples from Theodore Roszak, *The Voice of the Earth* (New York: Simon & Schuster, 1992); Iranian quanat from Ian R. Manners, "The Middle East," in Gary A. Klee, ed., *World Systems of Traditional Resource Management* (New York: V.H. Winston & Sons, 1980); South Pacific, including Mar-

quesas, from Gary A. Klee, "Oceania," in ibid.; Gitksan and Wet'suwet'en from Mike Morrell, "The Struggle to Integrate Traditional Indian Systems and State Management in the Salmon Fisheries of the Skeena River, British Columbia," in Evelyn Pinkerton, ed., *Co-operative Management of Local Fisheries* (Vancouver: University of British Colombia Press, 1989).

45. Owen J. Lynch, attorney, World Resources Institute, Washington, D.C., private communication, September 21, 1992.

46. Alaska from Michael Wright, Senior Fellow, World Wildlife Fund, Washington, D.C., private communication, April 20, 1992; Philippines from Linka Ansulang, Carmen, Philippines, private communication, July 9, 1992; general critique of indigenous resource management from Raymond Hames, "Wildlife Conservation in Tribal Societies," in Margery L. Oldfield and Janis B. Alcorn, *Biodiversity: Culture, Conservation, and Ecodevelopment* (Boulder, Colo.: Westview Press, 1992).

47. Shuar from Chuck Kleymeier, country representative, Inter-American Foundation, Rosslyn, Va., private communication, May 22, 1992.

48. Fondahl, private communication.

49. Lynch, private communication.

50. Pinkerton, *Co-operative Management of Local Fisheries*.

51. Ibid.

52. Robert K. Hitchcock, "Human Rights, Local Institutions, and Sustainable Development Among Kalahari San," presented at 90th Annual Meeting of the American Anthropological Association, Chicago, Ill., November 20–24, 1991; Robert K. Hitchcock, professor, University of Nebraska, Lincoln, private communication, October 1, 1992.

53. Inuvialuit from Dene Cultural Institute, "Amerindian Initiatives in Environmen-

tal Protection and Natural Resource Management: A Directory of Projects and Programs" (first draft), Yellowknife, N.W. Ter., Canada, 1992; Chinantecs from David Barton Bray, "The Struggle for the Forest," *Grassroots Development*, Vol. 15, No. 3, 1991; Miskitos from Armstrong Wiggins, attorney, Indian Law Resource Center, Washington, D.C., private communication, May 5, 1992.

54. Native Fish and Wildlife Service from Dene Cultural Institute, "Amerindian Initiatives"; Kuna from Chapin, private communication.

55. Mixe from David Bray, country representative, Inter-American Foundation, Rosslyn, Va., private communication, October 9, 1992; The Body Shop from Julia Preston, "Trial Spurs Debate on Brazil's Indians," *Washington Post*, August 17, 1992.

56. Mexico from Victor Toledo, "Green Economics and Indigenous Wisdom: How Many Products are Enclosed in a Tropical Forest?" presented at Can Nuts Save the Rain Forest? Symposium, Smithsonian Institution, Washington, D.C., March 26, 1992; Ecuador from Bennett, "Plants and People of Ecuador's Amazonian Rainforests"; risks of alternative trade from John C. Ryan, "Goods from the Woods," *World Watch*, July/August 1991.

57. Intellectual property rights from "Intellectual Property Rights: The Politics of Ownership," *Cultural Survival Quarterly*, Summer 1991; Jack Weatherford, *Indian Givers: How the Indians of the Americas Transformed the World* (New York: Fawcentine Columbine, 1988).

58. Shors from Kempe, *Siberian Odyssey*; Macushi from Mark J. Plotkin, Conservation International, Washington, D.C., untitled presentation at Can Nuts Save the Rain Forest? Symposium, Smithsonian Institution, Washington, D.C., March 25, 1992, and from Mark J. Plotkin, "Strychnos Medeola: A New Arrow Poison from Suriname," in Darrell A. Posey, ed., *Ethnobiology: Implications and Ap-*
plications, *Proceedings of the First International Congress of Ethnobiology* (Belém, Brazil: 1990).

59. Durning, "Last Sanctuary."

60. Maway, private communication.

61. Gatmaytan, private communication.

62. Mansayagan, private communication; Gatmaytan, private communication.

63. Situation at Mount Apo from Mansayagan, private communication, and from Gatmaytan, private communication; death threat and denial from Carol O. Arguillas, "PNOC Denies Offering Bounty for Tribe Chief," *Philippine Daily Inquirer*, July 13, 1992.

64. Foundation from Victor Mallet, "Getting into Hot Water," *Financial Times*, July 15, 1992; Maway, private communication.

65. Serafino, "Latin American Indigenous Peoples and Consideration for U.S. Assistance."

66. "March on Quito," *South and Meso American Indian Information Center Newsletter* (Oakland, Calif.), Spring/Summer 1992; area recognized from Douglas Farah, "Ecuador Cedes Amazon Lands to Indians," *Washington Post*, May 15, 1992.

67. Aid for Huaorani from Nina Orville, "Road Construction Threatens Huaorani in Ecuador," *Cultural Survival Quarterly*, Vol. 12, No. 3, 1988; Awa from Theodore Macdonald and Janet Chernela, "Politics, Development, and Indians" (draft), Cultural Survival, Cambridge, Mass., 1992.

68. Cameroon from Halpin, "Indigenous Peoples and the Tropical Forestry Action Plan."

69. Malaysia from Stan Sesser, "Logging the Rain Forest," *New Yorker*, May 27, 1991.

70. Chile from Alaka Wali, "Living *With* the Land: Ethnicity and Development in Chile," *Grassroots Development*, Vol. 14, No. 2, 1990; Sami from International Work Group for Indigenous Affairs, *Self Determination and*

Indigenous Peoples (Copenhagen: 1987); Mexico from Robert R. Alvarez, Jr., "The Paipai of Jamau: A Test Case for Constitutional Reform," *Cultural Survival Quarterly*, Vol. 14, No. 4, 1990; Brazil from Linda Rabben, Rain Forest Foundation, Washington, D.C., private communication, April 9, 1992; Colombia from Ted Macdonald, projects director, Cultural Survival, Cambridge, Mass., private communication, March 6, 1992; Canada from Mark Clayton, "Canada's Natives Exercise New Clout on National Scene," *Christian Science Monitor*, July 3, 1992.

71. Kayapó from James Brooke, "Rain Forest Indians Hold Off Threat of Change," *New York Times*, December 3, 1990; Australia from Ron Scherer, "Land Rights News Promotes Cause of Aboriginal People," *Christian Science Monitor*, March 11, 1992; radio from Vicki Elkin, "Radio Wave," *World Watch*, September/October 1992.

72. North American lawyers from Jose Barreiro, American Indian Program, Cornell University, Ithaca, N.Y., private communication, August 28, 1991; New Zealand from "Old Dreams, New Challenges," *Asiaweek*, December 23–30, 1988.

73. Earth Summit from Rabben, private communication.

74. Draft declaration text from Julian Burger, U.N. Working Group on Indigenous Populations, Geneva, Switerland, private communication, October 8, 1992.

75. Steve Tullberg, attorney, Indian Law Resource Center, Washington, D.C., private communication, May 5, 1992.

Chapter 6. Providing Energy in Developing Countries

1. Coloma situations from author's visits to Guamalán, and from Anne Quinlan Coloma and Carlos Coloma, Winsted, Conn., private communications, September 1992; energy statistics from United Nations, *1990 Energy Statistics Yearbook* (New York: 1992).

2. United Nations, *1990 Energy Statistics Yearbook*.

3. Amulya K.N. Reddy and José Goldemberg, "Energy for the Developing World," *Scientific American*, September 1990.

4. Figure 6–1 is based on British Petroleum (BP), *BP Statistical Review of World Energy* (London: 1992), on United Nations, *World Energy Supplies 1950–1974* (New York: 1976), on David Cieslikowski, International Economics/Socio-Economic Data Division, World Bank, private communication and printout, August 24, 1992, on Population Reference Bureau (PRB), *1991 World Population Data Sheet* (Washington, D.C.: 1991), and on PRB, "World Population Estimates and Projections by Single Years, Less Developed Regions: 1750–2100," Washington, D.C., unpublished printout, March 1992; J.M.O. Scurlock and D.O. Hall, "The Contribution of Biomass to Global Energy Use," *Biomass*, No. 21, 1990; U.S. Congress, Office of Technology Assessment (OTA), *Energy in Developing Countries* (Washington, D.C.: U.S. Government Printing Office, 1991).

5. Worldwatch Institute, based on United Nations, *1990 Energy Statistics Yearbook*, on BP, *BP Statistical Review*, and on PRB, *1991 World Population Data Sheet*. Commercial energy refers to oil, natural gas, coal, and electricity sources; it does not include biomass energy supplies, such as fuelwood and charcoal, for which insufficient data exist over time for reliable quantification, even though they may be sold in highly developed markets in some countries.

6. Income is based on purchasing power parity, from United Nations Development Programme (UNDP), *Human Development Report 1992* (New York: Oxford University Press, 1992), and from UNDP, *Human Development Report 1990* (New York: Oxford University Press, 1990); energy statistics, which include biomass energy for India and Pakistan, are from D.O. Hall, "Biomass Energy,"

Energy Policy, October 1991, and from United Nations, *1990 Energy Statistics Yearbook*.

7. OTA, *Energy in Developing Countries*; OTA, *Fueling Development: Energy Technologies for Developing Countries* (Washington, D.C.: U.S. Government Printing Office, 1992).

8. Andrew Hill, "Extracting the Benefits from African Oil," *Financial Times*, May 28, 1992; World Bank, *World Development Report 1992* (New York: Oxford University Press, 1992).

9. International Monetary Fund, *World Economic Outlook* (Washington, D.C.: May 1992); C. Rammanohar Reddy et al., "The Debt-Energy Nexus: A Case Study of India," International Energy Initiative, Bangalore, India, undated.

10. Percentage of debt for energy projects from Gunter Schramm, "Electric Power in Developing Countries: Status, Problems, Prospects," in *Annual Review of Energy 1990* (Palo Alto, Calif.: Annual Reviews Inc., 1990); tariffs in developing countries are in constant 1986 dollars, from Energy Development Division, *Review of Electricity Tariffs in Developing Countries During the 1980's*, Industry and Energy Department Working Paper, Energy Series Paper No. 32 (Washington, D.C.: World Bank, November 1990); OTA, *Fueling Development*.

11. "World Bank Funds Energy Efficiency Improvement in India," *Global Environment Change Report*, February 14, 1992; Mark D. Levine et al., "China's Energy System: Historical Evolution, Current Issues, and Prospects," in *Annual Review of Energy and the Environment 1992* (Palo Alto, Calif.: Annual Reviews Inc., in press); World Bank, Industry and Energy Department, "The Bank's Role in the Electric Power Sector: Policies for Effective Institutional, Regulatory, and Financial Reform" (draft), Washington, D.C., April 27, 1992.

12. Gita Piramal, "Power Generation a Thorn in the Side of Industrial Growth," *Financial Times*, September 16, 1991.

13. Edwin A. Moore and George Smith, *Capital Expenditures for Electric Power in the Developing Countries in the 1990s*, Industry and Energy Department Working Paper, Energy Series Paper No. 21 (Washington, D.C.: World Bank, February 1990); Schramm, "Electric Power in Developing Countries"; John E. Besant-Jones, senior energy economist, World Bank, "Financing Needs and Issues for Power Sector Development in Developing Countries During the 1990s," presented at the UPDEA-UNIPEDE Symposium on Financing Problems Facing Electrical Power Utilities in Developing Countries, Libreville, Gabon, January 1990.

14. Number of people without electricity from Derek Lovejoy, "Electrification of Rural Areas by Solar PV," *Natural Resources Forum*, May 1992; "Is Rural Electrification Such a Good Idea?" *Energy Economist*, July 1988; Gerald Foley, *Electricity for Rural People* (London: Panos Institute, 1990).

15. P.J. de Groot and D.O. Hall, "Biomass Energy: A New Perspective," prepared for AFREPREN, Third Workshop, University of Botswana, Gaborone, Botswana, December 1989; Gerald Leach and Robin Mearns, *Beyond the Woodfuel Crisis: People, Land and Trees in Africa* (London: Earthscan Publications Ltd., 1988); U.N. Food and Agriculture Organization citation is from OTA, *Energy in Developing Countries*.

16. OTA, *Energy in Developing Countries*; Kenneth Newcombe, "Economic Justification for Rural Afforestation: The Case of Ethiopia," in Gunter Schramm and Jeremy J. Warford, eds., *Environmental Management and Economic Development* (Baltimore, Md.: Johns Hopkins University Press, 1989).

17. World Bank, *World Development Report 1992*; number of deaths from World Health Organization, Division of Epidemiological Surveillance and Health Situation and Trend Assessment, *Global Health Situation and Projections* (Geneva: 1992); Catherine Gathoga, "Indoor Air Pollution," *Stove News*, Founda-

tion for Woodstove Dissemination, Nairobi, May/June 1991; OTA, *Energy in Developing Countries*; Bangkok from Victor Mallet, "Third World City, First World Smog," *Financial Times*, March 25, 1992; "Mexico City Sets Pollution Record," *Washington Post*, March 17, 1992; "Air Pollution Threatens Nairobi Residents," *Daily Nation*, January 9, 1991, reprinted in *JPRS Report: Environmental Issues*, May 7, 1991; "Chilean Capital Chokes on Smog," *Wall Street Journal*, June 13, 1991; Victoria Griffith, "São Paulo Engulfed in a Tide of Pollution," *Financial Times*, May 29, 1991.

18. William U. Chandler et al., "Energy for the Soviet Union, Eastern Europe and China," *Scientific American*, September 1990; John McBeth, "Heat and Dust," *Far Eastern Economic Review*, September 19, 1991.

19. Carbon numbers are based on Tom Boden, Oak Ridge National Laboratory, Oak Ridge, Tenn., private communication and database, July 28, 1992, and on Intergovernmental Panel on Climate Change (IPCC), *Climate Change: The IPCC Response Strategies* (Washington, D.C.: Island Press, 1991); IPCC, *Climate Change 1992* (Cambridge: Cambridge University Press, 1992); IPCC, *Climate Change: The IPCC Scientific Assessment* (Cambridge: Cambridge University Press, 1990).

20. Paul Lewis, "Danger of Floods Worries Islanders," *New York Times*, May 13, 1992; "Kenya, Other African Nations' Industry Seen Suffering Greatly from Climate Rise," *International Environment Reporter*, May 6, 1992; M.L. Parry et al., eds., *The Potential Socio-Economic Effects of Climate Change: A Summary of Three Regional Assessments* (Nairobi: United Nations Environment Programme (UNEP), 1991); "China Blames Global Warming for Drought," Reuters, March 24, 1992.

21. BP, *BP Statistical Review*; PRB, "World Population Estimates and Projections"; OTA, *Energy in Developing Countries*; Charles Campbell, Lawrence Berkeley Laboratory, Berkeley, Calif., private communication and printout, June 18, 1992.

22. Worldwatch Institute based on Organisation for Economic Co-operation and Development (OECD), International Energy Agency (IEA), *Energy Policies of IEA Countries: 1990 Review* (Paris: 1991); Mark D. Levine et al., *Energy Efficiency, Developing Nations, and Eastern Europe*, A Report to the U.S. Working Group on Global Energy Efficiency (Washington, D.C.: International Institute for Energy Conservation (IIEC), 1991); World Bank, "The Bank's Role in the Electric Power Sector." OECD countries saw energy grow slower than economic growth in part because of improvements in energy efficiency and, to a lesser degree, to structural changes in their industrial bases; for example, OECD countries now focus more on information technologies or "high-tech" products, and less so on energy-intensive industries such as aluminum and steel, which increased as a share of developing countries' output (and export to OECD countries). For a discussion of world energy use, structural changes, and intensity over the past 20 years, see Steven Meyers and Lee Schipper, "World Energy Use in the 1970s and 1980s: Exploring the Changes," in *Annual Review of Energy and the Environment 1992* (Palo Alto, Calif.: Annual Reviews Inc., in press).

23. United Nations Economic and Social Council, Committee on Energy, "Global Energy Efficiency 21: An Inter-regional Approach," New York, March 6, 1992; OTA, *Fueling Development*.

24. Industrial energy use and Indonesian example from Levine et al., *Energy Efficiency, Developing Nations, and Eastern Europe*; Paul Culbert, "Crisis Hits Huge Market," *Petroleum Economist*, July 1991; C.Y. Wereko-Brobby and John O.C. Nkum, Ministry of Energy, Ghana, "Goals and Means for a Sustainable Energy Development in Africa," presented to Conference on Global Collaboration on a Sustainable Energy Develop-

ment, Copenhagen, Denmark, April 25–28, 1991.

25. Roger S. Carlsmith et al., "Energy Efficiency: How Far Can We Go?" Oak Ridge National Laboratory, Oak Ridge, Tenn., January 1990; Levine et al., *Energy Efficiency, Developing Nations, and Eastern Europe*; World Resources Institute, *World Resources 1992–93* (New York: Oxford University Press, 1992); P.M. Nyoike and B.A. Okech, "The Case of Kenya," in M.R. Bhagavan and S. Karekezi, eds., *Energy Management in Africa* (Atlantic Highlands, N.J.: Zed Books Ltd., 1992); Moncef Ben Abdallah, President, Societé Tunisiènne de L'électricité et du Gaz Tunis, private communication and printout, August 11, 1992.

26. World Bank, "The Bank's Role in the Electric Power Sector"; Besant-Jones, "Financing Needs and Issues for Power Sector Development"; Amalesh Sarkar, "No Sign of Ending Power Crisis: Industries Hard Hit," *Holiday* (Dacca, Bangladesh), May 1, 1992.

27. Ashok Gadgil et al., "Advanced Lighting and Window Technologies for Reducing Electricity Consumption and Peak Demand: Overseas Manufacturing and Marketing Opportunities," Lawrence Berkeley Laboratory, Berkeley, Calif., March 1991; Evan Mills, "Efficient Lighting Programs in Europe: Cost-Effectiveness, Consumer Response, and Market Dynamics," *Energy—The International Journal*, forthcoming; Mark D. Levine et al., "Electricity End-Use Efficiency: Experience with Technologies, Markets, and Policies Throughout the World," Lawrence Berkeley Laboratory, Berkeley, Calif., March 1992.

28. Stephen C. Smith, "Industrial Policy in Developing Countries: Reconsidering the Real Sources of Export-Led Growth," Economic Policy Institute, Washington, D.C., 1991; Howard Geller, *Efficient Electricity Use: A Development Strategy for Brazil* (Washington, D.C.: American Council for an Energy-Efficient Economy (ACEEE), 1991).

29. Steven Nadel et al., "Opportunities for Improving End-Use Electricity Efficiency in India," ACEEE, Washington, D.C., November 1991; Govinda Rao et al., *The Least-Cost Energy Path for India: Energy Efficient Investments for the Multilateral Development Banks* (Washington, D.C.: IIEC, 1991); P.M. Sadaphal and Bhaskar Natarajan, "Constraints to Improved Energy Efficiency in Agricultural Pumpsets: The Case of India," *Natural Resources Forum*, August 1992; Jayant Sathaye and Ashok Gadgil, "Aggressive Cost-Effective Electricity Conservation," *Energy Policy*, February 1992; Michael Philips, *The Least Cost Energy Path for Developing Countries: Energy Efficient Investments for the Multilateral Development Banks* (Washington, D.C.: IIEC, 1991); Levine et al., "Electricity End-Use Efficiency."

30. Sathaye and Gadgil, "Aggressive Cost-Effective Electricity Conservation"; Feng Liu et al., "An Overview of Energy Supply and Demand in China," Lawrence Berkeley Laboratory, Berkeley, Calif., May 1992; Carl Goldstein, "China's Generation Gap," *Far Eastern Economic Review*, June 11, 1992.

31. Liu et al., "An Overview of Energy in China"; Jayant Sathaye and Stephen Tyler, "Transitions in Household Energy Use in Urban China, India, The Philippines, Thailand, and Hong Kong," *Annual Review of Energy and the Environment 1991* (Palo Alto, Calif: Annual Reviews Inc., 1991); Levine et al., "Electricity End-Use Efficiency."

32. Sathaye and Gadgil, "Aggressive Cost-Effective Electricity Conservation."

33. OTA, *Energy in Developing Countries*; Yu Joe Huang, "Potential for and Barriers to Building Energy Conservation in China," *Contemporary Policy Issues* (California State University, Long Beach), July 1990.

34. P.P.S. Gusain, *Cooking Energy in India* (New Delhi: Vikas Publishing House, 1990); Leach and Mearns, *Beyond the Woodfuel Crisis*; Jane Armitage and Gunter Schramm, "Managing the Supply of and Demand for Fuelwood in Africa," in Schramm and Warford,

eds., *Environmental Management and Economic Development*.

35. Erik Eckholm, *UNICEF and the Household Fuels Crisis* (New York: UNICEF, 1983); Ogunlade Davidson and Stephen Karekezi, "A New, Environmentally-Sound Energy Strategy for the Development of Sub-Saharan Africa," African Energy Policy Research Network (AFREPREN), Nairobi, January 1992; OTA, *Fueling Development*; "Energy IDEA Award for the Kenya Ceramic Jiko," *Stove News*, July/August 1990.

36. Motor Vehicle Manufacturers Association, *World Motor Vehicle Data* (Detroit: various years).

37. Mudassar Imran and Philip Barnes, "Energy Demand in the Developing Countries," World Bank Staff Commodity Working Paper No. 25, Washington, D.C., August 1990; Deborah Lynn Bleviss, *The New Oil Crisis and Fuel Economy Technologies: Preparing the Light Transportation Industry for the 1990s* (New York: Quorum Press, 1988); Yue-Man Yeung, "Great Cities of Eastern Asia," in Mattei Dogan and John D. Kasarda, *The Metropolis Era: A World of Giant Cities*, Vol. 1 (Newbury Park, Calif.: Sage Publications, Inc., 1989); "The Future of the Motor Car," *Energy Economist*, January 1992; Marcia D. Lowe, *Alternatives to the Automobile: Transport for Livable Cities*, Worldwatch Paper 98 (Washington, D.C.: Worldwatch Institute, October 1990); Marcia D. Lowe, *Shaping Cities: The Environmental and Human Dimensions*, Worldwatch Paper 105 (Washington, D.C.: Worldwatch Institute, October 1991); Michael Replogle, *Non-Motorized Vehicles in Asian Cities* (Washington, D.C.: World Bank, 1992).

38. Levine et al., *Energy Efficiency, Developing Nations, and Eastern Europe*.

39. Levine et al., "China's Energy System"; Mark D. Levine, program leader, Energy and Environment Division, Lawrence Berkeley Laboratory, Berkeley, Calif., private communication, August 19, 1992.

40. Levine et al., "China's Energy System"; Levine, private communication.

41. Geller, *Efficient Electricity Use*.

42. Worldwatch Institute based on BP, *BP Statistical Review*, on United Nations, *1990 Energy Statistics*, and on Scurlock and Hall, "The Contribution of Biomass to Global Energy Use."

43. BP, *BP Statistical Review*; OTA, *Energy in Developing Countries*; Edward L. Morse, "The Coming Oil Revolution," *Foreign Affairs*, Winter 1990/1991.

44. United Nations, *1990 Energy Statistics Yearbook*; BP, *BP Statistical Review*; Levine et al., "China's Energy System"; Indu Bharti, "Power Generation at Cost of People," *Economic and Political Weekly*, October 20–27, 1990.

45. Moore and Smith, *Capital Expenditures for Electric Power*; Daniel Deudney, *Rivers of Energy: The Hydropower Potential*, Worldwatch Paper 44 (Washington, D.C.: Worldwatch Institute, June 1981); John E. Besant-Jones, *The Future Role of Hydropower in Developing Countries*, Industry and Energy Department Working Paper, Energy Series Paper No. 15 (Washington, D.C.: World Bank, April 1989); John Dunn, "Water into Juice," *Financial Times*, July 31, 1992; Itaipu costs from Patrick Knight, "Power Rationing in Brazil by 1992?" *Energy Economist*, December 1989, and from Leonard Sklar, International Rivers Network, Berkeley, Calif., private communication, September 22, 1992; Dennis Anderson, *The Energy Industry and Global Warming: New Roles for International Aid* (London: Overseas Development Institute, 1992); Christopher Flavin and Nicholas Lenssen, *Beyond the Petroleum Age: Designing a Solar Economy*, Worldwatch Paper 100 (Washington, D.C.: Worldwatch Institute, December 1990).

46. Christopher Flavin et al., *The World Nuclear Industry Status Report: 1992* (London, Paris, and Washington D.C.: Greenpeace International, WISE, and Worldwatch Insti-

tute, May 1992); Chung-Taek Park, "The Experience of Nuclear Power Development in the Republic of Korea," *Energy Policy*, August 1992.

47. OTA, *Fueling Development*; Ben Ebenhack, University of Rochester, N.Y., private communication, July 13, 1992.

48. Edwin Moore and Enrique Crousillat, *Prospects for Gas-Fueled Combined-Cycle Power Generation in the Developing Countries*, Industry and Energy Department Working Paper, Energy Series No. 35 (Washington, D.C.: World Bank, May 1991); Nigeria example is a Worldwatch Institute estimate based on United Nations, *1990 Energy Statistics Yearbook*, and on Boden, private communication and database; India example is a Worldwatch Institute estimate based on U.S. Department of Energy (DOE), Energy Information Administration (EIA), *Monthly Energy Review April 1992* (Washington, D.C.: 1992), and on Boden, private communication and database.

49. Culbert, "Crisis Hits Huge Market"; Shri K.N. Venkatasubramanian, "Oil Conservation Opportunities in Transport Sector," Oil Conservation Week Supplement, *Indian Express*, February 16, 1992; René Moreno, Jr., and D.G. Fallen Bailey, *Alternative Transport Fuels from Natural Gas* (Washington, D.C.: World Bank, 1989); Moore and Crousillat, *Prospects for Gas-Fueled Combined-Cycle Power*.

50. José Roberto Moreira, Secretariat of Science and Technology, "Goals and Means of a Sustainable Energy Development in Brazil and South America," Brazil, undated; Bob Williams, "Latin American Petroleum Sector at Crossroads," *Oil & Gas Journal*, July 6, 1992; Government of Thailand, *Thailand National Report to the United Nations Conference on Environment and Development (UNCED)* (Bangkok: June 1992); "A Spat Between Neighbours," *Asiaweek*, April 10, 1992.

51. Liu et al., "An Overview of Energy in China"; P.T. Bangsberg, "Arco's 10-Year Effort Bears Fruit with Pact to Develop Field Off China," *Journal of Commerce*, March 16,

1992; Levine et al., "China's Energy System"; BP, *BP Statistical Review*; "China Stressing Onshore E&D to Spur Crude Output," *Oil & Gas Journal*, July 29, 1991.

52. Thomas B. Johansson et al., "Renewable Fuels and Electricity for a Growing World Economy: Defining and Achieving the Potential," in Thomas B. Johansson et al., eds., *Renewables for Fuel and Electricity* (Washington, D.C.: Island Press, in press); Flavin and Lenssen, *Beyond the Petroleum Age*; Anderson, *The Energy Industry and Global Warming*; Olav Hohmeyer, "Renewables and the Full Costs of Energy," *Energy Policy*, April 1992.

53. OTA, *Fueling Development*; Chris Neme, Memorandum to Mark Levine, Lawrence Berkeley Laboratory, Berkeley, Calif., March 28, 1992; Mario Calderón and Paolo Lugari, Centro Las Gaviotas, Bogota, Colombia, private communication, April 13, 1992; R. Aburas and J.-W. Fromme, "Household Energy Demand in Jordan," *Energy Policy*, July/August 1991; Christopher Hurst, "Establishing New Markets for Mature Energy Equipment in Developing Countries; Experience with Windmills, Hydro-Powered Mills and Solar Water Heaters," *World Development*, Vol. 18, No. 4, 1990.

54. Matthew L. Wald, "High-Tech Windmills Are Sold to the Dutch," *New York Times*, June 16, 1992; Pacific Northwest Laboratory, "World-wide Wind Energy Resource Distribution Estimates," Richland, Wash., 1981; Dennis Elliot, Pacific Northwest Laboratory, Richland, Wash, private communication, May 28, 1991; Neelam Mathews, "Enthusiasm Could Conquer All," *Windpower Monthly*, January 1991; Neelam Mathews, "Bringing Down the Trade Barriers," *Windpower Monthly*, June 1992.

55. United Nations, *1990 Energy Statistics Yearbook*; Ronald DiPippo, "Geothermal Energy: Electricity Generation and Environmental Impact," *Energy Policy*, October 1991.

56. Jorge M. Huacuz V. and Ana Maria Martínez L., Electrical Research Institute,

Non-Conventional Energy Sources Department, Cuernavaca, Mexico, "Rural Electrification With Renewable Energies in Mexico: Financial, Technical, Social and Institutional Challenges," presented to SADCC Annual Technical Seminar, Swaziland, November 26–28, 1991.

57. Lovejoy, "Electrification of Rural Areas by Solar PV"; Richard D. Hansen and José G. Martin, "Photovoltaics for Rural Electrification in the Dominican Republic," *Natural Resources Forum*, Vol. 12, No. 2, 1988.

58. Scurlock and Hall, "The Contribution of Biomass to Global Energy Use."

59. Robert H. Williams and Eric D. Larson, Center for Energy and Environmental Studies, Princeton University, "Advanced Gasification-Based Biomass Power Generation and Cogeneration," presented to International Symposium on Environmentally Sound Energy Technologies and their Transfer to Developing Countries and European Economies in Transition, Milan, October 21–25, 1991.

60. U.N. group's recommendations from Johansson et al., "Renewable Fuels and Electricity."

61. Leach and Mearns, *Beyond the Woodfuel Crisis*; Gerald Leach, "Agroforestry and the Way Out for Africa," in Mohamed Suliman, *Greenhouse Effect and its Impact on Africa* (London: Institute for African Alternatives, 1990); David Brooks and Hartmut Krugmann, "Energy, Environment, and Development: Some Directions for Policy Research," *Energy Policy*, November 1990.

62. Amulya Kumar N. Reddy et al., "A Development-Focused End-Use-Oriented Electricity Scenario for Karnataka," *Economic and Political Weekly*, April 6 and 13, 1991; Reddy and Goldemberg, "Energy for the Developing World."

63. Reddy et al., "A Development-Focused End-Use-Oriented Electricity Scenario for Karnataka"; Reddy and Goldemberg, "Energy for the Developing World."

64. Amulya K.N. Reddy, "Barriers to Improvements in Energy Efficiency," Lawrence Berkeley Laboratory, Berkeley, Calif., October 1991.

65. Rao et al., *The Least Cost Energy Path for India*; Bjorn Larsen and Anwar Shah, "World Fossil Fuels Subsidies and Global Carbon Emissions," World Bank, February 20, 1992; World Bank, Industry and Energy Department, "Energy Efficiency and Conservation in the Developing World: The World Bank's Role," Washington, D.C., March 18, 1992.

66. Ashok Gadgil and Gilberto De Martino Jannuzzi, "Conservation Potential of Compact Fluorescent Lamps in India and Brazil," Lawrence Berkeley Laboratory, Berkeley, Calif., July 1989.

67. Geller, *Efficient Energy Use*; Levine et al., "Electricity End-Use Efficiency."

68. Sathaye and Gadgil, "Aggressive Cost-Effective Electricity Conservation."

69. Levine et al., "Electricity End-Use Efficiency"; Sacramento Municipal Utility District, "SMUD Launches Solar Programs," press release, Sacramento, Calif., July 10, 1992.

70. Peter du Pont and Koomchoak Biyaem, "A Walk on the Demand Side: Thailand Launches Its Energy Efficiency Initiatives," in *ACEEE 1992 Summer Study on Energy Efficiency in Buildings* (Berkeley, Calif.: ACEEE, 1992); Mark Cherniack, IIEC, Washington, D.C., private communication, July 14, 1992.

71. Lovejoy, "Electrification of Rural Areas by Solar PV."

72. John Besant-Jones, senior energy economist, World Bank, Washington, D.C., private communication, August 24, 1992; Levine et al., *Energy Efficiency, Developing Nations, and Eastern Europe*.

73. World Bank, *Annual Report 1992* (Washington, D.C.: 1992); African Development Bank, *1990 Annual Report* (Abidjan: 1991); Asian Development Bank, *Annual Report 1991* (Manila: 1992); Inter-American Development Bank, *1991 Annual Report* (Washington, D.C.: 1992); Philips, *The Least Cost Energy Path*; World Bank, Energy Development Division, "FY91 Annual Sector Review: Energy," Washington, D.C., October 23, 1991.

74. "World Bank Board Critical of Staff Policy Papers," *Banknote*, IIEC, September 1992; Glenn Prickett, Natural Resources Defense Council, Washington, D.C., private communication, September 30, 1992; E. Patrick Coady, executive director to the World Bank, presentation to the Environment and Energy Workgroup, Society for International Development, Washington, D.C., October 15, 1992.

75. Philips, *The Least Cost Energy Path*; Cherniack, private communication.

76. Global Environment Facility (GEF), "Report by the Chairman to the April 1992 Participants' Meeting," Washington, D.C., March 1992.

77. GEF, "A Selection of Projects from the First Three Tranches," Working Paper Series Number II, Washington, D.C., June 1992; GEF, "Mauritius Sugar Bio-Energy Technology Project," Washington, D.C., January 1992; GEF, "Report by the Chairman."

78. GEF, "Report by the Chairman"; Philips, *The Least Cost Energy Path*.

79. Reddy, "Barriers to Improvements in Energy Efficiency"; Philips, *The Least Cost Energy Path*; Davidson and Karekezi, "A New, Environmentally-Sound Energy Strategy"; du Pont and Biyaem, "A Walk on the Demand Side"; Cherniack, private communication.

80. Anderson, *The Energy Industry and Global Warming*; Haig Simonian, "Gap Needs Bridging," *Financial Times*, October 20, 1991.

81. UNCED Secretariat, "154 Signatures on Climate Convention in Rio," press release, June 14, 1992; Michael Grubb, "The Climate Change Convention: An Assessment," *International Environment Reporter*, August 12, 1992; Committee on the Development and Utilization of New and Renewable Sources of Energy, "Solar Energy: A Strategy in Support of Environment and Development," Report to the Secretary-General, United Nations, New York, February 13, 1992.

82. Brazil example is from Geller, *Efficient Electricity Use*.

Chapter 7. Rediscovering Rail

1. "Railroads and Locomotives," *Encyclopaedia Britannica*, 15th ed. (Chicago, Ill.: 1976); Kenneth T. Jackson, *Crabgrass Frontier: The Suburbanization of the United States* (New York: Oxford University Press, 1985).

2. Amount of oil potentially displaced in the United States is Worldwatch Institute estimate based on Motor Vehicle Manufacturers Association (MVMA), *Facts and Figures '91* (Detroit, Mich.: 1991), on Stacy C. Davis and Melissa D. Morris, *Transportation Energy Data Book: Edition 12* (Oak Ridge, Tenn.: Oak Ridge National Laboratory, 1992), and on U.S. Department of Energy, Energy Information Administration, *Annual Energy Review 1990* (Washington, D.C.: 1991); potential U.K. carbon reduction is Worldwatch Institute estimate based on Transport and Environmental Studies of London (TEST), *Wrong Side of the Tracks: Impacts of Road and Rail Transport on the Environment* (London: 1991).

3. Kilojoules per passenger-kilometer are based on Deborah Gordon, *Steering A New Course: Transportation, Energy, and the Environment* (Washington, D.C.: Island Press, 1991), using average commuting occupancies of 50 passengers for intercity rail, 100 passengers

for commercial air, 65 for commuter rail, and 50 for urban rail. The energy efficiency of urban rail varies widely from system to system.

4. Energy intensity of freight modes from Davis and Morris, *Transportation Energy Data Book: Edition 12*; truck comparisons from U.S. Congress, Office of Technology Assessment (OTA), *Energy in Developing Countries* (Washington, D.C.: U.S. Government Printing Office, 1991).

5. Mark D. Levine et al., *Energy Efficiency, Developing Nations, and Eastern Europe* (Washington, D.C.: International Institute for Energy Conservation (IIEC), 1991).

6. TEST, *Wrong Side of the Tracks*.

7. Edson L. Tennyson, "Impact on Transit Patronage of Cessation or Inauguration of Rail Service," *Transportation Research Record 1221* (Washington, D.C.: National Research Council, 1989); Los Angeles study cited in Campaign for New Transportation Priorities (CNTP), "Urban and Suburban Transportation: Programs and Policies for More Livable Cities," CNTP Policy Series Paper No. 1, Washington, D.C., March 1991.

8. Gordon, *Steering A New Course*.

9. U.S. estimate from Joseph S. Cannon, "The Health Costs of Air Pollution," prepared for the American Lung Association, New York, 1990; European figures from TEST, *Wrong Side of the Tracks*.

10. OTA, *Delivering the Goods: Public Works Technologies, Management, and Financing* (Washington, D.C.: U.S. Government Printing Office, 1991).

11. U.S. General Accounting Office (GAO), *Traffic Congestion: Trends, Measures, and Effects* (Washington, D.C.: 1989); European Conference of Ministers of Transport (ECMT), *Private and Public Investment in Transport*, Report of the Eighty-First Round Table on Transport Economics (Paris: Organisation for Economic Co-operation and Development (OECD), 1990).

12. Carmichael cited in CNTP, "Intercity Freight Transportation: The Multiple Threats of Bigger, Longer Trucks," CNTP Policy Series Paper No. 4, Washington, D.C., March 1991; ways to increase rail capacity from Frank N. Wilner, "User Charges and Transportation Efficiency," Association of American Railroads, Washington, D.C., 1990.

13. Cost of air traffic congestion from U.S. Department of Transportation (DOT), *Moving America: New Directions, New Opportunities* (Washington, D.C.: 1990); Harriet Parcells, "Airport and Highway Expansion on the Line: The Rail Option," presented at Transportation for Sustainable Communities, conference sponsored by the Center for Neighborhood Technology, Chicago, Ill., December 13, 1991.

14. Parcells, "Airport and Highway Expansion on the Line"; CNTP, "Intercity Passenger Transportation: Neglect of Rail and Intermodal Facilities," CNTP Policy Series Paper No. 5, Washington, D.C., August 1991.

15. CNTP, "Intercity Passenger Transportation"; roadbuilding program remark cited in TEST, *Wrong Side of the Tracks*.

16. Center for Neighborhood Technology, "Plane Basics," Lake Calumet Airport Network Issue Paper Series, Chicago, Ill., November 1991.

17. Montgomery County Planning Department, *Montgomery County Comprehensive Growth Policy Study* (Silver Spring, Md.: 1989), cited in Michael Replogle, "Sustainability: A Vital Concept for Transportation Planning and Development," *Journal of Advanced Transportation*, Spring 1991.

18. All accident rates are for 1989; U.S. figures from National Safety Council, *Accident Facts, 1991 Edition* (Chicago, Ill.: 1991); European figures from European Communities Commission, *Transport Annual Statistics*

1970–1989 (Luxembourg: 1991), and from ECMT, "Trends in the Transport Sector 1970–1990," Paris, 1991.

19. British Department of Transport estimate cited in Jonathon Bray, *Transport: Policy Options*, Economic Alternatives for Eastern Europe Briefing No. 5 (London: New Economics Foundation, 1992); TEST, *Wrong Side of the Tracks*; U.S. estimate from The Urban Institute, *The Costs of Highway Crashes* (Washington, D.C.: 1991).

20. Wilner, "User Charges and Transportation Efficiency"; ECMT, *Freight Transport and the Environment* (Paris: 1991).

21. David Schwab, "Airport Noise Report is Again Postponed," *The Star-Ledger* (New Jersey), August 27, 1992; TEST, *Wrong Side of the Tracks*; U.S. example from Wilner, "User Charges and Transportation Efficiency."

22. MVMA, *Facts and Figures '92* (Detroit, Mich.: 1992); estimated share of population physically unable to drive from F.E.K. Britton, "Cars, Transport and Amenity in Urban Places: A Reader" (draft), Paris, 1990.

23. Number of passengers per year from Jackson, *Crabgrass Frontier*; Gordon, *Steering A New Course*; transport conspiracy described in Jonathan Kwitny, "The Great Transportation Conspiracy," *Harper's*, February 1981.

24. Nancy Heiser, "Federal Aid to Domestic Transportation: A Brief History from the 1800s to the 1980s," U.S. Congressional Research Service, Washington, D.C., August 1988; 1990 figures from CNTP, "Intercity Passenger Transportation."

25. 1925 figure from GAO, *Railroad Competitiveness: Federal Laws and Policies Affect Railroad Competitiveness* (Washington, D.C.: 1991); all other figures from International Road Federation, *World Road Statistics 1991* (Washington, D.C.: 1991).

26. DOT, *National Transportation Strategic Planning Study* (Washington, D.C.: 1990); OECD countries' investments from ECMT, *Investment in Transport Infrastructure in ECMT Countries* (Paris: 1988).

27. Rail's share of freight traffic from ECMT, "Trends in the Transport Sector 1970–1990"; Bruce Barnard, "EC Panel Takes Step to Shift Freight from Roads to Water, Sea and Rails," *Journal of Commerce*, February 20, 1992.

28. United Nations, Economic Commission for Europe (ECE), *Transport Information* (New York: 1991); *Financial Times* article cited in Bray, *Transport: Policy Options*.

29. ECE, *Transport Information*; Keith Rockwell, "EC Officials Lament Inaction On East Europe's Transit Crisis," *Journal of Commerce*, October 31, 1991.

30. Chris Bushell and Peter Stonham, eds., *Jane's Urban Transport Systems 1985* (London: Jane's Publishing Company, 1985); Moscow subway from Louis Uchitelle, "Moscow Subway Defies the Odds," *New York Times*, March 10, 1992.

31. Akiyoshi Yamamoto, Deputy Director, Japan Railways Group/East Japan Railway Company, New York, private communication, April 30, 1992.

32. A.E. Cullison, "Congested Roads in Japan Thwart Just-in-Time Efficiency," *Journal of Commerce*, March 16, 1992.

33. Share of passenger and freight traffic carried by rail from International Road Federation, *World Road Statistics 1991*, and from International Civil Aviation Organisation, *Traffic: Commercial Air Carriers, 1986–1990* (Montreal: 1991); government spending from Hennie Deboeck, financial analyst, World Bank, Washington, D.C., private communication, April 22, 1992.

34. Lincoln Kaye, "On the Right Track," *Far Eastern Economic Review*, July 28, 1988; demand projections from "Railways Going Hi-Tech in Every Area," *India Economic News*, October 1991; 1987 freight figure from International Road Federation, *World Road Sta-*

tistics 1991; 1950 figure from C. Rammanohar Reddy et al., "The Debt-Energy Nexus: A Case Study of India," International Energy Initiative, Bangalore, India, April 1992.

35. Calcutta and Bombay from Gerhard Menckhoff, "Urban Transit Options in South Asia," presented at the Mid-Atlantic Region of the Association for Asian Studies 17th Annual Meeting, Indiana University of Pennsylvania, October 21–23, 1988; Latin American networks from International Road Federation, *World Road Statistics 1991*.

36. Sweden from TEST, *Wrong Side of the Tracks*; "Germans to Invest More in Rail than Road," *International Railway Journal*, July 1992.

37. Alan Armstrong-Wright, *Urban Transit Systems: Guidelines for Examining Options* (Washington, D.C.: World Bank, 1986).

38. "A Streetcar Named Light Rail," *IEEE Spectrum*, February 1991; cost figures from Armstrong-Wright, *Urban Transit Systems: Guidelines for Examining Options*.

39. Richard Tomkins, "Manchester's Metrolink: A Testbed for Britain," *Financial Times*, April 6, 1992; number of U.S. cities with light rail from Chris Bushell, ed., *Jane's Urban Transport Systems 1991* (London: Jane's Publishing Company, 1991); length of Los Angeles's former streetcar network from William S. Kowinski, "There's Still Time to Hop a Trolley—Vintage or Modern," *Smithsonian*, February 1988; Karen Zagor, "Light Rail Systems: Revival of Interest in North America," *Financial Times*, April 6, 1992.

40. Bushell, *Jane's Urban Transport Systems 1991*; phasing out of streetcar lines in Tokyo from Tokyo Metropolitan Government, *Plain Talk About Tokyo* (Tokyo: January 1991); Tomkins, "Manchester's Metrolink"; number of light rail networks in Germany from Bushell, *Jane's Urban Transport Systems 1991*.

41. Richard Barrett, Africa Technical Department, Infrastructure Division, World Bank, Washington, D.C., private communication, October 10, 1990; Manila from "Breaking Up the Jams," *Asiaweek*, February 28, 1992; other cities from Bushell, *Jane's Urban Transport Systems 1991*.

42. Barrett, private communication.

43. DOT, *National Transportation Strategic Planning Study*.

44. London from Regional Plan Association, *The Renaissance of Rail Transit in America* (New York: 1991); other cities from Bushell and Stonham, *Jane's Urban Transport Systems 1985*.

45. Daniel Machalaba, "Longtime Symbols of Decay and Delay, Commuter Railroads Undergo a Revival," *Wall Street Journal*, October 1, 1991; ridership on Miami commuter trains from American Public Transit Association, "Commuter Rail Transport," Washington, D.C., 1991.

46. Details of project from Michael Bustamente, Public Affairs Officer, Los Angeles County Transportation Commission, Los Angeles, Calif., private communication, October 9, 1992; time needed to complete project from Annette Colfax, Director, Passenger Facilities Coordination, Southern California Regional Rail Authority, Los Angeles, Calif., private communication, October 9, 1992.

47. Joseph Vranich, *Supertrains: Solutions to America's Transportation Gridlock* (New York: St. Martin's Press, 1991).

48. Ibid.; French government's plans for TGV expansion from Walter C. Streeter, "The French Train à Grande Vitesse: Focusing on the TGV-Atlantique," Working Paper 558, Institute of Urban and Regional Development, University of California, Berkeley, March 1992.

49. Vranich, *Supertrains*; cost range from DOT, *National Transportation Strategic Planning Study*.

50. Michel Guyard, Transportation Counselor, French Embassy, Washington, D.C., private communication, May 18, 1990; passengers on Paris-Lyon route from Parcells, "Airport and Highway Expansion on the Line"; travel between Nagoya and Tokyo from Mamoru Taniguchi, "High Speed Rail in Japan: A Review and Evaluation of the Shinkansen Train," Working Paper 557, Institute of Urban and Regional Development, University of California, Berkeley, March 1992; Jessica Mathews, "Getting Back on Track," *Washington Post*, November 29, 1991; Lufthansa from Ross Capon, Executive Director, National Association of Railroad Passengers, Washington, D.C., private communication, October 5, 1992.

51. "High Speed Trains Protested," *IRT: The Energy News Brief* (IRT Publications, Aspen, Colo.), August 23, 1990; "Train à Grande Tristesse," *The Economist*, August 25, 1990.

52. Bray, *Transport: Policy Options*.

53. Gary Stix, "Air Trains," *Scientific American*, August 1992; cost per kilometer from Malcolm W. Browne, "New Funds Fuel Magnet Power for Trains," *New York Times*, March 3, 1992; fire incident described in Gary Stix, "Riding on Air," *Scientific American*, February 1992.

54. Vranich, *Supertrains*.

55. Mick Hamer, "The Second Railway Revolution," *New Scientist*, May 23, 1992; projected increase in air travel from Parcells, "Airport and Highway Expansion on the Line."

56. Lawrence H. Kaufman, "Truckers Turn to Rails For the Long Haul," *Journal of Commerce*, February 20, 1992; number of intermodal shipments from Association of American Railroads, *Railroad Facts* (Washington, D.C.: 1991).

57. ECE, *Transport Information*; European Community plan from Michael Terry, "On Track to Speed Up Network," *Financial Times*, September 3, 1992; John May, "World-Class Destruction," *New York Times*, February 18, 1992; Swiss plan from "Swiss Approve Rail Tunnels Under the Alps," *Washington Post*, September 28, 1992.

58. James J. MacKenzie et al., *The Going Rate: What it Really Costs to Drive* (Washington, D.C.: World Resources Institute, June 1992).

59. Gas taxes from OECD, International Energy Agency, *Energy Prices and Taxes, First Quarter 1992* (Paris: 1992); UK company cars from "New Cars for Old," *The Economist*, March 14, 1992.

60. Wilner, "User Charges and Transportation Efficiency," citing GAO Controller General, *Excessive Truck Weight: An Expensive Burden We Can No Longer Support* (Washington, D.C.: 1979); heavy trucks' share of damage in the United States from MacKenzie et al., *The Going Rate*; CNTP, "Intercity Freight Transportation"; West European countries from Wilner, "User Charges and Transportation Efficiency."

61. Apportionment of European fuel tax revenues from DOT, *National Transportation Strategic Planning Study*.

62. W. Graham Claytor, Jr., "A Penny for Amtrak," *Washington Post*, April 28, 1992.

63. Ian G. Heggie, *Designing Major Policy Reform: Lessons from the Transport Sector*, World Bank Discussion Paper (Washington, D.C.: World Bank, 1991).

64. James Bruce, "Brazilian Privatization Takes New Twist With Train Loan," *Journal of Commerce*, January 28, 1991.

65. San Diego trolley from Regional Plan Association, *The Renaissance of Rail Transit in America*.

66. David Alan Aschauer, "Transportation Spending and Economic Growth: The Effects of Transit and Highway Expendi-

tures," American Public Transit Association, Washington, D.C., September 1991.

67. The Urban Institute and Cambridge Systematics, Inc., "Public Transportation Renewal as an Investment: The Economic Impacts of SEPTA on the Regional and State Economy," Delaware Valley Regional Planning Commission, Philadelphia, Pa., May 1991.

68. For a thorough analysis of the potential for linking bicycle transportation with rail, see Michael A. Replogle, *Bicycles and Public Transportation: New Links to Suburban Transit Markets*, 2nd ed. (Washington, D.C.: The Bicycle Federation, 1988).

69. Peter Newman and Jeffrey Kenworthy, *Cities and Automobile Dependence: An International Sourcebook* (Aldershot, U.K.: Gower, 1989).

70. Mexico example from Mia Layne Birk and Deborah Lynn Bleviss, eds., *Driving New Directions* (Washington, D.C.: IIEC, 1991).

71. Peter Passell, "Czech Streetcars None Desire," *New York Times*, March 18, 1992.

72. Don Phillips, "Reawakening the Sleeping-car Giant," *The Washington Post National Weekly Edition*, June 1–7, 1992.

73. Gordon Dabinett, "Tanks into Trams?" *Transport Innovation*, September 1992.

Chapter 8. Preparing for Peace

1. For details of economic and environmental costs, see Michael Renner, *National Security: The Economic and Environmental Dimensions*, Worldwatch Paper 89 (Washington, D.C.: Worldwatch Institute, May 1989), and Michael Renner, "Assessing the Military's War on the Environment," in Lester R. Brown et al., *State of the World 1991* (New York: W.W. Norton & Co., 1991).

2. Melvin Small and J. David Singer, "Patterns in International Warfare, 1816–1965,"

in Richard A. Falk and Samuel S. Kim, eds., *The War System: An Interdisciplinary Approach* (Boulder, Colo.: Westview Press, 1980); J. David Singer, "Peace in the Global System: Displacement, Interregnum, or Transformation?" in Charles W. Kegley, Jr., ed., *The Long Postwar Peace. Contending Explanations and Projections* (New York: Harper Collins, 1991); William Eckhardt, "War-Related Deaths Since 3000 BC," *Bulletin of Peace Proposals*, Vol. 22, No. 4, 1991.

3. The Strategic Arms Limitation Talks treaties (SALT I and II) allowed the superpowers' combined strategic offensive nuclear warheads to grow from about 6,500 in 1969, when negotiations started, to more than 17,-000 in 1979, when SALT II was signed, and accommodated continued growth in their arsenals for another decade. Robert S. Norris et al., "Nuclear Weapons," in Stockholm International Peace Research Institute (SIPRI), *SIPRI Yearbook 1991: World Armaments and Disarmament* (Oxford: Oxford University Press, 1991).

4. Institute for Defense and Disarmament Studies (IDDS), *The Arms Control Reporter 1992* (Cambridge, Mass.: 1992).

5. Other supplier control groups include the Australia Group (chemical and biological agents) and the Nuclear Suppliers Group, noted in "The Techies vs. the Techno-Cops," *Business Week*, June 15, 1992; Andrew Mack, "Missile Proliferation, Proliferation Control and the Question of Transparency," in United Nations Department for Disarmament Affairs (UNDDA), *Transparency in International Arms Transfers*, Disarmament Topical Paper 3 (New York: United Nations, 1990); dual-use issue and *Finding Common Ground* from Greg Bischak and James Raffel, "Economic Conversion and International Inspection: Alternatives to Arms Exports and Militarism," presented at the International Working Conference on the Arms Trade, New York, October 31-November 2, 1991.

6. Norris et al., "Nuclear Weapons"; deeper cuts from Andrew Rosenthal, "Bush

and Yeltsin Propose Deep Cuts in Atomic Weapons," *New York Times*, January 30, 1992, and from Michael Wines, "Bush and Yeltsin Agree to Cut Long-Range Atomic Warheads; Scrap Key Land-Based Missiles," *New York Times*, June 17, 1992.

7. Norris estimate from William J. Broad, "Nuclear Accords Bring New Fears on Arms Disposal," *New York Times*, July 6, 1992; Jonathan Eyal and David Fairhall, "Britain Struggles to Defend Size of Arsenal," (London) *Guardian*, February 1, 1992; David White, "Britain Seeks Watertight Nuclear Deterrent," *Financial Times*, February 10, 1992; Alan Riding, "France Drops Plans to Build New Nuclear Missile System," *New York Times*, July 23, 1991; William E. Schmidt, "British Are Planning to Remove A-Arms From Ships and Aircraft," *New York Times*, June 16, 1992.

8. Keith Schneider, "Nuclear Disarmament Raises Fear on Storage of 'Triggers,'" *New York Times*, February 26, 1992; IDDS, *The Arms Control Reporter 1992*; for a proposal to dismantle and store weapons-grade materials under international verfication, see Michael Renner, "Finishing the Job," *World Watch*, November/December 1992.

9. David Albright and Mark Hibbs, "Iraq's Bomb: Blueprints and Artifacts," *Bulletin of the Atomic Scientists*, January/February 1992.

10. Robert S. Norris, "Known Nuclear Tests Worldwide, 1945 to December 31, 1991," Nuclear Notebook, *Bulletin of the Atomic Scientists*, April 1992; Serge Schmemann, "Gorbachev Matches U.S. on Nuclear Cuts and Goes Further on Strategic Warheads," *New York Times*, October 6, 1991; "Yeltsin Extends Russian Ban on Nuclear Tests to July '93," *New York Times*, October 22, 1992; Alan Riding, "France Suspends Its Testing of Nuclear Weapons," *New York Times*, April 9, 1992; evolving U.S. position from Eric Schmitt, "House Votes to Ban A-Bomb Tests," *New York Times*, June 5, 1992, from Michael R. Gordon, "U.S. Tight-

ens Limit on Nuclear Tests," *New York Times*, July 15, 1992, from Michael R. Gordon, "Senate, in Defiance of Bush, Votes to End All Nuclear Tests in '96," *New York Times*, August 4, 1992, and from Andrew Rosenthal, "White House Ready to Make Deal to Accept Curbs on Nuclear Tests," *New York Times*, September 25, 1992; Barbara Crossette, "Chinese Set Off Their Biggest Nuclear Explosion," *New York Times*, May 22, 1992.

11. Halt in fissile materials production from Michael R. Gordon, "It's Official: U.S. Stops Making Material for Nuclear Warheads," *New York Times*, July 14, 1992; Yeltsin from David Albright and Peter Gray, "Fissile Material Production," in *Facing Reality: The Future of the U.S. Nuclear Weapons Complex* (San Francisco, Calif.: The Tides Foundation, May 1992).

12. A similar approach has been proposed by Arjun Makhijani and Katherine Yih, "What to Do at Doomsday's End," *Washington Post*, March 29, 1992.

13. Jozef Goldblat and Thomas Bernauer, "The US-Soviet Chemical Weapons Agreement of June 1990: Its Advantages and Shortcomings," *Bulletin of Peace Proposals*, Vol. 21, No. 4, 1990.

14. Ibid.; the full text of the Agreement on Destruction and Non-Production of Chemical Weapons and on Measures to Facilitate the Multilateral Convention on Banning Chemical Weapons is reprinted in SIPRI, *SIPRI Yearbook 1991*; for provisions of the international convention, see IDDS, *The Arms Control Reporter 1992*; Frances Williams, "Hopes High for International Chemical Weapons Treaty," *Financial Times*, August 26, 1992.

15. IDDS, *The Arms Control Reporter*, 1990, 1991, and 1992 editions; Jane M.O. Sharp, "Conventional Arms Control in Europe," in SIPRI, *SIPRI Yearbook 1991*.

16. Sharp, "Conventional Arms Control in Europe"; Michael R. Gordon, "Soviets

Shift Many Tanks to Siberia," *New York Times*, November 15, 1990; Ian Anthony et al., *West European Arms Production* (Stockholm: SIPRI, 1990); IDDS, *The Arms Control Reporter*, 1990, 1991, and 1992 editions.

17. The 1986 document of the Stockholm Conference on Confidence- and Security-Building Measures and Disarmament in Europe entails notification of and greater transparency about military maneuvers, including the use of observers; see Henry J. van der Graaf, "The Stockholm Document on Confidence- and Security-Building Measures and Disarmament in Europe (1986)," in Serge Sur, ed., *Verification of Current Disarmament and Arms Limitation Agreements: Ways, Means and Practices* (Aldershot, U.K.: Dartmouth, 1991). The March 1992 Open Skies accord permits flights by unarmed surveillance aircraft over the territory of NATO and former Warsaw Pact states; see IDDS, *The Arms Control Reporter 1992*.

18. Ian Anthony et al., "The Trade in Major Conventional Weapons," in SIPRI, *SIPRI Yearbook 1992: World Armaments and Disarmament* (Oxford: Oxford University Press, 1992).

19. Herbert Wulf, "Recent Trends in Arms Transfers and Possible Multilateral Action for Control," and Alessandro Corradini, "Consideration of the Question of International Arms Transfers by the United Nations," both in UNDDA, *Transparency in International Arms Transfers*. U.S. arms sales abroad nearly quadrupled between 1987 and 1992. See Eric Schmitt, "Arms Makers' Latest Tune: 'Over There, Over There,' " *New York Times*, October 4, 1992.

20. Lack of attempts to restrain arms transfers from Susan Willett, "Controlling the Arms Trade: Supply and Demand Dynamics," Faraday Discussion Paper No. 18, The Council for Arms Control, University of London, November 1991. On the recipient side, in 1974, for instance, eight Latin American countries signed the Ayacucho Declara-

tion, which was intended to negotiate regional limitations on arms transfers and on military expenditures. But the declaration was never implemented. Wulf, "Recent Trends in Arms Transfers"; Michael Brzoska, "The Nature and Dimension of the Problem," in UNDDA, *Transparency in International Arms Transfers*.

21. Willett, "Controlling the Arms Trade"; Stephanie G. Neuman, "Present and Future Arms Trade Prospects for Control and Limitation," in UNDDA, *Transparency in International Arms Transfers*; the text of the arms register resolution can be found in "Transparency in Armaments," U.N. General Assembly Document A/RES/46/36, 66th Plenary Meeting, New York, December 9, 1991.

22. Natalie J. Goldring, "UN Arms Register Takes Shape," *BASIC Reports*, August 17, 1992; for a private-group effort to draft a treaty on a mandatory arms register and a comprehensive program for the eventual eliminatation of arms transfers, see "Draft Convention on the Monitoring, Reduction, and Ultimate Abolition of the International Arms Trade," *Alternatives. Social Transformation and Humane Governance*, Winter 1992.

23. Joachim Badelt et al., "Disposing of Chemical Weapons: A Common Heritage Calls for a Cooperative Approach," *Bulletin of Peace Proposals*, Vol. 23, No. 1, 1992; Frans Berkhout et al., "Disposition of Separated Plutonium," prepared for Workshops on Disposal of Plutonium in Bonn, June 15–16, and London, June 18, 1992; C.H. Bloomster et al., "Options and Regulatory Issues Related to Disposition of Fissile Materials from Arms Reduction," prepared for U.S. Department of Energy, Pacific Northwest Laboratory, Richland, Wash., December 1990; Arjun Makhijani, "Options for Plutonium from Dismantled Nuclear Weapons," *Science for Democratic Action*, Winter 1992.

24. Sur, *Verification of Current Disarmament and Arms Limitation Agreements*; J.B. Poole, ed.,

Verification Report 1991. Yearbook on Arms Control and Environmental Agreements (New York: Apex Press, 1991); Patricia Lewis, *Verification and Disarmament* (London: Scientists Against Nuclear Arms, 1991); Joseph F. Pilat, "Iraq and the Future of Nuclear Nonproliferation: The Roles of Inspections and Treaties," *Science*, March 6, 1992.

25. IDDS, *The Arms Control Reporter 1992*; S.J. Lundin and Thomas Stock, "Multilateral and Bilateral Talks on Chemical and Biological Weapons," in SIPRI, *SIPRI Yearbook 1991*; Stephen J. Ledogar, "Destruction of Weapons Systems Under Multilateral Arms Control Agreements," *Disarmament*, Vol. 14, No. 4, 1991; staff and budget from Williams, "Hopes High for International Chemical Weapons Treaty."

26. IDDS, *The Arms Control Reporter 1992*; Paul Lewis, "Chemical-Arms Ban Written; Fast Action Asked," *New York Times*, June 25, 1992; R. Jeffrey Smith, "Stricter Verification Measures Backed for Chemical Arms Ban," *Washington Post*, July 16, 1991; Amy E. Smithson, "Tottering Toward a Treaty," *Bulletin of the Atomic Scientists*, July/August 1992; Williams, "Hopes High for International Chemical Weapons Treaty."

27. Stevenson quoted in Robert C. Johansen, *Toward a Dependable Peace: A Proposal for an Appropriate Security System*, World Policy Paper No. 8 (New York: World Policy Institute, 1983).

28. De Cuéllar quoted in Paul Lewis, "U.N. Chief Warns of Costs of Peace," *New York Times*, December 11, 1988; William J. Durch and Barry M. Blechman, *Keeping the Peace: The United Nations in the Emerging World Order* (Washington, D.C.: The Henry L. Stimson Center, 1992).

29. Table 8–4 based on Durch and Blechman, *Keeping the Peace: The United Nations in the Emerging World Order*, on Marjorie Ann Brown, "United Nations Peacekeeping: Historical Overview and Current Issues," *CRS Report for Congress*, Congressional Research Service, Washington, D.C., January 31, 1990, on Jeff Laurenti, *The Common Defense: Peace and Security in a Changing World* (New York: United Nations Association of the United States, 1992), on U.N. Department for Public Information, private communications, and on numerous news clips.

30. Past U.N. spending from Durch and Blechman, *Keeping the Peace: The United Nations in the Emerging World Order*; 1992 spending from Lucia Mouat, "UN Grapples with Cost of Expanding Peace Role," *Christian Science Monitor*, May 18, 1992; cumulative spending and number of peacekeepers from Boutros Boutros-Ghali, *An Agenda for Peace: Preventive Diplomacy, Peacemaking and Peacekeeping*, Report of the Secretary-General Pursuant to the Statement Adopted by the Summit Meeting of the Security Council on January 31, 1992 (New York: United Nations, 1992); cumulative military spending from Michael Renner, "Military Expenditures Falling," in Lester R. Brown et al., *Vital Signs* (New York: W.W. Norton & Co., 1992); number of countries from Brown, "United Nations Peacekeeping: Historical Overview and Current Issues"; 1990 and 1992 strength of peacekeepers from Lewis, "U.N. Chief Warns of Costs of Peace," and from Lucia Mouat, "UN Peacekeepers Face Tough, New Challenges," *Christian Science Monitor*, March 25, 1992.

31. Durch and Blechman, *Keeping the Peace: The United Nations in the Emerging World Order*.

32. For further discussion, see Indar Jit Rikhye, *Strengthening UN Peacekeeping: New Challenges and Proposals* (Washington, D.C.: United States Institute for Peace, 1992), and Laurenti, *The Common Defense*.

33. Rikhye, *Strengthening UN Peacekeeping*.

34. These issues are explored in David J. Scheffer et al., *Three Views on the Issue of Humanitarian Intervention* (Washington, D.C.: United States Institute of Peace, 1992); Edward G. Luck and Tobi Trister Gati, "Whose Collective Security?" *The Washington Quarterly*, Spring 1992.

35. For example, among the governments providing forces for the U.N. in Bosnia, those of Ukraine and Egypt have indicated a strong intention to pull out their contingents due to the increased danger and confused mandate; Hella Pick, "Knee-Deep in the Imbroglio," (London) *Guardian*, September 11, 1992.

36. Rikhye, *Strengthening UN Peacekeeping*; Durch and Blechman, *Keeping the Peace: The United Nations in the Emerging World Order*; Mark Sommer, "Who Should Keep the World's Peace?" *Christian Science Monitor*, August 29, 1991; Thomas L. Friedman, "Bush, in Address to U.N., Urges More Vigor in Keeping Peace," *New York Times*, September 22, 1992.

37. Robert C. Johansen, "UN Peacekeeping: The Changing Utility of Military Force," *Third World Quarterly*, April 1990; Paul Lewis, "Europeans Urge the U.N. to Act More Aggressively to Prevent War," *New York Times*, September 23, 1992.

38. Boutros-Ghali, *An Agenda for Peace*; Paul Lewis, "U.N. Chief Seeking 1,000-Troop Units," *New York Times*, June 20, 1992; Paul Lewis, "U.N. Set to Debate Peacemaking Role," *New York Times*, September 6, 1992.

39. Already, there are signs that some governments providing troops are increasingly intent on retaining influence over their use. In Bosnia, for instance, the United Kingdom and France "insist on more control over operations than is customary in U.N. peacekeeping operations"; Pick, "Knee-Deep in the Imbroglio." This might lead to a situation in which powerful countries officially act on behalf of the U.N. but in reality according to their national perspectives.

40. Brian Urquhart, "Foreword," in F.T. Liu, *United Nations Peacekeeping and the Non-Use of Force*, International Peace Academy Occasional Paper Series (Boulder, Colo.: Lynne Rienner Publishers, 1992).

41. Boutros-Ghali, *An Agenda for Peace*.

42. Liu, *United Nations Peacekeeping and the Non-Use of Force*.

43. "Security Council Summit Declaration: 'New Risks for Stability and Security,'" *New York Times*, February 1, 1992; Boutros-Ghali, *An Agenda for Peace*.

44. Robert C. Johansen, "Lessons for Collective Security," *World Policy Journal*, Summer 1991; Johansen, "UN Peacekeeping: The Changing Utility of Military Force."

45. Rikhye, *Strengthening UN Peacekeeping*; cost estimate cited by Daniel Deudney, "The High Frontier of Outer Space in the 1990s: Star Wars or Spaceship Earth?" in Michael T. Klare and Daniel C. Thomas, eds., *World Security: Trends and Challenges at Century's End* (New York: St. Martin's Press, 1991).

46. De Cuéllar quoted in Paul Lewis, "U.N.'s Fund Crisis Worsens as Role in Security Rises," *New York Times*, January 27, 1992.

47. Margaret P. Karns and Karen A. Mingst, "Multilateral Institutions and International Security," in Klare and Thomas, *World Security*; Ethan Schwartz, "U.S. Plans to Pay U.N. Nearly All of '89 Dues," *Washington Post*, January 14, 1989; "The United Nations: Seriouser," *The Economist*, January 27, 1990; "Status of Contributions as at 31 December 1991," United Nations Secretariat, Document ST/ADM/SER.B/364, New York, January 8, 1992; Paul Lewis, "With U.S. the Biggest Debtor, President Finds U.N. Skeptical," *New York Times*, September 22, 1992; for examples of how funding shortfalls almost derailed some recent peacekeeping undertakings, see Enid C.B. Schoettle, "U.N. Dues: The Price of Peace," *Bulletin of the Atomic Scientists*, June 1992.

48. Schoettle, "U.N. Dues: The Price of Peace"; Ann Gertler, "UN Reports on its Varied Roles," *Ploughshares Monitor*, March 1991; Brandt Commission from Wulf, "Re-

cent Trends in Arms Transfers and Possible Multilateral Action for Control."

49. Durch and Blechman, *Keeping the Peace: The United Nations in the Emerging World Order*; Boutros-Ghali, *An Agenda for Peace*. The U.N. General Assembly is expected to approve the $50-million start-up fund soon; Frank J. Prial, "U.N. Seeks Signal on Troop Notice," *New York Times*, October 30, 1992.

50. There is no formal link between possession of nuclear weapons and permanent Security Council membership, but the U.K. and French governments have made it clear that they will not relinquish their nuclear arsenal because that might endanger their international status as great powers and thus their hold on a Council seat. See Glenn Frankel, "Britain to Expand Nuclear System," *Washington Post*, January 30, 1992; Bruno Barrillot, "French Finesse Nuclear Future," *Bulletin of the Atomic Scientists*, September 1992.

51. For the official text of the U.N. Charter, see U.N. Office of Public Information, *Charter of the United Nations and Statute of the International Court of Justice*; for a more detailed discussion of how U.N. Charter provisions were ignored, see Erskine Childers, "The Gulf War: Lessons for the United Nations," *Bulletin of Peace Proposals*, Vol. 23, No. 2, 1992, and Johansen, "Lessons for Collective Security."

52. Paul Lewis, "West Acts to Defer Issue of New U.N. Council Seats," *New York Times*, January 3, 1992; Paul Lewis, "Germany Tells the U.N. It Wants a Permanent Seat on the Council," *New York Times*, September 24, 1992.

53. Laurenti, *The Common Defense*. Among the few countries that have not been involved in wars in recent decades are Costa Rica, Venezuela, Iceland, Sweden, Switzerland, and Côte d'Ivoire, but Sweden and Switzerland have significant domestic arms industries.

Chapter 9. Reconciling Trade and the Environment

1. François Nectoux and Yoichi Kuroda, *Timber from the South Seas: An Analysis of Japan's Tropical Timber Trade and Its Environmental Impact* (Gland, Switzerland: World Wide Fund for Nature (WWF), 1989); batteries from Center for Investigative Reporting and Bill Moyers, *Global Dumping Ground: The International Traffic in Hazardous Waste* (Washington, D.C.: Seven Locks Press, 1990); Sally Johnson, "Indians in Canada Cross Border to Fight Utility," *New York Times*, June 4, 1989.

2. Nicholas Lenssen, "Third World PVs Hit the Roof," *World Watch*, May/June 1992; Ed Ayres, "Whitewash: Pursuing the Truth About Paper," *World Watch*, September/October 1992.

3. Information on services from General Agreement on Tariffs and Trade (GATT), *International Trade 90–91, Vol. II* (Geneva: 1992), and from United Nations Development Programme (UNDP), *Human Development Report 1992* (New York: Oxford University Press, 1992); investment growth from United Nations Center on Transnational Corporations, *World Investment Report 1991: The Triad in Foreign Direct Investment* (New York: 1991).

4. For a discussion of the many interactions between trade and the environment, see Kym Anderson and Richard Blackhurst, eds., *The Greening of World Trade Issues* (Ann Arbor: University of Michigan Press, 1992).

5. For statements of the need for trade to contribute to the goal of sustainable development, see Organisation for Economic Co-operation and Development (OECD), "Trade and Environment: A Progress Report," Paris, May 1992, and United Nations Conference on Trade and Development, "The Outcome of UNCTAD VIII in the Field of Sustainable Development and the Environment," United Nations, undated.

6. U.N. Food and Agriculture Organization (FAO), *Forest Products Yearbook 1990* (Rome: 1992); FAO, *Production Yearbook 1990* (Rome: 1991); FAO, *Trade Yearbook 1990* (Rome: 1991); FAO, *Fishery Statistics Yearbook 1989* (Rome: 1991); Fearnresearch, *World Bulk Trades 1990* (Oslo: 1991); United Nations, *1990 Energy Statistics Yearbook* (New York: 1992).

7. GATT, *International Trade 90–91, Vol. II*; Jim MacNeill et al., *Beyond Interdependence: The Meshing of the Earth's Economy With the Earth's Ecology* (New York: Oxford University Press, 1991).

8. FAO, *Trade in Tropical Timber, Monthly Bulletin: Annual Totals* (Rome: various years); MacNeill et al., *Beyond Interdependence*; Sandra Postel and John C. Ryan, "Reforming Forestry," in Lester R. Brown et al., *State of the World 1991* (New York: W.W. Norton & Co., 1991); FAO, *Forest Products Yearbook 1990*.

9. Postel and Ryan, "Reforming Forestry."

10. Tropical hardwood exports from FAO, *Trade in Tropical Timber: 1988. Monthly Bulletin: Annual Totals* (Rome: 1988); FAO, *Forest Products Yearbook 1990*.

11. FAO, *Forest Products Yearbook 1990*; John C. Ryan, "Plywood vs. People in Sarawak," *World Watch*, January/February 1991; Victor Mallet, "Guarding a Dwindling Asset," *Financial Times*, August 28, 1992.

12. Postel and Ryan, "Reforming Forestry"; Adam Raphael, "Earth Summit Casts Shadow Over Timber Talks," *Financial Times*, May 15, 1992.

13. Ann Misch, "Can Wildlife Traffic Be Stopped?" *World Watch*, September/October 1992; Sarah Fitzgerald, *The International Wildlife Trade: Whose Business Is It?* (Washington, D.C.: World Wildlife Fund, 1989).

14. "World Trade in Wildlife," Fact Sheet, TRAFFIC USA, World Wildlife Fund, Washington, D.C., February 1992; Fitz-gerald, *International Wildlife Trade*; Misch, "Can Wildlife Trade Be Stopped?"

15. Task Force on Environment and the Internal Market, *"1992": The Environmental Dimension* (Bonn: Economica Verlag, 1990); Debra A. Rose, "A North American Free Trade Agreement: The Impacts on Wildlife," WWF, Washington, D.C., 1991.

16. GATT, *International Trade 90–91, Vol. II*; Michael Zielenziger, "Free-Trade Agreement Could Uproot Thousands of Mexican Farm Workers," *Journal of Commerce*, August 18, 1992; Mark Ritchie, "Free Trade versus Sustainable Agriculture: The Implications of NAFTA," *The Ecologist*, September/October 1992.

17. "Trade and the Environment," in GATT, *International Trade 90–91, Vol. I* (Geneva: 1992); U.S. Congress, Office of Technology Assessment (OTA), *Trade and the Environment: Conflicts and Opportunities* (Washington, D.C.: U.S. Government Printing Office, 1992); Robert Repetto, World Resources Institute, memo to the NACEPT Trade and Environment Committee, December 16, 1992; Letter of Justin Ward, Senior Resource Specialist, Natural Resources Defense Council, Washington, D.C., to Carla A. Hills, U.S. Trade Representative, and Edward Madigan, U.S. Secretary of Agriculture, March 20, 1992; Mark Ritchie, "GATT, Agriculture, and the Environment: The US Double Zero Plan," *The Ecologist*, November/December 1990.

18. Annual sales loss from UNDP, *Human Development Report 1991* (New York: Oxford University Press, 1991); Charles Arden-Clarke, *The General Agreement on Tariffs and Trade, Environmental Protection and Sustainable Development* (Gland, Switzerland: WWF, 1991).

19. Alan B. Durning, "Fat of the Land," *World Watch*, May/June 1991; Alan B. Durning and Holly B. Brough, *Taking Stock: Animal Farming and the Environment*, Worldwatch Paper 103 (Washington, D.C.: Worldwatch

Institute, July 1991); FAO, *Production Yearbook 1990*; FAO, *Trade Yearbook 1990*.

20. FAO, *Fisheries Statistics 1989*; "Iceland Faces Calls for 40% Cut In Cod Catch," *Financial Times*, June 3, 1992; Robert Corzine, "Iceland Finds Enemy to Replace Soviet N-subs," *Financial Times*, October 8, 1992; figure on developing countries from Nicholas Lenssen, "The Ocean Blues," *World Watch*, July/August 1989.

21. Chris Hellier, "The Mangrove Wastelands," *The Ecologist*, March/April 1988; Robin Broad and John Cavanagh, *Plundering Paradise: The Stuggle for the Environment in the Philippines* (Berkeley: University of California Press, in press).

22. John E. Young, *Mining the Earth*, Worldwatch Paper 109 (Washington, D.C.: Worldwatch Institute, July 1992).

23. Ibid.; Information Research Limited, "Trends in Relocation of Potentially Polluting Chemical Industries" (draft), London, June 1992.

24. United Nations, *1990 Energy Statistics Yearbook*; Lucille Langlois, "The Environmental Effects of Trade in the Energy Sector," OECD, Paris, forthcoming.

25. British Petroleum, *BP Statistical Review of World Energy* (London: various years); Murray Feshbach and Alfred Friendly, Jr., *Ecocide in the USSR: Health and Nature Under Siege* (New York: Basic Books, 1992).

26. Jim Vallette and Heather Spaulding, *The International Trade in Wastes: A Greenpeace Inventory* (Washington, D.C.: Greenpeace, 1990); for numerous ongoing instances of waste export see Greenpeace's *Toxic Trade Update*, Second Quarter 1992.

27. United Nations Environment Programme, "Basel Convention on the Control of Transboundary Movements of Hazardous Wastes and their Disposal," Final Act, Basel, Switzerland, March 21, 1989; "United Nations Officials See Basel Treaty As 'Limping'

Into Effect With Limited Support," Special Report, *International Environment Reporter*, May 6, 1992; "Basel Convention Now in Force," *Toxic Trade Update* (Greenpeace USA), Second Quarter 1992.

28. Task Force, *"1992": The Environmental Dimension*; Simon Caroll, *The Single European Dump* (Amsterdam: Greenpeace International, 1991); Office of the U.S. Trade Representative (USTR), "Review of U.S.-Mexico Environmental Issues," Washington, D.C., February 25, 1992.

29. "EC Court Ruling May Allow Restrictions on Waste Imports," *International Environment Reporter*, July 15, 1992; "Euro-Court Rules on Waste Trade" and "EC Waste Trade Legislation Passes to U.K. as France Stands Against Waste Trade," *Toxic Trade Update* (Greenpeace USA), Second Quarter 1992.

30. Jonathan Dahl, "Canada Encourages Mining of Asbestos, Sells to Third World," *Wall Street Journal*, September 12, 1989; Mario Epelman, "The Export of Hazard in the Third World: The Case of Asbestos in Latin America," *New Solutions*, Summer 1992; Ray Sentes, Professor of Political Science, University of Regina, Saskatchewan, Canada, private communication, October 15, 1992; U.S. General Accounting Office (GAO), "Export of Unregistered Pesticides is Not Adequately Monitored by EPA," Washington, D.C., April 1989.

31. United Nations Industrial Development Organization (UNIDO), *Industry and Development: Global Report 1990/91* (Vienna: 1990); UNDP, *Human Development Report 1991*. Two recent studies examine the question of location trends in "environmentally dirty" industry. One paper shows the importance of "environmentally dirty goods" in production in various countries, demonstrating that exports are declining somewhat in the industrial world and growing in the developed. A second notes a growth in toxic-intensive industries in developing countries,

particularly ones rather protected from the international market. Patrick Low and Alexander Yeat, "Do 'Dirty' Industries Migrate," and Robert Lucas et al., "Economic Development, Environmental Regulation and the International Migration of Toxic Industrial Pollution: 1960–1988," both in Patrick Low, ed., *International Trade and the Environment*, World Bank Discussion Papers (Washington, D.C.: World Bank, 1992).

32. H. Jeffrey Leonard, *Pollution and the Struggle for the World Product* (Cambridge: Cambridge University Press, 1988); OTA, *Trade and the Environment*.

33. Leonard, *Pollution and the Struggle for the World Product*; OTA, *Trade and the Environment*; U.S. Bureau of the Census, *Manufacturer's Pollution Abatement Capital Expenditures and Operating Costs* (Washington, D.C.: 1988), cited in USTR, "Review of U.S.-Mexico Environmental Issues."

34. Leonard, *Pollution and the Struggle for the World Product*.

35. Roberto Sanchez, "Health and Environmental Risks of the Maquiladora in Mexico," *Natural Resources Journal*, Winter 1990; GAO, "Some U.S. Wood Furniture Firms Relocated from Los Angeles Area to Mexico," Washington, D.C., April 1991.

36. Gary Clyde Hufbacher and Jeffrey J. Schott, *North American Free Trade: Issues and Recommendations* (Washington, D.C.: Institute for International Economics, 1992).

37. Justin Ward and Glenn T. Prickett, "Prospects for a Green Trade Agreement," *Environment*, May 1992; "Nafta May Bring 'Import' of Pollution to Mexico," *Journal of Commerce*, August 20, 1992; "Hazardous Waste from U.S.-Owned Plants in Mexico Dumped Illegally, Panel Told," *International Environment Reporter*, December 4, 1991; GAO, "U.S. Mexico Trade: Assessment of Mexico's Environmental Controls for New Companies," Washington, D.C., August 1992.

38. S.J. Lewis et al., *Border Trouble: Rivers in Peril* (Boston: National Toxics Campaign Fund, 1991); Council on Scientific Affairs, American Medical Association, "A Permanent U.S.-Mexico Border Environmental Health Commission," Chicago, June 27, 1990; John Holusha, "Trade Pact May Intensify Problems at the Border," *New York Times*, August 20, 1992; USTR, "Review of U.S.-Mexico Environmental Issues."

39. Lic. Patricio Chirinos, Secretary of Urban Development and Ecology, speech on Mexican Integrated Environmental Border Plan, Ciudad Juarez, Mexico, October 23, 1991; Governments of Canada, Mexico, and the United States of America, "The North American Free Trade Agreement," September 6, 1992.

40. "Japan, Malaysia Embroiled in Dispute Over Alleged Pollution From Chemical Firm," *International Environment Reporter*, July 29, 1992; Mohamed Motala, "Bayer Poisons South Africa" and "Thor Chemicals Reopens Mercury 'Recycling' Facility in South Africa," *Toxic Trade Update* (Greenpeace USA), Second Quarter 1992.

41. OECD, *The OECD Environment Industry: Situation, Prospects and Government Policies* (Paris: 1992); capacity of wind turbine exports from Strategies Unlimited, *International Market Evaluations: Wind Energy Prospects* (Mountain View, Calif.: California Energy Commission, undated); value of wind turbine exports from Kevin Rackstraw, American Wind Energy Association, Washington, D.C., private communication, August 21, 1992, based on ibid.; photovoltaic exports are a Worldwatch Institute estimate, based on Rick Sellars, Solar Energy Industries Association, Washington, D.C., private communication, September 9, 1992; Terry McGowan, Manager of Applications Development, General Electric Lighting, Cleveland, Ohio, private communication, October 14, 1992.

42. Amy Vickers, Amy Vickers & Associates, Boston, Mass., private communication,

October 16, 1992; Curtis Moore, "Bush's Nonsense on Jobs and the Environment," *New York Times*, September 29, 1992.

43. Nancy Birdsall and David Wheeler, "Trade Policy and Industrial Pollution in Latin America: Where Are the Pollution Havens?" and David Wheeler and Paul Martin, "Prices, Policies, and International Diffusion of Clean Technology: The Case of Wood Pulp Production," in Low, *International Trade and the Environment*.

44. Birdsall and Wheeler, "Trade Policy and Industrial Pollution in Latin America."

45. Seaborne freight trade tonnage from Fearnresearch, *Fearnleys Review 1990* (Oslo: 1991); energy used in shipping is a Worldwatch Institute estimate, based on ibid. and on Stacy Davis and Melissa Morris, *Transportation Energy Data Book: Edition 12* (Oak Ridge, Tenn.: Oak Ridge National Laboratory, 1992); energy equivalents from U.S. Department of Energy, Energy Information Administration, *International Energy Annual 1990* (Washington, D.C.: 1992); airfreight energy use is a Worldwatch Institute estimate based on data supplied by the International Civil Aviation Administration, Quebec, Canada, and by Larry C. Benton, Avmark, Inc., Arlington, Va., private communication, September 23, 1992.

46. Task Force, *"1992": The Environmmental Dimension*; USTR, "Review of U.S.-Mexico Environmental Issues."

47. Task Force, *"1992": The Environmental Dimension*; USTR, "Review of U.S.-Mexico Environmental Issues"; H. Landis Gabel, INSEAD, Fontainbleau Cedex, France, "The Implications of International Trade Liberalization for the Environment: The Case of the Transport Sector," OECD, Paris, forthcoming; Gregory S. Johnson, "Shippers, Truckers Hope NAFTA Cuts Time, Losses," *Journal of Commerce*, August 12, 1992.

48. Task Force, *"1992": The Environmental Dimension*; Gene M. Grossman and Alan B. Krueger, "Environmental Impacts of a North American Free Trade Agreement," Working Paper No. 3914, National Bureau of Economic Research, Cambridge, Mass., November 1991; U.S. Environmental Protection Agency (EPA), *1990 Toxics Release Inventory Public Data Release* (Washington, D.C.: 1992); Grossman and Krueger's estimate is most likely on the low side, as it assumes that the industries in Mexico produce the same amount of pollution per unit of output of a given product as U.S. industries do.

49. OECD, *Environmental Data Compendium 1991* (Paris: 1991); Swedish pulp production and chlorine use from K. Karlsson, Swedish Pulp and Paper Association, Stockholm, private communication, November 2, 1992.

50. Grossman and Krueger, "Environmental Impacts of a North American Free Trade Agreement"; $12 billion estimate from study cited in "Poor Odds, High Stakes," *The Economist*, June 27, 1992; $90 billion estimate from Ian Goldin and Dominique van der Mensbrugghe, *Trade Liberalisation: What's At Stake?* Policy Brief No. 5 (Paris: OECD Development Centre, undated).

51. OTA, *Trade and the Environment*. The EC has a somewhat different set of rules than GATT and NAFTA. In the EC, the goal is mutual recognition of member-country environmental standards, meaning that a product that is legal for sale in one country should in theory be accepted throughout the Community. In GATT and NAFTA, the only requirement is that national producers be subject to the same rules as importers and that the rule not be a disguised trade barrier. Though the EC rule is in theory more restrictive, environmental measures can be a legitimate reason for exceptions to the "mutual recognition" rules. See Task Force, *"1992": The Environmental Dimension*.

52. For a description of the controversy over bovine growth hormone, see OTA, *Trade and the Environment*; Nancy Dunne and Bernard Simon, "Canada-U.S. Beer War

Gets Green Tinge," *Financial Times*, July 31, 1992; Hufbacher and Schott, *North American Free Trade*.

53. David Wirth, Assistant Professor of Law, Washington and Lee University School of Law, Testimony before the Committee on Science, Space, and Technology, U.S. House of Representatives, Washington, D.C., September 30, 1992; Steve Charnovitz, "Trade Negotiations and the Environment," *International Environment Reporter*, March 11, 1992.

54. "Commission of the European Communities v. Kingdom of Denmark—Case 302/86," *Report on Cases Before the Court, Vol. 8* (Luxembourg: Office for Official Publications of the European Communities, 1988); "Landmark EEC Court Case on Returnable Bottles Gives Boost to Environment," *ENDS Report*, September 1988; Jesper Hostrup, NOAH, Copenhagen, private communication, May 29, 1991.

55. "Commission of the European Communities v. Kingdom of Denmark"; OTA, *Trade and the Environment*; Charnovitz, "Trade Negotiations and the Environment"; Wirth, Testimony.

56. GATT, "United States—Restrictions on Imports of Tuna: Report of the Panel," Geneva, September 3, 1991; David Phillips, Earth Island Institute, "Statement on the Implications of the GATT Panel Ruling on Dolphin Protection and the Environment," U.S. House of Representatives, Subcommittee on Health and Environment, Washington, D.C., September 27, 1991; Eric Christensen and Samantha Geffin, "GATT Sets Its Net on Environmental Regulation: The GATT Panel Ruling on Mexican Yellowfin Tuna Imports and the Need for Reform of the International Trading System," *Inter-American Law Review*, Winter 1991–1992.

57. GATT, "Report of the Panel"; OTA, *Trade and the Environment*. Some analysts have suggested that the judges in the tuna-dolphin case used an extremely narrow interpretation of GATT's exceptions clause, Article XX.

Charnovitz, for instance, argues that the drafting history of the GATT suggests that the GATT founders meant to cover import bans based on process. See Steve Charnovitz, "Exploring the Environmental Exceptions in GATT Article XX," *Journal of World Trade*, October 1991.

58. GATT, "Report of the Panel."

59. David Clark Scott, "Stung by US Tuna Ban, Mexico Protects Turtles," *Christian Science Monitor*, May 14, 1992; Christensen and Geffin, "GATT Sets Its Net"; "U.S. Bans Importing Fish Caught With Drift Nets," *Washington Post*, September 20, 1992; Steve Charnovitz, "Environmental and Labour Standards in Trade," *World Economy*, May 1992; Arden-Clarke, *The General Agreement on Tariffs and Trade, Environmental Protection and Sustainable Development*; Sara Oldfield, "The Tropical Chainsaw Massacre," *New Scientist*, September 23, 1989.

60. Nigel Dudley, Earth Resources Research, *Importing Deforestation: Should Britain Ban the Import of Tropical Hardwoods?* (Godalming, Surrey, U.K.: WWF-UK, 1991); Arden-Clarke, *The General Agreement on Tariffs and Trade, Environmental Protection and Sustainable Development*; Emily Schwartz, "Ravaging Resources: GATT and the World's Forests," *Multinational Monitor*, November 1990; William Bown, "Trade Deals a Blow to the Environment," *New Scientist*, November 10, 1990.

61. Todd Campbell, "B.C. Fishermen Pay a High Price for Free Trade," *The New Pacific*, Winter/Spring 1990; OTA, *Trade and the Environment*.

62. OTA, *Trade and the Environment*; Jeffrey R. Vincent, "The Tropical Timber Trade and Sustainable Development," *Science*, June 19, 1992; Edward B. Barbier et al., London Environmental Economics Centre, "Environmental Effects of Trade in the Forestry Sector," OECD, Paris, forthcoming; Charles Arden-Clarke, "South-North Terms of Trade, Environmental Protection and Sus-

tainable Development," WWF, Gland, Switzerland, February 1992.

63. Arden-Clarke, "South-North Terms of Trade"; "Synthesis Report: The Environmental Effects of Trade," OECD, Paris, forthcoming; Young, *Mining the Earth*.

64. GATT report on trade and the environment, in GATT, *International Trade 90–91, Vol. I*; OTA, *Trade and the Environment*.

65. J.O. Cameron et al., "Relationship Between Environmental Agreements and Instruments Related to Trade and Environment," U.N. Conference on Environment and Development, Research Paper No. 35, Geneva, February 1992; Governments of Canada, Mexico, and the United States of America, "The North American Free Trade Agreement."

66. OTA, *Trade and the Environment*; Steven Shrybman, "Trading Away the Environment," *World Policy Journal*, Winter 1991–92; Charnovitz, "Trade Negotiations and the Environment."

67. Lori Wallach, "Trading Away the Environment," *Pesticides and You*, June 1992; James Cameron and Halina Ward, Foundation for International Law and Development, "The Multilateral Trade Organization: A Legal and Environmental Assessment," WWF, Gland, Switzerland, May 1992.

68. Governments of Canada, Mexico, and the United States of America, "The North American Free Trade Agreement."

69. John H. Jackson, University of Michigan School of Law, unpublished memorandum of November 7, 1991, on "Changing GATT Rules"; Christensen and Geffin, "GATT Sets Its Net"; Peter Uimonen and John Whalley, "Trade and Environment: Setting the Rules," draft, Institute for International Economics, Washington, D.C., July 1992; Charles Arden-Clarke, "International Trade, GATT, and the Environment," WWF, Gland, Switzerland, May 1992;

"Trade and the Environment," Statement of Senator Max Baucus, Chairman, International Trade Subcommittee, Committee on Finance, U.S. Senate, Washington, D.C., September 17, 1992; "U.S. Senator Urges New GATT Round to Consider Inclusion of Environmental Code," *International Environment Reporter*, November 6, 1991.

70. Cameron et al., "Relationship Between Environmental Agreements"; Governments of Canada, Mexico, and the United States of America, "The North American Free Trade Agreement."

71. Peter Weber, "Green Seals of Approval Heading to Market," *World Watch*, July/August 1990.

72. Robert Thompson and David Lascelles, "Tax May Run Into Political Sands," *Financial Times*, May 15, 1992; Bruce Barnard, "EC Executive Seeks to Impose Energy Tax to Curb Emissions," *Journal of Commerce*, May 13, 1992.

73. OECD, *The Polluter Pays Principle: Definition, Analysis, Implementation* (Paris: 1975); David A. Wirth, School of Law, Washington and Lee University, Remarks at Conference on Environmental Quality and Free Trade: Interdependent Goals or Irreconcilable Conflict, School of Law, Lexington, Va., September 25, 1992; "Rio Declaration on Environment and Development," U.N. Conference on Environment and Development, Rio de Janeiro, June 3–14, 1992.

74. Hilary F. French, "The EC—Environmental Proving Ground," *World Watch*, November/December 1991; Cameron Keyes, *The European Community and Environmental Policy: An Introduction for Americans* (Baltimore, Md.: WWF, 1991); Philippe Sands, "European Community Environmental Law: The Evolution of a Regional Regime of International Environmental Protection," *Yale Law Journal*, Vol. 100, No. 1, 1991.

75. "Monitoring the Implementation of Community Law on the Environment: An

Initial Report by the Commission," Information Memo, Commission of the European Communities, February 8, 1990; "The Dirty Dozen," *The Economist*, July 20, 1991; David Wilkinson, "Greening the Treaty: Strengthening Environmental Policy in the Treaty of Rome," Institute for European Environmental Policy, London, October 1990.

76. Governments of United States, Mexico, and Canada, "Draft Outline for Trilateral Environmental Commission," Washington, D.C., September 16, 1992; Justin Ward, Natural Resources Defense Council, and Stewart J. Hudson, National Wildlife Federation, Testimonies before the Subcommittee on International Trade, Committee on Finance, U.S. Senate, Washington, D.C., September 16, 1992.

77. U.S. International Trade Commission, *International Agreements to Protect the Environment and Wildlife Agreements in the Field of the Environment* (Washington, D.C.: 1991); for a discussion of international environmental treaties, see Hilary F. French, *After the Earth Summit: The Future of Environmental Governance*, Worldwatch Paper 107 (Washington, D.C.: Worldwatch Institute, March 1992).

78. Roosevelt quote from George E. Brown, Jr., et al., "Making Trade Fair," *World Policy Journal*, Spring 1992; on the history of linking trade to respect for labor and human rights, see Charnovitz, "Environmental and Labour Standards."

79. Walter and Loudon study cited in World Commission on Environment and Development, *Our Common Future* (New York: Oxford University Press, 1987); Arden-Clarke, *The General Agreement on Tariffs and Trade, Environmental Protection and Sustainable Development*.

80. OTA, *Trade and the Environment*; Arden-Clarke, "South-North Terms of Trade"; Konrad Von Moltke, "Free Trade and Mutual Tariffs: A Practical Approach to Sustainable Development," *EcoDecision*, June 1992. Export tariffs are consistent with

GATT in its current form, while import tariffs are not.

81. Congressman Richard A. Gephardt, Address on the Status of the North American Free Trade Agreement, Institute for International Economics, Washington, D.C., July 27, 1992; Senator Max Baucus, Policy Address, National Association of Manufacturers Special Forum on Trade and the Environment, Washington, D.C., August 12, 1992; Nancy Dunne, "Mexico May Impose Environmenal Tax," *Financial Times*, July 24, 1992.

82. Brown et al., "Making Trade Fair"; "New Fund to Provide 400 Million ECUs Through 1995 for Environmental Efforts," *International Environment Reporter*, August 12, 1992; USTR, "Review of U.S.-Mexico Environmental Issues"; William K. Reilly, Administrator, EPA, Testimony before the Committee on Ways and Means, U.S. House of Representatives, Washington, D.C., September 15, 1992.

83. Paula L. Green, "International Trade Talks Likely to Be Greener," *Journal of Commerce*, August 19, 1992; Mark Magnier, "Power of Environmentalists Called Trade Issue of '90s," *Journal of Commerce*, July 20, 1992; Jay D. Hair, "Environmentalism and Free Trade," *Conservation Exchange*, National Wildlife Federation, Washington, D.C., Spring 1991.

Chapter 10. Shaping the Next Industrial Revolution

1. Figure for 1950 from Herbert R. Block, *The Planetary Product in 1980: A Creative Pause?* (Washington D.C.: U.S. Department of State, 1981); figure for 1991 from International Monetary Fund (IMF), *World Economic Outlook October 1992* (Washington D.C.: 1992).

2. Organisation for Economic Co-operation and Development, "The OECD Environment Industry: Situation, Prospects, and Government Policies," Paris, 1992; gross national product of Belgium from IMF, *Interna-*

tional Financial Statistics Yearbook, Washington, D.C., 1991.

3. Cities failing to meet U.S. air standards from Marcia D. Lowe, *Alternatives to the Automobile: Transport for Livable Cities*, Worldwatch Paper 98 (Washington, D.C.: Worldwatch Institute, October 1990); U.S Environmental Protection Agency, Office of Air Quality Planning and Standards, *National Air Quality and Emissions Trends Report 1991* (Research Triangle Park, N.C.: U.S. Government Printing Office, 1992); for an overview of global air pollution problems, see Hilary F. French, *Clearing the Air: A Global Agenda*, Worldwatch Paper 94 (Washington, D.C.: Worldwatch Institute, January 1990).

4. California Clean Air Act, Chapter 1568, Statutes of 1988 (AB 2595, Sher); Southern California Association of Governments, *1991 Air Quality Management Plan* (Los Angeles: Southern California Air Quality Management District, 1991) (approved by the California Air Resources Board, Ocotber 15, 1992).

5. Matthew L. Wald, "California's Pied Piper of Clean Air," *New York Times*, September 13, 1992; Robert Reinhold, "Ford Unveils Cleanest-Running Cars for California," *New York Times*, April 15, 1992; Terry Box, "Electric Cars May be Poised to Enter the Mainstream," *Journal of Commerce*, September 18, 1991; Bavarian Motor Works, "Electric Cars at BMW—E1, E2: Quietly the Future Draws Near," Munich, February 1992; Charles Mendler, energy and transportation analyst, Energy Conservation Coalition, Takoma Park, Md., private communication, October 20, 1992; Volkswagen, "Research for the Future of Recycling at Volkswagen: Product Recycling and Recycling in Production," Munich, undated; Nissan, "Symbiosis: Harmonious Coexistence of People, Automobiles and Nature," Tokyo, 1992.

6. Marcia D. Lowe, "Bicycle Production Outpaces Autos," in Brown et al., *Vital Signs*.

7. John E. Young, *Mining the Earth*, Worldwatch Paper 109 (Washington, D.C.: World-watch Institute, July 1992); Sandra Postel and John C. Ryan, "Reforming Forestry," in Lester R. Brown et al., *State of the World 1991* (New York: W.W. Norton & Co., 1991); John C. Ryan, *Life Support: Conserving Biological Diversity*, Worldwatch Paper 108 (Washington, D.C.: Worldwatch Institute, April 1992).

8. Postel and Ryan, "Reforming Forestry."

9. For information on trends in materials use, see Marc H. Ross and Robert H. Williams, *Our Energy: Regaining Control* (New York: McGraw-Hill, 1981), Eric D. Larson et al., "Materials, Affluence, and Industrial Energy Use," *Annual Review of Energy*, Vol. 12 (Palo Alto, Calif.: 1987), Peter F. Drucker, "The Changed World Economy," *Foreign Affairs*, Spring 1986, Robert U. Ayres, "Industrial Metabolism," and Robert Herman et al., "Dematerialization," in Jesse H. Ausubel and Hedy E. Sladovich, eds., *Technology and Environment* (Washington, D.C.: National Academy Press, 1989), and United States Bureau of Mines, *The New Materials Society, Volume 3: Materials Shifts in the New Society* (Washington, D.C.: 1991); the share of U.S. municipal solid waste recovered for recycling rose by one third between 1988 and 1990, according to U.S. Environmental Protection Agency (EPA), *Characterization of Municipal Solid Waste: 1992 Update* (Washington, D.C.: 1992); potential for reducing U.S. wood consumption and share of raw wood from Southeast Asia made into finished products from Postel and Ryan, "Reforming Forestry."

10. Ed Ayres, "Whitewash: Pursuing the Truth About Paper," *World Watch*, September/October 1992; Renate Kroesa, *The Greenpeace Guide to Paper* (Vancouver, B.C.: Greenpeace International, 1990).

11. Donald F. Barnett and Robert W. Crandall, *Up From the Ashes: The Rise of the Steel Minimill in the United States* (Washington, D.C.: Brookings Institution, 1986).

12. U.S. production of organic chemicals has increased more than tenfold since World

War II, according to David J. Sarokin et al., *Cutting Chemical Wastes: What 29 Organic Chemical Plants Are Doing to Reduce Hazardous Wastes* (New York: INFORM, 1985); EPA, *1990 Toxics Release Inventory Public Data Release* (Washington, D.C.: 1992).

13. Union Carbide from Kenneth Scott, Council on Economic Priorities, New York, private communication, October 8, 1992.

14. Stephan Schmidheiny, with the Business Council for Sustainable Development, *Changing Course* (Cambridge, Mass.: The MIT Press, 1992).

15. Ibid; Ecover, *The Ecological Factory* (Oostmalle, Belgium: 1992).

16. National Research Council, *Alternative Agriculture* (Washington, D.C.: National Academy Press, 1989); Peter Weber, "A Place for Pesticides?" *World Watch*, May/June 1992.

17. Sandra Postel, *Last Oasis: Facing Water Scarcity* (New York: W.W. Norton & Co., 1992).

18. Fish catch from U.N. Food and Agriculture Organization, *FAO Production Yearbook: Fishery Statistics* (Rome: various years); aquaculture from U.N. Environment Programme (UNEP), *Environmental Data Report 1991–92* (Oxford: Basil Blackwell, 1991).

19. Douglas Cogan, *Stones in a Glass House* (Washington, D.C.: Investor Responsibility Research Center (IRRC), 1988); CFC production from Mack McFarland, E.I. Du Pont de Nemours & Co., Wilmington, Del., private communication, April 15, 1992.

20. Richard Elliot Benedick, *Ozone Diplomacy* (Cambridge, Mass.: Harvard University Press, 1991); Du Pont from Rogene A. Buchholz et al., *Managing Environmental Issues: A Casebook* (Englewood Cliffs, N.J.: Prentice-Hall, 1992).

21. Benedick, *Ozone Diplomacy*; CFC production from McFarland, private communication; Matthew L. Wald, "Staying Cool and Saving the Ozone," *New York Times*, June 22, 1992.

22. Intergovernmental Panel on Climate Change, *1992 IPCC Supplement: Working Group I Scientific Assessment of Climate Change* (Geneva and Nairobi: World Meteorological Organization and UNEP, 1992); British Petroleum (BP), *BP Statistical Review of World Energy* (London: 1992); statement on need to leave fuels in the ground based on fossil fuel resources from Eric Sundquist, "Geological Perspectives on Carbon Dioxide and the Carbon Cycle," in E.T. Sundquist and W.S. Broecker, eds., *The Carbon Cycle and Atmospheric CO_2: Natural Variations Archean to Present* (Washington, D.C.: American Geophysical Union, 1985).

23. Douglas Cogan, *The Greenhouse Gambit: Business and Investment Response to Climate Change* (Washington, D.C.: IRRC, 1992); Karen Schmidt, "Industrial Countries' Responses to Global Climate Change," *Environmental and Energy Study Institute Special Report*, Washington, D.C., July 1, 1991; Karen Schmidt, program associate, Environmental and Energy Study Institute, Washington, D.C., private communication, October 21, 1992; BP, *BP Statistical Review*.

24. Arnold P. Fickett et al., "Efficient Use of Electricity," *Scientific American*, September 1990; Arthur H. Rosenfeld, "Energy for Homes and Buildings," *Scientific American*, September 1990; Howard Geller et al., *Energy Efficiency and Job Creation* (Washington, D.C.: American Council for an Energy-Efficient Economy, 1992).

25. Mark D. Levine et al., "Electricity End-Use Efficiency: Experience with Technologies, Markets, and Policies Throughout the World," Lawrence Berkeley Laboratory, Berkeley, Calif., March 1992.

26. Gregg Marland, "Carbon Dioxide Emission Rates for Conventional and Synthetic Fuels," *Energy*, Vol. 8, No. 12, 1983; "Fuel Cells for Urban Power," *EPRI Journal*, September 1991.

27. The Alliance to Save Energy, American Gas Association, and Solar Energy Industries Association, *An Alternative Energy Future* (Washington, D.C.: 1992); "World Status: A Grid for East Asia," *Energy Economist*, February 1992.

28. Christopher Flavin and Nicholas Lenssen, *Beyond the Petroleum Age: Designing a Solar Economy*, Worldwatch Paper 100 (Washington, D.C.: Worldwatch Institute, December 1990).

29. American Wind Energy Association, *1992 Wind Technology Status Report* (Washington, D.C.: 1992); Christopher Flavin, "Wind Power Soars," in Brown et al., *Vital Signs*; "Europe To Out-Install U.S. in New Wind Energy Capacity," *The Solar Letter*, March 6, 1992; Paul Maycock, *PV News*, February 1992; "PV Shipments Up More Modestly Than Had Been Anticipated," *The Solar Letter*, February 7, 1992; A.E. Cullison, "Japanese Solar Cell Producers Expand to Meet Demand Abroad," *Journal of Commerce*, March 18, 1992.

30. Joan M. Ogden and Robert H. Williams, *Solar Hydrogen: Moving Beyond Fossil Fuels* (Washington, D.C.: World Resources Institute, 1989).

31. "World Status: The Electricity Utility," *Energy Economist*, August 1992.

32. Lead from Barry Commoner, *Making Peace With the Planet* (New York: Pantheon Books, 1990); asbestos from Joel S. Hirschorn and Kirsten U. Oldenburg, *Prosperity Without Pollution* (New York: Van Nostrand Reinhold, 1991); Bringer quoted in Joel Makower, *The E Factor* (New York: Times Books, 1993).

33. A discussion of the limits of traditional regulation can be found in Alvin L. Alm, "A Need for New Approaches," *EPA Journal*, May/June 1992.

34. Russell Mokhiber, *Corporate Crime and Violence: Big Business Power and the Abuse of the Public Trust* (San Francisco, Calif.: Sierra Club Books, 1988); General Accounting Office cited in Robert W. Adler and Charles Lord, "Environmental Crimes: Raising the Stakes," *George Washington Law Review*, April 1991.

35. Lowe, *Alternatives to the Automobile*; Ernst U. Von Weizsäcker and Jochen Jesinghaus, *Ecological Tax Reform* (London: Zed Books, 1992); Schmidheiny et al., *Changing Course*; "Business Group Raises Stakes on Transport Policy," *ENDS Report*, September 1992.

36. Tax exemptions for U.S. mining and timber industries from Executive Office of the President, *Budget of the United States Government* and *Special Analyses: Budget of the United States Government* (Washington, D.C.: U.S. Government Printing Office, various years); below-cost timber sales from "Forest Service Is Mismanaged, Costing Taxpayers Money While Catering to Timber Industry, Congressional Panel Told," *Corporate Crime Reporter*, April 6, 1992; aluminum prices from Merton J. Peck, ed., *The World Aluminum Industry in a Changing Energy Era* (Washington, D.C.: Resources for the Future, 1988), and from Ronald Graham, *The Aluminum Industry and the Third World* (London: Zed Books, 1982); "Who's For the Chop—Coal or the Economy Minister?" *Energy Economist*, May 1991.

37. Sanford E. Gaines and Richard A. Westin, *Taxation for Environmental Protection* (New York: Quorum Books, 1991).

38. U.S. Congress, Office of Technology Assessment, *Superfund Strategy* (Washington, D.C.: U.S. Government Printing Office, 1985); "Revenue Service Issues Guidance on Ozone-Depleting Chemicals Tax," *International Environment Reporter*, January 10, 1990; U.S. House of Representatives, "Omnibus Budget Reconciliation Act of 1989, Conference Report to Accompany H.R. 3299," Washington, D.C., November 21, 1989; Joint Committee on Taxation, "Estimated Reve-

nue Effects of Conference Agreement on Revenue Provisions of H.R. 3299," Washington, D.C., November 21, 1989; "Race to Ban Ozone Destroyers Accelerates After U.S. Announcement of Earlier Action," *International Environment Reporter*, February 26, 1992.

39. Roger C. Dower and Mary Beth Zimmerman, *The Right Climate for Carbon Taxes: Creating Economic Incentives to Protect the Atmosphere* (Washington, D.C.: World Resources Institute, 1992); "Carbonated Growth," *The Economist*, August 8, 1992.

40. Dower and Zimmerman, *The Right Climate for Carbon Taxes*; U.S. Congressional Budget Office, *Carbon Charges as a Response to Global Warming: The Effects of Taxing Fossil Fuels* (Washington, D.C.: U.S. Government Printing Office, 1990).

41. "WP&L Gets $6.5 Million for Allowance Sales," *Compliance Strategies Review*, August 31, 1992; Scott Armstrong, "For Cleaner Skies, L.A. Considers Free-Market Pollution Solution," *Christian Science Monitor*, March 4, 1992.

42. California Public Utilities Commission, "CPUC, Major Utilities Promote Energy Efficiency and Conservation Programs," San Francisco, Calif., August 29, 1990.

43. Government of Germany, "Ordinance on the Avoidance of Packaging Waste of 12 June 1991," Bonn, undated; Duales System Deutschland, "Der Grüne Punkt," Bonn, undated; Ferdinand Protzman, "A Nation's Recycling Law Puts Businesses on the Spot," *New York Times*, July 12, 1992; James O. Jackson, "Breaking the Trash Habit," *Time*, April 20, 1992; Hahn quoted in Schmidheiny et al., *Changing Course*.

44. Derek Denniston, "From Murky Politics, A Bright Idea," *World Watch*, July/August 1992; EPA, *Green Lights Update*, July 1992; "Ambitious Efficiency Programs Target Manufacturers Rather Than End Users," *The dsm Letter* (International Institute for Energy Conservation, Washington, D.C.), August 3, 1992; Intel Corp., "Intel Brings Energy-Saving Technology to Desktop Computers: Firm to Support EPA's Energy Star Computer Program," Santa Clara, Calif., press release, October 14, 1992.

45. Greenpeace International, *The Greenpeace Book of Greenwash* (Amsterdam: 1992).

46. Global Environmental Management Initiative, *Total Quality Environmental Management: The Primer* (Washington, D.C.: 1992).

47. Sony example in Schmidheiny, *Changing Course*; IRRC, *Corporate Environmental Profiles Directory: Executive Summary and Findings* (Washington, D.C.: 1992); Tom Decker, BankAmerica, San Francisco, Calif., private communication, September 29, 1992.

48. Dinner table criticism point from John Collins, Chairman, Shell U.K., London, private communication, February 18, 1992.

49. Hurwitz from Kenneth Scott, Council on Economic Priorities, New York, private communication, May 19, 1992; James C. Abegglen and George Stalk, *Kaisha: The Japanese Corporation* (Tokyo: Charles E. Tuttle Company, 1987).

50. Ecological Management Foundation, "Prospectus on International Senior Management Programmes for Ecologically Responsible Decision Making," Amsterdam, February 1992; Buchholz et al., *Managing Environmental Issues*.

51. Schmidheiny, *Changing Course*.

52. John Elkington, *The Environmental Audit: A Green Filter for Company Policies, Plants, Processes, and Products* (Godalming, Surrey, U.K.: World Wide Fund for Nature-UK, 1989).

53. Ibid.; UNEP, Industry and Environment Office, *Environmental Auditing*, Technical Report Series No. 2 (Paris: 1989); Cameron Keyes and Christine Ervin, "Environmental Review of U.S. Industrial Facilities: A Survey of Information Tools" (draft), World Wildlife Fund, Washington,

D.C., 1991; "The CERES Principles (Formerly the Valdez Principles)," Coalition for Environmentally Responsible Economies, Boston, Mass., amended version, April 28, 1992; "A Matter of Principles," *The Green Business Letter* (Tilden Press, Inc., Washington, D.C.), February 1992.

54. British Standards Insitute, "Specification for Environmental Management Systems (BS 7750)," London, 1992; "Proposal for a Council Regulation (EEC) Allowing Voluntary Participation by Companies in the Industrial Sector in a Community Eco-Audit Scheme," *Official Journal of the European Communities*, March 27, 1992; Keyes and Ervin, "Environmental Review of U.S. Industrial Facilities."

55. Keyes and Ervin, "Environmental Review of U.S. Industrial Facilities."

56. EPA, *1990 Toxics Release Inventory Public Data Release*; Monsanto from Bruce Smart, ed., *Beyond Compliance* (Washington, D.C.: World Resources Institute, 1992); reports using Toxics Release Inventory data from Alair MacLean, OMB Watch, Washington, D.C., private communication, October 20, 1992.

57. "Pollution Damage Claims Threaten Corporate Profits," *Greenpeace Business*, August 1991; Liz Spayd, "Judge Approves Plan on Asbestos Claims," *Washington Post*, May 17, 1991; Samuel C. Florman, "Asbestos: Hindsight Is 20/20," *Technology Review*, July 1987.

58. Calvert from Terence B. Lee, Shearson Lehman Brothers, New York, private communication, August 10, 1992; Global Environment Fund, *1991 Annual Report* (Washington, D.C.: 1992); figures from Frances Cairncross, *Costing the Earth* (Boston: Harvard Business School Press, 1992); Swedish example from Gunter Pauli, General Manager, Ecover, Oostmalle, Belgium, private communication, November 3, 1992.

59. Tom Burke, U.K. Ministry of Environment, London, private communication in Washington, D.C., October 8, 1992.

60. Waste Reduction Task Force, McDonald's Corporation and Environmental Defense Fund, *Final Report* (New York: 1991); Environmental Defense Fund, "Environmental Defense Fund Initiates Policy Dialogue with General Motors," press release, Washington, D.C., July 8, 1992.

61. John Elkington and Julia Hailes, *The Green Consumer Guide* (London: Victor Gollancz, 1988); Günter Berger, *Ökotest*, Frankfurt, Germany, private communication, May 19, 1992; Peter Weber, "Green Seals of Approval Heading to Market," *World Watch*, July/August 1990.

62. Schmidheiny, *Changing Course*.

63. Abegglen and Stalk, *Kaisha*; among the recent contributions to the U.S. industrial policy debate are Robert B. Reich, *The Work of Nations: Preparing Ourselves for 21st Century Capitalism* (New York: Alfred A. Knopf, 1991), and Lester Thurow, *Head to Head: The Coming Economic Battle Among Japan, Europe, and America* (New York: William Morrow, 1992).

64. Research Institute on Technology for the Earth, "New Earth 21," Tokyo, 1990; Keidanren, "Keidanren Global Environment Charter," Tokyo, April 23, 1991; H. Shoep, Ministry of Industry, The Netherlands, private communication, October 21, 1992; Sematech from "Sematech's New Mission Is Defined," *New York Times*, October 5, 1992, and from Ted Smith, Silicon Valley Toxics Coalition, San Jose, Calif., private communication, October 9, 1992.

65. Olaf Hohmeyer, Fraunhofer Institute for Systems and Innovation Research, Karlsruhe, Germany, private communication, October 20, 1992.

66. International Finance Corporation, *Investing in the Environment* (Washington, D.C.: 1992).

67. Michael E. Porter, "Green Competitiveness," *New York Times*, June 5, 1991.

Index